D0024524

FIRST-LINE MANAGEMENT
APPROACHING SUPERVISION EFFECTIVELY

FIRST-LINE MANAGEMENT

APPROACHING SUPERVISION EFFECTIVELY

HF
5549
.S 84286
1986

Lawrence L. Steinmetz
President
High Yield Management, Inc.

H. Ralph Todd, Jr.
American River College

ST. JOSEPH'S UNIVERSITY

3 9353 00269 5748

1986   Fourth Edition

**BPI
IRWIN**

Homewood, Illinois 60430

© BUSINESS PUBLICATIONS, INC., 1975, 1979, 1983, and 1986

All rights reserved. No part of this publication may be
reproduced, stored in a retrieval system, or transmitted,
in any form or by any means, electronic, mechanical,
photocopying, recording, or otherwise, without the prior
written permission of the publisher.

ISBN 0-256-03376-5

Library of Congress Catalog Card No. 85-73700

Printed in the United States of America

2 3 4 5 6 7 8 9 0 ML 3 2 1 0 9 8

Preface

Since it's first edition in 1975, *First-Line Management* has undergone many changes. Most changes were designed to keep pace with the impact of shifts in societal values, modifications in management philosophy, and the effects of new technologies. Input from instructors, managers of organizations, and students has been an important part of the text's redesign.

In the fourth edition, we have taken a hard look at the new realism that many managers at all levels are developing. Survival of the United States as a world economic and social force will depend, to a large extent, on the decisions made by managers of organizations—perhaps more than any set of political actions that occur in Washington, D.C. As in the past, we have avoided advocating any special techniques or schools of thought. Buzz words, fad practices, and transient methods have also been shunned. Based on our experience as managers and consultants to management, as well as our association with the academic world, the new fourth edition of *First-Line Management* continues to view the world of work from the perspective of "how it is" rather than the more wishful "how it should be."

Management theory and practice is treated much the same as in past editions. Theory is, we believe, an attempt to explain why things occur in certain ways and why different actions may lead to different results. Practice is the application of theoretical findings to everyday activities. Our intent is to present a blend of theory and practice that is useful for both students and practicing managers. We continue to find copies of *First-Line Management* in hospitals, automotive repair garages, department stores, engineering companies, police stations, and even in the bookcases of college administrators. Although it is intended to be primarily a classroom text, *First-Line Management* is also a guide to management action. Evidence indicates that it is being used both ways.

We continue to stress that supervison is a true management position and that first-line managers are no longer one of the girls or one of the boys of a work team or group. It is necessary that supervisors, as managers, have different sets of responsibilities and must view the organization in ways quite different from nonmanagement employees.

In the fourth edition, two chapters have been added. A new Chapter 6 extends the discussion of leadership to reflect current research and its relationship to writings in three popular management books. Power and politics as realities of organizational life are reviewed in Chapter 14. Again, in the new chapters, a reflection of the real world is more important than any particular popular theoretical position.

Significant changes have been incorporated in most other chapters as well. We retained material that is still applicable and assists students and professional managers in understanding the importance of key management functions. A completely new Instructor's Manual has been prepared that will be of significant assistance to instructors who use such manuals as guides to classroom activities and test materials.

It is our hope that users of the text will find it interesting and useful not only in college classes or management seminars, but in day-to-day work activities. Comments from instructors and students who use the text are always welcome.

Lawrence L. Steinmetz, Ph.D.
H. Ralph Todd, Jr. , Ed.D.

Contents

PART ONE

Introduction

First-Line Management: Linking the Organization

1

Thought Starter

In every computer there is a vital chip called the CPU or Central Processing Unit. A major function of the CPU is to link instructions from the keyboard, which are typed in by the computer operator, to the components of the computer that translate the typed instructions into directions for ultimate use. That is, the CPU is the brains of the computer.

Like CPUs, supervisors, or first-line managers—as supervisors are called in this text—are an essential part of the brains of an organization. Supervisors (first-line managers), like CPUs, are responsible for interpreting and implementing policies and procedures into directions for the operating components, usually nonmanagement employees, of an organization.

First-line managers are the vital links between the producing segments of an organization and the policymaking, objectives-determining, and strategic-planning components. Supervisors are the first line of management. Computers will not function without CPUs, and organizations will not function without first-line managers.

Chapter 1 discusses first-line management, or supervision, as it exists today and as it will probably exist between now and the end of this century. A brief history of supervisory practices as well as some of the basic steps that lead to success or failure of individuals responsible for the activities of others are also introduced.

In Chapter 1 you will learn:

- **The meaning and importance of first-line management.**
- **The importance of contributions made by early management theorists.**
- **The identification of major fields of "classical" management thought impacting today's organizations.**
- **The complexity of change on supervisory responsibilities.**
- **The causes of supervisory success and failure.**

Patricia "Pat" Showalter had worked hard to become a part of management. Fresh out of a local community college, Pat's first assignment was in the statistical analysis department of HOP (Health Organization Partnerships), a large international hospital and health care conglomerate. Three months later, a reorganization placed Pat in the position of senior analyst and group leader for a new human resources management research group. She found herself the newly appointed supervisor of a group that promised to be a key component of HOP's long-range planning effort.

"Hard work and luck will get you anywhere," she joked. Underlying her lighthearted statement, however, was the uneasiness she felt in anticipation of supervising people who had formerly been her peers, as well as a total unfamiliarity with basic management principles. "I'll have to learn fast," Pat thought. "It's going to be a real change."

For people who have made the vital shift from nonmanagement to management assignments the change can be exciting, challenging, and frequently difficult—especially for those not fully prepared for the change.

LINKING OPERATING EMPLOYEES AND MANAGEMENT

Supervisors are the first line of management. Their jobs differ from others' in work organizations in many ways. As the level of management directly responsible for planning, organizing, controlling, and directing the activities of nonmanagement employees, they are the primary contact most employees have with the total organization and its objectives. To be effective, first-line managers, the supervisors of employees who perform the work that produces the services or products of the organization, must be human relations specialists, coaches, technical advisors, disciplinarians, evaluators, motivational experts, team builders, records keepers, and the vital link between the work of the organization and its upper levels of management.

A WORLD OF CHANGE

Throughout most of its history, the United States has been a leader in the productivity of both manufactured products and services. Beginning in the late 1960s, and continuing until the late 1970s, the traditional styles of leadership began to decline and by 1980, many countries, such as Japan, West Germany, France, Italy, and Switzerland, registered much higher productivity gains than were achieved in the United States. Prior to the end of the leadership decline, managers throughout the United States were beginning to show increased concern not only for the loss of productivity but for improving their basic management practices. In addition to the concerns of managers, the country was recovering from a severe recession as well as a prolonged period of intolerable inflation. It became increasingly apparent that in an era of profound social change and accelerating technological development, many of the management practices and attitudes of the past were no longer applicable.

TYPES OF MANAGERS

In all but the smallest organizations there are usually several layers of responsibility and authority. Top-level management, frequently called **executive management,** is responsible for formulating policies and goals of the organization. **Mid-level management,** those managers who report to top management, interpret policies and goals in terms of their own areas of specialization. Some examples of mid-level areas of specialization are marketing, procurement, production, finance, maintenance, and employee relations. In large organizations, there may be several levels of mid-level managers. Reporting to these mid-level managers are first-line managers, who convert policies and goals into reality through the efforts of the nonmanagement employees they supervise. First-line managers (supervisors) deal directly with employees who make a product or provide a service; the procurement supervisor is responsible for the activities of buyers and contract specialists; the marketing supervisor is responsible for the activities of sales, advertising, and research specialists; production supervisors are responsible for completion of products; and in each area of specialization, other supervisors are equally concerned with the performance of those who report to them.

There are literally thousands of different work organizations. Employees reporting to a supervisor may perform tasks as simple as counting boxes or as complex as writing a new computer program for determining costs of operating a construction facility in Saudi Arabia. The type of organization and the area of specialization largely determine the type of employee the first-line manager has on his or her work team. First-line managers are responsible for seeing that schedules are met, services and products are provided, costs are controlled, quality is maintained, and that work flows smoothly through their part of the organization—whether its a computer chip development facility, a hospital, or a water purification plant.

SUPERVISION AND MANAGERS AT ALL LEVELS

Supervision occurs at every level of an organization. First-line managers supervise employees who directly produce services or products. Mid-level managers supervise first-line managers and top-level managers supervise mid-level managers. Supervision encompasses directing, planning, leading, controlling, and coaching the activities of others. When supervisor is discussed as a job title, however, it is usually in reference to the activity of first-line management. Supervision is the only level in an organization that deals directly with nonmanagement employees producing products or services.

In most work situations, first-line management is a difficult, complex, challenging, sometimes frustrating, and often rewarding assignment. The task of these supervisors is not to make people happy, although effective supervisors' employees frequently like their work; nor is their task to please everyone, although frequently they will please many people. Supervisors have the task of accomplishing work effectively and efficiently through the efforts of the employees who report to them.

First-line management requires working with all kinds of resources, such as materials, methods, money, time, space, equipment, and most importantly, people. It is a job that has been studied, analyzed, and written about for years.

INTO THE PAST

No one knows when the control and direction of the efforts of others, the act of supervision, began. In all probability, management started with the beginning of humankind. Studies of the most primitive and isolated societies reveal that there is nearly always a structure of leadership and discipline that includes many of the activities that are associated with managing. Ancient civilizations such as the Sumerians, the early Greek states, and the Egyptians evolved sophisticated methods of organizing and directing the activities of workers long before the beginning of the Christian era some 2,000 years ago. Since many of the early civilizations depended on slave labor, supervision was frequently harsh and punitive. Those who failed to meet the supervisor's requirements were whipped and sometimes put to death by having their heads chopped off. In some situations, the heads were mounted in a prominent workplace as a warning to others who might defy the expectations of a first-line manager. For many centuries, the system of absolute power was the prevalent people management system in numerous cultures, and in some countries, it still exists to a limited degree.

As time passed and absolute power declined, the stick and carrot evolved into major management symbols. Like a jackass stubbornly standing between the punishment of being beaten by a stick and the reward of eating a delicious carrot, employees were first offered incentives such as approval, recognition, higher pay, promotion, and better assignments if they excelled in their work. Employees who failed to meet the highest expectations of management were reprimanded, demoted, given unfavorable performance reviews, and they received both verbal and nonverbal supervisory disapproval. As societies became more complex and employees became more knowledgeable, the carrot and the stick as well as the whip and the sword failed to work as well as they had in the past. Threat of punishment and promise of reward, while still in use, became less effective. Managers were forced to look at the personal values of employees that extended beyond pay and benefits. It was not enough to tell people what to do, pay them for their efforts, and demand their loyalty. New approaches were needed and are still being developed today. It is an interesting commentary on our times that we have learned there is no one best way to manage.

Although there has been some recent improvement, the United States, traditionally the world leader in yearly productivity gains, no longer holds that position. Prior to the Korean War, in the early 1950s, the United States nearly always had a positive balance of trade. The United States sold more to other countries than it bought from them. Since the early 1970s, we have bought more from other countries than we have sold to them. Factors such as our dependency on oil from other countries, the decline of manufacturing in our country, and managerial bad judgment have led to this difficulty. Like a store that buys more than it sells, we are continually buying from other more productive and innovative sources than our own. Some examples are shocking. None of the world's most modern steel plants are in the United States. Korea leads in new steel technology, with Japan, Sweden, and West Germany close behind. Yet, we want to protect old, worn-out U.S. steel mills while our management fails to invest in facilities and equipment that will make us more competitive. Product after product, from typewriters and sewing machines to electric irons and television sets, all hallmarks of American productivity, are being made in other countries. A resurgence of the "can-do" philosophy is sorely needed in the United States. It will depend on managers at all levels. Employees know what is needed and are ready to respond.

GETTING WHERE WE ARE

Little research in management effectiveness occurred prior to 85 years ago. With only a few exceptions, employees were mostly slaves to the whims of employers. Wages were paid at a subsistence rate. Enough money to eat, to pay rent in a substandard dwelling, and to buy meager necessities was the stark reality for most workers. Little thought was given by most managers to the real needs of workers. Novels of the times— such as *A Christmas Carol* by Charles Dickens—depicted the worldwide practice of management's absolute power over employees. Bob Cratchit was required to respond to Scrooge's every demand. While exaggerated, *A Christmas Carol* reflected a great deal of the truth of early management-employee relations.

Shortly after the Civil War, as the Industrial Revolution began to rapidly spread, it became apparent that more than simple prodding and threats were needed to improve productivity. Although industrial managers such as Charles Babbage and Andrew Ure had recognized management's responsibilities to employees, profits, and the impact of humanistic management on productivity, their concepts were frequently ignored.

As the 1900s began, Frederick W. Taylor, a native of Germantown, Pennsylvania, was the first person to apply scientific principles to management, the way organizations work, and the methods of production. In his studies at the Midvale Steel Company, where he was chief engineer, and later as the United States' best-known management consultant, Taylor earned the title "Father of Scientific Management." For almost 40 years, from 1890 to 1930, *Scientific Management* was the dominant management direction. Many of Taylor's concepts are still given serious consideration. Briefly summarized in Figure 1–1 are some of Scientific Management's major assumptions as developed by Taylor. It is interesting that large unions, as well as management, have adopted many of Taylor's concepts over the years, even when they were apparently inappropriate. Strict job descriptions that describe the limitations of job assignments is a Taylor concept. It is also a rule in many of today's labor organizations. By adhering to this nearly 70-year-old management rule,

**FIGURE 1–1 Some of Scientific
Management's Basic
Assumptions that Influence
Work Today**

1. There is one best way to do every job. It is management's responsibility to study each job, define the best way, and instruct workers so that every job is performed in a manner that reflects the results of scientific analysis.

2. Both managers and employees work for money. If both are shown how improved effectiveness will improve their income, they will both beneift from the application of Scientific Management.

3. Management is a science, not a game of chance. It is motivated by both service and profits.

4. Employees must know the amount and quality of work (standard) expected of them. Work standards must be developed by scientific methodology.

5. Optimum effort, a level that can be maintained for long periods of time, is always more productive than maximum effort that can be maintained only for short periods.

unions have effectively restricted the kinds of assignments that employees may be given.

MANAGEMENT SCIENCE

As in all studies of human activities, the Scientific Management movement was a function of its times. The Scientific Management period began in the late 1800s and continued through the late 1920s.

A basic concept of the Scientific Management era was that people tried to satisfy economic needs by working. People's interests at work were believed to be compatible with organizational needs. In short, it was believed that there was a mutual interest between the employee and the employer: both wanted money.

A primary objective of the manager at that time was to lay out, arrange, or organize work so that the person responsible for doing the task could produce the maximum amount in a given period. During the Scientific Management era, most of those who concentrated on productivity or quality did so by either conducting studies or reviewing others' studies. A primary interest was discovering the best way to perform a particular task. Frank and Lillian Gilbreth identified the most basic units of movement necessary to perform a given assembly job. If it took one second to move a hand and they could determine how to save that second, they would change the work process. If a thousand workers could save one second each, they reasoned, then a thousand seconds in a day would be saved. By learning how to save many seconds, they could ultimately save many hours of time required to complete a task. The results were improved productivity and greater profits.

Several concepts formed the basis for Scientific Management approaches to improving productivity. In his early studies of workers who shoveled pig iron before it was converted into steel, Taylor developed improved shovel designs and more effective methods and pacing of work. In some instances, employees were able to triple their previous output. He became convinced that there was only one best way to do any given task. For many years, industrial engineers who felt Taylor was right spent endless hours developing the one best way for tasks performed at companies all over the United States. Many of today's industrial engineers use the principles of time and motion study as well as workplace layout developed by Taylor and his followers.

Perhaps more important in its long-range effectiveness was the concept of *optimum standards.* In his early work, Taylor realized that the average worker could perform a certain amount of work in a given period. After reviewing the efforts of many employees doing the same basic tasks, he was able to develop realistic standards. A **standard** is the amount of work an average employee can do under normal working conditions for a given period such as an hour or a shift. Workers who produce more than the average exceed the standard and those who produce less than the average are doing less than the expected amount of work. Taylor's concept also included standards based on the amount of effort a person could sustain for long periods. A person who tries to lift several 100-pound sacks of fertilizer into a truck may tire rapidly while the same person lifting smaller, 20-pound sacks can work all day without becoming exhausted. In this case, the optimum is 20 pounds while the maximum is 100 pounds. Optimum standards were developed to help people be productive for long periods rather than to exert all their energy in a short time and, in the long run, be less productive.

Taylor was also an advocate of **piece rates.** If a person exceeded the standard during a normal work period, they would be paid more than a person who just met the standard. In the garment industry today, it is common to pay people by the number of units of work completed compared to a standard. If the standard is 40 shirt collars sewn in a regular work day, the employee who sews 50 shirt collars will be paid an extra amount for each collar in excess of the standard. In addition to being paid for the amount of time worked, employees are also paid by the piece. While not as popular as it once was, piece-rate payment, similar to what was advocated by Taylor, is still used in some organizations where numerical standards can be set and where workers control the amount accomplished. Few tasks are still employee controlled as directly as they once were, and piece-rate incentives have largely disappeared.

Henry Gantt, follower of Taylor, developed a method for charting productivity that is still used today, even though it is done primarily by computers. Although these early Scientific Management advocates' ideas have long been surpassed by more recent approaches, their influence continues.

Under the assumptions of Scientific Management, it was believed that all people could maximize the benefits of working: employees could lead more productive lives, employers could maximize the utilization of their employee's services, and employees could make more money because they could work more productively.

Although Scientific Management was one of the most influential forces of its time in changing the way people worked and how they were managed, it ignored questions about the human side of both work and management. Do employees work for other items in addition to money? Are easy jobs more satisfying than difficult ones? Why do people behave differently? Why do some people consistently outperform others? Are men and women really alike in the job environment? Do ethnic minorities respond to management in the same ways as other employees? These and hundreds of similar questions related to managerial effectiveness and the depth of responsibility required for good management remained unasked and unanswered.

Contributions of the pioneers of the Scientific Management movement should not be ignored or forgotten. Productivity improved and managers began to look at work differently than in any previous period of history. Problems of working women, equality of opportunity, environmental concerns, rigid safety standards, chemical exposure and contamination, the impact of technological change, and a host of similar modern concerns were almost totally absent from the thoughts of managers—especially first-line managers—of the period.

Ultimately, attitudes and values changed, some of the Scientific Management era's doctrines were questioned, and a quest for even better ways to manage began. That quest is still going on today. One of the early turning points in the development of management thinking began in 1926 as a by-product of a Scientific Management study. It was the beginning of a long period of management thinking influenced by the **Human Relations movement.**

The Hawthorne Studies

The Hawthorne Studies were a series of experiments conducted at the Hawthorne plant of the Western Electric Company near Chicago. Initially the studies were an attempt to determine the relationship between working environment and productivity. Conceptually, the studies were typical Scientific Management designs. They were investigations of factors that affected productivity other than worker ability. It was known that poor ventilation, inadequate lighting, excessive noise, poor temperature control, and contamination of the air could all depress productivity. What was not known was the degree to which productivity was affected by negative environmental factors. An additional concern was how much change in environmental factors was required before productivity noticeably changed. Researchers at the Hawthorne plant were attempting to define optimal working conditions. What were the temperature, lighting, ventilation, and noise levels that provided optimal productivity? With some well-designed experiments, they believed, optimal environmental factors could be defined. People were regarded as machines. Train them, tell them what was needed, and correct them when something went wrong. Like defective machines, if people did not work properly or respond to corrective action, they would be replaced with more effective workers. Human considerations were largely ignored.

One of their most highly publicized experiments involved female assembly employees who tested electrical relays used in telephone equipment. In order to study the effect of lighting in the relay test room, productivity was measured under normal lighting conditions. As the amount of light was increased, productivity also increased. Immediately the researchers reasoned that there was a direct relationship between the amount of light and productivity. To test their concept, they lowered the amount of light in the test room and again carefully measured productivity. Much to their surprise, productivity continued to improve, and even under poor lighting conditions, it did not decrease below the original levels measured when the experiment began. It was obvious that factors other than lighting were affecting productivity.

To help understand some of the unpredicted outcomes of their experiments, Elton Mayo, a Harvard University psychologist originally from Australia, was asked to join the research team. Mayo interviewed all of the employees in the relay test room and found that for the first time they felt management was interested in what they were doing. They were being treated as people rather than as machines. Since they were part of a select group and they had come to know the experimenters, they believed that management was interested in their welfare and was trying to improve work conditions.

In other similar experiments, Mayo and his team found the same results. People responded to actions that appeared to be attempts by management to improve their working conditions. One of Mayo's most dramatic findings was that productivity improved after his interviews with employees—whether an environmental factors experiment was in progress or not. His conclusion that productivity was related more to how employees are treated as human beings than it is to work conditions changed management thinking as significantly as Taylor's earlier work in Scientific Management. From these studies came the supervisory principle that *effective first-line managers take a sincere interest in employees and treat them like people rather than machines. They build success on improved human relations.*

Attitudes and Job Performance

A major contribution of Elton Mayo, F. J. Roethlisberger, William Dickinson, and other earlier developers of the Human Relations movement was that organizations do not exist only for production. They also permit people to satisfy other needs. Organizations, they reasonsed, are social systems. Employees work together, become friends, develop skills, achieve goals, and have feelings. Positive attitudes toward work, management, and their organization lead to greater satisfaction, loyalty, and continued productivity. While managers can get people to work simply by paying them to do a job, they can get better results if they establish effective interpersonal relations with their employees. Human Relations experts suggested that supervisors who understand people and their motivations, who genuinely appreciate employee efforts, and who learn to deal with workers who report to them on a person-to-person basis are more likely to be successful.

Basic Human Relations Movement Problems

While there is little doubt that the Human Relations movement had a profound impact on management, the findings of Elton Mayo and other researchers were frequently misinterpreted. The concept of building effective interpersonal relationships between employees and managers came to mean "A happy employee is a productive employee." In many instances, this is far from the truth. Some people can be happy at work drinking coffee, visiting with other employees, and generally avoiding work. Others can be equally happy performing work inefficiently and sometimes ineffectively. In jobs paced by machines, there is little relationship between happiness and work under any circumstances. While common sense dictates that employees who derive some degree of satisfaction from their work tend to like their place of employment better than those who are dissatisfied, it is difficult to fully justify that happiness alone leads to improved performance. For many employees, interesting job assignments that are challenging and that demand utilization of their training and skills lead to increased job satisfaction.

Effective human relations is dependent on more than making people happy or trying to build a friendly set of relationships. It requires an understanding of the complexity of human behavior and the realization that all employees are different. Some employees respond to challenge, some employees do not. Other employees like friendly relations with their employer, and a few want to be left alone. No one method of supervisory relations with employees works in all cases.

Although many managers used what they thought was human relations to try to manipulate employees, many were puzzled by the lack of improved performance from their best human relations efforts. The movement continued until the late 1950s and, to some extent, it still influences managerial thinking. Overall, the human relations movement was a positive trend. Its decline was the result of oversimplification of beliefs about human behavior.

In addition to the oversimplification of basic human relations concepts, three other problems, common in organizations, also contributed to ineffective relationships between managers and employees:

1. Some Managers Are Not Effective in Human Relations. When supervisors are chosen, it is frequently because of their aggressiveness, their willingness to work hard, their tendency to be loyal to management's objectives, and their ability to accept added responsibilities. They are frequently high achievers with a strong need to be known in the organization. Many of these potential supervisors are good workers, loyal employees, and they have ambition and drive. However, they do not relate very effectively to lower-level employees. They tend to be impatient with people who are less effective than they are, people who see themselves as more knowledgeable, and people who are more interested in accomplishing the tasks of their section or department rather than building effective organizational relations. In a crisis, they inevitably revert to hard-nosed, authoritarian policies that frequently lead to job success but very poor relations with nonmanagement employees.

2. Some First-Line Managers Attempt to Buy Effective Human Relations. Several years ago, Daniel Bell said that "trying to make people happy" was an ineffective way to increase employee performance. Bell stated that the type of human relations that many managers practiced was **"cow psychology."** It was an attempt to manipulate employees by giving them good working conditions, good pay, fair management, and good fringe benefits. Such employees are treated well, have good benefits, know that management has generally low expectations, and eventually settle into a pattern of work that is neither inspired nor uninspired. Like cows, and especially like contented ones, they do their jobs but little more. They work, like millions across the United States and in other countries, for Fridays. Friday is payday and the beginning of the weekend. Many supervisors thought, unfortunately, that good management was using the tangible benefits of work to make employees happy and, as a consequence, more productive. It simply did not work. There was no evidence that "human relators" were able to achieve more than tough-minded managers who believed their major task was accomplishing work rather than building a contented work force.

Claude Swanke, a vice president of Johnson & Johnson, stated that "We have got to find some place to hang this human relations business onto so it will produce more, not just make people contented." Like Daniel Bell, Swanke was concerned with employees not only liking their work but being fully productive as well. People will, Swanke thought, often concern themselves with maintaining happiness rather than with accomplishing tasks that are the real lifeblood of an organization.

Managers need to realize that getting work accomplished is a more important emphasis than making people happy. Productive employees are frequently more satisfied with the knowledge of accomplishment than employees who work to minimum standards under the direction of managers with low expectations.

3. Some People Don't Like to Be "Human-Related with." Bosses, to some employees, are appreciated most when they are not around. Because of past experiences or suspicions based on what they've been told, many employees work best when left alone to complete their assignments. The less they see and hear from their immediate first-line manager, the better. Frequently, their feeling is that supervisors are friendly only to increase output or to pour oil on troubled waters. Sincerity is both disbelieved and disdained. To these employees, polite remarks such as "How is your family?" are viewed suspiciously. Their expectations are that management is dedicated to exploiting employees and that they would rather be left alone to do their assigned work. Dedicated and skilled first-line managers can gradually build climates of trust and confidence when confronted with such attitudes, but it is a slow and often frustrating task.

A Note on Sincerity

Attempts to manipulate employees rather than lead, support, coach, and encourage is nearly always viewed with suspicion by many employees. The "let them think it was their idea" philosophy is nearly always doomed. People know when their supervisors are being sincere, honest, and truly appreciative of their efforts. Faking pride and concern does not work. There is little, if any, evidence that employees who become supervisors are more intelligent, have greater knowledge, or have greater skills than the average employee supervised. Ideally, they are chosen because of their willingness to lead, to make decisions, and, most of all, to accept responsibility. They are not chosen to make people happy, to manipulate, or to provide a "happy atmosphere." Effective supervisors are expected to direct the efforts of others in accomplishing the work of their organizations.

Bragging about minor accomplishments, compliments about work that is mediocre, and rewarding achievement of generally low standards reinforces the belief that it's only necessary to meet the minimum required at work. It is unfortunate that in the United States attendance is rewarded as much as accomplishment. In organizations with employees that have the same job classifications, some seniority, and same basic experience, all have the same rate of pay even though some work harder and more effectively than others. Rewards are based not on accomplishment but on attendance.

Trends and Promises

Although Scientific Management and Human Relations, as schools of thought, have been replaced by a succession of other theories and practices, their impact on management thinking will linger for many years. Taylor was correct in his concern for more effective work methods and Mayo was equally right in emphasizing the importance of psychological and social aspects of employment. Neither school of thought could predict the technological, social, political, and economic changes of the future. Led by a number of thoughtful and highly skilled management observers, many new and more sophisticated approaches to improving management action have emerged. Beginning in the late 1950s and continuing since then, the development of new concepts of effective management have had a major impact.

While not all of the major movements that formed a basis for much of modern management thinking are listed here, five significant contributions are worth examination:

1. **Management by Objectives.** In 1954, Peter Drucker, then a professor at New York University, stated in his text, *The Practice of Management,* that managers can be judged only by their achievements. He expressed the belief that if managers set measurable, attainable objectives with realistic time lines, they could evaluate their own performance. Managing by self-developed objectives, usually in conjunction with an immediate higher-level manager, could be a form of self-control as well as a method for measuring achievement. In later years, Drucker's original concept was enlarged and developed by others. Eventually, the objec-

tives-setting concept was applied to all levels of organizational employees and managers. Later in this text, the value of setting and utilizing objectives is discussed more fully.

2. Recognition of Needs. In the same year that Peter Drucker was proposing Management by Objectives, A. H. Maslow, at Brandeis University, published his famous text, *Motivation and Personality*. Although Maslow did not write specifically for managers until his later book, *Eupsychian Management,* his concepts of the strength of human need under various conditions have had a long and lasting effect on management thinking. Over time, many other theories of motivation have emerged and, to some extent, they have replaced Maslow's original thinking. In a later chapter dealing with motivation, the impact of Maslow's famous **hierarchy of needs** is presented in detail.

3. Assumptions about People at Work. One of the most influential management texts ever published was written by Douglas McGregor in 1960. Like Maslow, McGregor recognized human needs in a work environment. In *The Human Side of Enterprise,* he stated that the assumptions managers make about their employees profoundly influence how employees perform. His famous **Theory Y** and **Theory X** sets of managerial assumptions, included in our later discussions of leadership theory, are still part of management language.

4. Contingency-Based Management. A consistent theme throughout this text is that no one management system or style works for all organizations, managers, or situations. Effective managers must vary their styles and approaches to problem solving depending on many conditions. No one person is responsible for the total development of contingency-based management but, in all probability, studies conducted by Joan Woodward during the early 1960s of management styles in British industries had a major influence on the development of contingency-based management. She found that in different industries, different management styles and organizational patterns seemed to evolve and work well for each setting. Study after study by other management specialists have expanded and verified the implications of Woodward's early findings. Many factors affect the type of management most appropriate. Not only the type of industry, but the degree of crisis in the organization, expectations of employees, manager personalities and preferences, and current social values all contribute to the way organizations can be most effectively managed.

5. Recognition of the Importance of Job Design. Frederick Herzberg has many publications, including his famous article originally published in the *Harvard Business Review* entitled "One More Time: How Do You Motivate Employees?" Herzberg has been the chief advocate of the concept that increasing employee control and responsibility for their own work is a primary method of improving performance. His concepts have been challenged many times, but their contributions to the development of current management thinking is undeniable. While his theories require lengthy explanation, a primary focus of them is that good job design gives employees a high degree of control over their own activities and makes them accountable for their actions. A word-processing specialist who checks and signs the reports he or she produces or a craftsperson who inspects his or her finished work are examples. This is especially true if a mechanism is built into the work system that requires people doing a particular job to correct their errors when a product or service is found to be defective at some later date.

Herzberg also pointed out that in most jobs there are two types of motivational conditions or needs. Needs for security, adequate conditions of work, acceptable pay and benefits, fairness, and good relations with other employees are important considerations for employees, but they do not necessarily affect performance. These were classified by Herzberg as maintenance needs. They are necessary for survival and comfort but not for improved performance. Recognition, responsibility, interesting work, achievement, and opportunity are another set of needs that, if present, tend to improve performance. They were designated as motivational or growth needs. These are the needs that tend to satisfy people most when they are achieved.

MANAGEMENT IN A WORLD OF CHANGE

Supervisors are confronted with change on a constantly increasing scale. Technological change in the increased use of computers, social change in the attitudes and demands of employees, organizational change in the form of restructuring and new assignments with different responsibilities, and external political and economic changes all affect the way managers must act. (See Figure 1–2.)

For most organizations, the most visible and easily identified change has been increased reliance on computer-based technology. The Automated office, an interesting concept only five years ago, is now a reality.

Computer-assisted design and drafting and computer-assisted manufacturing have changed the types of skills, training, and management needed for many organizations. New patterns of work are beginning to emerge that were unheard of in the past. Management, especially first-line management, is faced with challenges different from those of any other era.

While changes associated with technological development help create new management challenges, social changes are far more significant in their impact. Regardless of criticisms about the educational systems of the United States, employees are more knowledgeable, frequently better

FIGURE 1–2   Influences on Management Thought

Classical theory—1910–1926	
Taylor	One best way—Scientific Management.
Gantt	Modern production control.
F. and L. Gilbreth	Time and motion study.
Fayol	Principles of administration.
Follett	People are management's greatest resource.
Human Relations—1926–1962	
Mayo	Human Relations.
Bernard	Authority relationships.
Maslow	Need satisfaction.
Whyte	Communication patterns—organizations.
McGregor	Management assumptions.
The Revisionists—1962–1972	
Argyris	Personality and organizations.
Likert	New patterns in management.
Drucker	Results-oriented management.
Herzberg	Job enrichment.
Continuing trends—1972–	
Vroom	The situation, type of work, and employees all
Fiedler	help determine management style. There is
Katz	no one best way. Increased worker involve-
Sayles	ment and sharing with management in deci-
Ouchi	sions leads to improved performance.
Schmidt and Tannenbaum	
Etc.	

Note: Many, many researchers in management thinking have contributed to modern methods of running organizations. This figure lists only a few. At present, the number of qualified management analysts and developers of concepts helpful in understanding factors that lead to managerial effectiveness is greater than ever. Only time will determine the most prominent contributors to management thinking of the era between now and the year 2000.

educated, and have different attitudes and expectations than workers of any other period. Authority and status do not impress employees to the degree they once did. Many employees are more willing to question management decisions and directives. Studies indicate that companies that decrease the social distance between management and nonmanagement employees, that view employees as their most important resource, and that demonstrate a willingness to view work from the perspective of those who actually perform the daily activities of the organization tend to be successful. They are able to meet most employee expectations by making them part of the organization rather than being viewed by both management and themselves as ''hired hands.''

Economic uncertainties, compliance with federal and state regulations, organizational changes, increases or decreases in union activities, market requirements, shortages and oversupply, and a host of other factors all result in management adjustments. An important lesson is that in a dynamic environment, there is no one best way to manage. It is necessary to choose the best approach for each situation from various alternatives.

The Invasion of the Future

There is no accurate way to precisely predict the future. We can, however, carefully examine a number of current trends and make some intelligent estimates. Between now and the beginning of the next century, some of the factors that will affect management of work organizations include:

1. Continued Decline of the Traditional ''Blue-Collar'' Work Force. With a general decline in factory production in the United States have come major alterations in the types of work needed. Traditional assembly work, even in automobile factories, which are the largest single employer of assembly line efforts, is rapidly disappearing. Computer-assisted manufacturing, computer-based production control, and even computer-driven quality control in all types of industries have increased the need for employees who supervise machines rather than operate them or assemble their components. Newer, more technically trained work forces employed in factories with far fewer people and dramatically different assignments will continue to replace the older style, semiskilled personnel. Where employee skills, once acquired, were good for a lifetime of application in the past, today's employees and employers can look forward to a lifetime of learning new and constantly changing job requirements needing equally new and changing patterns of work, knowledge, and expertise.

2. Less Insistence on "Bottom-Line" Management and Increased Emphasis on Longer-Range Objectives. During a large part of the 1970s and early 1980s, many work organizations have stressed immediate profits as their primary goal. A growing number of organizations are beginning to stress building more effective work forces, designing quality into their services and products, and emphasizing long-range goals rather than immediate bottom-line profits. Strategic planning and strategic management have become full-fledged management buzz words. While the terms may rapidly become dated, they express the concept that survival depends on long-range objectives more than on emphasis on immediate profits.

3. Periodic Retraining and Updating Current Training Will Become a Major Educational Effort. With increased technological change and new types of job emphasis, skills will become obsolete more rapidly than in the past. Retraining, similar to the current change from typing to word processing, will be necessary for employees to retain current employment and even more important for promotion to higher-level jobs. Many skills and areas of expertise will disappear and be replaced by others not yet anticipated. In a recent speech, Austin Kiplinger, publisher of the famous *Kiplinger Letter* and the magazine *Changing Times,* stated that the business of America is not business, as so often quoted, but the business of America is education. Kiplinger was referring to the necessity of education to meet the requirements of a constantly changing world and economic climate.

4. Emergence of National Industrial, Business, Educational, and Government Organization Goals. Reindustrialization of the United States has been a concept since it became evident in the late 1970s and early 1980s that manufacturing had virtually left the United States. In a democratic, capitalistic society, government goals for work organizations are viewed with a great deal of suspicion. As industries and businesses increasingly operate in foreign countries, buy from foreign countries, and sell in the United States, we become more dependent on outside sources than on ourselves for the means of assuming a productive economy and a healthy long-range economy. Government will eventually be forced to take the leadership in building incentives into the country's productive and support systems.

5. Emphasis on Increased Competency of Management. Many organizations realize that the current demands on managers are more complex than ever. Carrot and stick approaches that rely on simple incentives such as praise as well as fear of punishment simply do not work for long periods. Managers who are *proactive* rather than *reactive* are in increased demand. Proactive managers are those who are able to anticipate needs, able to develop workable plans for future activities, and able to concentrate efforts on coordination rather than control. They understand the necessity for effectiveness by every part of the work force. Reactive managers use most of their energy solving problems that would not have occurred had they taken time to effectively plan and anticipate potential problems.

A CONTINUING CHALLENGE

In the late 1970s and early 1980s, it became apparent that something was drastically wrong with much of the United States' management systems. For several years, Japanese management styles were looked upon as models. Gradually it became apparent that while many of the Japanese approaches to management were excellent, they met with mixed success in this country. Managers began to examine American organizations that operated exceptionally well. Like the Japanese, the excellent United States organizations, as they are popularly known, value employees as members of the organization. They have high expectations and frequently set difficult goals. Recognition of the basic human charac-

teristics that most people like to be on a winning team and be recognized as part of that team is one of the important factors of well-run, successful organizations. Management has been going through profound changes and will continue to do so in the search for true excellence. We are experiencing one of the most challenging and exciting periods in the history of people in work organizations.

Managers are people who direct the efforts of others toward achieving organizational goals. They are responsible for accomplishing work through the efforts of others. Sometime in the beginning of mankind, it was realized that no one person can do all of the work that needs to be done in almost any endeavor. From gathering agricultural crops to operating a hospital, organizations depend on people working in an organized, planned, and coordinated effort. This is an ancient concept that has a more complex meaning and perhaps is more important now than at any time in our past.

Things to Remember

1. First-line managers are the vital link between the work of an organization and its upper-level management.

2. Supervisors are the first line of management. Supervisors are first-line management.

3. Top-level or executive managers formulate policy.

4. Mid-level managers interpret policy.

5. First-line managers implement policy.

6. Scientific Management was developed by Frederick W. Taylor. Scientific Management was based on these principles:
   a. There is one best way to do any given task.
   b. Optimum standards are necessary to measure performance.
   c. Piece-rate structures encourage performance.
   d. Management is a science motivated by profits and service.
   e. Both employees and managers work primarily for money.

7. Human Relations, as a management movement, began at the Hawthorne, Illinois plant of Western Electric Company in 1926.

8. Elton Mayo and his Hawthorne team founded the Human Relations movement with the discovery that productivity improved when employees felt that management was genuinely interested in their welfare.

9. Some managers are not effective "human relators."

10. Some first-line managers attempt to buy effective human relations.

11. Some people don't like to be "human related" with.

12. Modern management theory was preceded by Management by Objectives, theories concerning assumptions about people at work, contingency-based management, recognition of the importance of job design, and other research-based theory.

13. Future trends include decline of the blue-collar work force, less insistence on bottom-line management, emphasis on reeducation, and improvement of management competence.

Key Words

supervisor
first-line management
mid-level management
executive management
Scientific Management
standard
optimum standards
piece rates
Human Relations movement
Hawthorne Studies
cow psychology
attitude
need psychology
MBO management by objectives
contingency-based management
job design

Self-Assessment

Listed below are statements about supervisory competence. Rate yourself as honestly as possible to determine how well you rate as a supervisor or whether you have supervisory potential. If you do not perform or do the actions described, or disagree with the statement, rate yourself as 1, 2, or 3 depending on how much you dislike the actions or disagree. If you like or perform well in the actions described, or agree with the statement, rate youself 4, 5, or 6 depending on the strength of your preference or actions.

1. I usually take full responsibility for my own actions and the performance of those who report to me.

| 1 | 2 | 3 | 4 | 5 | 6 |

2. When faced with an unpleasant decision, I tend to enlist the support of a higher authority before acting.

| 1 | 2 | 3 | 4 | 5 | 6 |

3. Happy people are productive people. A supervisor's first responsibility is to make people happy.

| 1 | 2 | 3 | 4 | 5 | 6 |

4. Supervisors should realize that they are not part of management, and they should try to be "another employee" as much as possible to reduce resentment between them and other employees.

| 1 | 2 | 3 | 4 | 5 | 6 |

5. In spite of all the writing and talk, a supervisor must learn to manipulate employees in ways to ensure productivity and quality.

| 1 | 2 | 3 | 4 | 5 | 6 |

6. A contribution of Scientific Management was that it established the one best way to manage in all organizations.

| 1 | 2 | 3 | 4 | 5 | 6 |

7. Less knowledge is required by employees today than in the past.

| 1 | 2 | 3 | 4 | 5 | 6 |

8. The Hawthorne studies proved that people work for bread and bread alone.

| 1 | 2 | 3 | 4 | 5 | 6 |

9. In recent years, the rate of change experienced in the past has slowed significantly.

| 1 | 2 | 3 | 4 | 5 | 6 |

10. Social changes are more significant, in the long run, than technological changes.

| 1 | 2 | 3 | 4 | 5 | 6 |

CASES

**Rhome on
the Range**

Bonnie Rhome had been a top personnel specialist for two years, specializing in employment and promotional problems for women in the
giant Municipal Interstate Supply System, Corp. commonly known as
MISS. She was just promoted to supervisor of General and Professional
Employment. With nearly 8,000 employees in its central facility alone,
Bonnie felt she had been assigned a significant job. Most of the people in
her department were ones she knew and had worked with for the past few
years. Many were still loyal to George Krupp, who Bonnie replaced when
he accepted a job with a competing organization.

While some of the 20 new employees in her department seemed to
accept her, Bonnie felt resentment from others.

In order to establish herself, Bonnie called a meeting of the entire staff.
"Here are some of the things I'd like to do," she began. "First, I'd like to
appoint two group leaders, one to head general employment and the
other to head professional recruitment. I also feel many of our procedures
need revising and I'll need your help in getting the project started. To
improve our overall flexibility, we will also have a job rotation plan so
that everyone will have an opportunity to learn more than one job."

Instead of the approval she expected, Bonnie was greeted with complete silence. From the back of the room she heard someone whisper,
"George sure wouldn't have done it this way."

1. Even though she was sincere, what could Bonnie have done differently?

2. How should change be introduced?

3. Can new supervisors usually expect some resentment? Explain.

On the Road Again

Part of the functions of Bonnie's group was to recruit professional
personnel such as engineers, top technicians, accountants, management,
writers, physicists, chemists, and highly trained people for other job
classifications. Much of the recruitment required travel to cities all over
the United States to contact and interview qualified applicants.

Bonnie's recruiters were a mixture of men and women who took their
jobs seriously and had helped MISS build an enviable professional staff.
When a need arose for physicists, Bonnie assigned Steve Salz and Anne
Stewart as the recruiting team being sent to attend the Western Physics
Association meeting in Denver. They were to set up an interviewing

arrangement in one of the convention hotels to talk to physicists who might be interested in joining MISS.

On the day following the assignments, Bonnie received a call from Al Stewart, Anne's husband. "I don't know you very well but you must have a hole in your head," he began. "Don't you know better than to send a mixed-sex team out on the road? Steve's a single guy who plays around a lot, and I don't want him around Anne, especially in Denver."

1. What would you do if you were in Bonnie's role as supervisor?

2. Does Al have a legitimate concern?

3. How will Steve and Anne feel if the assignment is changed?

2

The Supervisor's Role and Functions While at Work

Thought Starter

No two organizations are exactly alike (not even highly standardized ones like McDonald's and Kentucky Fried Chicken), and no two supervisors have exactly the same job. Nearly all supervisors, however, have a common body of knowledge and skills that they must draw on. All deal with people, all have some responsibility for the planning and direction of others' work and all are accountable to higher levels of management for the performance of employees under their supervision. Front-line management, the act of supervising, is a frequently challenging, difficult, and rewarding task. Effective supervisors have high expectations of themselves and others. They also recognize that there is a great deal to learn.

Some years ago, Bradford Boyd, a management professor and writer, asked the question, "What is a supervisor's real job? Employees ultimately determine how much work is actually done, not supervisors." Although the quote is not exact, the sense of Boyd's statement is that first-line managers get work done through the energy and efforts of others. But how is that done? That's the question Chapter 2 answers.

In Chapter 2 you will learn:

□ **What supervisors do that is different from nonmanagement employees.**

□ **Some basic concepts that all supervisors need to know.**

□ **Why planning is such an important function of all levels of management.**

□ **Some common causes of supervisory failure.**

□ **Essential requirements of effective organization of work, control of activities, and delegation.**

One of Houston Office Products and Equipment, Inc.'s (HOPE) larger customers was the Columbia Area Regional Transit (CART). As a private transportation company that specialized in both passenger bus services from the city of Columbia to outlying residential communities and commercial delivery for several major businesses, CART was an important segment of the community.

In an effort to improve both its passenger business as well as commercial trucking, CART's top managers felt that better training of supervisors responsible for day-to-day operations would be an effective starting place. Many existing supervisors were promoted as the organization grew and most learned what management required "the hard way." Some top managers realized that, although experience is necessary, learning the hard way can also be the wrong way if new supervisors are not properly trained and coached. As a starting point, CART's top management wanted their first-line managers to understand the basic role and functions of on-the-job supervision.

YOUR ROLE AND FUNCTION
AS A BOSS

The supervisor's role in any company or organization varies with the nature of that company or organization. If the enterprise is a service industry such as a restaurant, car wash, medical facility, or consulting firm, the emphasis will be on helping employees provide the desired service directly to the customer. In contrast, in a construction business, the supervisor's subordinates may never see the customer, and the emphasis will be on putting things together correctly. In a manufacturing company, however, the boss may be mostly concerned about getting subordinates to do repetitive, redundant work for days, months, or years. In the retail business, the emphasis might be on having an employee do a series of different tasks accurately, such as marking merchandise correctly.

Any supervisor is faced with a variety of problems and that variety often occurs because of the nature of the work that the supervisor's subordinates must do. Let's look at how these things change in the supervisor's job.

THE SUPERVISOR'S ROLE
IN THE ORGANIZATION

People began to study the job of supervision seriously years ago. It was not until recently, however, that the functions of the supervisor were clearly identified and investigated in this country. Today, the study of supervision is an international undertaking with most of the developed— that is, industrialized—countries contributing to the body of literature and knowledge about supervision. However, we are now changing from an industrialized society to a service society.

In the beginning, the supervisor's tasks studied were **planning, organizing, directing,** and **controlling.** Since then, numerous other functions have been added to the supervisor's job—motivating, communicating, **delegating,** and staffing (see Figure 2–1). These functions must be mastered for a supervisor to be an effective people manager. This book is not concerned with higher-level management processes and will not analyze their functions in great detail. We will, however, analyze how supervisors can and must integrate their actions with the activities planned by top and middle management.

FIGURE 2–1   The Supervisor's Functions

Planning	Motivation
Organizing	Communication
Directing	Delegating
Controlling	Staffing

WHAT SUPERVISORS DO

It is estimated that there are at least 10 million supervisory people at work in the U.S. economy. That means that hundreds of people are appointed as new bosses every day. An increasing percentage of the newly appointed supervisors are women. But, male or female, few people who become supervisors for the first time are well prepared for the job. No one has told them what the supervisors job really entails.

There are many activities that supervisors must perform. A partial list of these includes the following:

1. See that people under the supervisor's control work together in a reasonably acceptable fashion.

2. Motivate employees to perform their jobs both as the company or organization requires the work be accomplished and in a manner compatible with employees' expectations.

3. Provide job instruction to emloyees, give them assistance in performing work, and explain assigned tasks.

4. Develop employees to assume additional responsibilities and train them in new activities.

5. Maintain control and discipline.

6. Coach and counsel employees when they fail to understand their job or when they have personal problems that affect their work.

7. Resolve differences between workers.

8. Plan, schedule, and coordinate work activities.

9. Recognize and reward employees when they consistently do a good job or when they make a significant contribution in terms of ideas or effort.

10. Coordinate operations and ensure that work procedures are conducted in a safe and orderly manner.

11. Ensure that high-quality products and services are delivered by employees.

12. Develop people to ensure that work is done as efficiently and economically as possible.

Supervisors are busy people, as a quick review of the foregoing list might indicate. To be effective, they must devote time and attention to their jobs. It is not enough for supervisors to be knowledgeable about the job they supervise. It is not even enough to be sufficiently educated or intelligent to do the job. To be effective, good supervisors must have an intense desire to succeed. They must also know how to obtain assistance and cooperation from other supervisors and managers they work with as well as from the people they supervise. In addition, they must also be knowledgeable about the machinery, equipment, tools, and materials that their subordinates utilize. They must also integrate their unit's activities with other parts of the organization and with the requirements of their bosses.

WHAT SUPERVISORS NEED TO KNOW

There have been many studies concerning what supervisors need to know to do their jobs. Practically all studies indicate that typical new supervisors are most lacking in the knowledge and skills necessary to relate effectively to other people, in particular, their own work force. A common, visible symptom of this lack of skill is found among supervisors and first-line managers who are having difficulty because they don't know how to give job assignments and work orders. As a result, employees are often confused and sometimes angered.

Problems with subordinates, of course, do not arise only because the supervisor lacks human relations knowledge and skills. Sometimes the supervisor lacks skills in effective communication. As stated in Chapter 12, typical supervisors probably spend about 70 percent of their time in some form of communication mostly talking or listening. When supervisors are inept at explaining ideas or expressing themselves effectively, difficulty in accomplishing work through their subordinates is certain.

Supervisors also need to know personnel procedures and policies, record-keeping, planning and scheduling techniques, work-improvement methods and techniques, the control of quality and quantity, and the handling and processing of work. There are many and varied activities in which the effective supervisor must engage. These functions, in a nutshell, contain the ingredients for success as a supervisor. Lack of knowledge or skill in doing these activities usually guarantees failure. However, simply possessing the appropriate skills will not assure success. Thinking and action-oriented implementation of these skills are also required.

THE BASIC FUNCTIONS OF A SUPERVISOR

In a classical sense, there are four primary functions that a supervisor performs: planning, organizing, directing, and controlling. These functions are conducted daily by supervisors, even though supervisors may not realize it when they are performing a particular activity. Because all supervisors must perform these functions, it is imperative that they understand the tasks. This is true for supervisors involved in manufacturing, retailing, wholesaling, or service industries—whether they supervise large or small numbers of people.

While we tend to say that the basic functions of the supervisor occur in the sequence of planning, organizing, directing, and controlling, experienced supervisors rarely look at their activities in any particular order. The reason is that all activities seem to need to be done constantly. The following sequence is not the only order in which the various functions can be performed.

Planning

Planning means formulating a course of action for the future. The future may be short term or long term. A department head in a factory making ferromagnets may plan only one day's work at a time if most orders are for small quantities that can be produced in an hour or two. On the other hand, the department head may be simultaneously making long-term plans about phasing out an obsolete line of stamping mills while phasing in replacement machinery without a loss of production. In making the long-range plans to phase in the new machinery, the department head must integrate his or her plans with the plans of others. For example, the department head in charge of maintenance will need to know *when* and *how* to prepare the maintenance schedule on the new machinery, and the shipping department will need to be informed about how the new equipment will affect their operations.

Planning is the selection of objectives, policies, procedures, and pro-

**FIGURE 2–2 Plans Will Help Get Your
Job and Your Workers
from How or Where
Things Are to How or
Where You Want Them
to Be**

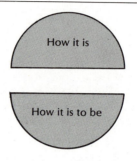

grams from various alternatives to be conducted by the supervisor's
department or unit. The ability to plan effectively is the keystone among
the essentials of effective leadership and supervisory practice. Effective
planning is not, however, always a formal process. Planning can be and
often is done effectively by experienced supervisors.

However, planning is often done poorly by new or inexperienced
supervisors. One reason for this difficulty is that some people don't
understand what planning involves or how to do it. Also, many supervisors fail at planning because they don't integrate their plans with the
plans of other supervisors and workers who are involved.

Planning can be done in a variety of ways. The best way is to address
the problem formally. One gimmick used by many experienced supervisors is sitting down with a scratch pad and trying to define two areas—
how things are and how things ought to be (see Figure 2–2). Once those
two areas are defined, then this question is raised: "How can my department get to the desired situation?" The answer is a plan of action, and the
supervisor is then performing the tasks of planning! The next step is to
carefully analyze the plan's workability and suitability based on the
needs and requirements of others in the business.

By nature, planning is necessary at all levels in the organization. It is
perhaps most important at the line or operational level, even though
planning is usually far less formal at that level. Planning is important
because the operational level is the "go or bust" level. Unfortunately,
many supervisors are not effective in making formal operational plans;

effective, tangible plans for implementing jobs are the key to successful productivity figures.

Just as important as planning is the need to communicate the supervisor's plans to the people responsible for implementing them and anyone else affected by the plans. To be effective at planning, supervisors must understand what requirements planning places upon them to communicate their plans to others. It is essential that supervisors be able to: (1) see the work situation as a whole, (2) break down the whole situation into workable parts, (3) use imagination and be creative with ideas, (4) be objectively analytical, (5) measure the effectiveness of their units and their people at implementing plans, and (6) avoid being bogged down by details.

Principles of Organizing Work

Organizing is the second basic function of the supervisor. Organizing is the ability to systematically arrange one's personnel, material, equipment, machinery, and work area or office into a viable, effective work unit that can accomplish the plans established for the unit by the supervisor. Thus, in attempting to organize a group of employees well, supervisors have the primary task of assigning the right person to the right job so that the most efficient and effective work situation is realized.

The basic principles of organization, according to most supervisory texts, are as follows:

1. The form of organization that supervisors must develop is largely a function of what their organization is designed to accomplish. That is, the nature of the work dictates what organizational form will work best. There is no evidence that one organizational form is superior to another. For example, a supervisor who is managing a highly creative unit—such as an advertising department or an interior design department for a large decorating store—will develop a form of organization totally different from another supervisor who is in charge of a "do" organization such as an assembly line. Supervising "thinkers" also requires different organizational talents than supervising "doers." Consider the problem of organizing an effective work team of mechanics tuning a race car as compared to supervising a group of busboys in a restaurant. The mechanics must be specialists who do precise functions, but the busboys can be generalists who can trade jobs and cover for each other if someone is sick or on break. Thus, a fundamental principle

of good organization for new supervisors is understanding what their unit or department is in business for; this will affect how the work is arranged.

2. Another principle of well-organized work performed by experienced supervisors can be stated as "one employee, one boss." Although many organizations are well-organized in terms of job descriptions performed by employees (they write advertising copy, prepare food, or sell tires), there is often confusion about who is whose boss in these organizations. It is almost impossible for one person to effectively report to two, three, six, or even eight supervisors, yet this often happens in poorly organized situations. As an illustration, think of the kinds of problems that advertising agency copywriters can run into if their supervisor tells them to make an advertisement funny, but the client (another boss, in effect) asks for a serious ad. Should the ad be seriously funny, serious, funny, or both? What happens if the cartoonist who is scheduled to draw a filmstrip to go with the copy says it can't be done unless the copy is changed? These problems help explain why advertising people are often thought to be ulcer-prone. These concerns show the need for *unity of command* and decision making in any organizational unit! It is inhuman to expect one person to please numerous supervisors. The saying "too many cooks spoil the broth" applies here. Someone will always say the broth tastes bad if there are several people ready to judge its quality.

The basic test of well-organized work for supervisors in this situation is to assess their ability in this area by answering the question, "Is there unity of command?" The effective supervisor tries to eliminate an organizational arrangement where there is more than one manager to whom a subordinate must report. About the only exception to this principle is the special case where some people working as integrators on jobs where many organizational lines must be crossed to get the job done. The concept of matrix management addresses this problem. But that concept is too specialized in its adaptation to be treated here. However, even in those cases, the integrator in the matrix organization usually has a primary supervisor to whom he or she reports.

3. To ensure effective organization, the supervisor must also be a person who can delegate. Delegation means assigning people to jobs and giving them the required authority and responsibility for getting the job done. Delegation will be treated as a separate

supervisory action later in the book. Delegation of responsibility requires giving a subordinate the authority to use and commit resources of the organization.

4. In units that are effectively organized, the boss seldom decides all matters to be accomplished by the unit. The supervisor depends on responsible subordinates to make decisions in areas where they have competence. This type of action frees the supervisor for other matters, and it is the primary reason that experienced supervisors can find time to plan. This may be the primary reason, too, that people who are considered good supervisors are good at delegating.

To understand why good managers do not decide all matters themselves, consider the benefits of supervisors of boosting the morale of their subordinates. True, supervisors can save time by relying on subordinates to make decisions. But, more importantly, knowledgeable supervisors using delegation, give their employees that all-important good feeling of making their own decisions, carrying them out, and seeing how things work out. Managers who do not let their subordinates make their own decisions and have the responsibility for carrying out those decisions deprive their employees of morale-enhancing benefits, and they also fail to help their subordinates develop their capabilities and prepare for more responsible jobs in the future.

The Increasing Significance of Planning for the Supervisor

Management expert Franklin G. Moore once said that "before you can plan what to do in the future, you have to decide what the future will be like." Thus, good supervisory planning requires the manager to look toward the future. If you want all your employees to be left-handed, you must know that in advance, not after the fact.

At one chemical plant, it was found that most people with light complexions reacted with violent illness to materials used in some work areas. A plan was developed to only hire people who had dark complexions and who showed no toxic reactions to the critical work areas. In another company, which manufactured transformers it was found that only about 8 people out of 10,000 had the necessary hand-eye coordination to wind certain small coils. A lot of planning went into how to find and hire the people possessing this refined talent.

Practical supervisors recognize one thing about planning: The future is not perfectly predictable, and even the best plans may not be fulfilled.

We know that people will engage in various forms of recreation in the future. But will they necessarily continue to swim, ski, or ride trailbikes? Computers and electronic technology have had a significant impact on recreation. Just as many traditional recreational activities have changed in popularity simply as a result of ecological pressures or because they have been replaced by newer, more appealing electronic interests and activities, the same process is true at work. Just because the clerks in your favorite store currently write up sales slips by hand does not mean that they will do so next year. Twenty years ago, joggers and runners were considered weird, yet today it is estimated that 10 percent of all adults jog and run. Technology is constantly changing. If your company is mechanizing retail sales operations, as a company supervisor, you must plan to meet those changes. For example, soft drink dispensing machines long ago replaced the soda jerk, and your great grandfather may well have gone to the pub with a bucket for carrying his beer home.

Why You Must Plan

There are many reasons why a supervisor must plan (See Figure 2–3). One reason is that planning helps gain the coordination needed to accomplish a particular task. Planning helps ensure that things get done, and it also may enable the supervisor to see when things may not get done, why they may not be done right, or where there is a duplication of effort.

Good planning also means sound control of operations. Supervisors can compare organizational results with plans to determine whether their unit is on schedule and to determine what might be done to improve operations, reduce costs, improve schedules, and improve the quality of the work or services to the customer. Planning also provides the supervisor with the opportunity to analyze operations. It enables the front-line manager to ask questions: "Who is going to do what?" "How much can be accomplished in a given time?" Planning helps supervisors make the most economical use of their people and equipment. Supervisors can, in so doing, economize on labor costs and equipment operations.

Do You Always Need to Plan?

Some supervisors feel that it is not necessary to plan. After all, history shows that some supervisors and companies get along well with little planning. One way or another things seem to get done. Furthermore, one can certainly say after it's all over that it was for the best—no matter how it worked out. Manufacturers of metal ice chests who did not plan ahead

FIGURE 2–3 Benefits of Good Planning

1. When jobs and work are coordinated, work gets done on time.
2. Duplication of efforts by employees can be avoided.
3. Good relations and coordination can be achieved among different units in the organization.
4. People are assigned to jobs that use their highest skills.
5. Greater job control is attained.
6. Costs can be reduced or minimized.
7. Employees know how their jobs fit into the total pattern of operations.
8. Quality of work performed can be improved.
9. Wage costs can be reduced.
10. Equipment and materials can be ordered on time.
11. Waste can be minimized.

and anticipate the coming of Styrofoam ice chests can always claim, for example, that the drying up of their market was for the best—even though they were caught short when the market for steel chests collapsed.

Saying it was all for the best, however, is rationalizing. Few companies can afford to be flip about poor planning—especially poor planning done by operating supervisors. As Franklin G. Moore has indicated, successful companies get where they are by planning. Not only do they plan, they engage in a variety of serious financial, product, market, and service planning, as well as performance and people planning. Successful companies also require supervisors to plan for implementing overall corporate goals.

Evidence of Poor Planning

Some bosses like to check themselves out as planners, so they ask themselves questions such as "What might be evidence of poor planning?" Questions that can give such evidence include these:

1. Are schedules and delivery dates not met and work not done?

2. Are crash programs and overtime work required to complete a job or work arrangement?

3. Are machines idle or employees idle with nothing to do?

4. Are supervisors making work for employees to keep them busy?

5. Are employees dragging out a job?

6. Are quarreling, bickering, and passing the buck common among emloyees?

7. Is there duplication of work?

If you answer many of these questions affirmatively, you are probably not planning as effectively as possible.

What to Do about Plans that Fail

The reasons for plans that fail are myriad. Missing the mark with plans is not always the result of incorrectly guessing what an employee or even what a machine will do. At times, it is the result of unforeseeable and uncontrollable events—a customer cancels an order, or a river goes on a rampage and floods the operation. In other cases, plans fail because they were poor. Also, lack of drive by the supervisor may cause failure because no one pushes the required tasks to completion. Supervisors must recognize that the planning phase of work must be followed up with a strong implementation phase, which really means the organizing, directing and controlling of the job.

Supervisors have difficulties in planning for a variety of reasons. Sometimes they fail because they don't possess sufficient knowledge of what really needs to be done in a job. As a result, their planning is inadequate. Other times, plans may fail because the supervisor has too much knowledge and this interferes when preparations are too detailed.

There are many other reasons why plans fail (see Figure 2–4). Even though the plan is satisfactory, there may be a lack of time. For example, it may be impossible to plan the construction and opening of a 100-mile freeway in one year. It takes too long for certain processes to occur—for roadbeds to settle, for concrete to cure, and so forth. A good manager cannot plan to serve Thanksgiving dinner at noon and expect to start preparing the meat at 10 A.M. Even in microwave ovens, it takes longer than that to roast a 23-pound turkey, let alone prepare the trimmings.

Planning may also fail because of outside pressure or the pressures of other competing work. Most businesses try to react or adapt favorably to

FIGURE 2–4 Why Plans Fail

1. Unforeseen circumstances.
2. Uncontrollable circumstances.
3. Poor planning.
4. Lack of knowledge and information.
5. Failure to make appropriate time considerations.
6. Outside pressures, pressures for completing work.

customers and their wishes. As a result, they usually try to deliver special orders or squeeze in special projects to satisfy a major client. This rushing, however, creates demands that totally abuse the work schedules of even the most organized supervisors.

Directing

Many inexperienced first-line supervisors fail to understand the importance of being skilled in leading and directing employees. Frequently their attitude is, "Employees are paid to work, so all the manager needs to do is tell them what to do, and they damn well better do it."

Directing (or leading) is the third of the basic supervisory jobs. Good supervisory direction means helping employees to get the right resources on the right job so that it can go in the right direction. The working environment of most supervisors, however, is often not conducive to making it easy for the supervisor to be a good director of work. Whether in an office or in a plant, on a sales floor or on a newspaper beat, most work situations are a subtle maze of relationships. There is a tangled mass of people's ambitions and abilities, mechanical systems and equipment, physical facilities and geographical dimensions, not to mention problems of competition, weather, and other uncontrollables.

Directing means more than giving instructions like a coach or an instructor. It means effectively leading employees to do a job by assigning tasks and using established policies, procedures, and techniques to optimize the efforts of the people, material, machines, and money for which the supervisor is responsible. Therefore, directing requires that the manager can effectively communicate, counsel, assign, train, motivate, and discipline subordinates.

Simply telling one to do something is not effective in directing people in their jobs. For example, what happens if a supervisor gives an order to an employee, and the employee doesn't understand—or misinterprets—what the order is? Employees can't do what they were told if they didn't understand the message. Also, some people react negatively to being commanded to do something rather than being requested to do something. People who are pompous or overbearing in telling others to do things seldom get the cooperation necessary for a good working relationship.

Occasionally, employees may refuse to comply with their supervisor's instructions. At times, they may carry out job instructions but do so haphazardly. In these cases, direct, forceful behavior may be required. Typically, however, the supervisor who uses tactful communication will get more work done because employees will be more willing to work for that supervisor than one who constantly uses threatening or demeaning approaches.

There are many mistakes made by first-line managers in directing people. Generally, these mistakes are caused by the supervisor's insensitivity to the critical importance of how job directions and instructions should be given. Some common mistakes are discussed below.

1. Not Appearing to Be Serious. Some supervisors are rather flip or cavalier in how they give instructions to employees. If the supervisor does not appear serious about the job, the worker probably will not take it seriously either.

2. Using Hard-to-Understand Terminology. Sometimes first-line supervisors fail to direct their employees because they use words or terms that employees do not understand. One sure way to confuse workers is to talk in language they do not understand or to use terminology that has little or no meaning to them. For example, would you know what a supervisor meant by telling a worker to "get off the skip"?

3. Making the Assumption that the Worker Understands Things. Sometimes, first-line supervisors assume that their employees know a good deal about a job when they do not. Often supervisors give job directions and instructions to an employee and later find out that the employee did not have the foggiest notion what the supervisor was talking about—and, perhaps, the employee was afraid to say so.

4. Giving Too Many Directions at Once. It is possible for an employee to remember a week's worth of work assignments. But, unless the work assignment involves repeating the same task all week, it is unlikely that the employee will remember everything. There is no reason to tell employees on Monday what they have to do the following Friday. This is particularly true if what needs to be done on Friday may change.

5. Being a Big Deal. Attitudes have a lot to do with whether or not employees are mentally tuned in and listening to the supervisor's instructions. A supervisor who needs to impress employees or who acts self-important will fail to effectively communicate job instructions and directions to subordinates.

6. *Giving Conflicting and Confusing Instructions.* It is impossible for first-line supervisors to assign work effectively unless they fully understand what the employee needs to do. The problem can become especially acute when the first-line supervisor tells the employee to do a job one way and later tells the same worker to do it differently. Whenever supervisors do not know what they want accomplished, it is best to analyze what needs to be done and then give clear instructions to the employee rather than simply "get somebody started on something" for the sake of assigning activities.

There are many reasons why first-line supervisors and managers fail to direct employees effectively. A supervisor however, can fail for reasons other than the inability to give clear directions and job instructions. One of those reasons is the failure to follow up or control. Let us now look at the control function of supervisors.

Controlling

The fourth function of a good supervisor is controlling. Basically, the function of control is the establishment of a feedback system for the supervisor in terms of employee performance. Feedback can be in the form of oral reports, written reports, personal observation, or any other form of information designed to apprise the supervisor regularly of how the job is going (see Figure 2–5).

Often, the supervisory function of control is thought of as authoritarian or dictatorial. Supervisory control should not be thought of in negative terms. Actually, the supervisory function of control can be used in a positive vein. After all, how can a supervisor give a sincere compliment to an employee who performs well on a job if some checking up via an inspection, report, or information-gathering activity does not occur? If a boss doesn't check up on employees, he or she doesn't know what is

---

FIGURE 2–5 Requirements for Good Control

1. Accurate information.
2. Cover separate units or people.
3. Give current state of affairs.
4. Prevent making things look good (or bad) when such is not the case.
5. Indicate actions taken and actions to be taken.
6. Highlight comparisons of people's job performance.

going on, and if that boss says, "Thanks, you did a great job," the subordinate is apt to think, "How the hell do you know?"

Experienced supervisors usually learn to use feedback as a basis for taking corrective action when things are not going well. For example, supervisors of airline flight attendants use many feedback methods to find out how well employees are doing their job and how improvements might be made in any particular performance. The supervisor may go on a flight to observe an individual's performance. Or the supervisor may screen letters of complaint and praise received concerning the attendant. The information obtained can be used to coach, counsel, train, and help improve the flight attendant's job effectiveness. Thus, solid information will be developed by the supervisor, and recommendations for improvement can be made from that information.

The important point here is recognizing *how control is attained*. Supervisory control is not the same as the control a corporate comptroller exercises in issuing annual reports to stockholders or in cutting off credit to a customer. It is the control achieved through a system of formal or informal reports and observations that ensures the correct work is done on time and as required.

Requirements for Control

Some of the basic requirements for a good control situation include the following:

1. Reports and observations must provide accurate information about the status of the work for which the supervisor is responsible. *Accurate* information is not necessarily precise or complete information. Information that is sufficiently accurate to alert the supervisor that work is going poorly may not be complete. For example, it is usually unnecessary for automobile drivers to know precisely how many miles they can drive before they run out of gas. Usually it is adequate to know that one can drive *about* another 25 miles, or that the car has *about* 2 gallons of gasoline left in the tank. Similarly, for control purposes, supervisory information does not have to be precise—a department manager does not need to know that worker A will run out of material to work on at 10:30 A.M., but the department manager probably does need to know that worker A is likely to run out of material about mid-morning.

2. If reports are to help give good supervisory control, they must cover separate employees. Information about the performance efforts of individuals must be available if the supervisor is to have usable informa-

tion for making judgments for corrective action. It is undesirable and useless to lump the performances of several people together in one report. Such a report does not permit the supervisor to identify and understand who is performing adequately and who is not. To a grocery shopper, how useful is the knowledge that the average price of a pound of meat is $2.75 when the shopper is trying to decide whether or not to serve T-bone steaks? While $2.75 may be true, average prices are not meaningful. What the shopper wants to know is the price of T-bone steaks. In the same vein, bosses need to know what each person under their guidance is doing—how many sales per person, how much production per person, and so forth. Knowing that the average typist in a work unit types 80 words per minute (wpm) meaning nothing if the real typing speeds are as follows: employee A, 100 wpm; employee B, 100 wpm; employee C, 100 wpm; and employee D, 20 wpm. The supervisor who knows only the average typing speed will never be in a position to work with employee D to develop his or her typing skills.

3. Reports of an individual's performance must contain current information. Any report, no matter how good, no matter how formal or informal, is worthless in today's dynamic business world if it highlights a bad situation six months after it began. This is one of the reasons that today's supervisor must learn how to use computer-generated and/or other electronically generated data. Learning that a shipment was missent to a customer six weeks after the fact indicates poor management. Reports must be prompt, up-to-date, and understood by the supervisor if the supervisor is to take corrective action or exercise control over the work performed. The boss must know *when* a bad situation is getting worse in order to take immediate action. Timeliness is the key to good supervisory control.

4. Another basic requisite for effective supervisory control is that the formalized reporting of facts be mechanically designed to minimize the possibility that reports can be used to make a person or situation look good or bad. Loading the dice or whitewashing anyone's job performance cannot be tolerated. A teacher should not ask only favorite students how they liked the teacher's class, and the supervisor should not rely on arbitrary or biased judges for reports about an employee's performance. Asking the local bigot to evaluate a minority group employee's performance is only going to get one answer, and asking people to critique their own performance may not be much better. The purpose of using reports is to maintain supervisory control. Any device that can be used to

manipulate or distort facts—either good or bad—is useless because it is fraudulent.

A common problem for beginning supervisors is the desire to look good in the eyes of *their* supervisor. They often permit reports to be made that tend to hide or otherwise modify poor performances. Ultimately, when the inaccurate nature of the poor report is disclosed, it is often too late to take corrective action. No effective supervisor will tolerate inaccurate reporting procedures.

5. Reports from or about employees and work performance must always be designed to include notes regarding actions that are taken and/or planned to be taken. Reporting procedures should not only highlight the fact that things are getting out of control or that bad situations are developing, but they should also include ways to remedy the problems. This is the reason that supervisors must also learn to put information into data-processing terminals. Informing other affected people in the organization is the flip side of being informed and it is an important ingredient in control.

6. The final aspect of a good supervisory control system includes the principle that reports must be designed to highlight comparisons of performance among various organizations, units, and individuals. Supervisors who hope to evaluate the individual performance of their subordinates must have reports that highlight critical elements of differences among individual performances. Reports must also underscore performance elements that can be compared. Reports should not be designed to group together or otherwise cover up, exonerate, or embellish poor performance. Reports alone do not assure control, but they do form a basis for corrective action, and they are an important part of the control function.

WHY SOME SUPERVISORS FAIL IN THEIR ROLES AND FUNCTIONS

Most people who are appointed to a supervisory position succeed largely because they are ambitious, dedicated, and hard-working. They usually have been selected as supervisors for their intelligence and alertness. Most supervisors have a lot of innate talent. Some supervisors, however, fail. Let's take a brief look at some reasons why they fail:

Rigidity and Inability to Change. Some supervisors simply will not change anything—not their ideas, methods, or outlooks. They are rigid because they think their way is the *only* way of doing anything right, or because they cannot see the need to change, alter, or rearrange methods and techniques they have learned. This is especially true when the methods or techniques they are using have worked well for many years. The supervisor must recognize that supervision is an ever-changing, ever-challenging activity. Methods and techniques constantly change, even methods that are tried and proved. Excessive rigidity is the bane of any would-be successful supervisor.

Poor Interpersonal Relationships.   A supervisor must understand the need to relate well to employees, fellow supervisors, and superiors. No one is an island; no one can work alone. According to one study, the most important reason for supervisor failure is the inability to build workable interpersonal relations.

Lack of Organization.   Planning requires predicting the future. Supervisors must know how they want the future to look in order to help that future materialize. The supervisor's functions—planning, organizing, directing, and controlling—are an ongoing series of activities that are interdependent. Supervisors who are disorganized, who do not know where they are going, who do not know how to get there, and who are confused about what the future will bring cannot be effective in accomplishing the supervisor's job.

An I Don't Care Attitude.   Sometimes supervisors will fail because they do not care about success. Such instances, however, are infrequent. Most people have too much pride to fail in supervisory roles. In fact, Jim Hayes, as president of the American Management Association, argued that fear of failure is the most important motivational attribute a supervisor can have. When supervisors do not care, they are doomed to failure.

Lack of Commitment.   Another reason why some people fail in a supervisory capacity is that they are unwilling to devote the time and effort required for success. Good supervision is not easy. It can be a rewarding and exhilarating activity, but it is also a tiring and sometimes thankless activity. Some people want the good but not the bad. Because of this, when the going gets rough, they sometimes develop a "quitter" mentality. Quitters are seldom long-term winners.

Lack of Vision.   A final reason why some supervisors fail is that they do not clearly see what they are trying to accomplish. Top-level management may be at fault as much as the first-line supervisor in such cases. Frequently, top-level management fails to communicate its ideas to first-level supervisors. Sometimes this is on purpose. Other times, top management may take first-line supervision for granted, a problem that the first-line supervisors may have, in turn, with their subordinates. It is hard to argue that the first-line supervisor should not know what is happening in the work situation. First-line supervisors are the first rank of management. They are the persons to whom nonmanagement employees look for guidance and direction. The first-line manager must know what is happening. It is important that first-line supervisors learn where the organization is going and how it is going to get there, as well as whether or not such information is initiated by top-level management and/or communicated to the first-line supervisor.

HOW THE SIZE OF THE ORGANIZATION AFFECTS THE SUPERVISOR'S JOB

One last issue to be addressed is the impact that the size and nature of the organization have on the supervisor's job. In small organizations, the supervisor's job is usually far more difficult than in large organizations. The reasons for this are twofold, and they can be an advantage or a disadvantage depending on the supervisor.

First of all, in the small organization, supervisors are in charge of almost everything from hiring to firing; actually, they are responsible for everything from recruiting efforts that go on before hiring to processing the paperwork after someone is terminated or quits. Individuals who like broad challenges inevitably prefer to be supervisors in smaller organizations because of the job's diversity, but many individuals are terror-stricken at the thought of such broad areas of responsibility.

The second reason that the supervisory job is so different in smaller organizations is that professional assistance/requirements are so much more available/demanding. This aspect, too, is a double-edged sword. In the larger organization, there are inevitably bountiful numbers of professional people available to help the supervisor in his/her functions. There are legal and labor experts, financial advisers, medical departments, counselors, training facilities and advisers, and even people to help you buy a new home or decide where to send your kids to school. Persons who thrive in large structures relish these forms of assistance. But persons who like small organizations tend to think of this "advice" as meddlesome, confining, and restrictive of individual growth; it creates too many limitations for them.

Supervision is not the same in organizations of different sizes. The organization's size may largely determine if a supervisory aspirant will be successful. Some people work well within delineated boundaries, while others can't abide such constraints. Some persons like to sing harmony, some like to sing melody, and some don't like to sing at all. Supervision is the same. The reader should not think in absolutes about what is required of a supervisor; instead, he or she should think about personal expectations for any supervisory job. In this text, we attempt to classify the requirements for successful supervision, but these efforts are only a beginning. All supervisory talents must be molded to fit and be applied correctly in each supervisory situation by the individual supervisor.

Things to Remember

1. The supervisor's role in any company varies because of the nature of the company or organization for which he or she works.

2. Today the study of supervision is an international undertaking.

3. There are four primary management functions in which supervisors are involved:
   a. Planning.
   b. Organizing.
   c. Controlling.
   d. Leading (motivating).

4. Not all managers are necessarily good leaders, and not all leaders are necessarily good managers. Leadership and managership are separate skills. Excellent managers, however, are also good leaders.

5. Planning is the keystone of both management and leadership. It is related to organizing, controlling, decision making, leading, and the entire range of management activities. It is a look into the future.

6. Organizing involves the systematic arrangement of personnel, equipment, materials, work area, methods, and other work variables into a coherent sequence to accomplish the goals of an organization.

7. Directing involves more than planning. It includes all activities associated with letting people know what is required to accomplish goals of an organization.

8. Control involves setting standards, measuring to determine if the

standards are being met, and taking corrective action to ensure that they are.

9. Primary reasons supervisors fail include rigidity, lack of organization, and an I don't care attitude.

10. Supervision in small organizations often differs vastly from supervision in large organizations.

Key Words

planning
organizing
controlling
directing
communication skills
long-range plans
short-range plans
delegating
supervisory control
reasons for failure
unity of command

Self-Assessment

Evaluate your knowledge of first-line management skills by answering the questions below on a scale of 1–6. Answers 1, 2, or 3 mean that you disagree or would give the question a negative response with 1 being the most negative and 3 the least negative. Answers 4, 5, or 6 indicate agreement or positive responses—with 4 being the least positive and 6 the most positive.

1. Most supervisory jobs are alike regardless of the organization.

      1   2   3   4   5   6

2. Currently, serious study of supervision is limited largely to the studies made in the United States.

      1   2   3   4   5   6

3. It is estimated that there are at least 10 million supervisors at work in the U.S. economy.

      1   2   3   4   5   6

4. Most inexperienced supervisors lack the skills and the knowledge in effectively relating to their own work forces.

1	2	3	4	5	6

5. Planning is the one management function that is not necessary at all levels in an organization.

1	2	3	4	5	6

6. Directing means giving instructions.

1	2	3	4	5	6

7. Sometimes direct, forceful behavior is required in a supervisor.

1	2	3	4	5	6

8. Are you usually serious when you direct the activities of others?

1	2	3	4	5	6

9. Control, if properly applied, is essentially a negative management function since most people resent control.

1	2	3	4	5	6

10. Do you consider yourself dedicated, ambitious, and hard-working?

1	2	3	4	5	6

CASES

Tough-Minded or Tough Headed?

As crew chief for Columbia Area Telephone System (CATS), Randy Guerrero felt he knew his business. While enrolled in Columbia College, Randy had started as a system installation helper, was promoted to installer before completion of his first year on the job, and shortly after graduating become crew chief, the primary first-line management title used by CATS. Randy and his crew were responsible for the installation and maintenance of commercial and business telephone systems.

Driven by a need to succeed, Randy became a demanding but generally fair first-line manager. His crew members admired his ambition but none felt close to him as a person. All crew members were cautious when they talked to him, and they tended to avoid making on-the-job decisions unless they checked with him first.

In day-to-day operations, Randy would carefully review installation plans with sales engineers and analysts, make out a materials and equipment list, check equipment loading, and give his crew of eight installers and helpers a general outline of what needed to be done. On the job, Randy would assign work to each person on the crew and tell them to check with him as soon as an assignment was completed. If there was an especially difficult system hookup, Randy would frequently do the job himself rather than assign it to an installer. Eventually, Randy felt he was working harder and harder, and his crew, although competent, seemed to take too long to complete required work.

In looking at his own performance, Randy felt he was supervising correctly. He was careful, worked hard, treated his employees fairly, and tried to make work go smoothly. Yet, he was dissatisfied.

1. What might Randy want to improve?

2. How would your rate Randy as a first-line manager? Explain.

3. What will happen to Randy if he fails to change his current management style?

Growing Pains

Linda Tuttle knew about the expansion of Minden Electronic Service Systems (MESS) almost a week before it was publicized. As Supervisor of Shipping and Receiving, she attended weekly review meetings where preliminary discussions of the company's new undertaking took place. The company was enlarging its service area to include a number of nearby cities and communities as well as the city of Minden. As an electronics service company, MESS provided repair, special assembly, and standard maintenance for computers, disk drives, terminals, and related electronic equipment. Grace Gil, Linda's immediate manager, had asked each of the first-line managers to develop a plan for expanding their departments. "We are going to go from a single-shift operation to a double-shift operation as a first move. In addition, most departments, especially the receiving area, will be expanded to include more room for the increased volume of material we'll be handling. I would like a preliminary plan of what you feel will be necessary to make the expansion as successful as possible. Try to have a rough draft to me a week from today," instructed Grace.

As Linda returned to her office, she thought about Grace's instructions: second shift, more space, and handling a greater volume of materials. "It may be a little tougher than I thought," she mused, "but I have a few ideas."

1. In developing her preliminary plan, what major factors should Linda consider?

2. Why did Grace Gil want a preliminary plan rather than a final, detailed plan?

3. How would plans differ if MESS decided to decrease its operations rather than increase them?

PART TWO

Supervisory Skills

3

Making Effective Work Assignments

Thought Starter

Some years ago, Keith Davis, a major management writer and professor at Arizona State University, observed that Americans prefer general directions to specific directions from their supervisors. They would rather be told what to do than how to do it, especially if they are trained, experienced employees. Managers who insist on explaining precisely how to do a task to experienced employees are communicating a lack of confidence in employees' job knowledge. While such direction may be appreciated by an untrained or inexperienced person, it can create the opposite reaction from an experienced employee.

Making effective work assignments requires more than knowledge of what needs to be done and how to do it. In Chapter 3, pitfalls and promises of effective job assignments are explored. Making effective job assignments is a vital first-line management skill.

In Chapter 3 you will learn:

- Why delegation skills are essential to successful management.
- Reasons that some managers fail in making work assignments.
- How work assignments vary at different organizational levels.
- Ways that situational management can make giving orders largely unnecessary.
- Guidelines for effective delegation.

When Carl and Gail Smith started their foreign car repair service shortly after they were married, they had no idea it would grow as rapidly as it did. Specializing in repairing expensive European cars had paid off. Now they had six full-time repair specialists and three office employees. Their future looked bright as their reputation for quality work and fair prices grew.

To help keep the business on schedule, Carl kept his tools available, and he usually did the highly technical jobs himself. He was often irritated by frequent interruptions from employees who needed information or work directions. One of his pet dislikes was giving work assignments to people who were supposed to know what they were doing. Over time, both Carl and Gail were spending longer hours doing paperwork, even though the office workers did well with everyday tasks. "What are we doing wrong?" Carl asked Gail. "I take care of the shop, you take care of the office and even help in the shop, but we keep falling behind."

"Maybe we're spending too much time doing work and too little time managing work," responded Gail. "It's something I read in a book. We can start delegating more."

"You may be right, but there are many things I can do better than anyone else in the shop. Who is going to take care of those things?" Carl wondered.

"It ain't my job."

The foregoing sentence is not an unusual comment for a supervisor to hear. Usually when it is uttered, it follows a request—or order—from a boss to a subordinate to get something done.

Many supervisors are troubled by the prospect of giving orders to subordinates. They have learned it's not "right" to tell employees to do things; instead, supervisors should ask them. But, supervisors discover that even when they do ask, they are still told "It ain't my job."

How does a boss effectively assign work? Some bosses seem to have little trouble, while others seem to constantly battle with their subordinates. Is it a question of asking politely, a question of how one's hair is parted, or something more?

PEOPLE DON'T LIKE TO BE TOLD

People don't like to be told what to do. Or maybe it is more correct to say they sometimes don't like the way something is said. There is no evidence that people don't like to be told what to do when they like what they hear. Few people reject such direct orders as "Take a break," "Go inside and warm up for a few minutes," or "Why don't you move in the shade to work; it'll be cooler there."

Giving orders—telling—isn't the problem that creates difficulty for the supervisor in making work assignments. The problem comes from resistance to what is being said. That resistance can occur for a variety of reasons. Sometimes the problem is that the boss is not perceived as having the authority to give an order. Certainly, most company presidents do not have this problem. "Right or wrong, the big boss is still the big boss." But, for first-level supervisors, their authority isn't always perceived as unquestionable. The level of the individual in the organization may effect his or her ability to make effective work assignments. Other matters also affect the supervisor's ability to issue effective work assignments, even when supervisors are perceived by employees as having the authority to make assignments. Some of these limits come from the supervisor's self-image. Some problems come from the supervisor's lack of skills in organization and communication. Some concerns arise from what the boss doesn't say—errors of omission. Making effective work assignments is not an easy task.

Who Is at Fault in Failure to Assign Work Effectively?

Assigning work is one of the most important managerial functions affecting a supervisor's success or failure. Not all supervisors fail in assigning work to subordinates. However, the supervisor's failure to assign or delegate work effectively is not the only reason that many workers mishandle job assignments. Sometimes, supervisors can be completely clear in assigning work to subordinates; yet, the worker still fails.

Supervisors must be able to understand and recognize the reasons for failure in making work assignments effective so that they can pinpoint the reasons when they occur. They must also be able to overcome the problem of unresponsive employees. Failures in assigning and accepting work assignments are largely due to the behavioral outlook and attitudes of both the supervisor and the subordinate. A clear understanding of the psychology involved in making effective work assignments is essential.

HOW ORGANIZATION LEVEL AFFECTS WORK ASSIGNMENT

A person's supervisory level in the organization affects the way a manager, supervisor, or lead person assigns and delegates work. A front-line supervisor's problems in delegating and assigning work are different from the problems of top management. The reason for this lies partly in the nature of job assignments to be made and partly in the nature of individuals to whom the job assignments are to be made. For a graphic portrayal of the changing nature of work assignments among various levels of supervision, see Figure 3–1.

What Is Work Assignment and What Is Delegation?

There is a difference between **assigning work** and **delegating.** Assigning work, which is part of the supervisory function of direction, is the act of giving job instructions, directions, orders, and training to the person doing the job.

Delegation, on the other hand, is assigning to subordinates the duties, tasks, and responsibilities normally done by the boss. First-line supervisors assign work and delegate. Supervisors who expect to be promoted to higher levels of management usually develop delegation skills early in their supervisory careers. This makes them more promotable because it (a) frees up their time to take on more of their boss's responsibilities and (b) demonstrates their ability to get work done through others by being well-organized and competent in communicating with and training subordinates.

The First Phase— Direct Supervision

In the direct supervision stage, the supervisor's job is to plan, organize, direct, control, and motivate the activities of their employees. At this level in the organization, most of the supervised work is "doing" work.

FIGURE 3–1 The Changing Nature of Work Assignments

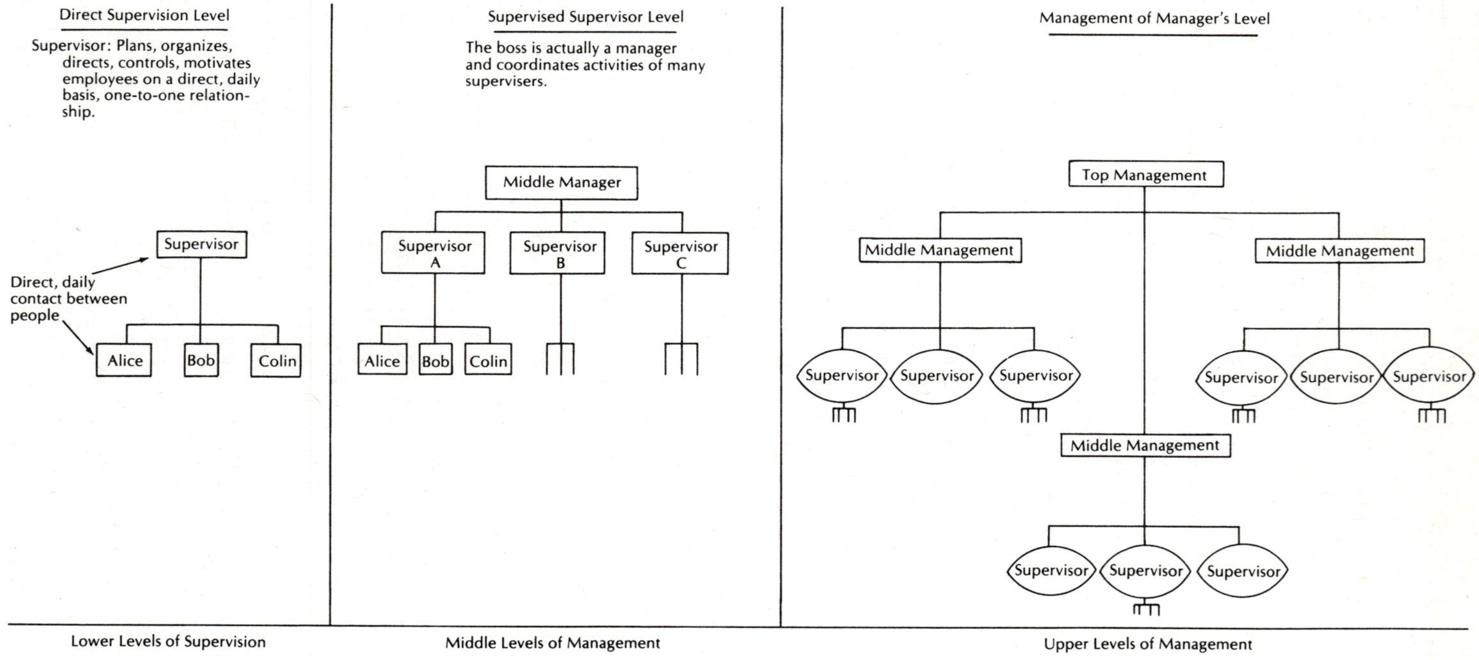

Direct Supervision Level
Supervisor: Plans, organizes, directs, controls, motivates employees on a direct, daily basis, one-to-one relationship.
Supervisor
Direct, daily contact between people
Alice
Bob
Colin
Supervised Supervisor Level
The boss is actually a manager and coordinates activities of many supervisers.
Middle Manager
Supervisor A
Supervisor B
Supervisor C
Alice
Bob
Colin
Management of Manager's Level
Top Management
Middle Management
Middle Management
Middle Management
Supervisor
Supervisor
Supervisor
Supervisor
Supervisor
Supervisor
Supervisor
Supervisor
Supervisor
Lower Levels of Supervision
Middle Levels of Management
Upper Levels of Management

This means almost everyone that the supervisor oversees and evaluates is involved in the mechanical function of the job—an employee is a welder, typist, salesclerk, or has an *operating* assignment. The front-line supervisor must understand what is required *mechanically* for the subordinate to function effectively on the job. The actual assignment of work is often relatively simple, because employees may have a written description of the activities that they are expected to perform.

The primary problem for the supervisor in the direct-supervision stage is organizing work so that it will flow as smoothly as possible. This in no way minimizes the problem of making work assignments. Supervisors must still get people to perform. Their job is to get results through their subordinates. But, at this level, supervisors have the advantage of close, daily contact with each employee. Rather than needing to engage in large, elaborate managerial schemes, they can quickly, easily, and regularly observe how work is going and make corrective work assignments where they are required. The supervisor must make work assignments that are understood by employees so that they can proceed independently without continual observation. Motivating the employee is an integral part of making work assignments in this phase.

The Second Phase—Supervising Supervisors

Supervising supervisors is different than supervising "doers." In this stage, the top supervisors' responsibility is to make work assignments to subordinates *who are supervisors*. Thus, the supervisor of supervisors, instead of making "doing" work assignments, makes project assignments. At this level, more delegation occurs than at the work assignment level. At this point on the organizational scale, the boss or superior actually becomes more of a general manager (versus a supervisor of one particular function and only a few people).

Figure 3–2 delineates how supervision changes as a manager grows from basic supervision to supervision of supervisors to being a manager of managers. The difference in job function between a line supervisor and middle and top-level manager is *primarily one of degree*. Figure 3–2 shows the changing job emphasis of each supervisor and manager as they command larger and larger segments of the organization.

As shown in Figure 3–2, the job of the nonsupervisory employees is almost totally technical and/or mechanical. Their job is, for the most part, accomplishing required activities with little responsibility or concern for planning or motivating people. Actually, the principal requirements for operational employees are that they come to work on time, do their job, and behave in a socially acceptable manner.

Figure 3–2 **The Changing Nature of Job Functions as People Grow in Organizational Rank**

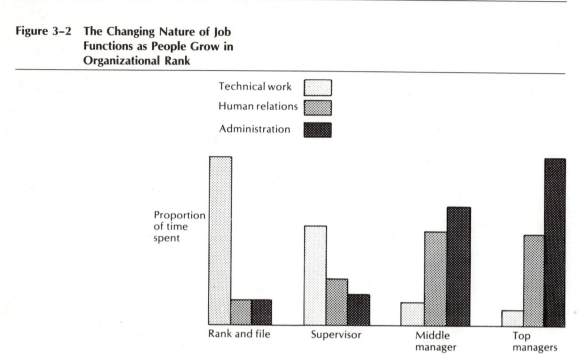

When an individual becomes a supervisor, however, the nature of the job changes. Figure 3–2 shows that front-line supervisors must know a great deal about the jobs they are supervising. A large percentage of the supervisor's work, however, is not mechanical or technical in nature. If a supervisor spends too much time actually doing the work or closely examining how it is done, not enough time can be spent directing and coordinating the efforts of operating employees. Line supervision is emphasizing and directing the efforts of subordinates rather than worrying about the how-to aspects of the job. From a technical standpoint, supervisors keep up-to-date on new processes and methods that can be used to get the best performance from their people. But, the supervisor's primary concern is planning and coordinating the efforts of employees.

In addition to effectively coordinating and controlling subordinates, the line supervisor also is responsible for effective interpersonal (human) relations. This duty is as important in the line supervisor's work as planning. The line supervisor must spend a lot of time with people who perform specific functions. While employees seldom go out of their way to sabotage each other's efforts deliberately, they do get into minor squabbles that often can be exceedingly bitter. Thus, the line supervisor's job is often directed toward keeping everyone working toward common goals with minimum destructive personal influences. The good line supervisor has more responsibility to promote harmonious working conditions (good human relations), as illustrated in Figure 3–2.

As supervisors grow in importance to the organizations, they have a slightly different role from that of the front-line supervisor in both technical and human relations functions. Supervisors of supervisors (called middle managers in Figure 3–2) are less concerned about the job's technical functions. From a technical standpoint, their primary responsibility is keeping abreast of the overall operation, relying on the line supervisor for overseeing the exact details of work accomplishment. Middle managers' technical job knowledge is often relatively limited in scope. They do not have to be an expert at the details and mechanics of doing the job. The manager in charge of the automotive parts section of a large retail store does not need to know the technical attributes of the various tires or batteries the store sells. However, the store's floor managers and salesclerks, who report to the floor managers, must know those details.

In the realm of interpersonal relations, the middle manager is ultimately responsible for handling major employee grievances and working effectively with and through subordinate supervisors. It is in this area of cooperation that line supervisors can be the most useful to their bosses. The middle manager can't be concerned with daily operating details but, instead, should be apprised of administrative, operational, and human relations problems that arise.

What supervisors of supervisors must be good at is the implementation of plans and the accomplishment of objectives. They have a tremendous amount of responsibility with respect to *administrative* functions. Middle managers must plan promotion schemes, oversee the scheduling of major contracts or work segments, and be concerned with budgetary constraints and controls. Middle-level managers must increasingly rely on the knowledge and expertise of the people who report to them as well as on their own administrative and managerial skills.

The Third Phase— The Management of Managers

The ultimate responsibility of managers of managers is to totally coordinate a major operation or organizational unit. In this capacity, they are required to devote practically all working time to administrative requirements. Managers of managers have, among their many responsibilities, requirements for procuring work, developing the capacity of the business or organization to produce, and delivering the finished product or service.

Managers of managers are seldom concerned with the technical functions of doing a specific job; instead, they usually spend their time delegating activities to responsible subordinates. Their interests lie in the overall effectiveness of the organization rather than in operational details. They coordinate the efforts of middle managers who, in turn, coordinate efforts of first-line supervisors, who see that the people with required technical skills perform their various tasks. Consider, for example, whether or not it would be proper for the president of a major electronics firm to know precisely how a computer is being manufactured, or if the director of research and development for a large oil company should be concerned with the procedures required to manufacture an antipollutant engine oil additive. Top management should not get involved in workaday details, yet they must be somewhat knowledgeable of them.

GROWING PROFESSIONALLY AS A SUPERVISOR

The nature of line supervisor's tasks are continually changing. Effective line supervisors also grow into more responsible jobs and find that they are increasingly accepting more administrative duties. The change in job duties toward more administrative responsibility is called the *vital shift* in supervision from the technical supervisor to the administrative manager. While first-line supervisors need not be overly concerned with this change in their job position, they must realize that over time it will occur, especially if they grow into more responsibile jobs. Facing this supervisory challenge requires that the line supervisor become adept at making effective job assignments. Yet, here is precisely where many line supervisors fail.

WHY SUPERVISORS FAIL AT MAKING EFFECTIVE WORK ASSIGNMENTS

One of the nation's foremost management consultants, Nathanial Stewart, several years ago conducted a poll of several hundred first-line supervisors from a cross section of retail and industrial firms to determine why supervisors failed to make effective work assignments. Some of the reasons he found included the following:

1. Some supervisors feel their subordinates are too inexperienced to do a job and they won't assign any work to them (the supervisors often prefer to do it themselves).

2. Many times the managers feel that it takes more time to explain the job than to do it themselves. Thus, they roll up their sleeves and do it themselves.

3. Some supervisors use the excuse that a mistake by subordinates would be too costly, thus, they don't assign work to them.

4. Sometimes supervisors feel that there are some items that simply should not be assigned to subordinates.

5. There is a feeling that many subordinates are detail specialists who lack the overall knowledge required for a job out of their specialty, so they shouldn't (or can't) be assigned additional job responsibilities.

6. Sometimes supervisors feel that their subordinates are too busy to take on any more work. (This, of course, can be true.)

7. Some managers feel that their subordinates are not ready to handle additional responsibility.

8. Some supervisors simply *like* doing detail work rather than administrative work, and they don't intend to assign certain jobs to their subordinates.

Of all nine reasons given for why line supervisors fail to assign more work than they do, there are only two reasons in this list that are ever partly valid—numbers 5 and 7. There are some items a boss should not assign (like motivational discussions, salary reviews, performance appraisals, and so forth), and there are times when an employee may have

**FIGURE 3–3 Why Supervisors Fail to
Assign Work Effectively
to Subordinates**

1. Subordinates are too inexperienced.
2. It takes longer to explain the work than to do it myself.
3. A mistake may be too costly.
4. I can get quicker action.
5. Some things just can't be assigned to my subordinates.
6. My people don't see the big picture.
7. My people are too busy.
8. My people just aren't ready.
9. I'd like to do it myself.

too much to do (like retail clerks at Christmas). For the most part, however, the reasons supervisors give for not assigning work are more often *excuses* rather than reasons.

The "I Can Do It Better Myself" Fallacy

Many supervisors are reluctant to assign work because they feel they can do the job better than their subordinates. By objective measurements, however, it is seldom true that supervisors can actually perform better than subordinates. In a study conducted by one of the authors, it was found that in over 80 percent of the cases where supervisors indicated they thought they could do the job better than their subordinates, the employee could do the job just as well as, if not better than, the boss.

The question of whether or not one can do the job better is not really an appropriate criterion on which to make work assignments. The criterion should be to assign work to the employee who can perform *satisfactorily, not necessarily best*.

Unfortunately, many supervisors find the idea of not doing the best possible job displeasing. This is especially true if they are proud of the quality of their work. While it is a good idea to encourage employees to do the job to required standards, it also must be recognized that projects can be overengineered or overplanned and that products and services can be overdone or overstressed in terms of quality. The consequences are cost increases with no benefit to either the producer or the user of the product or service. For example, in manufacturing a little red wagon as a child's toy, there is no need to machine the wagon's wheel bearings to one ten- thousandth of an inch tolerance, when one hundredth of an inch is more than satisfactory and will last the expected lifetime of the wagon. To go ahead and do the higher quality job will not make the red wagon last any longer. In all likelihood, something else will break, rust, or get bent long before the bearing wears out in the wheels, even if it is manufactured at a tolerance of one hundredth of an inch. Such overdone quality in manufacturing only increases production costs with no particular benefits. The same thing happens when a supervisor says "I'll do that job because I can do it better than anyone else." Even if the supervisor can do the job better than anyone else, if someone else who is paid less money per hour than the supervisor can do the job *well enough* in comparable time, that person should be assigned the work.

Lack of Ability to Direct

Many managers are unable to communicate what must be done. It is a proven maxim that before you can tell someone what to do, you must know what needs to be done. Supervisors who are incompetent at planning find it difficult to communicate job requirements to subordinates. Effective ability in assigning work to others requires that supervisors know specifically what to expect of their subordinates. This point was made patently clear by Lewis Carroll in his book *Alice's Adventures in Wonderland*, which was published more than 100 years ago. The reader might recall that Alice engaged in the following dialogue with the Cheshire Cat:

> **Alice:** Tell me, how can I get where I am going?
>
> **Cheshire Cat:** Well, that all depends upon where you want to go.
>
> **Alice:** I don't much care where.
>
> **Cheshire Cat:** Well then, my dear, any path will take you there.

Lack of Confidence in Subordinates

Lack of confidence in subordinates is a continual problem in the assignment of work. Supervisors lack confidence in their employees for a variety of reasons. They may feel the subordinate is too uninformed to understand what is required; they may be afraid that the subordinate doesn't possess sufficient judgment to handle the situation if a problem arises; or they may feel that the subordinate has failed to follow through on ideas in the past and, consequently, he or she might drop the ball and leave the job unfinished again.

Lack of confidence in subordinates also arises because of bigotry. Some managers lack confidence in subordinates because they feel that they are too young or too old. Other bosses lack confidence in subordinates (or at least refuse to assign them work) because they feel they are the wrong sex, race, or religion. The advent of the women's liberation movement in the early 1970s was partially triggered by managers with this attitude. Most jobs can be done equally well by women and men, young people and their elders. While wisdom does come with experience, and personal qualities may have a decided influence, these considerations are seldom valid reasons for failure to delegate or assign work.

Lack of Control

Many managers refuse to assign work because they need assurance that the work will be done correctly. Among some supervisors, "if you want a job done right, you must do it yourself," has almost become a creed. Unfortunately, most studies indicate that these managers are really saying that they are the only ones who can do the job correctly.

A common reason supervisors are reluctant to assign work is that they lack adequate control. If they do the job themselves, they can prevent anything from going wrong and institute immediate corrective action. Good control procedures ensure that the work is done correctly. Thus, good supervisors establish reports, observations, and control mechanisms by which they can determine whether or not subordinates are doing the job correctly.

Fear of Taking a Chance

Fear of taking a chance can be a real detriment to a supervisor in assigning work to subordinates. While there are some items an individual cannot effectively assign to others, most work done by supervisors can be delegated to subordinates. Supervisors who aspire to a more responsible job must remember that until they have delegated most detail work to subordinates, they will not be likely candidates for promotion. It is imperative that supervisors think in terms of delegating. Ideally, supervisors have their work organized and assigned so that there are few jobs left to oversee personally. Most top-level managers feel this is the ideal or desired situation—or at least it is the direction in which they encourage ambitious supervisors to develop their jobs. Seldom is the ideal attained, but many times it is approximated, and supervisors who do so are the supervisors who get promotions.

The Martyr Complex

Some supervisors fail to assign work to subordinates because they suffer from the *martyr complex*. The nature of the martyr complex is difficult to understand, but it can best be summarized as self-pity on the part of the supervisor. Such people are frequently called workaholics. They are supervisors who like to feel sorry for themselves because they have to work so hard. They enjoy being seen by others as working extraordinarily hard. Little do they realize that the people they think are feeling sorry for them are actually *making fun of them*. Employees seldom feel any real sympathy or pity for the boss who is a habitual martyr. More serious, however, is the attitude of the martyred supervisor's supervisor. Invariably, the supervisor of the martyred supervisor sees the martyr as poorly organized and incapable of performing supervisory duties satisfactorily.

The Guilt Drive

Some supervisors believe that "idle hands are the devil's workshop." The good employee, they think, always has something to do, and the bad employee is the grasshopper who has idle time. That many people believe they should be busy constantly is unfortunate, especially if they are supervisors. Supervisors should not hoard work. To do so means that subordinates are not accomplishing what they should be doing. Rather than feeling guilty for not having enough to do, it is far better for supervisors to plan for the future rather than to fear that they will be caught with little to do.

HOW SUBORDINATES MANAGE TO AVOID RESPONSIBILITY

It is not always the supervisor's fault when work is assigned but doesn't get done. Many times, supervisors are perfectly willing and quite able to assign work to their subordinates. However, the supervisor can still fail— many times subordinates are reluctant to (or at least fail to) accept responsibilities assigned to them by the boss. In some cases, the reasons why subordinates avoid responsibility are similar to the reasons supervisors fail to assign work. Reasons that employees are reluctant to cooperate or fail to cooperate with their supervisor's desires include the following:

1. It is often easier for employees to ask the boss than to decide to do something themselves. A characteristic of an *ineffective* boss is the willingness to solve *all* problems. An effective supervisor realizes that employees must develop the ability to solve most of their work problems *without* extensive supervisory help. Wise supervisors discourage dependence on their knowledge as supervisors and encourage employee problem solving. This must be done judiciously, of course. But a good supervisor is careful not to make decisions for subordinates concerning matters that subordinates should decide for themselves.

2. Many employees fear unjust or unreasonable criticism, and they will avoid responsibility if they feel a small mistake will result in embarrassment or harassment from their boss. For this reason, overly critical supervisors often have the least effective work force. There is a time, place, and method to correct employee mistakes, but shouting and screaming in front of customers or other employees is always an inappropriate time, place, and method.

3. Employees are reluctant to tackle work they do not understand. A good line supervisor is a good communicator. He or she lets the employee know what is expected and makes sure the employee is adequately prepared and equipped to complete the assignment.

4. Sometimes an employee is overloaded with work and cannot accept new assignments without failing. Successful supervisors look carefully at their staffing requirements and the distribution of work, and they determine if organizational problems are causing work overloads before they dump more work on an employee.

5. Employees may, at times, lack confidence in their ability to complete an assignment successfully. As a developer of people, the supervisor tries to inspire subordinates' confidence and helps them become confident in their own abilities.

6. When recognition of effort is lacking, most employees lose interest in assuming added responsibility. The feeling of being important and worthwhile is valued by everyone. A good supervisor regularly lets employees know where they stand and shows tangible appreciation for jobs well done.

7. Some employees think that certain types of work fall outside or beneath their skill level and, thus, they should be exempt from doing such work. Supervisors wise to the world of work recognize this and must often explain that many tasks are not as desirable as others but, in order for the organization and its employees to be successful, everyone must do some work he or she may not enjoy as much as other assignments.

8. Employees may neglect some assignments in favor of others that they see as having higher payoffs in terms of recognition, promotion, or status. As in the case of undesirable jobs, the manager has to distribute work equally and let all employees know that the mundane, dull, low-payoff jobs must also be accomplished.

9. In some situations, it is customary that the senior employee or employees in certain job classifications do not do particular assignments. A successful supervisor will minimize the formation of restrictive job customs and eradicate norms that tend to hurt the organization rather than help it.

10. Often for good reason, but most often because of distrust, employees will resist assignments because they lack confidence in their boss. Effective supervisors establish their roles strongly and purposefully in their organizations. They know that work effectiveness depends on *mutual* respect and confidence. They constantly work at increasing confidence and trust in their relationship with employees.

Uncertainty as to What to Delegate

Many times it is difficult for the supervisor to determine what can be effectively delegated. Remember that when a supervisor delegates, a

**FIGURE 3–4   Reasons Why Subordinates
Resist Work that the Boss
Assigns to Them**

1. It's easier to get the boss to do it.
2. They fear criticism.
3. They don't understand the job.
4. There is too much work to do.
5. They lack self-confidence.
6. They feel their efforts will go unrecognized.
7. They feel the work is beneath them.
8. Greater reward comes from doing other things.
9. The customary practice is that others have to do it.
10. They lack confidence in the boss.

subordinate will be doing the work ordinarily done by the supervisor. The following guidelines are designed to assist supervisors in determining activities they can delegate and activities they should do themselves.

What to Delegate

1. Problems that require only technical or mechanical skills.

2. Activities described in the subordinate's job description.

3. Jobs that the subordinate will ultimately be expected to do and jobs that provide individual development and growth for the subordinate in either mechanical, administrative, or semisupervisory skills.

4. Problems and/or activities that a supervisor feels the subordinate can handle; if the activities are done by the subordinate, it will conserve time.

**What Is Generally
Not Delegable**

There are many activities the supervisor really cannot delegate to subordinates, at least not until the subordinate has experience. These activities are exclusively supervisory. Examples include the following:

1.   Planning.   The supervisor has primary responsibility for his or her department's operational plans. This activity should not be delegated to a subordinate.

2.   Morale Problems.   These problems are extremely difficult to delegate. They are part of the supervisor's interpersonal responsibility.

3. *Conflict Resolution.* Usually, if there is a conflict between two immediate subordinates of the line supervisor, no one else should handle the problem. Such conflicts and attempts at reconciliation of differences cannot be assigned to anyone else.

4. *Coaching Employees.* This is also a difficult job that should not be delegated (unless it is akin to teaching mechanical job skills and someone else is a more qualified trainer). It is the supervisor's general responsibility to coach and help employees develop their capabilities.

5. *Personal Assignment.* Whenever the supervisor's boss assigns something that the supervisor is expected to do personally, it would be imprudent for the supervisor to delegate that work to a subordinate, even though the supervisor would like to do so.

6. *Exclusive Qualifications.* When there is no one else qualified to do a specific job other than the supervisor, the supervisor must take care of it.

These guidelines are not a foolproof standard for the supervisor to use in determining what can or cannot be delegated. They do, however, give a fairly clear indication about whether or not one should delegate some particular work to a subordinate.

MAKING WORK ASSIGNMENTS—
HOW TO DO IT RIGHT

There are some definite things the supervisor can do to make work assignments effective. For example:

1. Clearly explain to the employee what is expected.

2. Check that subordinates understand what has been assigned.

3. Give employees an opportunity to do the job the way they want to.

4. Be reasonable in what is expected of employees in accomplishing their job duties.

5. Be accessible to subordinates to explain items they do not understand.

6. Reinforce confidence in employees (but don't forget to check occasionally on how work is going and what might be done to help).

7. Demonstrate trust in the employee's capabilities, intelligence, and judgment.

8. Recognize and reward successful or outstanding performance.

9. Hold the employee responsible for poor work, but show him or her why the work was poor and where the mistakes were made.

10. Preclude any alibis—if you feel the subordinate is making excuses for unsatisfactory work, point out the difference between legitimate reasons and excuses.

11. Don't rush in and take over. Many bosses cannot resist the overwhelming urge to step in and straighten things out when a situation looks like it is getting out of hand. It's best to wait until the employee clearly needs help in solving a problem rather than jumping in immediately and engaging in corrective meddling.

12. Don't expect perfection. Few people will do the job the same way—remember the requirement is that the subordinate do the job adequately, not perfectly.

13. Don't assign work that you, as a supervisor, don't understand. Although you might hope that employees will be able to solve and complete the work successfully, unless you are sure of the employees' special skills and knowledge in a field different from your own, don't expect success.

Things to Remember

1. People don't like to be told what to do.

2. Assignment of work is one of the most important management functions.

3. Organization level affects the way work is delegated.

4. Delegation is the procedure for assigning work to employees that is normally done by the manager.

5. Supervisors fail in making work assignments for a variety of reasons.

6. Some things cannot be assigned to others.

7. Employees can be too busy to take on additional work.

8. Major delegation problems include:
   a. The "I can do it better myself" fallacy.
   b. Lack of ability to direct.
   c. Lack of confidence in subordinates.
   d. Lack of control.
   e. Fear of taking a chance.
   f. The martyr complex.
   g. Guilt drives.

9. There are at least 10 ways that employees avoid responsibility.
10. It is important to know both what to delegate and what not to delegate.

Key Words

delegating
assigning work
organization levels
direct supervision
supervising supervisors
management of managers
fallacies
avoiding responsibility

Self-Assessment

As in previous chapters, you may evaluate some of your own supervisory skills by answering the following questions. If you are not presently a supervisor or higher-level manager, answer the questions as if you were. A 1, 2, or 3 response means that you disagree, you are giving a negative response, and you rate the item low. Answers 4, 5, or 6 indicate agreement, a positive response, and a high rating.

1. Do you feel comfortable telling people who report to you what needs to be accomplished?

         1   2   3   4   5   6

2. When you are not busy on your job do you feel uncomfortable or guilty?

         1   2   3   4   5   6

3. Do you sometimes feel that you have to do all of the real work and can't really rely on others?

         1   2   3   4   5   6

4. Do you frequently have difficulty getting work organized so it will flow smoothly?

         1   2   3   4   5   6

5. For supervisors of supervisors, administrative matters are more important than technical aspects of accomplishing work.

1	2	3	4	5	6

6. It is better for a supervisor to do a job than try to explain it to a person who does not understand the requirements as well as the supervisor does.

1	2	3	4	5	6

7. It is not always necessary to assign work to the employee who can best perform a required task.

1	2	3	4	5	6

8. How well do people understand what you really mean when you give directions?

1	2	3	4	5	6

9. Fear of criticism can be a major reason for employees avoiding responsibility.

1	2	3	4	5	6

10. How much do you trust the judgment of employees who report to you.

1	2	3	4	5	6

CASES

Poor Richard

As manager of the Metropolitan Utility District's (MUD) Customer Relations section, Richard Beymer was responsible for handling customer complaints, routing repair and emergency requests to proper departments or agencies, recommending solutions to customer problems, and keeping upper-level management informed of probable trouble spots as well as occasional positive feedback from customers. It was a difficult job and it had to be done with 12 employees who spent most of their time either on the telephone responding to customer inquiries or typing letters of explanation for MUD's actions. Richard's unit was a busy and important part of the MUD central office.

"When you have a problem customer, transfer the call to me," Richard instructed his employees. "I also want to review all letters that go out and sign them myself. In addition, any reports you send to other departments should have my approval before they go out. If you have questions or need information, ask me directly and I'll get it for you. Please don't contact other departments without my approval."

Most employees quickly learned how to load Richard with work. Rarely would they make anything but the most routine judgments without first checking with him. All paperwork, as he asked, was sent to him for approval. Night after night, Richard found himself plowing through an unending pile of reports, letters, and memorandums. He was known as one of the hardest working supervisors at MUD and in many ways Richard was well liked by his employees since he made their jobs easy. Some employees, however, resented his need to review everything they did. "I wonder," Richard thought one night as he plowed through yet another stack of paper, "why I seem to be working harder than anyone else. I'm the only supervisor in the division that takes paperwork home. I'm sure one of them has a job as hard as mine." Poor Richard.

1. What is Richard's most obvious problem? Why?

2. Why does he want to check all the details in his department?

3. What activities can he delegate to reduce his load?

4. Rate Richard as a supervisor. Explain your rationale.

Lisa Wong Is Not Wrong

After three years as Supervisor of Statistical Analysis for the Municipal Utility District (MUD), Lisa Wong was promoted to Department Manager for Engineering Services. As a department manager, she found herself responsible for providing technical-report writing, graphics, statistical analysis, and research information to MUD's engineering departments. As a supervisor of supervisors, many of Lisa's functions changed. She spent most of her time in consultation with other department managers, in meetings with the four supervisors who reported to her, and in meetings involving long-range planning, status reports, and problem solving. It was a vital shift from her old assignment.

Lisa had been a popular and well-liked supervisor. One of her primary new tasks was developing an understanding of the four supervisors who reported to her. All of them, with the exception of her replacement in the statistical analysis section, were experienced, competent people. One of the most striking aspects of her new relationship with the supervisors was that she rarely told them what to do unless she received a new directive from top management. Lisa found that she discussed problems, evaluated how well the total department was performing, and relied on individual supervisors to determine if the day-to-day tasks were being performed correctly.

One of her primary objectives was to help her supervisors develop skills in managing. She refused, when asked to solve problems that she felt her supervisors could handle. Lisa also suggested sources of help and information but did not require that they be used. In her weekly meetings with the supervisory staff, she asked supervisors to review their major accomplishments for the week and to tell how they, in turn, helped other departments.

As higher level management reviewed Lisa's performance, they placed a star by her name in their confidential personnel file of supervisors on the move. Lisa Wong was not Wrong. Because of her abilities, one day she will make the next vital shift of management.

1. Why do you think Lisa was well liked by her employees as a supervisor?

2. Is coaching, as Lisa did when meeting with the supervisors who reported to her, a means of assigning work? Explain.

3. Is there a danger in supervisors encouraging employees to be as good or better than they are? Why?

4. How do you feel about Lisa's primary objective? Was it the correct one?

Decision Making

4

Thought Starter

Many of the decisions we make in daily life are the result of habits and routines. A red light at a street intersection signals us, and without a great deal of thought, we stop. When hungry or thirsty we seek food or drink. Again, our actions are almost automatic. In a job situation, if a familar report has to be completed, it is acted on much in the same way. When faced with a choice of alternatives, however, the process becomes more difficult. People faced with buying a new blouse or shirt may look at all sorts of styles and colors before making a final selection. Some people may become so frustrated with the process of choosing that they make no decision at all. When faced with many alternatives, decision making is difficult.

First-line managers must choose from alternatives constantly. While most decisions are reasonably routine, some decisions require a great deal of thought and careful evaluation before a choice is made. Like other management skills, effective decision making is essential. Indecisiveness means ineffectiveness. Techniques for systematic decision making can be learned. While they do not guarantee that all decisions will be good, they provide some assurance that the decisions will be better than guessing or intuition. Managers who rely on guesses and experience may fail to recognize that one experience does not fit all situations and that poor experience may be a poor teacher. Good managers learn to use information, analysis, development, evaluation of alternatives, and careful follow-up to develop effective decision-making skills.

In Chapter 4 you will learn:

☐ Why indecisiveness and failure go hand in hand.

☐ The cardinal sins of decision making.

☐ How to determine objectives.

☐ Development of alternatives.

☐ Choosing alternatives and implementing alternatives.

☐ The value of group decision making.

☐ Rules for ulcerless decision making.

Harry Arden was faced with a tough choice. As Supervisor of Florida and Texas (FAT) Gas Analysis Laboratories, he was good at his job, liked by his employees, had a stable home and work environment, and was paid an adequate salary with good benefits. Although problems arose from time to time, life was generally good. He was surprised and pleased when Sid Chase, corporate vice president for FAT, telephoned. Sid started the conversation by saying, "Harry, you've done an outstanding job and we would like for you to join the corporate staff as Director of Measurement Engineering. It will mean a sizable pay increase and we'll pay for your move to Orlando, where you'll be headquartered. What do you think?"

"Sid, I'm flattered, but I need a couple of days to think it over," answered Harry.

"I knew you would, and I've already had some additional information on the job mailed to your home address," said Sid.

Harry was faced with a tough decision. He liked where he lived and what he was doing. His family was involved with friends and community activities. His children were in good schools and were active in sports and other school-sponsored activities. In spite of the prestige and additional money, the offer also meant many more administrative responsibilities than before. When he discussed it with his wife, she stated, "You decide." Two days later, Harry made his decision.

Decision making is a critical supervisory skill. An executive of a major hotel chain was recently quoted as saying he would not have *any* supervisors on his payroll who were indecisive or who seemed incapable of making decisions. Unfortunately, being decisive is not a trait found in many people.

The ability to make decisions is highly regarded by so many upper-level managers because they recognize the importance of decision making. Making a decision can be defined as choosing a course of action from various alternatives. With the increasing complexity of business operations in the last few decades, there is an increasing emphasis on making *correct* decisions.

The need to make good decisions has underscored the importance of knowing what a decision is and the process of thoroughly analyzing the various (uncertain) alternatives. In studying decision making, many authorities have divided the process into a series of parts for detailed examination. As a result, tremendous amounts of data have been collected concerning how supervisors make decisions—ranging from the use of complex, computer-based information systems to the simplest of **go-no-go decisions**. Unfortunately, most concern has been focused on the mechanics of decision making, and little attention has been written about the understanding required for good supervisory decisions. We will, therefore, analyze how to develop a better feel for sound supervisory decision making.

THE KEY TO SUPERVISORY SUCCESS—BEING DECISIVE

Reliance on knowledge and supervisory acumen is the key to supervisory decision making. Many examples can be noted where decisiveness has carried the day in otherwise chaotic circumstances. Consider the chicken crossing the road. *If* it would decide to cross or not to cross, things would be simple—and safe. But by being indecisive, many chickens have ended up in the stew pot. Many supervisors have found themselves in a similar dilemma. Should a supervisor use a more expensive ingredient to keep the assembly line going, or is it better to shut down operations? Is it permissible to authorize unusual alterations (at company expense) for a customer, or is it best to ignore the customer's request? Should a person hire temporary help or ask regular employees to work overtime? Fortunately, some of these decisions are becoming less troublesome because of the electronic age and the benefits that computers provide in giving data to the decision maker. Making decisions, however, is still a tough job.

Being required to make decisions is not unusual. Decision making helps supervisors give guidance and direction to the people that work for them. Furthermore, being able to give guidance isn't the only reason for trying to develop skills in decision making. The more definite a supervisor is in deciding to do something, the more likely he or she will succeed. An air of decisiveness creates a situation that must be coped with, even if it is wrong. It also creates an air of confidence among one's subordinates—an invaluable ingredient in a supervisor's talents.

The Cardinal Sins of Decision Making

There are two cardinal sins in decision making—procrastination and vacillation. If a supervisor fails to decide—by procrastinating or vacillating—many things can go wrong. No one knows what is supposed to be done, and no one has any particular objective or goal to accomplish. Consequently, the work may not be completed. Furthermore, lack of direction causes additional problems. Supervisory indecisiveness results in the wasting of resources and time. Andrew Jackson once said, "Take time to deliberate; but when the time for action arrives, stop thinking and go on." To postpone a critical decision wastes time and energy. To fail to stick with a decision, once it is made, can be extremely expensive.

Why the Ability to Make a Decision Is Essential

Decisiveness is required for growth as a supervisor for two reasons: (1) supervisors who seem to know what is happening and what is to be accomplished will receive more respect from their subordinates, and (2) the supervisor who demonstrates the confidence derived from knowing what must be accomplished will be respected more by other managers.

Indecisive supervisors suffer from a variety of ills. Their subordinates lose confidence in their front-line manager's supervisory talents. So, too, will the supervisor's boss, who will be reluctant to assign significant new

tasks to the supervisor. Executives lack confidence in first-line managers who seem incapable of doing a job on time. It is for this reason that decision making, followed by action, is an important skill for the first-line manager to develop.

THE FIRST ELEMENT OF DECISION MAKING—DETERMINING OBJECTIVES

Supervisory decision making can be broken into various elements to analyze each step in the decision-making process, and the supervisor who is determined to be adept at making decisions will do this. The first step in the procedure is to determine objectives.

If supervisors do not know what their primary objectives are, they will experience great difficulty in making good decisions. These decisions will be even worse if supervisors are unaware of how their unit's goals fit into organizational goals. The difficulty that most supervisors have in making good decisions stems from a lack of clear objectives. Studies show that the supervisor who doesn't conceptualize the end results of decisions seldom makes correct decisions. More importantly, such first-line managers often make bad decisions and fail to make the best use of people's time and other resources in helping to accomplish work. For example, a supervisor in a TV repair store must decide which employee to send out on which service call. Not all calls can be responded to at the same time; but, if the supervisor doesn't consider the nature of the various calls (pickup versus on-the-spot repairs) to decide who should do what, there will be no way to effectively assign particular people or materials to a job.

To overcome the problems resulting from unclear objectives, the supervisor must ask analytical questions. These include: What am I trying to accomplish? What personnel, material, machinery, and money are available? When are these objectives expected to be accomplished? If supervisors have answers to such questions, they can move to the next phase in the supervisory decision-making process—determining which objectives are the most important.

Determination of Which Objectives Are the Most Important

When supervisors have clearly established what objectives they want to accomplish and how those objectives fit into overall organizational objectives, they are able to rank objectives. Some objectives are nearly always more important than others. Knowledgeable supervisors allocate their resources to jobs that must be done. Putting fuel on an airplane is more important than ensuring that there are enough meals for passengers, but getting ice for the bar in a restaurant is usually more important than starting a fire in the bar's fireplace.

The basic criterion to use in determining priorities is the question of wants versus needs. We often want things, but we do not always need them. A young woman might want a new dress, but she does not need that dress. A truck driver may want a new truck, but he or she does not really need one.

Of course, sometimes wants can become needs. Sooner or later, the young woman will outgrow all the dresses she has; the truck driver will ultimately wear out the truck. At that point, things—dresses or a truck—must be purchased. Although needs grow out of wants, wants really do not grow out of needs. A typist may want a new word processor. But as the typing work load grows, the typist may begin to need a word pro-

Is this chicken deciding to cross the road?

cessor. This would be particularly true if the typist's company becomes concerned with the typist's quality of work. In the same vein, other wants can become needs. A desire for a new, easier method of processing orders in a mail-order operation may become a need as business grows.

Thus, one way to make sound decisions is to use the priority-of-objectives method. This can be somewhat determined by answering the question of needs rather than wants. But, when using that criterion, one must know that wanted things are not *really* needed. Many successful supervisors intuitively array priorities along the lines of needs, sometimes ranking them in importance. An objective criterion, such as a rank order, is more meaningful than subjective feelings.

Developing Various Alternatives

Computers are useful tools. Furthermore, they help immensely in managerial decision making; effective decision making requires the supervisor to determine what action items are most important and what items are least important. Once that has been done, the supervisor can develop and analyze alternatives in attempting to resolve problems. Data provides the knowledge that is essential for making good decisions.

By reviewing the list of most important needs or performance duties, the supervisor can analyze the options available for each item. For example, with the aid of a computer, a supervisor could determine that it is possible to push a rush order through production by adding more people or by having employees work overtime. It can also be decided that getting the work done on time is important to the company. Thus, a decision must be made about adding overtime for present employees or hiring more workers. Complicating the problem, however, is the fact that while these two alternatives are available, the supervisor might not act on either one because of other constraints. These constraints might be the supervisor's management (who refuse to authorize overtime), or it might be the laws that preclude certain employees from working overtime. The supervisor must make decisions and implement them based on perceived priorities and work constraints. The supervisor may have to plan to *fail* to make production schedules *if* overtime is not authorized.

Supervisors must recognize that good decision making requires them to consider the alternatives that may help or hinder the decision. When supervisors have clearly spelled out the available alternatives, considered the objectives, and analyzed the alternatives in light of ranked objectives, they can choose alternatives that will make the work run smoothly.

EVALUATING THE ALTERNATIVES

After the supervisor has developed alternatives, each possible course of action must be examined. One of the first considerations that must be made in analyzing possible alternatives is whether or not they are realistic. Assessing the sensibility of alternatives can be worked out on a simple grid. Figure 4–1 is an example of such a grid.

As shown in Figure 4–1, the supervisor arrays the alternatives in the left-hand column. Then, the following questions are asked in assessing the alternatives: Is the cost sensible? Will the alternative contribute to accomplishing the objectives? Are there any desirable or undesirable side effects that might occur from selecting a particular course of action? What is the feasibility of implementing each alternative?

Decisions are not made to solve one problem over another simply because the action will accomplish the objective. A supervisor who wants to schedule a 10 percent increase in production might consider overtime, hiring new people, or taking people off maintenance and putting them on production, as demonstrated in Figure 4–1. Any of these alternatives would do the job. However, two of the alternatives, while capable of accomplishing the desired objective, contain other problems. Alternative A, working overtime, is expected to have a negative impact on morale. Furthermore, alternative C, taking people off maintenance,

**FIGURE 4–1   Sample Decision-Making
            Grid**

	Will it accomplish the objective?	Is the cost sensible?	Is it feasible?	Are there any desirable or undesirable side effects?
A. Work overtime	Yes	Not really	Yes	Poor morale
B. Hire additional help	Yes	Yes—for a short time	Yes	Yes—good— build up a reserve of people
C. Take people off maintenance and put them on as a new shift	Yes	Yes	Not for longer than two weeks	Yes—bad— neglects maintenance
D. _____				

means that problems are likely to occur as a result of poor maintenance.

The supervisor who is faced with similar alternatives will probably find the decision-making grid in Figure 4–1 helpful. It requires simultaneous consideration of all available alternatives and the grid puts them into a clear perspective regarding how they will do the job and whether there are other considerations.

CHOOSING THE BEST ALTERNATIVE

Once alternatives are evaluated, the next step in effective decision making is selecting the best solution from the alternatives for implementing the decision. While we *never know what will be the best way to do a job* or what alternative will get the best results, a systematic procedure, such as the grid is helpful. The rule is to minimize the problems that can occur in implementing that solution while maximizing the positive contributions.

The first column the supervisor should look at in selecting an alternative is the one entitled "Will it accomplish the objective?" Each alternative solution should be analyzed regarding its contribution to the desired objectives.

Once the supervisor has selected the two or three best alternatives, the cost of those alternatives should be examined (as directed by the Figure 4–1 column entitled "Is the cost sensible?"). It is usually possible to accomplish an objective if the supervisor is willing to spend the money and/or the time. Good supervisors try to economize. Consequently, the supervisor should look for alternatives that contribute *most* to objectives at the *least* possible cost.

Once a supervisor has selected the one or two best solutions at the lowest price, he or she should look at the feasibility of implementation (Figure 4–1, column 3). In Figure 4–1, transferring maintenance people to production is not really feasible, at least not in the long run, so the supervisor would be unwise to select that alternative.

Thus, the supervisor seeks the most feasible and least costly solution. However, one other question must be considered: Does the decision have any desirable or undesirable side effects? Obviously, it there are desirable side effects, all is fine, as in the example where hiring new people also has the advantage of building a reserve of people who are trained in doing the job.

On the other hand, the secondary effects could be undesirable. In that case, the supervisor may choose a less dramatic alternative (alternative C) even though it costs more or may not accomplish the total objective. The supervisor tries to keep a broad view of the decision's consequences.

Implementing the Decision

The next step in effective supervisory decision making is implementing the decision. Many supervisors establish the priority objective, develop alternatives to accomplish that objective, and they still drop the ball because they failed to implement their decisions actively and aggressively.

There is no substitute for taking deliberate action in implementing a decision. Leadership must be demonstrated, and instructions must be communicated. People must be motivated to do what is necessary. Yet, the supervisor must also determine what progress is being made toward the desired results—that work is done on time, customers are happy, personnel are effective, and that sales are being made. To do this effectively, the supervisor should have a definite concept of what must be done, in what sequence, by whom, and at what required standards. This leads to the last step in effective decision making: follow-up.

Follow-Up

Supervisors cannot make a decision and then expect to totally meet their objectives simply because they made a decision. The supervisor must also follow up to ensure that plans and decisions are implemented.

Effective follow-up means that the supervisor must carefully observe what is done and what happens. If necessary, it also means that the supervisor must reconsider certain elements of the decision if things do not occur as planned. While supervisors who make decisions observe what happens, they do *not* do so with the idea that they will necessarily change their decisions if problems occur. Experts know that good decision makers *seldom* change decisions—although they do so on occasion. Also, a supervisor should not be rigid and refuse to change a decision (or a course of action created by a decision). Sometimes, new information or a change in circumstances necessitates a change in plans and a new decision.

Should You Always Make Decisions Yourself?

Many first-line supervisors seem to know intuitively how to implement decisions on their own. But making one's own decisions is not the totality of supervisory decision making. Sometimes, decisions must include the feelings and aspirations of other people such as bosses, subordinates, or other supervisors. Some decisions, too, should be less concerned with being right, wrong, or even workable compared to how acceptable the decision is to the people it affects.

One problem that occurs for supervisors in today's computer world is that they sometimes adamantly insist on making data-based "correct" decisions that disregard employee feelings. This can be a major error in supervisory decision making.

Often, decision making is more a function of deciding between equally attractive or, at least, seemingly equally viable alternatives. When this is the case, it is necessary to evaluate the work team's needs and views before making a decision.

WHEN TO CONSULT OTHERS

Some decisions are best made by individuals, yet many decisions are best made by a group—perhaps informed nonmanagement employees. An example of the kind of decision that may best be made by an individual is when there is a critical time limitation. Decisions that are best made by a group are decisions where *acceptability* of the decision to the group is important, and the time needed to make the decision is secondary or incidental to the group.

Here are some examples of decision-making situations. Who should

make the decision concerning when a work unit schedules the production for a special equipment item wanted by both customer A and customer B on a given day. Many items must be considered before such a decision can be made. Are there materials and resources available for the job? Who is at work today and who is not? How important a customer is customer A compared to customer B? How often does customer A exaggerate the necessity of receiving the product immediately compared to customer B. Can customer A get by with a partial shipment while customer B cannot?

Obviously, in the foregoing example, the supervisor must make the schedule decision. Such decisions are considered managerial. A managerial decision is one concerned with the appropriateness of making a decision.

Sometimes, however, a group of workers can make a better decision than an individual supervisor. This is especially true when the *accep-*

tance of the decision is important. We will call this an acceptance, or group, decision. But an experienced individual can sometimes make a better decision than an inexperienced group. Furthermore, a cool head often makes better judgments than emotionally involved people. Where popular acceptance of a decision is important, however, letting the group make a decision usually works better.

When Group Decisions Are Most Productive

When acceptance of problem solutions that will affect others is desirable, group decisions work best. An example of a decision that is important to employees is who will go on a coffee break first (or when will someone take a vacation). Obviously, an experienced supervisor will see that all employees get their coffee break and that all employees are scheduled to get a vacation. That is simply a matter of fairness. But the issue goes beyond merely deciding who will go at what time.

In the eyes of concerned employees, coffee break or vacation schedules may be extremely important. One employee may prefer to go on a coffee break early in the day, while another employee may prefer to go late in order to make a telephone call to check on a babysitter or respond to a friend's telephone message. When the two workers take their coffee breaks may not matter to the supervisor, but it will matter to the workers involved.

The most experienced supervisor will never fully understand *nor be aware of* the reasons that employees vary in when they want to do things. Therefore, a supervisor who becomes "the almighty decision maker" sooner or later runs afoul of the wishes of individual employees.

Whenever the supervisor doesn't care who goes on coffee break first or who gets vacations scheduled early, it is foolhardy to make arbitrary decisions regarding those matters. In such cases, it is better that the decisions be left up to the individual.

Whenever it is important that an individual supervisor makes a decision acceptable to the group, it is a good idea for the supervisor to turn the decision-making process over to the employees. This process can be accomplished in a variety of ways. One way is to use majority vote. Another way is to let the group discuss alternatives and let a consensus emerge. The astute supervisor anticipates the acceptability of decisions that could emerge and then gives the decision-making process to the group. In such circumstances, the effective first-line supervisor will not make the decision for the group, and he or she will not load the dice by stating preferences or opinions to the group unless those preferences are imperatives or requirements.

**Handling
Disagreements
about Decisions**

How should a supervisor handle arguing and fighting? What should a supervisor do when employees cannot agree on how or when something should be handled? Should the supervisor decide? If the supervisor decides negative feelings will probably result. The answers to these questions are not simple. By using the following guidelines, however, the first-line supervisor should be relatively successful in coping with differences of opinion. Many supervisors get into difficulty when they turn decisions over to their employees. This typically occurs when two employees disagree over what needs to be done or how or when to do it. It becomes an acute problem if it leads to fighting and bickering. Whenever there is a difference of opinion between two or more employees (see Figure 4–2), the following guidelines will help resolve differences.

1. *Be descriptive, not judgmental.* The intelligent supervisor should never pass judgment on who is right or wrong in any conflict involving employee feelings or emotions. Rarely will one disputant agree that another is right in an emotional situation. Most of the time, there is no readily recognizable right or wrong, and, in such instances, the supervisor should *describe* the situation and withhold judgment. It is appropriate for the supervisor to say, "Jack has worked days and Mary has worked evenings for the past six months." Such a statement describes the facts. It is not appropriate, however, for the supervisor to say, "Jack *always* gets his way and doesn't let Mary work the day shift." Such a statement implies judgments about the appropriateness of Jack's working days and the length of time that he has worked in that manner.

2. *Be specific, not general.* Whenever there are conflicting opinions concerning right or wrong, the operating supervisor must describe what has happened *in specific detail*. It is one thing to say that "Jane is never late"; it is something entirely different to say that "Jane hasn't been tardy in the past two and a half months." The first statement is general. It is unusual for any employee to have *never* been late to the job unless he or she is relatively new. It is more specific to say that an employee has not

**FIGURE 4–2   How to Handle Differences
of Opinion between Two
Employees**

1. Be descriptive, not judgmental.
2. Be specific, not general.
3. Deal with what can be changed.
4. Focus on the problem, not the person.
5. Always ask, "To do or accomplish *what?*"

been tardy in a specified period. The latter statement clarifies who has been doing what and for how long. The former statement unnecessarily antagonizes the people involved.

3. *Deal with what can be changed.* No supervisor should ever encourage employees to question situations that cannot be changed. It is one thing for a supervisor to ask employees how they want to change a vacation schedule, given that a schedule can be changed. It is something else for the same supervisor to ask employees if they would like to have new machines to work on, especially if there is no way that management will authorize the purchase of new machines. Encouraging employees to make a decision in the second situation will only frustrate them. If there is no way that new machines can be purchased (or new methods or processes undertaken), there is no point in encouraging discussion to that effect. Some matters cannot be changed, at least in the short run. The false hope engendered by asking questions—such as "Would you like something?"—that aren't likely to happen only create false hope and may lead to antagonism and frustration from employees.

4. *Focus on the problem, not the person.* When two employees disagree, it is rarely effective to focus on the personalities involved. If a supervisor says, "Mary, you always want to have weekends off," a personal statement is being made. Mary is identified as the individual who *never* wants to work weekends. The fact is that the problem may have nothing to do with whether or not Mary wants to work weekends. It may be that the company simply requires its employees to work an inordinate amount of overtime hours, and Mary is the only one who is willing to express the fact that she doesn't wish to work overtime. Thus, a supervisor who has a meeting with employees to resolve the issue of who will work overtime can accidentally harm one employee's (in this case Mary's) relationship with other employees and the company. It would be far better to say, "The problem is that we have to figure out how to get the required number of hours worked."

5. *Always ask, "To do or accomplish what?"* A final guideline for allowing employees to resolve their own differences through decision-making is to ask them, "What do you want to accomplish?" Some people are uncertain: Do they want to eliminate a problem of overtime, for example, or do they simply want to have Saturday off to go to a football game? If it is simply to have a day off to go to a football game, it is entirely different from the desire to eliminate Saturday work. The supervisor can provide real assistance to employees when *acceptance* of a decision is important.

Successful supervisors determine the kinds of decisions that they must make alone. If it is a managerial decision requiring special knowledge or experience, the supervisor should use decision-making criteria developed in the first portion of this chapter. On the other hand, if the decision requires broad acceptance—that is, a decision of importance to employees with no particular correctness associated with it—it is important that the supervisor follow the guidelines developed in this section of the chapter.

Whether or not supervisors are effective group decision leaders, it is a must that first-line managers be effective at making their own decisions. Intelligent leaders, no matter how decisive, are concerned about the decisions they must make—but this is not to say they will be extremely anxious about these decisions.

RULES FOR ULCERLESS DECISION MAKING BY SUPERVISORS

Over the years, many writers have been concerned with the decision-making process. The following rules for making ulcerless decisions have been collected from such sources. Following these rules will neither necessarily make a supervisor decisive or successful, nor will it ensure that all decisions made by a supervisor are workable or practical. However, improved control over job performance, through clear-cut goals, may be enhanced.

Rule One: Differentiate between Big Decisions and Little Problems

Supervisors must determine what big problems merit decisions and what little problems shouldn't be worried about. Big problems require time and should be considered in detail. They merit the time it takes to complete a decision-making grid as well as careful scrutiny of alternatives related to cost, contribution to objectives, feasibility, and side effects as outlined in Figure 4–1.

Little problems, on the other hand, do not warrant time-consuming considerations. Inexperienced supervisors often worry little problems to death. Consider, for example, the mental anguish of the supervisor who worries over who to send on coffee break first or what to do when two rush orders arrive at the same time. Concern over improbable or unimportant decisions simply isn't worth the supervisor's time. Yet, such problems, if not recognized as minor, often distract the supervisor's attention from more important matters.

Rule Two: Rely on Established Procedures When Possible

Have established procedures for action in routine situations. This means that the supervisor must be prepared to implement practices that are known to work with particular, routine problems. For example, a supervisor in an airline luggage office will have a regular operating procedure for the situation where a traveler claims to have lost luggage but does not have the luggage claim check to prove it. Not having a set procedure means that the supervisor must personally handle every such claim. However, with already established procedures, the supervisor can delegate duties to subordinates and free supervisory time for other activities.

Rule Three: Consult and Check with Others

A third essential rule in supervisory decision making is to check with other people for their opinions. Other people who are well-informed—supervisors, managers, and specialists—cannot make a decision for the concerned supervisor, but they can offer insight and advice. Often, there is a commonality in decision-making experiences that can be shared by persons who have done similar jobs. The well-informed supervisor will practically always look to others for guidance if they have expertise in the problem area.

Rule Four: Avoid Crisis Decisions

Making decisions under stress is *not* an ideal situation. Whatever the decision, the result is often not a happy one. As a racecar driver in an uncontrolled skid, consider the need to decide between hitting a bridge or a building. Neither choice is appealing.

Unfortunately, crises often occur, and decisions must be made under tremendous pressure, even in routine jobs. For example, selling tickets at a theater is usually "ho-hum." But being the supervisor at a theater that has received a bomb scare adds a lot of stress to the job. Should you evacuate the theater? You're the boss! Decide! Now!

It is not always possible for the supervisor to avoid the stress and pressures of making job decisions. Thus, the supervisor must know how to handle stressful circumstances when they arise.

The advice given by experts to the supervisor faced with a crisis is (1) relax and *think*; (2) go through the decision-making steps as outlined in the first part of this chapter, carefully consider the alternatives available and analyze them as to cost, feasibility, contribution to objectives, and desirable or undesirable side effects; and then (3) decide! Going through the mechanics of the process of thinking logically should enable the supervisor to maintain a rational presence of mind and to avoid making an emotional decision in a crisis.

Rule Five: Don't Try to Anticipate All Eventualities

Many supervisors are inept at making decisions and suffer needless worry because they try to anticipate everything that can possibly happen. Obviously, it is impossible to anticipate all eventualities. While it is possible that a shipment of hair spray could explode in the cargo bay of an airliner, causing the plane to crash, it is highly unlikely. Yet, if one constantly thinks about what could go wrong while the shipment is in the airplane, even though a possibility of trouble exists, a supervisor will be worrying more than is necessary. The *probability* of such an occurrence, however, is extremely remote and should not be considered. While Murphy's Law states "Whatever can go wrong will go wrong," the odds are high that most items that could go wrong will never go wrong. Thus, the supervisor is well-advised to not consider everything that could happen as a result of implementing a decision, but to concentrate on the probable outcome. Such a choice will not always ensure that the supervisory decisions will be right, but it will help.

Rule Six: Don't Expect to Be Right All the Time

Some supervisors insist upon *always* being right. To them, it is a fetish that must always be satisfied—even at the expense of accomplishing the organization's overall goals.

Obviously, a good supervisor avoids demonstrating a need to be right at all times, at all costs. While it is nice to be right, human frailty must be recognized—sometimes wrong decisions will be made, even by the best supervisors.

As a General Electric executive once said: "I don't expect to be right all the time, I just don't expect to be totally wrong *at any time*." There is usually a wide divergence between being wrong and being right. Usually, a happy middle ground exists where a supervisor may not have selected the *best* of the solutions available, but he or she did not select the worst solution, either. While it is possible to be dead wrong, such flagrantly wrong decisions are seldom implemented in a workaday life. More often, it is a question of the *degree* of rightness. Usually, it is a question of whether or not one job should be started before another one or whether one customer should be waited on before another. As a result, wrong decisions are not made often—just poor ones. But the results of a *poor* decision are seldom as grim as the results of a *wrong* decision. Once the supervisor recognizes that rightness is practically always a question of degree rather than perfection, the supervisor shouldn't be troubled by undue indecisiveness.

Rule Seven: Cultivate Decisiveness

Indecision creates tensions in most people. Too much tension generates stress and further indecision. Consequently, indecisiveness is a self-feeding and self-destructive phenomenon. Good supervisors make decisions and cultivate decisiveness. They don't neglect making a choice when it is time to render a decision.

Since most good supervisors know that the two cardinal sins in decision making are procrastination and vacillation, they understand that a time comes when a decision must be made. Procrastination is the failure or inability to make a decision when all the input is there and a decision should be made. When no decision is made, time is wasted, and work goes unfinished, is done improperly, or is done later in haste.

Vacillation is as difficult to cope with as procrastination. To vacillate causes a person to switch among alternatives long after a course of action is selected. Vacillation causes a misallocation of resources and a poor distribution of people's time on various projects. This is because of the on-again, off-again nature of such decisions. Waste always occurs in these situations, and indecisiveness takes its toll. Again, supervisors do change their decisions. But a good supervisor does not vacillate and does not change a decision unless it has been proved wrong or ineffective.

Rule Eight: Once the Decision Is Made, Implement It

If decisiveness is the key to decision making, implementation is the lock. Most good decision makers argue that once a decision has been made, the implementation of that decision is critical for success. Some authors argue that good managers never change or reverse their decisions. It may be that poor managers are often the ones who reconsider and reassess decisions after the fact. However, it is probably unrealistic to argue that one should *never* change a decision. Yet, a strong push to implement a decision is crucial.

The reason for emphasizing tenacious implementation of a decision (as opposed to thoughtful, thorough decision making) is practical in nature. Observation of decision making and implementation by supervisors, managers, and executives demonstrates a lot about good and bad decision making. Good managers and supervisors will change a decision because of two circumstances—when there is an opportunity to capitalize on an unforeseen circumstance, or when the original decision is proved wrong. The implementation phase of a decision is far more important for its success than the correctness of the decision.

DECISION MAKING AND HOW IT FITS IN WITH OTHER SUPERVISORY FUNCTIONS

Our foregoing discussion on decision making can be analyzed by how it fits in with other supervisory functions. Good supervisory decision making requires planning or the establishment of objectives. After all, how can a manager make effective decisions if there is no overall plan? Deciding about approving an authorization for overtime may depend on the company's major objectives: does the company want to supply all demands for its product at all times (a situation that might warrant the use of overtime), or is economy in labor costs more important than customer good will? Practicing supervisors must be fully aware of company plans and how their unit's performance fits into those plans before effective decisions can be made. Supervisors must be good planners before they can be good decision makers.

There are other ways besides planning that decisions fit into supervisory functions. One of these ways is control. Deciding to do something will never ensure that it will be done. Some effort is also required to control or follow up to see that the decision is implemented correctly. Thus, a decision to approve a change in work schedules may be implemented quickly but poorly if no control is exercised by the supervisor. Again, here is a case where computer technology can help the supervisor. By providing information for the supervisor, the computer can facilitate the supervisor's maintaining control over what happens.

Decisiveness alone is not a true supervisory attribute; it only becomes desirable when coupled with other supervisory talents. Decisiveness, like most concepts about supervision, must blend into a workable whole.

Things to Remember

1. Decision making is a critical management skill.
2. Procrastination and vacillation are the two cardinal sins of decision making.
3. Determination of objectives is the first step in good decision making.

4. Establishing priorities is a key to effective decision making.

5. Effective decision making involves development and examination of alternatives before selecting the most appropriate course of action.

6. In some cases, group decision making is more accurate and more acceptable to the work force than managerial decisions.

7. Good decision makers rarely change their mind once a decision is made.

8. Planning and control are required for decision making and implementation.

Key Words

decisiveness
go-no-go decisions
procrastination and vacillation
determining objectives
alternative
decision implementation
group decisions
implementation techniques

Self-Assessment

To evaluate some of your knowledge about the decision-making process, as well as your decision-making characteristics, respond to the following questions or statements with a 1, 2, or 3 if your answer is low or negative. Positive or high responses should be answered with a 4, 5, or 6.

1. I rarely have difficulty making either personal or work decisions.

1	2	3	4	5	6

2. The first step in good decision making is to develop alternatives.

1	2	3	4	5	6

3. Good decision makers rarely change their mind once a decision has been made.

1	2	3	4	5	6

4. Side effects of selecting a particular alternative can be either positive or negative.

1	2	3	4	5	6

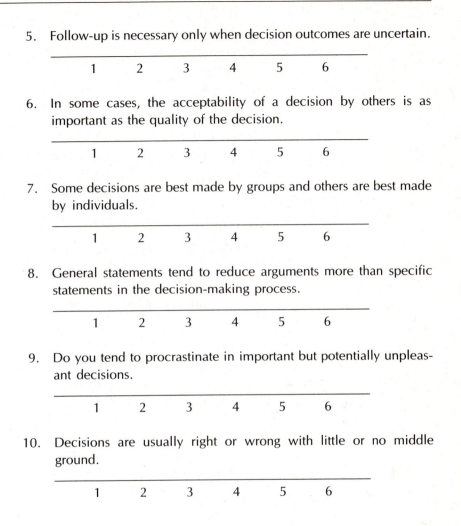

5. Follow-up is necessary only when decision outcomes are uncertain.

1	2	3	4	5	6

6. In some cases, the acceptability of a decision by others is as important as the quality of the decision.

1	2	3	4	5	6

7. Some decisions are best made by groups and others are best made by individuals.

1	2	3	4	5	6

8. General statements tend to reduce arguments more than specific statements in the decision-making process.

1	2	3	4	5	6

9. Do you tend to procrastinate in important but potentially unpleasant decisions.

1	2	3	4	5	6

10. Decisions are usually right or wrong with little or no middle ground.

1	2	3	4	5	6

CASES

Sophie's Choice

In just four hours, Sophie Lomax, Supervisor of New Product Research for American International Marketing (AIM) was scheduled to give a presentation on sales figures for new high-density computer laser disks. Sophie had the data, but the report was not typed, reproduced, stapled, or ready for distribution at the meeting. It would be embarrassing to her and her immediate boss if she attempted to give the presentation unprepared to distribute the report to the top-level managers attending the conference.

Sue Hoover, who normally did the word processing and reproduction follow-up, was late and had not called in. When Sophie called to learn why Sue was not at work, no one answered. All seven of her other employees were working on equally important projects and none were as familiar with the required format and the method of chart presentation as Sue. As minutes ticked away, Sophie became increasingly concerned. "There's not much that I can do about the report not being ready yet. Some of the data from sales offices around the country didn't get here until yesterday afternoon and it took time to put it in order," thought Sophie. "There's a lot to be done before the meeting, and I can't wait around for Sue all day. If the report is going to be completed by three o'clock, it will have to be started in the next hour."

As she sat thinking, Sophie wrote down alternatives. Her list included the following possibilities:

1. Call Sue again. If she can't be here in 30 minutes, forget this alternative.

2. Pull someone off other assignments and coach them through the report. It will take time, but it might work. Something else will slip.

3. Do the report myself. I can operate the word processor, but not as well as Sue or someone who is trained. If I do, some of my other work will go down the tubes.

4. See if I can reschedule the report for the next meeting. The boss won't like it, since it's an agenda item for the conference, but maybe I can explain.

5. Type out a quick summary of the full report and hand it out with the presentation. Explain that the full report will be issued in the next two days. The boss may not like this either, but it may be a way out.

There are probably some other alternatives, but I'll work with these for the time being, Sophie thought.

1. What alternative(s) would you choose if you were Sophie?

2. Are there any alternatives she has not considered? (Has she asked the advice of other supervisors or her immediate boss?)

3. In making an operational decision like Sophie's, how can a supervisor avoid a crisis atmosphere?

Norval's Nightmare   As manager of Baker-Air Regional Flight, Inc.'s (BARF) central terminal, Norval Wellsfry was faced with a tough decision. BARF specialized in short-range, critical freight shipments to cities with major air-transport facilities. Some of its biggest customers were oil-field drilling operations in remote areas of western states that needed quick delivery on core sample readings, replacement of special drilling bits, and electronic control equipment. In addition, BARF provided limited shipments of art goods, manufacturing equipment, and some agricultural products. Because of its specialized nature and ability to service small airports, its business grew rapidly. "We're going to start feeding into Benton, Park City, and Oiltown," announced Ken Almendo, general manager of BARF. "All of the material we gather will come here to the central terminal and then be shipped to major airports. For a while, at least, it will mean a greater load on the central terminal. Our service planes to the new small airports just don't have the capacity or range to make direct flights to the big carriers feasible. It's better for us to collect several flights' worth of goods together and load them on a larger airplane for transport to the major carriers. Norval, it will be up to you to decide the best way to handle the overload. We may have to rent additional space, put on a second shift, expand the existing space we rent at the airport, or take other actions. Let me know in a week what you intend to do."

Norval realized that planning and decision making are closely tied together, just as organizing is closely tied to planning. He saw that a plan is a series of decisions about the future.

1. What are some of Norval's key objectives in deciding what to do about the work overload? How should he prioritize them?

2. What are some potential side effects of the alternatives suggested by Ken?

3. Both costs and schedules are important to BARF. How should Norval approach ensuring prompt schedules without undue costs?

The Basics of Motivating Employees at Work

5

Thought Starter

Even though motivation has been a topic of serious research, and it has filled volumes of psychological and management literature for years, it is still not well understood. It is difficult to tell why some people are self-starters and seem to be high achievers at almost everything they do, while others need prodding and strong incentives to do anything productive. Equally puzzling is what may trigger energy and enthusiasm in some people may generate boredom and apathy in others.

From a management point of view, motivation is the key to increased productivity, quality, and lower operational costs. Although there are many theories ranging from the concept that people work for money alone to theories that state work can satisfy complex human needs, none seem to fully answer the question, "What can be done to get people to take a greater sustained interest in their work and become more involved in doing it well?"

In Chapter 5 you will learn:

☐ How the need for money motivates, and how it doesn't motivate.

☐ Ways that job assignments can increase motivation.

☐ Some older theories of motivation and their place today.

☐ Recent pragmatic and expectancy theories of motivation.

□ **Applications of motivational theory in the work place.**

"There are," began Jack Fujimoto, a well-known management consultant, "several problems in getting people to work effectively. Many people work in what I call a custodial climate. They are paid well, get good benefits, and only have to perform at a minimum level to retain their jobs. They work in an environment that has few rewards and even fewer punishments. Most employees neither like nor dislike their jobs, although they may develop close friendships with fellow employees. When these employees move to organizations with real motivational programs, their adjustment is long and difficult." As Jack continued his lecture to a group of top-level managers, some managers reflected on their own organizations.

"What do employees expect? If management expectations and requirements are low, employees will react in a similar fashion. Their expectations of meaningful rewards, incentives to perform, and results from job involvement will also be low. Most people would rather be productive members of a team than merely be paid for filling a slot five days a week." Jack continued, "What can managers do? If they are interested, willing, and can put their own egos aside, workable motivation programs can be built and employees will respond."

MOTIVATION

"How do I motivate my people?" is probably the question most asked by supervisors. Psychologists have studied this question for years and have developed a variety of explanations, interpretations, and understandings about what motivates people at work. Some of these explanations are plausible. Unfortunately, most line supervisors are not psychologists or even psychologically trained. Furthermore, experience has shown that some psychologists are unsuccessful in motivating people when they serve as supervisors.

We have a great deal of information about **motivation** of people at work. However, it is not easy for the supervisor to apply all the principles and rules that have been developed over the years. For example, psychologists might explain intellectually that the reason one employee doesn't get along well with another employee is because of some latent embryonic need. But the practicing supervisor has difficulty identifying this need, let alone determining beforehand that it exists. Even if supervisors recognize the source of the problem, they may have a difficult time determining what to do about it. In short, knowledge of what *causes* human motivation isn't nearly as important or useful a tool for the supervisor as is knowledge of what can be done about it.

WHAT WORKS IN MOTIVATING EMPLOYEES AT WORK

The reasons people work are simple and obvious in many cases. They may desire something special, such as a vacation trip or a new refrigerator. Their primary work motivation is to earn enough money to buy something they would otherwise not have. These motivations are real, honest, and simple to understand. But this only explains the motivations of *cakewinners*—the term used to describe people who have the need to get something extra as their primary work motivation. They are called cakewinners because their incomes are considered extra income above their primary source of income. They work for the "extras" in life.

On the other hand, the mainstay of our working population is the breadwinner. He or she works for another reason. Breadwinners are the *primary* support for themselves and their families. They work for the staples that will feed, clothe, and house their families in the manner to which they aspire. This motive is more compelling.

Money is the obvious motivation for both breadwinners and cakewinners. Yet, psychologists have long argued that people do not really work for money. More and more women have entered the work force in recent years—and not out of any compulsion to become breadwinners or any desire to become cakewinners, either. Many women want to have careers outside the home. Thus, the breadwinner-cakewinner explanation will not help the supervisor in understanding people's motivational drives. These people work because they value working as a manifestation of their worth and value to society.

MONEY IS NOT A MOTIVATOR— OR IS IT?

The evidence is clear that people have a variety of motives for working other than earning money. Yet, few people would work *if they were not being paid*. Most people cannot afford the luxury of working for nothing. Furthermore, even those people who can afford to work for nothing seldom decline their checks. In short, while it may be the ultimate put-down to be paid a dollar a year as the head of some large organization— like Calvin Coolidge, who, as president of the United States, did not accept his paychecks—there are few people in this country who practice the technique even when they can afford it.

The supervisor must recognize, therefore, that money is a prime motivator. Most people must earn money to stay alive and to do the things that satisfy their needs. The unfortunate problem with money as a motivator, however, is that while it may be one of the basic reasons a person works, it is *not* the reason why a person *works at a specific job*. Why is that? Because virtually all jobs pay, and most jobs (admittedly within a broad range) pay about the same, especially similar jobs in different companies and organizations.

THE DIFFERENCE MAY BE IN THE JOB

The jobs people look for are not necessarily a function of the money they need to live on. People may find jobs because they need money to pay their bills. But one person wants to be a nurse, another wants to be a dietician, another wants to be a trash collector, and another wants to be a mortician. Why does one person want to work for a business while another person wants to work for a governmental agency or a nonprofit organization?

Jobs that require a particular level of educational background, experience, and training pay roughly equivalent salaries. However, they are attractive to different people and for different reasons. Some people prefer a job making $4 an hour as a clerk in a hardware store or as an off-bearer on an assembly line. Others would prefer to work outdoors.

Consequently, the supervisor should recognize that the line of work an individual pursues depends on factors other than the money involved (depending on the availability of jobs, and certainly a *lot* of money may encourage some persons to take jobs that they don't want or that are considered dangerous).

THE OLDER THEORIES OF MOTIVATION

The "something else" other than money that causes a person to pursue one job over another is really a variety of items. In the early 1950s, Abraham Maslow was one of the first to receive recognition for assessing what motivates people at work. In his book, *Motivation and Personality*, Maslow established that people have a series of work motivations—what he called a **Hierarchy of Needs.**[1] The desire to satisfy these needs, according to Maslow, is what motivates people to work and do the things they do at work. Of primary concern are physical needs—getting enough money to stay alive, for example; next comes the need for safety, and finally, the need for self-fulfillment (see Figure 5–1).

Maslow's Hierarchy of Needs explains many motivational drives in simple terms. For example, the first two categories that Maslow identifies—**physiological needs** and **safety needs**—are really financial in their orientation. That is, if an individual has sufficient money, he or she usually can handle the needs for food, clothing, shelter, and be reasonably secure in old age. Consequently, the person who is independently wealthy is probably not highly motivated to work for money and will tend to be concerned with satisfying other needs higher in the order—to feel

FIGURE 5–1   Maslow's Hierarchy of Needs Concept

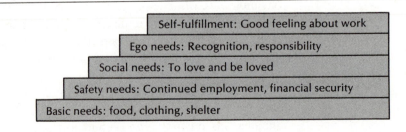

Self-fulfillment: Good feeling about work
Ego needs: Recognition, responsibility
Social needs: To love and be loved
Safety needs: Continued employment, financial security
Basic needs: food, clothing, shelter

[1] Abraham Maslow, *Motivation and Personality* (New York: Harper & Row, 1954).

accepted, to be liked, and to belong to a group; to be recognized and to feel important; and to enjoy doing work.

The need to like and be liked by co-workers is the next motivator in Maslow's analysis. When people feel reasonably safe and secure in their financial outlook, their next concern is with how well accepted they are among co-workers and whether or not they have friends to socialize with on the job.

Many authorities argue that some people never rise out of this third need for belongingness and acceptance, that some people spend most of their time being concerned with affectional needs and worrying about what other people think. However, this is not true in all cases and does not explain the behavior of all people. Some people have a relatively low need to be liked by other people or to try to capture people's affection. In addition, some people at work really seem to want something else, such as recognition for being in a responsible position or doing something important. These feelings are the highest order of needs that Maslow identifies.

MORE RECENT THEORIES OF MOTIVATION

Although the Hierarchy of Needs theory of motivation is somewhat antiquated, it was once widely accepted, and it is the theory upon which later motivation theories have been built. Many motivational theorists have utilized Maslow's concepts. They include Frederick Herzberg, M. Scott Myers and Susan S. Myers, David McClelland, Chris Argyris, Charles L. Hughes, Victor Vroom, Saul Gellerman, Morris Massey, John C. Talbot, and many others. All these people contributed to the knowledge concerning motivational drives at work. Their work ranges from merely elaborating on Maslow's work to explaining the changing values of our culture. The various concepts help the supervisor to determine what he or she can do to elicit improved performance.

THE SATISFIER–DISSATISFIER THEORY OF MOTIVATION

In the late 1950s, Frederick Herzberg asked 100 accountants and 100 engineers what they liked and disliked about their jobs. Herzberg recorded the *intensity* of their feelings as they responded, for as a psychologist, he knew that when people feel strongly about something they usually will talk at great length about it; but that when they are not interested in the subject or it is unimportant to them, they will generally gloss over the matter or perhaps not even mention it.

The Motivation-Hygiene Model

As a result of Herzberg's in-depth interviews with accountants and engineers, he determined that there are critical incidents that give most people feelings of pleasure or satisfaction on the job. These good feelings occur for people when they are recognized for special accomplishments; when they feel they are really achieving something; when they are proud of their responsibility; when they receive advancements, promotions, or increases in their pay; and when they experience intrinsic pleasure from just doing the work.

The other side of the coin was also found to be true. That is, Herzberg's subjects indicated that they also can be quite unhappy within their jobs. They mentioned environmental factors as the major cause of their displeasure. These factors were mostly company policy and administration (especially when it was ineffective or unfair), poor or undesirable working conditions, bad relationships with co-workers, lack of acceptable technical qualifications of a supervisor, and poor pay.

Figure 5–2 lists the factors that were considered both dissatisfiers and satisfiers by Herzberg's subjects. The dissatisfiers are decidedly different from the satisfiers, with one exception—pay. Yet, according to Herzberg, even the factor of pay is essentially dissatisfying. Herzberg found that the dissatisfaction an employee felt because of inadequate pay, or lower pay compared to a co-worker's salary, was *three times as intense* in bitterness as were the positive feelings engendered by high pay, especially when an employee's pay was higher than his or her co-workers. Thus, the one similar factor in sources of satisfaction and dissatisfaction is pay, and it is

FIGURE 5–2

Dissatisfier aspects about job (hygiene factors)	Satisfier aspects about job (motivational factors)
Company policy and administration.	Achievement.
Working conditions.	Recognition.
Peer relationships.	Responsibility.
Technical competence of boss.	Advancement.
Pay.	Interesting work.
	Pay.

decidedly more important as a source of dissatisfaction than as a source of satisfaction.

In summary, Herzberg discovered that there are satisfying and dissatisfying factors about a job, and that if the dissatisfying factors are grossly unfair or inequitable, they cause employees to be unproductive. Yet, if those factors are all acceptable and administered fairly, there is no reason to presume that people will be highly motivated to do a better job.

PRAGMATIC THEORIES OF MOTIVATION

One of the really pragmatic motivational theorists, Robert Presthus, in his book entitled *The Organizational Society*, said that employee attitudes and outlooks toward their company and their jobs can roughly be divided into three different groups.[2] Ambitious go-getters who want to get ahead and make a name for themselves are called **ascendants.** They have high achievement-power drives. Employees who are not interested in finding achievement or accomplishment in their jobs, who only see work as a way to derive income and the friendship of co-workers, thereby satisfying their desires for affiliation, are known as **indifferents.** People who are really interested in their jobs but do not aspire toward monetary success and power are **ambivalents.** Let's look at how these attitudes are manifested by people at work and how supervisors might recognize these motivational drives and therefore work more successfully with their employees (see Figure 5–3).

Ascendants

Ascendant individuals are people who really want to get ahead in their organization. They identify and associate with the company or organization. They tend to feel that their company is the best one to work for and that its products are the best on the market. In fact, ascendants identify so closely with their organization that, in a way, they adopt their company. They feel they must grow with the organization, and they hope that the organization will reward them with more responsibility. They have a long-run identification with their organization and tend to resent it when anyone else finds fault with their organization.

Because of their strong need to be powerful and achieve, ascendants are easy to supervise. They will usually do anything and everything their

---

[2] Robert Presthus, *The Organizational Society* (New York: Alfred A. Knopf).

FIGURE 5–3 Differences in Work Attitudes

Ascendants:

Identify closely with the company.

See failure as reflecting personal inadequacies.

Want feedback from superiors.

Engage in ritualistic behavior to conceal resentments.

Want power for its potential influence.

Tend to be procedure- and rule-oriented.

Place personal success above acceptance by co-workers.

Have high-visibility drive.

Go down hard when they fail.

Indifferents:

Withdraw from identification with the company.

Prefer not to compete for rewards.

Avoid ego involvement with the company.

Gravitate toward off-the-job satisfaction.

Reject those who strive for success and power.

Demand individual treatment and recognition.

Get upset by anything not routine.

Frequently deprecate the things they produce.

Seek immunity to discipline by joining unions and otherwise identifying with immediate work group.

Tend to have satisfactory interpersonal relations.

Usually adjust slowly to change.

Ambivalents:

Creative but anxious about the work.

Tend to rise to marginal positions and have limited career opportunities.

Cannot reject a promotion even if they do not want it.

Tend to be neurotic.

Always want change from the status quo.

Have high intellectual interests but low interpersonal skills.

Subjective, withdrawn, introverted, and given to displays of anger and temper.

Make it a rule to resist rules and procedures.

Have idealistic and usually unrealistic career expectations.

Avoid psychological involvement with the company.

Tend to feel that success comes from luck and is a denial of talent, wisdom, or morality.

Usually are out-of-step in the company.

Reject fellow workers and what they view as compromises that co-workers accept in their relationships to the company.

Become disturbed that they are successful (if they get a promotion).

Tend to display a compulsive interest in the job in an effort to gain recognition.

Are poor decision makers.

supervisor asks of them. They delight in getting feedback from their supervisors so that they know how they are doing and how they might do a better job. They like to have their performance appraised, especially if they feel they are doing a good job. However, they will listen carefully to any criticism or critique about how to improve their performance. Almost always, ascendants feel badly when things go wrong. They cannot do enough for their boss or for the organization, and they never seem to get overworked. They are always willing to do more as long as they see the payoff at the end of the road in increased prestige, power, and job recognition.

Indifferents

Indifferents have a totally different orientation from ascendants. Indifferents have a high affiliative drive and need to be socially accepted among co-workers. Consequently, indifferent employees tend to manifest a relatively low achievement, power, and competence need. As a result, they do not share the ascendant's interest in and ambitions toward getting ahead, especially if it involves working extremely long, hard hours.

These employees are called indifferent because they are usually not excited about working or striving to make a notable career. It's not that they *dislike* their jobs; they just are not excited about their jobs like the ascendant and seldom derive any enriching experiences from their jobs—nor do they expect to.

Indifferent employees seldom have any zeal for the organization, and they do not identify closely with the company. Rarely, if ever, do they have any ideas about becoming a supervisor and when they do think about it, they usually do not like the idea. They do, however, like their co-workers, and they are primarily concerned with how they relate to them and the friendships they find at work.

The indifferent employee is basically a noncompetitive individual, in contrast to the ascendant, who is extremely competitive and tries to get ahead no matter what. Because indifferent employees are noncompetitive, they are seldom offered promotions and advancement. This is good, however, because it is *the way they want it*. Their association with the company may be only from the standpoint that they happen to work there—as a welder or an electrician, as a desk clerk or a telephone operator. Primarily, they want to be identified by the job skill or title they have rather than by the company or organization for which they work. "I am a computer programmer" is more important than "I work at XYZ Corporation."

One problem that causes turmoil for supervisors in managing indifferent employees is that the indifferent employee thinks the ascendant (who is likely to be the supervisor) is an insensitive and power-hungry individual. Because of this, indifferents often reject a supervisor whom they feel is willing to do anything to accomplish a mission or complete a job. In fact, indifferents actually feel that something is wrong with ascendants who are highly motivated. As a result, indifferents frequently manifest a general reluctance to do anything unusual in work performance or job duties, especially in the eyes of supervisors. Consequently, indifferents are usually perceived by supervisors as being a motivational problem at work.

The supervisor and the indifferent employee will also often clash over attitude differences regarding punctuality and regularity of attendance. Attendance and tardiness problems nearly always originate with indifferent employees, who really do not care about being at work. Many times they will not come to work because they "don't feel like it" or they feel that the company owes them time off. Naturally, the supervisor does not agree.

Ambivalents

Other things being equal, ambivalent employees would like to get ahead. However, they are not willing to go out of their way to *ensure* getting ahead. Ambivalents are primarily interested in being competent at what they do. Power over others can be a bother—and so are other people who are too friendly and get in the way. In short, the ambivalent personality is a cross in attitude between the ascendant and the indifferent. The ascendant wants to get ahead, be powerful, knows it, and is more than willing to do so. The indifferent doesn't seriously desire to get ahead, knows it, and isn't afraid to admit it. Consequently, indifferents do not try to get ahead; they are reasonably content with their position in the work community. Ambivalents, on the other hand, think they deserve and have the talent to be successful and, to some degree, they resent it when others do not see or appreciate those talents. As a result, a tremendous amount of friction can arise between ascendant, ambivalent, and indifferent employees.

The ambivalent is the most challenging employee from a supervisory standpoint. The indifferent is easy to manage but must be closely supervised. Ascendants are easiest to supervise because they identify with management and will not do anything to harm their chances of getting ahead. Inevitably, the ascendant personality is the one that best fits into the organization so far as top management is concerned. Yet, indifferents are usually good workers—and happy—because they are content with the job and do not aspire to bigger positions. The most unhappy individuals are usually ambivalents, who desire something they are not likely to attain.

ADAPTING TO THE NEW WORK
ETHIC–EXPECTANCY THEORY

The explanation about ascendants, ambivalents, and indifferents by Presthus has one shortcoming: It develops stereotypes. Ascendants, ambivalents, and indifferents are known to everyone, but the analysis unfortunately leaves it up to individual supervisors to decide what category an employee is in, and Presthus does not give much guidance or instruction on motivation. Many people reject his ideas as impractical because his analysis only points out that some people are ambitious, some people are not, and some people are somewhere inbetween. For this reason, we must consider two other recent theories on employee motivation. One theory focuses on employee values, the other focuses on worker expectations.

Expectancy Theory

A new body of literature has emerged since Presthus did his work that nicely supplements the theories about ascendant, indifferent, and ambivalent personality types. The new work, called **expectancy theory**, concerns an employee's perceptions of self, superiors, subordinates, associates, and the total job environment. An employee's expectations of his or her own role and the roles of others in an organization tend to define how one thinks and relates with others at work. What a person expects influences how one is treated and how one treats others. An individual who expects to be treated with respect usually will engender that respect. An individual who expects to be treated disrespectfully usually will receive little or no respect. Generally, supervisors who expect to be respected manage with dignity, while other supervisors who don't feel worthy of respect manage with difficulty. Likewise, employees who feel competent to do their jobs normally expect to be treated as highly skilled individuals, while employees who feel uncomfortable about their competence often expect to be treated like children rather than workers.

Expectancy is the perceived probability of an individual realizing something he or she anticipates. Thus, a supervisor may hope an employee is ascendant-oriented; thus, the supervisor may give him or her ample opportunity to demonstrate leadership and supervisory talents, and to aspire to a more responsible job.

Unfortunately, the supervisor who has high expectations of subordinates may nevertheless see them fail because working conditions deny that individual access to necessary tools, materials, machinery, and equipment. The worker is *expected* to do the necessary work but, because of lack of resources and tools, an *availability* problem develops and an otherwise qualified individual is prevented from accomplishing the job. Thus, expectations are important, but the *availability* of resources to do the job is also imperative if success is to occur.

THE PYGMALION EFFECT

Expectancy and availability can work either for or against the supervisor in his or her attempt to accomplish organizational goals. For example, the **Pygmalion effect** occurs in the relationships between a superior and a subordinate. If a boss has high expectations, the employee may perform well if resources are available. Conversely, if expectations are low, high performance may not occur.

The Pygmalion effect, as applied to supervision, is a loose adaptation of George Bernard Shaw's play *Pygmalion*. In the play, Eliza Doolittle says, ''You see, really and truly, apart from the things anyone can pick up (the dressing and the proper way of speaking and so on), the difference between a lady and a flower girl is not how she behaves but how she's treated. I shall always be a flower girl to Professor Higgins, because he always treats me as a flower girl, and always will; but I know I can be a lady to you, because you always treat me as a lady, and always will.''

As Jay Sterling Livingston has stated, the Pygmalion effect, as it operates in supervisory management, may well behave in the following fashion:

> Some managers always treat their subordinates in a way that leads to superior performance. But most managers, like Professor Higgins, may intentionally treat their subordinates in a way that leads to lower performance than they are capable of achieving. The way managers treat their subordinates is subtly influenced by what they expect of them. If a manager's expectations are high, productivity is likely to be excellent. If his expectations are low, productivity is likely to be poor. It is as though there were a law that caused a subordinate's performance to rise or fall to meet his manager's expectations.[3]

From the foregoing statement, one can conclude that the typical manager, in attempting to motivate subordinates, probably will realize the following experiences:

---

[3] Jay Sterling Livingston, ''Pygmalion in Management,'' *Harvard Business Review*, July–August 1969, pp. 81–82.

1. The way a manager treats subordinates and what the manager expects of them will largely determine their performance.

2. Most superior managers have the ability to create high performance expectations that their subordinates fulfill.

3. Less effective managers develop lower-level expectations of their employees and, as a consequence, cause their subordinates' productivity to be less than acceptable.

4. Employees often appear to do what they perceive they are expected to do rather than what really is needed to be done.

In short, supervisory expectations of subordinates tend to dictate subordinates' performance. It is an upward or downward spiral. High expectations elicit high performance, and low expectations elicit poor performance.

Once the expectations elicit a certain performance, there is a compounding effect. That is, when a supervisor expects high performance and gets it, that supervisor continues to expect high performance and continues to realize it. Likewise, when a supervisor has low expectations of subordinates, the usual result is inferior performance, which reinforces the low expectations, which tend to elicit yet poorer performance.

The Downward Spiral of Ineffective Performance. The supervisor who is saddled with a low-performing organization has two choices: (1) fire the poor performers (which may be difficult to do because of union contracts or other reasons) and hire employees of whom the supervisor has high expectations, or (2) respond to the less than acceptable low performance with high expectations and trust.

It is not easy to fire someone because they do not measure up to expectations. Furthermore, firing someone is not necessarily the best alternative in a marginal performance circumstance, not to mention the fact that competent replacements are not always readily available. The second choice, responding with high expectations and trust, is usually more advisable.

In that situation, the supervisor works to upgrade expectations concerning the performance and behavior of subordinates. Thus, because it is extremely difficult to put high expectations on poorly performing employees, a boss who wishes to turn around an ineffective organization must think developmentally.

DEVELOPING SUBORDINATES

A supervisor using the technique of high expectations develops a poorly performing subordinate by first requiring some responsible work and then, as soon as the subordinate does a decent job, the supervisor rewards him or her for improved results. This must be done incrementally and regularly, and the process must continue as the subordinate's behavior comes closer to the supervisor's expectations. This concept, of course, has some limitations. Certainly, the supervisor must be careful not to assign too much work too rapidly to the subordinate.

Employees rarely change dramatically in their job performance from day to day, and the supervisor must be cautious not to give rewards *without first getting the desired performance improvement.* Efforts designed to bribe an employee into superior performance usually give the supervisor a "soft touch" label in the eyes of subordinates, and they end up playing games with the supervisor.

The supervisor should recognize that it may take time to turn a poorly performing individual into an individual who can perform adequately. It may take a few months, half a year, or more; however, the supervisor who perseveres is apt to be successful as expectations are raised.

Using Positive Reinforcement to Develop Subordinates

One recent concept concerning employee motivations that is consistent with expectancy theory and is useful in developing employee performance is positive reinforcement. Many interpretations of positive reinforcement have been developed. Original pioneers in positive reinforcement for developing employees were B. F. Skinner and Edward J. Feeney. However, recent activity has surrounded the work of Dr. Kenneth Blanchard and the concept of the one-minute manager.

The One-Minute Manager

The notion of the one-minute manager is that employees should be commended briefly and to the point whenever they do something right. Therefore, they are given positive reinforcement that encourages them to continue to do that portion of their job correctly.

The one-minute-manager concept argues that many bosses wait to commend people on their job performance until the subordinate is doing the entire job correctly. The one-minute-manager idea states that if a supervisor waits until an employee does the whole job satisfactorily, it may never occur, and the employee must wait indefinitely to get any positive reinforcement regarding his or her job performance. Because positive reinforcement does not occur, the employee never knows whether he or she is doing anything right or wrong or whether what he or she is doing has any meaning. As a consequence, the employee may never learn to do the job entirely right and, perhaps, may decide that he or she is worthless and can never do the job satisfactorily. The people become chronically poor employees who must be terminated.

By using the idea that all employees can learn to do parts of the job correctly, the one-minute-manager concept expects the employee to ultimately be able to do the entire job correctly. When the employee begins to do part of the job correctly, always acknowledge (with one minute of praise) the portions of the job that the employee does correctly. This not only confirms for the employee that certain parts of the job are being done correctly, but it futher motivates him or her to realize that progress is being made toward performing the complete job correctly.

Ultimately, it is expected that the employee will master all portions of the job (and, of course, he or she is adequately recognized or praised for total job performance). The employee is finally satisfactorily performing all portions of the job and the supervisor has developed what might have been a poorly performing employee into one whose job performance is totally adequate.

Most employees can be developed to do a satisfactory job, but they must be developed properly. Some of that development includes giving them positive reinforcement as assurance that they can do the job satisfactorily. Additionally, the boss must totally expect individuals to "come up to speed" and perform their jobs completely satisfactorily. Therefore, leadership ties in with motivation and the development of employees.

Using Expectancy Theories and the One-Minute-Manager Notion to Motivate Employees

Losing, as well as winning, can be contagious. People who win continue to expect to win. People who lose usually continue to expect to lose. Futhermore, teamwork is gained or lost by the use of such motivational strategies as those found in the one-minute-manager idea.

Workers can be motivated to be winners or losers. It is extremely important for a supervisor to develop a motivational climate that makes it possible for employees to be winners; that is, the supervisor must set goals for employees that will enable them to be successful. Whether the goals are couched in Maslow's Hierarchy of Needs; Herzberg's satisfiers or dissatisfiers; Presthus' ascendant, ambivalent, and indifferent personality styles; or ideas about the one-minute manager, employees will want to succeed. The more that employees find it possible to reach the goals they are expected to reach, the more likely they will try hard to attain those goals.

However, if employees feel there is no opportunity to attain those goals, and if they are not expected to be successful, frustration will occur. Frustration is stultifying, and if it continues, it can paralyze an organization *and* its people. It is for this reason that supervisors must understand the role that his or her expectations play in eliciting desired performance from employees.

Listening—A Critical Skill

Effective listeners are successful at motivating employees. They listen to their subordinates and attempt to interpret what they really want and expect based on their actions and needs, as well as upon what they say. Chapter 11 contains some suggestions on how to enhance your listening skills as a supervisor, for it is only by listening carefully that a supervisor can determine what his or her employees' expectations are for co-workers, the supervisor, and the organization. Effective supervisors use that information in a constructive way, constantly trying to keep their expectations high for subordinates and encouraging subordinates to keep their expectations of the job high.

It is extremely important that the supervisor understand the interrelationship between expectancy and availability. It is one thing to have high expectations, either as a supervisor or as a subordinate, but there must be an opportunity to realize those expectations in tangible, measurable, and identifiable ways. If the organization and/or the supervisor does not provide adequate tools, materials, and resources to do a job with, success cannot be attained—even with high expectations. Therefore, the supervisor must understand that the total environment, including facilities and resources, has much to do with employee motivations. Some employees, like the ascendant, always want to get ahead, while other employees do not care. But that does not mean the indifferent employee, who might be classified as having lower expectations, has no way of attaining adequate performance levels. A supervisor needs to understand how expectations affect job performance, what is expected in the form of supervisory leadership, and what acceptable job performance is.

EMPLOYEE VALUES

One final set of supervisory and employee expectations needs to be discussed: employee values. Research by Clare W. Graves, Charles L.

Hughes, Vincent Flowers, M. Scott Myers, and Susan S. Myers led to another set of theories concerning why some people do not behave as they should at work. That is, many supervisors—particularly older supervisors—are prone to say that "things are wrong with today's youth," or that younger workers "don't do what they are supposed to do," or that they "don't care anymore."

Values and You

Jobs need to have meaning if people are to be motivated. But different people want and need different things. Just to say that one expects something is not enough. "What is expected?" is the question.

Many psychologists believe that the new work ethic is shaped in terms of personal values. For example, Dr. Morris Massey, while at the University of Colorado, pinpointed some definite facts about human motivation and work behavior in his discussion, "What You Are Is What You Were When." In Massey's analysis, employees and their value systems are a

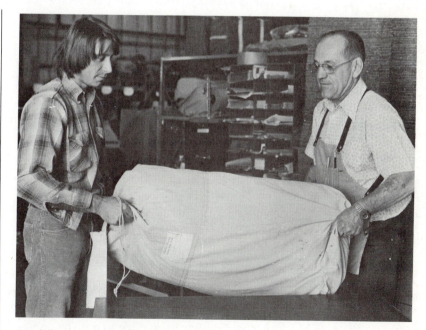

Do different workers have different values? Do younger workers often socialize with younger fellow workers, while older workers do the same with older fellow workers?

function of what they were *when they were young teenagers*. According to Massey's thesis, whatever code of values young teenagers are exposed to in their formative years will determine the code of values and the standards of conduct they will adhere to as they grow older and begin to work. This applies not only to what employees expect to do at work, but also to what they expect work to do for them. Therefore, we often see older employees who have difficulty with younger employees because of different value systems. It may be as simple as what kind of music they like to listen to or as complex as disdain for each other's values. Their inability to tolerate each other is a function of the values they hold as individuals—values they learn in their early teens, for the most part.

In analyzing employee values, Dr. Charles L. Hughes states that "if it's right for you, it's probably wrong for your employees." Dr. Hughes means that most supervisors tend to have a different value system from their employees, largely because of age differences. Dr. Hughes and other psychologists have identified seven different value systems held by employees. Each system causes different behavior and, therefore, explains some of the various expectations—and behaviors—people have at work. Let us briefly look at the resulting types of behavior to better understand employee motivation.

Values and Understanding Motivation

According to researchers who attempt to understand employee motivation based on employee values, there are seven different behavioral patterns that people at work manifest because of their value systems. These behavioral patterns are significant indicators that explain what might be expected from employees by a supervisor concerned about motivation. Essentially, they are as follows:

Reactive. Reactive individuals are childlike. A supervisor must expect to relate to them viscerally. They are only interested in the physiological aspects of working—pay, safety, benefits, comfortable working conditions, and so forth.

Tribalistic. Usually, tribalistic employees are impressed by power and authority and, they will react only to a boss who is willing to use power in telling them what to do. They have a strong need to be directed, and they expect the supervisor to provide them with direction. A supervisor who is unwilling to use power with these individuals will probably be unsuccessful.

Egocentric. Egocentric individuals are nearly always suspicious and are inclined to engage in disruptive behavior at work. They will respond well only to the supervisor who is willing to control their behavior. Inevitably, egocentric individuals place themselves ahead of others and generally have difficulty living within the constraints of society and its dictates. To relate well to this kind of an individual, communications must be direct, authoritarian, and specific in explaining the consequences of both good and bad behavior. Printed directives are probably not a good form of communication with these individuals because egocentric workers often discredit memos or do not believe them. This individual needs to be treated on a one-to-one basis if the supervisor is to be effective in getting results.

Conformist. Conformists are people who subscribe to classic notions of the work ethic. They believe in duty, loyalty, and whatever they *should* do. They are the employees who will subscribe to the written word and embrace policies, standard operating procedures, job descriptions, and work duties. These people go by the book, and any supervisor who is not willing to boss them by the book—particularly any supervisor who doesn't go by the book—is apt to have trouble and find these people not being motivated at work. Perhaps it would be nice if all employees were conformists, but employees come in a variety of shapes and sizes— as well as motivations and value systems—and because of that, what works well in motivating one employee will not necessarily work with another person.

Manipulative. The manipulator is the wheeler-dealer. This is the individual who sees everything as a game and tries to take advantage of the system or figure out the shortest or slickest way to beat the system. The manipulator is constantly striving to get ahead and therefore must be motivated to excel in an environment that is conducive to this kind of behavior. Manipulators respond best to a boss who gives them the opportunity to achieve, advance, and get the psychological payoff of more money. Typically, strong manipulative people are found in marketing and sales jobs, and the number of successful American businesspeople who are manipulative is legendary.

Sociocentric. Sociocentric individuals feel that people are most important. Their value system revolves around interpersonal relationships, human relations, friendly supervision, and harmony within the

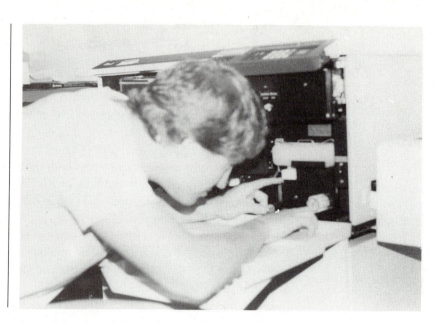

work group. Anything a supervisor does to create disharmony or dissatisfaction will be viewed badly by them. Because of this, if sociocentric
individuals have a manipulative supervisor who does not value social
relationships, there is apt to be a dramatic clash between subordinate and
boss. Unfortunately, of course, manipulative personality types tend to
become the boss (because they are more ascendant-oriented, in terms of
Presthus' analysis). There may be plenty of misunderstanding between
what motivates a subordinate and what motivates the boss.

Existential. Existential individuals are basically concerned about
themselves as individuals. They believe in job enrichment and the mean-
ingfulness of work. They are inclined to set their own standards of
performance, and they inevitably like the opportuntity to solve problems
and engage in any kind of meaningful task that is challenging, imagina-
tive, or that requires initiative or creativity. People who are existential
perform as big question marks in the minds of manipulative bosses. This
is because bosses do not really understand the desire of existential
individuals to concern themselves solely with the satisfactions of work.

HOW DO YOU MOTIVATE PEOPLE AT WORK?

Ideas about the one-minute manager and the analysis of values and expectations help supervisors understand basic motivations at work. One can argue that Presthus' work concerning the ascendant, ambivalent, and indifferent personality types can be superimposed over the work of Dr. Hughes, Dr. Graves, Dr. Myers, et al. But, like it or not, there *are* different values, outlooks, motivations, and expectations that people have at work—and different ways they perform.

Some people argue that nothing new has been invented under the sun. In fact, at one major U.S. university a few years ago, there was a preliminary examination question for doctoral students to the effect of: "Eclectically synthesize the findings of the motivational theorist, beginning with the work of Abraham Maslow and ending with the current time." In responding, there were students who found many common themes underscoring the basic motivational theories and interpretations, as well as students that developed many differences. Our purpose is not to say that any given theory is right or wrong, or that any particular belief can be supported while another belief cannot be supported. Practically all theories of motivation somewhat reinforce each other. Some theories are more practical; others are more theoretical. But they all come down to this: It is one thing to recognize and understand a person's motivations and expectations; it is something else to actually know *how*, as a supervisor, to lead and direct people to the desired results. That question concerns leadership and how to be an effective leader.

Things to Remember

1. Motivation depends on more than money, although money is an important factor.

2. Abraham Maslow stated that we have different levels of needs, and that lower-level needs must be at least partially satisfied before higher-level needs become motivational factors.

3. More recent motivational theories include:
   a. Frederick Herzberg's motivation-hygiene model.
   b. Robert Presthus' ascendant-ambivalent-indifferent approach.
   c. Expectancy theory.

4. The way people are treated (the Pygmalion Effect) is a powerful motivational tool.

5. Personal values, as described by Charles Hughes, are factors that affect motivation. Values described by Hughes include:
   a. Reactive.
   b. Tribalistic.
   c. Egocentric.
   d. Conformist.
   e. Manipulative.
   f. Sociocentric.
   g. Existential.

6. All theories of motivation, to some extent, seem to reinforce one another.

Key Words

motivation
Abraham Maslow
Hierarchy of Needs
physiological needs
safety needs
social needs
Ego needs
self-fulfillment needs
Frederick Herzberg
motivation-hygiene model
Robert Presthus
pragmatic theories of motivation:
   a. ascendants
   b. ambivalents
   c. indifferents
expectancy theory
Pygmalion effect

Self-Assessment

Evaluate your knowledge of motivational theory and how well you understand its application by responding to the questions or statements listed below. Remember that a 1, 2, or 3 means a low or negative response and a 4, 5, or 6 means a positive or high response.

1. With effort and a knowledge of motivational theory, indifferents can be changed into ascendants.

| 1 | 2 | 3 | 4 | 5 | 6 |

2. I tend to procrastinate on jobs I don't especially like, and I work hard on jobs that I find interesting.

 1 2 3 4 5 6

3. Giving everyone a pay increase, such as a cost-of-living increase, improves productivity.

 1 2 3 4 5 6

4. Existential employees tend to like easy jobs, short hours, and high pay.

 1 2 3 4 5 6

5. Most employees will work only as hard as required to keep from getting fired.

 1 2 3 4 5 6

6. A good motivational technique is to instill fear. Employees who are afraid of being fired or receiving disapproval will work harder.

 1 2 3 4 5 6

7. A good management technique is to concentrate on making people happy at work. Happy employees are more productive.

 1 2 3 4 5 6

8. People who win continue to expect to win. People who lose continue to expect to lose.

 1 2 3 4 5 6

9. Most motivational techniques are an attempt by management to manipulate people and employees see right through them.

 1 2 3 4 5 6

10. Few, if any, managers are really interested in their employees any

more than they are interested in machinery. They want their machines to work well, require little maintenance, and not bother them. They feel the same way about people.

1	2	3	4	5	6

CASES

Are American Employees Motivated?

In negotiations of its first contract with United Manufacturing, Inc., the General Motors-Toyota plant in Freemont, California, the United Automobile Workers (UAW) union made work load a primary issue. American workers, the UAW argued, especially older ones, are not accustomed to the pace of work that Japanese management expects from employees in Toyota's home plants. Until recently, Japanese workers have assembled nearly twice as many comparable automobiles in a single day as their U.S. counterparts. As a consequence, Japanese automakers have lower labor costs, not necessarily because of lower wages, but because of greater productivity. Although improved technology in the United States has erased some of the Japanese advantage, there is little doubt that Japanese employees are still more efficient, on the whole, than workers in this country.

A critical question for management is whether U.S. workers can become as highly motivated as workers in other countries. There are many examples of U.S. companies where management has adopted programs that encourage greater participation, higher productivity, and a will to be the best. It is unfortunate that these companies are a small minority of the total work force.

Can we operate at peak performance only if threatened, as in an emergency, or can programs be designed to change our seemingly "get all you can for as little as you can" attitude to a philosophy of desiring to always be the best. Many serious observers of organizations believe that employee motivation can be improved, but only if all levels of management have a serious commitment to the concept of excellence in every aspect of work.

1. What kinds of programs can management adopt to improve employee motivation?

2. Can first-time managers take specific actions to improve motivation in their work units?

3. Why would unions resist programs that increase productivity even if the existence of the organization depends on higher productivity and lower costs?

Down Towne

Drew Towne, one of six sales managers for Valley Area Distributors (VAT), finally convinced Nancy Ribordy, Sales Director for VAT, that an improved financial incentive plan would pay off in increased sales. VAT distributed a variety of carbonated and noncarbonated beverages to supermarkets, restaurants, and beverage stores throughout the central area. Sales personnel were paid a 5 percent commission for all sales in excess of $1,000 per day or $5,000 per week. Most salespeople exceeded the standard and the average salary for one of Drew's employees was $520 per week.

"What I would like to do," Drew stated in his meeting with Nancy, "would be to give them increasing percentage increments above the $1,500 per day level or $7,500 per week. They would continue to receive the current 5 percent for sales in excess of $1,000 per day or $5,000 per week. Sales in excess of $1,250 a day or $6,250 per week would receive a 7 percent commission and that would be increased 1 percent for each additional $250 in sales per day or $1,250 per week to a maximum of 10 percent."

"It might eat into our profits a little," returned Nancy, thoughtfully, "but it also may be a real incentive."

Drew's salespeople accepted the plan enthusiastically, and during the first two weeks, most salespeople were averaging $540 per week. After three months, the average dropped to approximately $535, where it seemed to stabilize. Some salespeople made slightly more than others. Drew knew that just one or two more customer calls made each day by salespersons would increase their income, yet apparently the calls weren't being made. He wondered why such a good plan had such modest returns.

1. What are some of the reasons sales did not increase as much as Drew expected?

2. Can you devise a plan that may work better than Drew's plan?

3. In a nonsales organization, where financial incentives are not practical, what other systems could improve productivity?

PART THREE

The Supervisor's Role in Leadership

The Supervisor as a Leader

6

Thought Starter

Like the word love, the terms *leader* and *leadership* can be used in many ways. There are many theories about leadership and its development, but none seem to fully answer all questions. Is the leader of a group of children playing "follow the leader" different from a supervisor who inspires a mediocre work group to excellence? Do successful generals make successful leaders in nonmilitary assignments? Is a successful professional football quarterback, the leader on the field, automatically a good leader in other types of work?

Leadership is closely related to the concepts of power and authority. Leaders must be able to influence followers and be recognized as being in charge. Followers of a particular leader believe that the leader can help them accomplish goals that they cannot achieve by themselves. Regardless of whether we fully understand what makes leaders, they are necessary in most situations, and first-line managers who have strong leadership characteristics, as well as sound management skills, are most likely to succeed.

In Chapter 6 you will learn:

- Why the role of leadership in work organizations is changing.
- Traditional leadership roles such as the "bull of the woods."
- McGregor's Theory X and Theory Y.
- How modern theories of leadership emerged.
- Basic dimensions of leadership.

□ **Contingency and situational leadership approaches.**

□ **Multicratic leadership.**

Approximately 35 years ago, right after the end of the Korean War, one of the most significant studies in leadership of that time was based on the reactions of prisoners captured by the North Korean army. North Koreans were diligent in separating leaders from other prisoners. Officers, both commissioned and noncommissioned, were moved to separate quarters. American prisoners became demoralized, suffered disease, and many died of no apparent cause other than hopelessness. Turkish prisoners, however, had a high survival rate. When officers and noncommissioned officers were separated from imprisoned Turkish soldiers, the most senior soldier became the recognized leader. Turkish prisoners were never without a leader who helped organize, arrange care for the ill, and lead the group in activities that helped them survive. Many current courses in prison-camp survival taught by various defense organizations are based on the Korean experience.

Similar studies made in many other conditions, less dramatic than a prison camp, indicate that leadership is necessary. Groups will either formally elect a spokesperson or acknowledge leaders by common consent if they are engaged in some kind of activity where they feel there is a need for representation. There is a great deal that is not known about leadership. We do know, however, that for most efforts involving groups, leaders are both necessary and desirable.

Most people can recognize leaders, but few people can satisfactorily define what makes leaders different from followers. We know that successful leaders in one organization may not be successful in another. A successful general may be a poor corporate president, just as a successful business manager may be a poor educational leader. Research shows that the situation, the expectations of followers, and the personal characteristics of the leader all contribute to leadership effectiveness.

THE CHANGING ROLE AND NATURE OF LEADERSHIP

There are different motivational attitudes toward work. Some people—ascendants—want to get ahead in their careers. Others, the indifferents, aren't really interested in seeing how high they can rise in their organization; they are content to be one of the group. Yet, the ambivalents have a different outlook. To them, demonstrating their intellect is often more important than their relations with co-workers or a supervisor.

Value systems play an important role in worker motivations. Sociocentric people, for instance, often strongly rebel against manipulative bosses, as will many people with conformist values. Yet, tribalistic people may demand manipulative behavior from the boss.

Attempting to be an effective supervisor by relating well to employees and respecting their attitudes toward work can be exceedingly difficult.

One of the problems is that employees cannot be treated the same way: They have different motivations and ambitions; their expectations are different; what they perceive as meaningful work varies tremendously. Furthermore, not all employees could be treated indentically even if they had similar motivations because no two work situations are identical. Employee interests, personalities, ambitions, and work situations are always different to some degree. It is the supervisor's duty to cope with varying employee interests, ambitions, attitudes, and personalities while achieving results through people. That is the problem of leadership.

Leaders must also be concerned with employee productivity—or the lack of it. Much has been written about how supervisors can interact more effectively with employees. Current ideas about leadership, such as the use of quality circles, have begun to revolutionize ideas about leadership. Some of the writings are founded on solid logic, some of the ideas are couched in theoretical concepts of what ought to be, and some ideas are based on practical experience. How can this thinking be used by supervisors to improve their leadership capabilities?

THE TRADITIONAL LEADER

Originally, the supervisor was expected to be hard-nosed. The job of supervisor was considered simple—the only requirement was to get results desired by top management. In doing so, the supervisor could behave like a traditional bull of the woods—issuing orders, handing out rewards and punishments. However, this supervisory leadership gave way to more tolerant approaches. Ultimately, as the human relations movement took hold in the 1930s and 1940s, supervisors began to be more considerate of employees' feelings and interests at work. However, this practice had some problems. Recently, however, changes in social values, worker expectations, and the emphasis on the quality of life have significantly changed what it takes to be an effective leader.

HISTORICAL APPROACHES
TO LEADERSHIP

After the human relations movement became de-emphasized in the early 1950s, other supervisory philosophies emerged. One pioneering work, which won a great deal of popularity in the 1960s, was Douglas McGregor's *The Human Side of Enterprise*.[1]

---

[1] Douglas McGregor, *The Human Side of Enterprise* (New York: McGraw-Hill, 1960).

Can you identify the leader?

McGregor's concepts serve as a springboard for studying the leadership behavior of supervisors. McGregor suggested that supervisors typically hold one of two primary attitudes toward employees in the way that they supervise (See Figure 6–1). What McGregor said was that the **Theory X** supervisor (McGregor argued that supervisors *traditionally* were Theory X types) believes that most employees are lazy, indolent, and would avoid work if they could. McGregor believed that the average person supervised in a tightly controlled manner would limit production to the bare minimum required. McGregor argued, therefore, that the better way to supervise was in a **Theory Y** fashion.

Theory Y supervisors, according to McGregor, are more open in their behavior and expect people to experience enriching aspects of their jobs. Theory Y bosses feel that people like work, they find working as natural as play or rest. Theory Y supervisors believe that their subordinates will demonstrate drive, initiative, and diligence in pursuit of organizational goals, especially if the goals are compatible with employee goals.

The concepts of Theory Y supervisory practices took the nation by storm in the 1960s. Most supervisory training sessions at the time were devoted to debates and discussions about whether Theory X or Theory Y was the best supervisory leadership pattern. The outcome of such debates

FIGURE 6–1 Two Sets of Assumptions about Human Nature and Human Behavior*

Theory X: the traditional view of direction and control
Assumptions:
1. The average human being has an inherent dislike of work and will avoid it if possible.
2. Because of this human characteristic for disliking work, most people must be coerced, controlled, directed, or threatened with punishment to get them to put forth adequate effort toward achieving organizational objectives.
3. The average human being prefers to be directed, wishes to avoid responsibility, has relatively little ambition, and wants security above all.

Theory Y: A new theory of direction and control
Assumptions:
1. The expenditure of physical and mental effort in work is as natural as play or rest.
2. External control and the threat of punishment are not the only means for achieving adequate effort toward organizational objectives. People wil exercise self-direction and self-control in the service of objectives to which they are committed.
3. Commitment to objectives is a function of the rewards associated with that achievement.
4. The average person learns, under proper conditions, not only to accept but to seek responsibility.
5. The capacity to exercise a relatively high degree of imagination, ingenuity, and creativity in solving organizational problems is widely distributed in the population.
6. Under the conditions of modern industrial life, the intellectual potentialities of the average person are only partly utilized.

*Source: Douglas McGregor *The Human Side of Enterprise* (New York: McGraw-Hill, 1960), pp. 33-34, 47-48.

was generally in favor of Theory Y—people would work harder to accomplish goals that they were committed to.

As a result of these ideas, supervisors were told that it would be best if they followed Theory Y in relating to employees. Also, note the similarity between Theory Y and the expectancy theories. While Theory Y is perhaps a bit more superficial in implying that thinking good thoughts about employee motives will make them more highly motivated, it does represent a good, fundamental foundation for appropriate supervisory activities.

There were, however, some problems that materialized when supervisors tried to implement Theory Y ideas, which essentially boiled down to "think good thoughts about your employees' motives." Many supervisors who were trained to implement Theory Y supervision became confused by the resulting employee behavior. While it is easy to accept the logic of Theory Y, *it is hard to implement*. For example, in trying to implement the supervisory practices suggested by Theory Y, supervisors often found that employees did work incorrectly or not as accurately, rapidly, or thoroughly as expected. Many supervisors were amazed to see their best intentions go unheeded; others doubted their supervisory skills in implementing Theory Y assumptions and blamed themselves for failing to realize the results. As a result, as early as the mid-1970s, there were some serious studies made regarding the appropriateness of applying Theory Y behavioral and supervisory standards. Many studies indicated that Theory Y practices might not result in the job performance desired by employers. At that time, too, concern about the general decrease in employee productivity began to seriously concern bosses and executives, and the quest for other solutions began.

THEORIES AFTER McGREGOR

A strong movement developed in the late 1960s and early 1970s to bring certain practical realities forward in studying leadership styles and behavioral patterns because of the experienced problems with Theory Y supervisory practices. This drive was the logical culmination of many independent efforts by persons such as William J. Reddin, Fred E. Fiedler, Jane S. Mouton, Robert R. Blake, Paul Hersey, and Kenneth H. Blanchard, to name a few. Many of these researchers, including Robert Presthus, were not convinced that everyone is ambitious at work or would respond to only one leadership style. Researchers found that people responded differently to various leaders in various situations. Thus, researchers studying supervisory styles and practices in the 1960s, 1970s, and early 1980s established that operating supervisors might be faced with situations where they would be ineffective, *even if* they were playing a supervisory role as taught by McGregor and other theorists. The big breakthrough came when many consultants, educators, and supervisory trainers began to accept that supervisory effectiveness depended on a multiplicity of factors, only one of which is the assumptions the supervisor makes about employee behavior and motivation. So, today, we have many more useful ideas and guidelines on how to supervise and lead effectively.

WHAT MAKES EFFECTIVE LEADERSHIP?

In determining what makes effective leadership, one must understand the difference between leadership and management. Leadership is influencing people to strive to attain the goals of the organization. Management, on the other hand, is the function of running an organization from a conceptual or policy standpoint. Leadership is the business of an individual boss influencing people to accomplish the organization's plans and purposes.

A manager needs to be a good leader, but a good leader does not need to be a good manager. For example, a good leader may be able to get people to produce on an assembly line, but he or she may be inept at budgeting, cost control, or making decisions concerning the company's marketing efforts. On the other hand, a good manager may design and develop a well- run organization policywise, but that manager may not be able to implement plans or sell products because, being a poor leader, he or she cannot get the required results from workers.

FACTORS IMPINGING UPON LEADERSHIP

Persons who have studied leadership have historically looked at it from the standpoint of traits manifested by good leaders. Researchers have looked at successful leaders and used them as models to be emulated. However, according to people like Eugene E. Jennings, those studies have *never* revealed any *individual qualities* that can be used with certainty to predict leadership capability. They only look at traits. As a result, the focus is currently on the situational nature of leadership and attempting to document exactly what makes for an effective leader in a given situation.

In recent years, authors who have delved into leadership processes have generally concluded that leadership effectiveness is largely a function of (1) the individual leader (traits and personalities included); (2) the subordinates or followers of that leader and the workers' outlook toward working and other personality and socioeconomic interests; and (3) situational variables in which the leader and followers find themselves. For example, a supervisor who has just been appointed to take over a poorly managed work unit has all the authority necessary to influence employee action. If, however, the employees resent the new supervisor's presence and perceive their work situation as unchanged, they may deliberately make things difficult. This may be due to unchanged worker expectations. Furthermore, even if expectations are changed and employees want to please their new boss, they may fail to do so because of a lack of training, materials, or other conditions (which we call the availability problem) that they have no control over, which are situational problems.

Leaders and Followers

Many trainers and educators in supervisory techniques have stated, "Leaders are only as effective as their subordinates want them to be." Or, to put it another way: "You aren't a leader unless you have followers who will do what you want." Leadership effectiveness is seldom a function of the individual leader. A leader in a position of power can strongly influence individuals in an organization, but this is true only if the leader's followers want and expect the leader to hold sway over their working activities. In addition, even if followers *do* want and expect the leader to hold power over them, the leader may still fail in accomplishing the organization's goals because the situation precludes the people from doing so. For example, an airline pilot may want to fly an airplane to a destination designated by the boss. But if weather conditions make this impossible, the pilot will fail no matter how willing and able the pilot is to fly the plane. The situation simply won't permit the job to be done.

The Two Basic Dimensions of Leadership

Recent leadership studies indicate that there are at least two basic dimensions of leadership. One is concern for a task to be done, that is, a primary concern for the **structure** of the organization. The other dimension is a regard for the people who do the task, that is, **consideration** for the workers. Prior to recognizing the importance of these two dimensions, it was generally held that the leader who related well to employees would be effective. That is, until the importance of the structure or the situation (task) was accepted, many people felt that all a good boss needed was a capability to tell people what to do with a pleasing demeanor. It was not imperative for the successful leader to attempt to control the situation.

THE MANAGERIAL GRID

Robert R. Blake and Jane S. Mouton[2] were leadership experts who helped popularize ideas about the situational structure (versus consideration for employees). They viewed leadership effectiveness as a function of either emphasizing task accomplishment or stressing the manager-employee relationship. Their analysis of leadership styles is depicted by the well-known Managerial Grid® (see Figure 6–2).

As seen how in Figure 6–2, the vertical axis plots the concern a leader demonstrates for subordinates, while the horizontal axis plots the structural concern that a leader demonstrates for getting the job done. The lower left-hand corner, therefore, is for leaders who have *little* concern for both people *and* production; the upper right-hand corner is for leaders who have a *high* concern for both people *and* production.

The quadrants in Blake and Mouton's Managerial Grid are reasonably descriptive of leadership style and associated expectations of job performance. The five primary styles are described below.

Country Club Leadership Style. The individual who demonstrates high concern for people and low concern for production is classified a

**FIGURE 6–2   Blake and Mouton's
          Managerial Grid®**

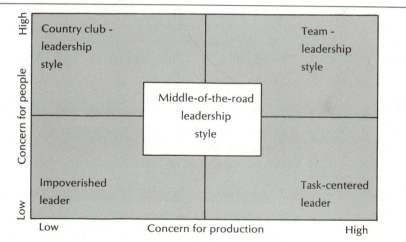

[2] Robert R. Blake and Jane S. Mouton, *The Managerial Grid* (Houston: Gulf Publishing, 1964).

country club leader. This style might represent total consideration of employees and very little concern for structure. This type of leader gives thoughtful attention to the needs of people and tries to develop relationships into a comfortable, friendly, working organization. He or she is more concerned about the congeniality of the work environment than whether or not production is accomplished. In this leader's eyes, everyone should be happy.

Task-Centered Leader. The polar opposite of the country club leader is the **task-centered leader.** This style is the epitome of the totally structure-oriented leader. The task-centered leader is an individual who is mainly concerned with efficiency of operation and getting the job done. Results are all that matter to task-centered leaders. Any problems that hinder production, especially problems with a human element, only interfere with effective operations. Concern for the individuals who do the work is minor. People are treated, at best, as equal to machines.

Impoverished Leader. The **impoverished leader** has little concern for either people or production. The basic attitude is "don't rock the boat at all." The impoverished leader exerts minimal effort in getting the work done, yet demonstrates no concern for personal relationships and the human dimensions of the job. This individual might best be characterized as both unfriendly and lazy when having a good day, and grouchy and obstinate on a bad day.

Middle-of-the-Road Leadership Style. **Middle-of-the-road** supervisors have a modicum of concern for people and production. This leader usually gets acceptable organizational performance in trying to balance getting the work out while maintaining an acceptable level of employee morale. Such a balance in leadership style produces a supervisor who is *not* overly energetic or overly enthusiastic about either job performance or employee satisfaction.

Team Leadership Style. The **team leader** is ideal. The team leader has high concern for people and for production. Consequently, he or she can be plotted on the Managerial Grid as scoring high in consideration and structure. The team leader is successful at motivating employees to achieve. Persons working for team leaders are committed to doing the job. The team leader also has the ability to get people to recognize the interdependence between job satisfaction and work achievement. Thus, the team leader succeeds in promoting mutual trust and respect between himself or herself and subordinates.

THE MANAGERIAL GRID: A LAUNCHING POINT FOR TODAY'S LEADERSHIP STYLES

The Managerial Grid is a convenient way to assess how well a leader will behave and succeed in managing people. Supervisors with a high concern for people (consideration) and a high concern for production (structure) ought to get the best results. The prescription, however, that one receives from the managerial grid—that there is a best leadership style, the team leader—may not be reliable. There have been some disquieting indicators that suggest there is no best leadership style.

The problem with the idea of a best style of leadership is that experience shows some leaders are quite effective when they have low concern for people, yet other leaders are effective when they have low concern for production. Other leaders are effective when they have low concern for both people *and* production.

Once it became commonly accepted that a single best style of leadership was *no guarantee* for either getting the best results or for being the most appropriate in any particular situation, the time was right to accept the idea that leadership effectiveness is contingent upon leadership methods and expectations, followers' attitudes and expectations, and situational constraints in the organization. This contingency theory, as it is called, as well as the research proposed by Fred E. Fiedler and William J. Reddin, who have enhanced our understanding of the subject[3], have become more accepted as a result of this movement.

CONTINGENCY THEORIES OF LEADERSHIP

The idea that one's effectiveness as a leader is contingent upon many variables is commonly accepted and can help supervisors at all levels to cope more effectively. The **contingency theory of leadership** rejects the notion that there is a best style of leadership; rather, it suggests that there are many leadership styles. How effective these styles are depends on

---

[3] Fred E. Fiedler, *A Theory of Leadership Effectiveness* (New York: McGraw Hill, 1967); and William J. Reddin, *Managerial Effectiveness* (New York: McGraw-Hill, 1970).

each situation, employee expectations, and the leader's expectations and power.

Fiedler's Theory

According to Fred Fiedler, there are three major variables that affect a leader's effectiveness in a given situation: (1) how well the individual leader gets along with subordinates, (2) the degree of structure in the task that subordinates are trying to accomplish, and (3) how much power and authority the leader's subordinates attribute to the leader in the situation.

If, for example, a leader has high expectations and excellent personal relationships with subordinates, if subordinates are engaging in a highly structured task where the end result can be clearly seen, and if the leader is perceived as having plenty of power and authority to accomplish objectives, the leader will be extremely effective. There are, of course, situations where the relationship between the leader and the group is weak, the task to be accomplished is unclear, and/or the leader's perceived power is low. A situation like that may emerge when an unpopular boss gives directions to subordinates who perceive the boss as having little or no authority to issue such orders. The classic example is a boss who appoints himself or herself to tell workers who report to another supervisor that they need to be more efficient. If the individual is truly unpopular, perceived as having no authority, and has a vaguely defined work objective, the boss is unlikely to be successful in that situation.

Effective leadership style depends on many circumstances, which include the situation in which the leader operates, if the leader has any power (as perceived by subordinates), and whether or not the leader has a reasonably good working relationship with subordinates. Above all, the leader's effectiveness depends on the consideration that he or she gives to subordinates.

Reddin's Theory

William J. Reddin was among the first researchers to suggest that leadership effectiveness depends on a variety of styles in any situation. Redding argues that the situational demands of a specific environment may determine the leader's effectiveness. If a leader's style is appropriate in a given situation, he or she will be effective; if the style is inappropriate, the leader will be ineffective. Reddin's theory adapts well to the ideas developed in Chapter 5 about different employee motivations in terms of value systems and attitudes.

Perhaps the major importance of Reddin's work is best seen in a work situation involving a union. For example, in the construction industry, a leader may have an excellent relationship with employees and be working to accomplish a clearly defined task like erecting a brick wall. The supervisor may have all the authority required to order the employees to erect the wall as well as all the materials and equipment required—bricks, mortar, trowels, and so forth. If, however, the bricklayers who are to erect the wall are on strike, the job will not be accomplished. In this case, whether or not the leader exercises a task-oriented approach is immaterial. In this case, *no* leadership style is appropriate because employees are not on the job.

Now, however, let's say that no strike exists, and while the supervisor has a close working relationship with most employees (assuming that no other dimension has changed), one problem still exists: a particular worker has a great dislike for the supervisor. Remember, of course, that the individual worker who dislikes the boss is protected under the union contract, just like all the other workers. Now let's say that the supervisor asks the worker in question, a bricklayer, to do something that would greatly help the other workers in doing their jobs, but the task is under a question of jurisdiction—should it be done by a bricklayer or by a member of another building trade—say an iron worker? In this case, the bricklayer may *refuse* to do the job and rely on the protection of the union agreement to be excused from having to do it because of the murky situation under the labor contract.

In this case, the leader—the supervisor—will be ineffective unless a strong approach is exercised in dealing with the bricklayer. The reason this is needed is that the supervisor may be perceived as having little or no power in the situation and, because of the personal antagonism from the bricklayer, the leader will not get the results that he or she might otherwise expect. Such jurisdictional disputes often occur in construction industries, and if this example seems far-fetched, the reader should investigate what is called a *wobble* in construction trades. A wobble is a situation where it is unclear which union craft has jurisdiction over what work, and individual workers may refuse to do the job or, in some cases, walk off the job because another craft "stole" work that they felt was under their jurisdiction.

Reddin's contribution to the study of leadership is the observation that leadership effectiveness is nearly always a *matter of degree* in any situation. Furthermore, he shows that there are numerous ways for a leader to be effective. A leader may come on strong in either task orientation or in relationships with people. Regardless of how the leader comes across, he or she may still fail.

Furthermore, the success or failure of a leader to get people to do something may not emanate from that leader's style. It may come strictly from the situation.

SITUATIONAL LEADERSHIP

Situational leadership involves altering the work environment so that an individual not only wants to do what is expected, but he or she may do so without being ordered. It is a form of leading without giving orders. It relies heavily on expectations, expectancy theory, and the fact that people will do what is expected of them. The technique involves designing the work environment so that it is obvious that (1) something needs to be done and (2) the time and resources are available to do it. For example, one task that many employees mentally rebel against is housekeeping. Dislike of routine housekeeping and maintenance functions, such as cleaning off the workbench or putting away tools, is common. Yet, few people like to work in a dirty, cluttered environment. The problem is that everyone wants a clean work area, but no one wants to do the cleaning.

The situational leader can make people *want* to clean off a workbench by providing ready access to trash barrels. Have you ever finished taking a drink in a public place and then tried to find a place to dispose of your drink container? Have you ever had the dissatisfying experience of not finding a place to dispose of the container? Have you then (presumably unnoticed) abandoned the container? The point is, you would have been happy to properly dispose of the container, but you didn't because it wasn't convenient to do so—the situation wasn't conducive to proper disposal.

Situational leaders know that refuse containers must be provided if refuse is to be controlled. Supervisors who have a good housekeeping situation do so by making it as convenient as possible. This process of engineering the situation is extremely useful for first-line supervisors in making work assignments. It is not leadership by orders or example—it comes merely from engineering the situation to get the desired results.

How the Environment Dictates Our Behavior. Situational leaders recognize that our environment affects our behavior. It has long been known by psychologists that whenever young children are put in big, empty buildings—such as a barn or a gymnasium—there is a native instinct for the children to run, scream, and shout. Have you ever seen children sit quietly when left unattended in a gymnasium? If you have, they must have been sick. The same idea is true at work. Some work situations are virtually designed to cause employees *not* to do what you want them to do. Whenever working conditions are too crowded, too hot, or too noisy, people become hostile. When people are upset, they frequently avoid work and may interfere with the work of others.

Understanding how people react to their work environment and then managing that environment will encourage workers to accomplish their assigned tasks. Engineering the work environment requires an acknowledgment that people are "triggered" to do things and that this triggering is, for the most part, a learned response. When we are asleep and hear an alarm clock ring, we wake up. When the telephone rings, we answer it. Furthermore, when someone politely says "Excuse me," we step out of the way. All of these behaviors result from the training we have had in reacting to our environment. We do things because we were trained to do them. Situational leaders understand how triggering activities can cause the worker to do what is desired.

Triggering the Situation. All workers have "hot buttons," or triggers. Usually, when employees act or refuse to act, it is because their hot button has been pushed. Effective managers try to tune into these triggering situations. Situational leadership is concerned with initiating desired behavior. Consider how you react, for example, when you read a sign that says, "Keep off the grass," or "Trespassers will be prosecuted to the fullest extent of the law," or "Smokers, if caught, will be fined." Do rude, abrupt, and insensitive directives cause you to arch your back in defiance? These communiques are negative triggers. Could they be changed to get compliance—perhaps even willing compliance instead of resentment? It would be easy to word the signs to read, "Please stay on the sidewalk," or "Please respect our need for privacy," or "Smokers are encouraged to smoke only in the coffee shop." Note, too, that providing sidewalks (to stay off the grass), installing privacy barriers (walls, door, and dividers), and supplying ashtrays are situational engineering techniques that make it easy for people to comply with a request.

When a situation is engineered to encourage compliance with orders or wishes, signs or instructions must not be sarcastic, and work situations must not be demeaning. If the situational leader's goal is true cooperation, an offensive tone should not be used, and active compliance with the supervisor's wishes problably will be realized. One does not want to be either solicitous or overbearing.

Why Situational Leadership Works

There are many advantages to engineering the situation so that people will want to comply with work assignments, orders, and directives. Some of the primary advantages are:

1. There will be less resistance to work assignments when the situation is conducive to work rather than when an individual is directly ordered. People generally don't mind cleaning workbenches when it's easy to dispose of the trash. However, they resent it bitterly when it becomes a difficult task.

2. Employee behavior is more likely to change if the *situation* seems to issue the order *rather than the boss*. Things are usually less offensive than people. If it is obvious that something needs to be done (everybody else's workbench is clean), then there will be a compulsion to do what is desired. But if someone tells you to do something, you may get mad.

3. If directives are presented in a way that appears to be dictated by the situation rather than by personal motivation, they are better accepted. A duty roster posted on a bulletin board that shows all people are assigned to the same dirty detail will be far more readily accepted by workers than will the same duty assignment given on a "by the way, it's your turn" basis. Consider, for example, when the boss says, "Hey, George, it's your turn to cover the phones at lunch today." It may well be George's turn to cover the phones that day. If, however, George wanted to leave the office during the lunch hour, he might feel that the boss was treating him unfairly, even though it was his day to cover the telephones. When a regular schedule listing telephone assignments during lunch is published knowledge, less antagonism results—and the option of making other arrangements is easier to invoke.

4. Managing the situation reduces authoritarian orders. No one likes to be ordered by someone who is very authoritative. When the first-line supervisor becomes threatening, ill will usually results. By managing the situation, authority doesn't have to be used. When it's obvious that something must be done and the subordinate is compelled to do so by the situation, the situation becomes far more palatable than orders and directives.

5. Situational management accentuates the positive and deemphasizes the negative. Positive instructions get better results than negative ones. The boss who threatens an employee is far less likely to achieve compliance than the boss who encourages compliance in a positive manner. The supervisor who says, "If you drive your forklift outside the yellow line and I catch you, I'm going to give you a three-day layoff" is

far more likely to find the forklift driver operating the forklift outside the yellow line than the supervisor who sincerely says, "Try to stay inside the yellow line for your own safety and the safety of other people." Both statements carry the same message. The second statement, however, doesn't carry the threat of punishment. It avoids a negative emphasis and the probability of creating resistance.

6. Situational leadership permits the supervisor to avoid issuing ultimatums and threats which, if acted on, will hurt the supervisor and/or the organization *more* than the employee. In the example concerning the forklift truck, the supervisor threatened the employee with a three-day layoff if the forklift was driven outside the yellow lines. When a supervisor makes a threat, it usually elicits a negative response from the threatened employee. Psychological studies also indicate that some employees see threats as a challenge, and they react accordingly: "You said you'd give me a three-day layoff if you caught me. Now let's see if: you can catch me and if you really meant what you said about a three-day layoff. I know that the layoff will disrupt production and hurt you (the supervisor) more than it will hurt me, because I'd like to have three days off to go fishing anyhow."

Situational leadership is the engineering of work situations, either physically or by using positive directions, to cause an employee to want to carry out the manager's orders or directions. It requires avoiding saying or doing things that will result in resistance to job instructions. Being a situational leader is not something that first-line supervisors learn intuitively. It must be studied and practiced before it works effectively. Studies of situational leaders who have refined their skills show that they are considered popular leaders and usually attain the highest productivity, best safety records, and best employee morale ratings of any supervisors. Consider situational leadership as an integral part of your job and you'll find that the principles begin to work automatically.

LEADERSHIP STYLES REVISITED— AN APPENDIX

A Pragmatist's Approach to Determining the Most Suitable Leadership Style

Because there was so much debate in the early 1970s over the many practical thoughts concerning the best supervisory behavior, pragmatic writers developed some interesting insights into supervisory style. The three basic ideas that shaped this thinking were: (1) some people may be lazy and wish to avoid work if they can, (2) a particular leadership style may not be the most effective in all cases, and (3) people who do not share the same values will relate differently to bosses with different leadership styles.

Many writers attempted to synthesize these ideas into a workable whole or guideline for line supervisors. However, while these prescriptions are useful, they are sometimes viewed as scholarly works that are not very helpful for the practicing supervisor. To bridge this gap, let's explore a mundane yet pragmatic approach to understanding leadership and how this approach can be integrated into a practical supervision scheme. This material is for practicing supervisors and is placed here to germinate ideas; it is not meant to be a purely academic exercise.

The Multicratic Approach to Leadership

Several years ago, a real pragmatist, Clark C. Caskey, described his **multicratic approach to leadership style**.[4] Remembering that most ideas developed by theorists on leadership styles use dichotomous approaches such as Theory X verus Theory Y, work centered versus employee centered, structure versus consideration, expectations versus availability, and so forth, Caskey suggested that there are only two approaches to supervisory style analysis—the hard-nosed approach and the soft-nosed approach. He argued that there are supervisors who take the hard-line, crack-of-the-whip approach, and there are other supervisors who take softer approaches—to the point of practically not bossing at all. Consequently, Caskey developed the **nosecator** to identify supervisory styles from the hard-nosed to the "no-nosed" (see Figure 6–3).

From Caskey's nosecator approach, supervisory styles can range from the hard-nosed autocratic style, where individuals tend to derive power from themselves in a dictatorial fashion and tell everyone what to do, to the extreme soft-nosed or abdicator style. The abdicator derives power from the informal organization and communicates on a random basis. The abdicator style is inappropriate in most instances of management, but it might be suitable in situations where no guidance from the boss is desired, such as when a subordinate has a personal problem that he or she needs to decide and in which the supervisor is powerless to be helpful. A similar situation might occur if a subordinate says, "Hey, boss, I'm thinking about calling up my old girlfriend for a date. What do you think I should do?"

Besides the supreme hard-nose and the no-nose, Caskey says, there are four types of leaders somewhere between those extremes. They are

---

[4] Clark C. Caskey, "Developing a Leadership Style," *Supervision*, April 1964.

FIGURE 6–3 Management Styles

	Theory X hard nose					Theory Y no nose
Style	Autocrat	Authoritarian	Bureaucrat	Democrat	Participative	Abdicator
Source of power	Self	Position	Rules, policies, procedures	Majority	Group	Informal organization
Mode of comunication	Orders and directions	Orders and directions	Explainer	Discusser	Joint determiner	Random

Source: Clark C. Caskey, "Developing a Leadership Style," *Supervision,* April 1964.

the authoritarian, who derives power from the formal organizational structure and who communicates autocratically by giving orders and directives; the bureaucrat, who derives power from company rules, regulations, and policies—who communicates by explaining why one must cooperate with established rules; the democrat, who derives power from the majority and who believes in discussing various issues and matters; and the participative leader, who derives power from the group and believes in joint decisions as to who will do what and when.

A careful study of Figure 6–3 indicates that the six leadership styles identified by Caskey can be divided into two groups—those styles primarily on the hard-nosed side and those styles primarily on the soft-nosed side. If one makes such a distinction, the leadership styles on the hard-nosed side of the nosecator are primarily structure-oriented supervisors, people who are far more concerned with getting the job done than with what employees think about them as bosses. About the only concern or consideration that hard-nosed supervisors demonstrate for what employees think of them occurs in the bureaucrat's role. The bureaucrat is the nice guy of hard-nosed management. Bureaucrats can blame decisions on someone else as they explain to employees why they must do something that they don't especially want to do (or can't do something they want to do).

A corollary can be seen on the soft-nosed side of the nosecator. Clearly, the democrat is the most hard-nosed of the soft-nosed styles, for the democrat tells people what to do once *the group* decides what its members are to do. The democrat implements the wishes of the group in a relatively hard-nosed fashion. However, the democrat cannot be classified as hard-nosed in a pure sense because he or she takes subordinates' wishes into consideration during the process of group decision making.

Relating the Nosecator to Employee Types

The nosecator, as a means of determining one's supervisory style, can be useful if one is pragmatic. Its usefulness is not because of the multiplicity of styles it identifies or because it is easily understood, but because it can be more effectively related to the three kinds of employee attitudes developed in Chapter 5, the ascendant, ambivalent, and indifferent attitudes. Ascendants like to work and view the opportunity to work as a chance to get ahead. They will respond more readily to a boss who has high expectations of them. Ascendant employees like being given the opportunity to be left to their own devices to do a job. Fortunately, the supervisor can rely on ascendants to do the job as well as possible *because* they want to get ahead. They feel miserable as failures and, more than anything, they want to succeed and do a good job.

A similar type of analysis can be established for the ambivalent's attitude toward work. Compared with ascendants, ambivalents do not have a tremendously high achievement drive, they do not need the high degree of recognition, and they do not demonstrate the extreme need for power. They do, however, have a high order of ego needs. Furthermore, ambivalents are intelligent and *do* wish to win recognition on the technical side of their job. The ambivalent wants to be recognized as a researcher, developer, or other technically proficient individual, and he or she will demonstrate plenty of professionalism toward the job. Consequently, the ambivalent personality, too, will respond better to the soft-nosed styles of leadership that include the democratic, participative, and even abdicator styles if practiced intelligently by the supervisor.

Supervisors must recognize that the indifferent employee is one who logically responds best to the hard-nosed leadership styles identified by Caskey. The indifferent employee often does not like the job (and does not *expect* to), tends to view it simply as a source of income, and does not especially aspire toward getting ahead. As a result, indifferents often respond better to being told what they are expected to do, when, and under what circumstances. The supervisor in charge of primarily indifferent employees might obtain better results by supervising them in a more hard-nosed fashion, be it autocratic, authoritarian, or bureaucratic.

Relevance to the Real World of Work

Let's look at an example of this analysis. Assume that your instructor is a boss and that you and your fellow students are co-workers who work for the instructor. Your "boss" wants to be an abdicator and tells your class to "study hard for I know you will want to do a good job." Will your fellow students study hard? What will they study? Will some students goof off?

What would happen if your instructor told your fellow students that they could do anything they wanted—any day and all day? Would they volunteer for work? Or would they spend most of their time engaging in activities of more interest to them—talking, sleeping, watching television, drinking beer, playing tennis, and boy- or girl-watching?

The answers to the above exercise are obvious: Some students would do a lot of work; some wouldn't do any work. In contrast, what would happen if a manager who is supervising ascendants or ambivalents came on strong as a hard-nosed autocrat? What would happen if the dean of a university advised a professor to teach the Darwinian notion of evolution as a hoax, or to proclaim that the world was flat? What would happen (as, in fact, it did) if the president of a major television network told an entertainer how to tell a joke, what kind of jokes to tell, and what songs to sing? Repercussions that have been created by similar issues in our society in prior years make the answer clear. When a person is managing people who do the job because they *want* to, because they *like* to, and because they expect to do it *their way*, the soft-nosed styles of supervision work best. But when a person is supervising people who do not enjoy their jobs or who view working only as a means toward an end, the soft-nosed styles of supervision will not be as effective in many cases. In those situations, supervisors must recognize that the hard-nosed line may be necessary.

Key Words	**leadership**
	traditional leaders
	Theory X
	Theory Y
	structure
	consideration
	Managerial Grid
	country club leadership
	task-centered leaders
	impoverished leaders
	middle-of-the-road leadership
	team leadership
	contingency theory of leadership
	Fred Fiedler
	William Reddin
	situational leadership
	Clark Caskey

multicratic approaches to leadership style
nosecator

Self-Assessment

How much do you know about your own leadership characteristics and leadership theory? To evaluate yourself, respond to the following questions or statements with a 1, 2, or 3 if you disagree, have a negative response, or rate the item low. If you agree, have a positive response, or rate the item high, answer 4, 5, or 6.

1. Are you willing to take responsibility for being the spokesperson for a group when others are reluctant to do so?

   1   2   3   4   5   6

2. Team leadership has been fully demonstrated as the best leadership style.

   1   2   3   4   5   6

3. According to expectancy theory, employee expectations have little to do with the appropriate leadership style.

   1   2   3   4   5   6

4. William J. Reddin was one of the first people to recognize that there is one best leadership style for each person instead of each situation.

   1   2   3   4   5   6

5. Are you willing to take a stand on a principle you believe even though others you know or work with do not agree.

   1   2   3   4   5   6

6. In a crisis situation, a task-oriented leader is most likely to be successful.

   1   2   3   4   5   6

7. Every manager should learn the leadership formula.

    1   2   3   4   5   6

8. It has been demonstrated that environmental factors have a strong effect on appropriate leadership style.

    1   2   3   4   5   6

9. Clarke Caskey demonstrated the type of leadership that works best when dealing with indifferents also works best when supervising ascendants.

    1   2   3   4   5   6

Things to Remember

1. The traditional role of leaders in work organizations has undergone many changes.

2. During the 1950s and 1960s, the theories of Douglas McGregor, based on managerial assumptions about people, were dominant:

   a. Theory X was considered the traditional view of leadership. It was based on the belief that people needed both strong direction and strong control.

   b. Theory Y was considered an enlightened style of leadership that was based on the assumption that good leaders helped people develop their own sense of direction and control. Punishment, threats, and external controls were not necessary for effective leadership.

3. Blake and Mouton identified consideration for people and consideration for the task to be accomplished as the two most important components of leadership.

4. Blake and Mouton developed a Managerial Grid that depicted five leadership styles depending on the degree of consideration for people and tasks.

5. Contingency theory, such as that developed by Fiedler and Reddin, points out that there is no best leadership style for all situations.

6. Clark Caskey's nosecator is a pragmatic approach to job leadership.

7. Situational leadership is based on the concept that situations can be developed that largely determine employee activities. When such situations exist, little direction and control by managers is necessary.

CASES

It Always Hurts

Ellie Yapundich was a professional nurse for Health Underwriters Research Teams (HURT), a health service group sponsored by a group of related insurance companies that had pooled their resources to sponsor a medical facility for treatment and research of rare medical problems. Although she had been offered promotions on several occasions, Ellie saw her role as a professional nurse with a Master's degree who was part of a treatment/research team.

Early in her career with HURT, Ellie received a set of X-ray photographs of a patient with a rare type of spinal tumors. Instead of the recommended side view as well as the view taken directly of the patient's back, the X-ray laboratory had taken only the direct picture. When the attending physician asked for the side view and it was unavailable, Ellie rushed the patient back to the laboratory and supervised a new round of exposures.

During a conference on the patient's illness the next day, Ellie voiced the need in a positive and somewhat aggressive manner that a procedure was needed to prevent such an incident from recurring. Over the objections of the head of the X-ray laboratory, the procedure was enacted.

After the incident, other nurses were to voluntarily let Ellie know where mistakes were being made and when procedures were not being followed properly. She would investigate and bring problems to the attention of management at regular weekly conferences. Although some managers grew irritated with what they saw as her constant attacks, few denied that she was wrong. Among nurses and technicians, she became highly respected as a person willing to take risks and correct faulty practices.

1. What type of leader was Ellie? Describe her style according to theories presented in the text.

2. It is possible to be an effective leader in an organization and not be part of management? How does this develop? Give some examples.

3. Do leaders seek followers or followers seek leaders? Explain your answer.

Good Old Carl   Carl Washington was well-liked, a hard worker, and loyal to upper management. When a vacancy occurred as head of administrative housekeeping for HURT (Health Underwriters Research Teams), Carl was a natural choice. As a first-line manager, Carl was designated Head of Administrative Housekeeping. In a health-care facility, it is an important job. Responsibility for the cleaniness of a health-care facility is different from that of any other organization. A knowledge of proper materials, their applications, disposal of contaminated materials, handling of infectious matter, and other related matters are as important as the actual cleaning operations. Technically, Carl was well qualified.

In his weekly reports, budget planning, inventory maintenance, equipment readiness, and emergency planning, Carl was excellent. His employees liked him and many thought he was a perfect boss. If an employee needed time off, Carl would grant it. When employees made mistakes, they were excused. If someone was late to work, Carl always understood. Absences were rarely questioned. When employees fell behind in their work, Carl would pitch in and help. Everyone liked Carl and many people were surprised when he was moved from first-line manager to administrative assistant to the Chief of Plant Services. There were too many mistakes being made, too many absences being recorded, and too many complaints about housekeeping personnel goofing off being heard.

1. Was Carl a leader? Explain your answer.

2. Why was Carl selected and what did management overlook?

3. Do leaders have to be hard-nosed and autocratic in some situations?

4. Who is respected more by employees: a task-oriented manager or a people-oriented manager? Why?

Action in Leadership

7

Thought Starter

Even though there is a long way to go, U.S. management is beginning to pay more attention to leadership and excellence in work organizations than at any time in the past. People are paying attention to management. Underlying this popularity in watching management is the concern that we, as a nation, must find ways to regain our leadership in business and industry that was somehow lost during the turbulent late 1960s and early 1970s when an antiestablishment philosophy was accepted by a large portion of our population. It was a period when workers developed an ethic far different from most managers; an ethic that may, in the long-run, be one of the most positive social movements ever experienced. Personal responsibility, rather than reliance on established authority, was the ultimate focus for many young people who are now in positions of leadership and authority nationally. As times have changed, business and industrial leaders, like Lee Iacocca of Chrysler, have become heroes rather than villains. We've come a long way. We have a long way to go.

In Chapter 7 you will learn:

- Good managers are developers of people. They select and make winners.
- It pays to praise good work, especially when a job is done for the first time.
- Why leadership is not always a bed of roses.
- Excellence is practiced in at least 62 top companies and is based on eight principles.

□ **How quality circles work.**

□ **What theory Z really means.**

"It's going to be tough. That's why you were picked as the new supervisor of the computer supply section," stated Tom Bradley, Distribution Manager for Lyle-Edmunds Office and Computer Supply Company. His conversation was directed at Maria Mendez, who had worked in the inventory control section for the past nine months. "Our primary goals," continued Tom, "are to get schedules back on-line, make sure orders are filled correctly, and improve the overall discipline of that section's employees. They've got, as you know, the worst reputation in the company."

Marie thought about his words for a few seconds. "I know it will be rough, but I have a few ideas. There have been three supervisors in the past year assigned to the section. All left for different reasons. I intend to be there a while and make it the best section at Lyle-Edmunds."

"She just might make it," thought Tom, "She probably will." Two weeks later, Marie started the company's first quality circle and instituted a set of goals for the section. Things were already improving.

One problem that frustrates many supervisors is the question of "How do I actually become an effective supervisor or leader in my organization?" Leadership theories are good. Any student of supervision must be knowledgeable in the many ideas that people have offered over the years concerning success in a leadership and/or supervisory role. Finally, the time comes to supervise. Then, all the good books don't seem as valuable as they once were. Facing the dragon is never the same as talking about it.

SOME REALISTIC APPROACHES TO SUPERVISORY LEADERSHIP

In recent years, there have been several outstanding books published concerning success in leadership and supervisory roles. One is the book by Kenneth Blanchard and Spenser Johnson entitled *The One–Minute Manager*. Another is *In Search of Excellence*, by Thomas J. Peters and Robert H. Waterman, Jr. Yet another book, albeit not a primer for supervisory leadership, is *Managing*, by Harold S. Geneen. Each of these books has made the nonfiction best seller list and they contribute to supervisory leadership. All have a practical base to them because they deal with what real, successful supervisors do.

THE ONE–MINUTE MANAGER

Supervisory leadership has to do with one's skills and ability to motivate employees. In fact, maybe one effective definition of leadership is the ability to motivate people to do what needs to be done. But the one-minute-manager concept is more than merely how to motivate people. It's more of a leadership idea—how to get appropriate action and behavior from subordinates in accomplishing the goals and objectives that you must accomplish as a supervisor.

The one-minute-manager idea is that a boss should take a minute, at whatever moment, to develop people to do the right thing. This includes taking time to praise people and to provide them with positive reinforcement. However, it also includes taking a minute to critique or discipline people to get them to correct poor performance or unacceptable work behavior. The supervisor is committed to continually taking advantage of opportunities to help employees achieve the desired performance.

DEVELOPING PEOPLE

The One–Minute Manager states that a supervisor has three choices as a boss in managing and developing people. The first choice is that you can hire people who are winners. But hiring winners is usually expensive. Moreover—and probably much more difficult—winners are extremely hard to find. We'd all like to hire winners, but we can't.

Second, if you can't find a winner, then you must hire someone who has the *potential* to be a winner. Hiring people who have the potential to become winning employees is probably the best alternative because there are many potential winners available. Blanchard and Johnson recommend that once you have hired someone with the potential, systematically train that person to be a winner. Your third choice, they say, is prayer.

Most supervisors know what they want their people to do. The problem is that supervisors often don't tell their people what they want them to do in a way they understand. Perhaps the problem is communication, but, for whatever reason, supervisors tend to assume that employees should know what the boss wants them to do without the boss having to "tell them a million times."

Perhaps the key to actually leading someone to do a task properly, according to the one-minute-manager concept, is, in the beginning, *to catch them doing something right*—particularly if it is a new task that they have never done. People can rarely do any job exactly right the first time. But they can probably do a portion of that job correctly. This portion is what should be praised.

Accentuate the Positive

Whenever employees do something desirable, particularly when they are in the learning phase, they must be praised—the boss must take a minute to praise them. Thus, the boss should accentuate *positive leadership*. The effective leader helps subordinates reach their full potential as employees by catching them doing something correctly and positively reaffirming the fact that they are doing that job correctly. Then, the supervisor can focus attention on other aspects of the job that are not going correctly and help the employee bring those performance expectations "up to speed."

It's a Problem of Leadership

The primary problem of leadership, particularly in motivating people to perform their work the way we want them to do it, occurs because most bosses will wait until their employees are doing something exactly right before they praise them. As a consequence, many people never become high-level performers at work because their bosses concentrate on catching them doing something wrong—that is, doing things that fall short of the final desired performance. Many bosses chastise employees for their failures, rather than commending them on their successes.

Bosses should not emphasize negativism—what's wrong—but rather the positive side—what the employee is doing right. If you catch people doing work correctly—and praise them for it—they will continue to work correctly. Then, over time, workers can concentrate on improving items that are not right while continuing to do the other items correctly. Ultimately, they will do everything correctly, and they will be totally satisfactory employees. The emphasis, therefore, is for the supervisor to help (and catch) the employee doing each aspect of the job correctly until they can do the whole job correctly rather than focusing attention on poor performance and failure.

Giving a One-Minute Praising

Supervisors always try to create situations from the beginning of any job relationship where they can give a subordinate a **one-minute praising** for doing jobs or functions correctly. It may be an old commercial, but the breakfast of champions, when it comes to supervisory leadership, is effective feedback to employees. Primarily, however, the emphasis should be on the positive—because the number one motivator of people at work is feedback on how they are doing things and whether or not they are working correctly.

Most people are potential winners when it comes to performing their jobs adequately. The bulk of employees are not only competent, but they enjoy doing a good job. A one-minute manager is a boss or leader who gets good results without taking much time in the process. They are devoted to getting people to perform as well as possible.

Leading Your People into Satisfactorily Performing Their Jobs

People who feel good about themselves on the job tend to produce good results. Helping people feel good about themselves is the key to getting more work done correctly, and it is a hallmark of a one-minute manager. Good one-minute managers will always say that the best minute they spend at work is the one that they invest in their people. Misguided supervisors get in a hole (by destroying employees' dignity and their desire to ever successfully perform on the job) by being critical in attempting to discipline people who are not performing well.

One fundamental aspect of good discipline from the supervisory standpoint, when you have a problem performer or behavior at work, is that discipline must occur as close to the problem behavior or performance as possible. This is particularly important if the alternative is to not implement any disciplinary action until after the problem has occurred. Waiting too long to discipline someone is similar to the situation where misbehaving children are told at the day-care center that they are "going to be in trouble" when they are picked up at the end of the day. When the end of the day rolls around, the kid has completely forgotten what the misbehavior was, the day-care center people can't remember what the problem was, but everyone knows that the parent must be apprised of the misbehavior and that some punishment must be rendered.

Blanchard and Johnson refer to this "you'll-pay-later" form of discipline as "gunnysacking." It is not appropriate for supervisors to "gunny sack" or save up negative feelings about someone's poor performance. They indicate that such behavior causes supervisors to become antagonistic toward the employee, and the employee is given little opportunity to correct a poor performance, especially if the employee is not told about it when it immediately occurs—the time when he or she can most learn something and do something about the problem.

BEING TOUGH AS A LEADER

One point that must be understood by any leader is that leadership is not always a bed of roses. Sometimes a good leader has to care enough to be really tough with employees—tough enough on poor performance to be sure that it gets corrected. But toughness should be toward the individual's performance not toughness toward the person. Good leaders do not tolerate poor performance. They don't, however, get tough on people by personalizing their toughness. Being tough on a person simply causes resentment and creates undesirable aftereffects in interpersonal relationships between supervisor and subordinate.

The idea of **tough leadership** is that a supervisor must be tough on behavior and then be supportive of the person. If the supervisor keeps that in mind, there is a high probability that he or she will be an effective leader.

The foregoing ideas are fundamental to the notion of the one-minute manager. The one-minute-manager concept, however, is not the only action-oriented supervisory leadership behavior that is being espoused today. There are other good ideas associated with effective leadership and supervision. One of those ideas comes from Peters and Waterman in their book *In Search of Excellence*.

IN SEARCH OF EXCELLENCE

In the early 1980s, *In Search of Excellence* appeared in the United States. It took no great genius to realize that something was terribly wrong with how management and leadership were operating in U.S. business and industry. The U.S. economy was in bad economic condition, the country was in a severe recession (perhaps depression), and seemed well on its way to becoming a second-rate industrial power. Foreign competition was rampant, there was an onslaught of foreign automobiles, steel, and so forth, and no end seemed to be in sight.

Many managers and executives, not to mention first-level supervisory people, worried about the decline in corporate success and in personal self-respect that individuals working, supervising, and managing in those organizations were noticing. People were extremely uncomfortable with what they perceived as a real shift in employee values and "the work ethic." The attitude seemed to be that the customer really doesn't matter or certainly matters less than maximizing profits. Personal advancement within the organization seemed more important than organizational loyalty or job performance. Management theories indicated that complying with theory was more important than understanding the lessons of experience and the impact that experience had on people's job performance. Managers and leaders were very unhappy about the situation, and there seemed to be no alternative solutions in sight.

Perhaps the one-minute-manager concept somewhat helped to alleviate this problem. However, the book *In Search of Excellence* hit the market and immediately became a best-selling book that again made it acceptable for managers and leaders to think in terms of caring not only about their customers, but also about their employees, products, and corporate values.

The notion of excellence in management was enormously exhilarating. The authors listed eight **excellence attributes** in management, including some that have important repercussions for supervisory leadership roles.

In Search of Excellence confirms what many people had observed or suspected about American management. That is, the key to success, survival, and prosperity in American organizations lies not in a rational, quantitative approach to problem solving (a technique that was extremely popular in the 1960s and 1970s), but in a basic commitment to perhaps irrational and certainly difficult to measure items like concern for people and the quality of one's products, services, and relationship with customers.

A Basic Philosophy in Management

In Search of Excellence showed that many managers thought of employees as variables that mess up a nice, clean, rational model of management. In addition, managers often regarded customers as uncooperative factors that refused to perform as agreed. These managers tended to view quality as something that an organization could only afford to provide so much of.

However, people are very important. Furthermore, the supervisor must relate with the people in the organization. It is paramount that supervisors understand the implications of this all-important theory. It concerns how the supervisor manages people, how the supervisor is responsible for quality control and assurance, and what the supervisor's responsibilities are in relationship to customers and others outside the organization.

The book states that managers at 62 of America's "best-run" companies have operated differently than most companies—these "excellent" companies believe in both the importance of superior quality and service to customers and the value of their people as individuals and as employees.

The Eight Attributes of Excellence

According to *In Search of Excellence*, there are eight attributes that emerged in the authors' study of the best-run companies in the United States that distinguish the excellent, innovative companies from other companies. Those attributes included the following:

1.   A Bias for Action.   Excellent companies "get on with the work." These organizations may be analytical in their decision making, but they are not paralyzed by the process. In many of these companies, standard operating procedure is "Do it, fix it, try it."

2.   Closeness to the Customer.   The excellent companies learn from the people and customers that they serve and work with. They provide unparalleled quality, service, and reliability to customers—things that work, things that last.

3.   Autonomy and Entrepreneurship.   The excellent companies foster many leaders and innovators throughout the organization. They are essentially a beehive for champions of business organization. The excellent companies don't try to hold everyone on so tight a rein that they cannot be creative. They encourage practical risk taking and support good efforts even though they may fail.

4.   Productivity through People.   Most of the excellent companies treat their employees—the rank and file as well as the executives—as the source of quality and productivity within their organizations. They try to avoid a we/they, good guy/bad guy attitude with respect to various levels of people in the organization. Furthermore, these companies feel that people are the fundamental source of improved efficiency.

5. A Hands-On, Value-Driven Operation. The attitude here is that a basic philosophy of organization is far more important than technological or economic resources. The excellent companies' people subscribe to this philosophy by getting their hands on work, getting involved, and they are driven to provide value to the organization and the organization's customers.

6. A Tendency to "Stick to the Knitting." The excellent companies stick to the business they know—they don't get involved in activities they are inexperienced with or don't know how to operate successfully. They don't necessarily pursue a diversity of products and services unless they can be successful and have experience in doing so.

7. A Simple Form, a Lean Staff. Most of the really successful organizations studied have an underlying structural form consisting of simplicity. Top-level staffs are lean in these organizations. All levels of management are required to be leaders and to be involved with their people.

8. A Simultaneous Loose-Tight Quality. This idea is that excellent companies combine autonomy at lower levels in the organization with virtually frenetic adherence to certain ideals. The excellent companies are both centralized and decentralized at the same time. For the most part, they push autonomy down to the lowest levels in the organization— where the real action occurs—productivity, quality, and concern for people.

Application for the Supervisor's Leadership

Some have suggested that the *In Search of Excellence* ideas are essentially observations and that the ideas are not detailed enough to follow. Furthermore, they suggest that the supervisor should not look for a grocery list of activities to be successful.

The theories and ideas espoused by *In Search of Excellence* relate to this book in how the supervisor can fit into the organization, and what the supervisor needs to do daily to obtain the objectives and goals established by his or her organization. The *structure* of these ideas probably has little to do with how well an organization is run by supervisors. The *goals* and the *people* pursuing those goals are far more important. One clear-cut idea that emerged from the study is the meaning of the word *champion*, a word used by both the authors of *In Search of Excellence* and *The One-Minute Manager*.

In today's world, the champion is probably a person who is not necessarily a dreamer or an intellectual giant, but he or she is someone who gets work done. Tenacity of purpose is the key to success. The individual who succeeds perseveres against all odds, long after everyone else has given up.

Yet another aspect of success as a supervisor implied by *In Search of Excellence* is that supervisors must raise questions rather than give answers. Instead of offering new structures or strategies of supervisory behavior, the supervisor can, by raising questions, get far more successful results. If supervisors developed more patterns and habits of questioning, rather than providing answers about "how to do it," supervisors would be more effective. Perhaps the overall idea behind *In Search of Excellence* is that the answers to business questions are found in the same way that answers to other questions are found: by thinking and feeling one's way into a situation rather than using a pat formula.

NO-BRAINER LEADERSHIP

One of the most unsatisfying aspects of applying *In Search of Excellence* to the supervisor's role is that many supervisors tend to apply some pat formula to their job performance. They like to pigeonhole actions and behaviors and believe that complying with certain actions or behaviors makes them good leaders. People have a fatal attraction for turning ideas into a formula response, and problems have occurred when supervisors have tried to apply notions from *In Search of Excellence* in their supervisory roles. Good leadership is a *human* art and not a science. Mindless adherence to formulas for successful leadership almost certainly will produce opposite results. One cannot be a no-brainer supervisor. If a supervisor doesn't think and doesn't apply the human art of management, he or she will be in trouble. There is no single patented or fool-proof way to be a successful leader in any organization. The only constraints are the supervisor's flexibility and willingness to change as situations require. So, while the lessons from both *The One-Minute Manager* and *In Search of Excellence* are important, there is still room for improvement in the application of these concepts by effective leaders.

THEORY G

An organization can't be run on a series of accidents. Otherwise, an organization will be accident-prone. Many successful people have good ideas about how they led their organization to success. Harold S. Geneen, formerly the Chief Executive Officer of ITT recently published a book about his ideas on managing and some concepts of theoretical management. To paraphrase some of Geneen's ideas and his astounding success in running his organization, he states that theories are like the paper hoops that one sees in a circus: they seem solid until the clowns crash through them. Once that happens, one realizes that the paper hoops were tissue-paper thin and that there was little or nothing going on at the event—it was all an illusion.

Geneen states that one problem many leaders have is that they always look for simple formulas to solve complex problems. Unfortunately, almost anything can fit into a neat little package, given an attractive label, and be swallowed like a sugar-coated bill. He says that many business and leadership theories have similar problems.

From a pragmatic standpoint, Geneen suggests that aspiring supervisors should know that while it may be desirable to buy into ideas about how one should behave as an effective leader, all ideas are simply theories and, until correctly implemented, they are no more than that. Even if they are implemented, they can lose much of their usefulness.

Perhaps the real benefit of **Theory G,** Geneen's theory, is that, when viewed in light of such concepts as Theory X, Theory Y, Theory Z, Japanese management, the one-minute manager, and *In Search of Excellence,* supervision is like all fads and fashions—theory. Business theories come and business theories go. One basic idea is required for success in leadership, according to Geneen's concept. The supervisor should not implement any pat formula. Rather, he or she should think in terms of dollars and cents, facts and fiction, and objective performance standards in determining expected results in the work place.

According to Geneen's concepts, most experienced leaders quickly discover that pat formulas really do not work like immutable formulas used by chemists and physicists in laboratories. Leadership is not a science; it follows no immutable laws. There is no predictability in what an individual will do.

A machine can cut a piece of steel with extreme accuracy, and a computer can retrieve a specific tidbit of information. One can throw all kinds of raw materials into a mechanized work area and quickly get an impressive finished product.

However, the supervisor must remember that the employee is not a robot. Employees must remember that supervisors are people, too. In any organizations, with all the official machinery, equipment, and computer technology, people still run the organizations—people who have all sorts of faults and frailties. These people must be led by thinking, concerned leaders rather than by bosses who are too busy to manage and lead. It is with this admonishment that we now turn to other current leadership theories about effective supervision.

OTHER CURRENT LEADERSHIP ACTIVITIES

Theory Z

While analyzing what works in the real world, one must be aware of **Theory Z.** As mentioned earlier, Theory X and Theory Y, popular supervisory concepts in the early 1960s, tended to focus on the supervisor's thoughts about workers. Theory Z, popularized by William Ouchi, states that employees can contribute much to productivity if they are only asked and are decently considered as having something to contribute.

Theory Z, and the concept of quality circles, which it spun off, became important in the latter part of the 1970s and early 1980s, when there was unanimous agreement that U.S. employee productivity had declined. At that time, evidence indicated that the productivity of employees in the United States was not nearly as high as in some European countries and in Japan. Therefore, many scholars attempted to analyze how and why some countries, especially Japan, seemed to achieve much greater productivity from their firms than their U.S. counterparts.

Ironically, Theory Z and quality circles can be traced to the United States. By using quality circles and Theory Z, many companies in the United States and abroad have experienced increasing productivity from employees. The way quality circles work is that a group of workers voluntarily meet on a regular basis to identify, analyze, and solve quality and other productivity problems. Ideally, people who participate in quality circles are from the same work area or at least do similar work so that the problems they attempt to solve are familiar to all participants.

Quality Circles: One Key to Employee Productivity and Morale

The reason there is so much interest in Theory Z and quality circles rests heavily on current leadership theory: Most workers want to be part of a team. They *expect* to be part of a team. In addition, they expect to be treated reasonably—that is, they want adequate consideration.

Employees like to take pride in their team and their company, in most cases. In virtually all instances, they want to be involved. The idea behind quality circles is to put your employees on your team. A company's employees are the most powerful and expensive resource that a company has—powerful in that their ideas can make or break an organization (especially when coupled with their attitudes and expectations); expensive in that labor is usually the largest expense for any organization.

Quality circles tap this resource not only for the organization's use, but also for the benefit of employees. Workers almost always enjoy their jobs more when they feel they belong to a team. Furthermore, they usually take pride in doing their jobs. How do you get them committed to participate in resolving problems facing the organization? In most cases, these are problems associated with doing the job, but they can be behavioral and morale problems as well.

Most supervisors are surprised at the sincerity, dedication, and loyalty that result when employees are asked to participate in making decisions that affect both their workaday lives and their livelihood. This is one of the most important reasons that quality circles and Theory Z have caught on as well as they have.

Building People

The success of quality circles is based on the supervisor's trust, respect, and caring for his or her subordinates. There are no human characteristics more powerful than trust, respect, and caring for developing self-reliance, confidence, and cooperation in subordinates. Some guidelines for quality circle performance are given in Figure 7–1.

Integrating quality circles into an organization is based on the hope of making employees better than they are. It means that the supervisor believes that they have the capacity to grow and develop at work. It also means that the opportunity to grow and develop is made available to employees. Accomplishing these ends requires that the supervisor be patient enough to allow growth to happen. There is no short cut to success in using quality circles and Theory Z.

Objectives Sought by Supervisors Employing the Theory Z–Quality Circle Concept

Primary objectives that supervisors seek in employing quality circles and Theory Z are to:

1. Inspire teamwork.
2. Reduce errors and improve quality.
3. Increase employee motivation.

FIGURE 7–1   Circle Code of Conduct

1. Attend all circle meetings and be on time.
2. Listen to and show respect for the views of other members.
3. Criticize ideas, not persons.
4. Accept results of circle votes.
5. Everyone is equal during circle meetings.
6. The only stupid question is the one that isn't asked.
7. Participate according to the golden rule.
8. Carry out assignments on schedule.
9. Ensure that credit is given to those to whom it is due.
10. Show thanks and appreciation to nonmembers who give assistance.
11. Avoid criticism and sarcasm toward the ideas of others.
12. Don't indulge in disruptive side conversations.
13. Always strive for "win-win" situations.
14. Don't belittle the ideas or opinions of others—you are not the judge.
15. Before you criticize, give praise and honest appreciation.

Source: © Quality Circle Institute, 1980, form 27.

4. Get people involved on the job.

5. Solve productivity and morale problems.

6. Develop an attitude of preventing problems.

7. Improve safety procedures at work.

8. Improve superior-subordinate communications.

9. Promote and develop personal and leadership development.

10. Develop harmonious relationships between workers and bosses.

A quality circle program is organized around the work group members, the leaders of the circles, the program coordinator (sometimes called the facilitator), and the steering committee. In most situations, quality circles are composed of six or eight persons who voluntarily join together to consider problems of mutual interest concerning their work situations. Usually, people meet in a small circle once a week for an hour, they identify the problem they wish to address, analyze it, and make recommendations to management for improvements.

In many companies, 80 percent or more of the recommendations made by quality circles to management are approved (and some reports run higher than 95 percent). In many cases, the circles meet during regular work hours, although this is not always convenient. Some companies, therefore, have circle meetings after or before regular working hours. Many companies compensate their employees with overtime when meetings are held after (or before) normal working hours. Savings

Does your company have a quality control department or are you responsible for quality control?

that result from improved productivity more than offset the cost. Any supervisor who contemplates establishing a quality circle, however, need not feel that work time be sacrificed or that overtime must be approved to initiate such a program.

How to Implement a Quality Circle Program

Any supervisor who wants to implement a quality circle program should do a little research. Writing for the Quality Circle Institute's booklet, *Quality Circles—Answers to 100 Frequently Asked Questions*, would be a good start. Then, making a presentation to one's boss about the advantages of having a quality circle instituted at work might be a good idea. The main reasons for implementing a quality circle program are leadership-based—to seek improvement in quality, productivity, and employee morale. It would be desirable to get top-level management support—the stronger the better—for the program. The supervisor must realize that what he or she *does* will do more to convince others of the usefulness of quality circles than what he or she *says*. So, to maintain vigorous management backing and genuine cooperation from other supervisors, the quality circle organizer must expend a little effort.

The usual members of a quality circle are the employees, the leaders, the facilitator (circle coordinator), and the steering committee. Any supervisor who wishes to employ a quality circle would ordinarily be the facilitator. Essential qualifications for a facilitator are listed in Figure 7–2.

The facilitator (the supervisor) trains the circle leader, who usually is an employee. It is important that the circle leader be someone held in high esteem by other circle members. The supervisor can be, and often is, the circle leader. In most cases, when quality circles are formed, the circle leader is also the facilitator and the supervisor. That usually changes, though, as real trust in the members fully develops.

As time passes, other circle leaders will emerge. This usually poses no

FIGURE 7–2   A Facilitator's Essential Qualifications

Experience in organizing, training, and directing volunteer groups.
Ability to accept and understand people and to wholeheartedly support them. Must truly care for people.
Experience in one or more industrial training programs.
Knowledge and/or experience in quality control.
Knowledge of elementary statistics.
Ability to organize and conduct conferences, presentations, and meetings.
Ability to train group leaders.
Ability to set aside own ego and give full credit to members, leaders, and management.
Overall view of organization's methods of doing business and managing.
Ability to set and follow standards, establish priorities, and give directions.
Ability to be creative, to innovate, and to improvise.
Ability to stimulate people emotionally.
Ability to communicate with and influence supervisors and all levels of management, and the ability to promote quality circle activity with them.
Ability to follow directions and adhere to the quality circle philosophy. Must be "manageable."
Ability to express the quality circle philosophy well both orally and verbally.
Complete commitment to the quality circle concept as a way of life—as a route to personal and organizational success.
Ability to promote, implement, operate, and mange quality circle activity in any other part of the organization.
Ability to become involved in his or her work and the work of others while, at the same time, relating it to the philosophy of both the program and the employing organization.

Note: Experience as a production worker may be helpful in some instances, but it is not essential.
Source: Quality Circle Institute.

problem once all people in the circle understand that the quality circle is neither a gripe session nor a group of employees meeting to take potshots at a despised boss. It is an organization designed to minimize or eliminate problems. When all circle members accept that they are there to discuss serious problems, and when each participant feels secure, they will feel more free to share their opinions, ideas, questions, and to join in brainstorming sessions.

DO QUALITY CIRCLES REALLY PAY OFF?

If one reads recent literature concerning quality circles, one is inclined to believe that quality circles *always* pay off. This is, perhaps, unfortunate. Some theories get overplayed. For example, there are reports of thousands (and even millions) of dollars saved by companies employing quality circles on a full-scale basis. These results usually are obtained only when there is a full-blown program and when a steering committee has been appointed in the organization.

Usually, steering committees are made up of representatives from major departments in an organization. For example, in a manufacturing operation, it is common to have representatives on the steering committee from such diverse areas as production, quality control, personnel, finance, and marketing. In these situations, the steering committee can actually facilitate implementing major ideas (particularly ideas involving heavy expenditures, which are usually necessary to achieve the large savings reported).

SOME WORDS OF CAUTION

The use of quality circles in the United States is booming. However, Robert E. Cole, a recognized authority on quality circles and Japanese managerial styles, has some words of caution about using quality circles. He points out that ritualism can blunt the effectiveness of quality circles—going to meetings for the sake of going to meetings, for instance. Furthermore, Cole says, the Japanese report that one third of their quality circles have a ritualistic flavor, one third function pretty well, and only the remaining third consistently tackle new problems.[1] Anyone who

---

[1] See "Researcher Cautions against Seeing Quality Circles as Miracle Cures," *Training/HRD*, August 1980, p. 94.

wants to employ quality circles must realize that they are not an instant cure for productivity or morale problems. One can't start a quality circle and assume it will perpetuate itself and/or that it will necessarily succeed. Cole says that there is no truth to the myth that a superior work ethic counts for high Japanese productivity relative to U.S. productivity: "I've worked right on the production line in both countries, and I find new differences on a person-to-person level. . . . the big difference is that, almost out of necessity, the Japanese organizations have developed an environment that encourages worker contribution and participation."[2]

Things to Remember

1. The one-minute manager stresses ways to develop people at work.
2. Good bosses hire potential winners and then help them become winners.
3. Most supervisors know what they want people to do, but often they don't tell them what to do.
4. Positive emphasis of work is more beneficial than negative emphasis.
5. Excellent organizations are concerned with employees, product quality, and customer needs and relationships.
6. There are no management formulas that work in all situations.
7. Theory Z and quality circles both emphasize building strong teamwork and a high degree of employee involvement in day-to-day job decisions.

Self-Assessment

Good leaders have to know what to do, how to make organizations function well, and how to build a climate of trust and confidence. You can evaluate yourself by responding to the following questions or statements. Remember that a 1, 2, or 3 answer is an indication of disagreement or low response. A 4, 5, or 6 answer is an indication of agreement or high response.

1. Managers who see one of their primary goals as developers of people are fooling themselves and their employees. Adult behavior doesn't change.

	1	2	3	4	5	6

---

[2] Ibid.

2. Many managers assume that employees know what the manager wants without being told.

| 1 | 2 | 3 | 4 | 5 | 6 |

3. I usually praise people rather than the work they do.

| 1 | 2 | 3 | 4 | 5 | 6 |

4. Helping people feel good about themselves is a form of "cow psychology."

| 1 | 2 | 3 | 4 | 5 | 6 |

5. Good discipline requires correcting mistakes as soon after they occur as possible.

| 1 | 2 | 3 | 4 | 5 | 6 |

6. Good managers learn from their employees, their customers, and other companies.

| 1 | 2 | 3 | 4 | 5 | 6 |

7. In excellent companies, supervisors use established formulas to assure success.

| 1 | 2 | 3 | 4 | 5 | 6 |

8. Geneen points out that employees are essentially robots. Train them, program them to do certain work, maintain them, and you have managerial success.

| 1 | 2 | 3 | 4 | 5 | 6 |

9. Quality circles originated in the Japanese automobile industry and have now spread all over the world.

| 1 | 2 | 3 | 4 | 5 | 6 |

10. Supervisors should be the facilitators, rather than the leaders, of quality circles.

1	2	3	4	5	6

Key Words

one-minute manager
In Search of Excellence
Geneen's managing
positive leadership
one-minute praising
tough leadership
excellence attributes
no-brainer leadership
Theory G
Theory Z
quality circles

CASES

The Case of TAG

   Tri-state Aggregates Group (TAG) started as a gravel and sand company supplying major road-building contractors and gradually expanded into cement, construction steel supplies, cranes and lifting equipment, and finally into one of the largest heavy equipment leasing concerns in the country. Some of its major contracts were in foreign countries where multinational construction companies were building dams, roadways, and bridges for emerging nations.

   A newly formed and vital human resource management specialty began to develop into a full-fledged department called International Policy Development. Members of the team worked with a variety of nationalites in formulating policies that would work universally. Highly skilled employees from the United States, Japan, Korea, Italy, and Germany frequently worked together. Each person, however, was accustomed to pay scales, benefits, and work rules of his or her own country. In some cases, the host nation had built-in legal mandates regarding pay and benefits.

   As prime contractor with overall management responsibility, TAG international policy members were constantly pioneering new types of personnel policies. Jim O'Shea, the International Personnel Policy Manager, was constantly trying to recruit people with foreign experience, especially people who had worked in a multinational environment. He was also concerned with developing a sensitivity in his people to the customs, laws, and general practices in other countries. As his team became more adept, they were called on by other companies to act as consultants for their foreign projects. When asked the secret of his success, Jim replied, "It's no secret at all. My primary task has been to bring out the full potential of the people in our unit. There's not a single one who knows less than I do about some aspect of our work."

1. In what ways do TAG and Jim illustrate aspects of an excellent company?

2. Why does Jim want his employees to know more than he does about at least some aspect of their job?

3. Jim's team is obviously full of winners. What makes a winning team in any organization?

Short Lesson in Building Confidence

Debbie Pittman didn't wait for a six-month or yearly period to evaluate the performance of her production control staff. Daily, she visited each employee on a random basis. If she saw someone with a problem she would usually ask, "Tell me what the difficulty is." After getting a response, her follow-up question was one of four: "What are you doing to solve the problem?" "Who have you asked for help?" "Let me know if you still can't work it out," or "See if anyone else has had a similar problem." Rarely would she solve an employee's problem, even when she knew the answer almost as soon as she spotted a difficulty. She would always follow up later and usually the employee had solved the difficulty. When that happened, Debbie immediately told the employee, "Thats good work, it was done the way it should have been."

In cases where employees were performing a task incorrectly but did not fully recognize their error, she would again go into a series of questions to test the employee's understanding. Sometimes she arranged for the employee to work with a more experienced person, and other times she conducted a short, on-the-spot training session. When Debbie spotted work that was being done correctly, she always commented with, "That looks the way it should" or a similar remark.

After she had been a supervisor for a few months, employees began to take pride in telling her how they solved their problems, what they were doing to improve their jobs, and sometimes, how much they liked working in the department. A number of her employees received promotions, and almost none quit or asked for transfers to other units.

1. Debbie used a number of effective confidence-building techniques. What were they?

2. Why did she avoid solving employee problems, even when it would have saved time and effort?

3. When Debbie praised, she praised work, not people. Comment on this practice.

Supervising for Results

8

Thought Starter

When Peter Drucker first wrote that the only way managers can be judged is by results in his famous *Practice of Management*, he started a major movement. Results can be measured in only one way: Specifically, what objectives were accomplished? From Drucker's early work in 1954, management by objectives (MBO) grew as a management philosophy and then a system. As a system, it gradually died in some companies because it was misused in a vast, burdensome paperwork system. Some managers, not fully understanding their purpose, used objectives set by lower-level managers as a basis for punishment, usually by withholding pay increases when the objectives were not achieved—regardless of the conditions that caused failure.

While incorrect usage has caused some rejection of MBO, it is still a valuable tool to assist in determining how well an organization, department, individual manager, or employee is doing.

In Chapter 8 you will learn:

☐ A way supervisors can make things happen.

☐ The kinds of objectives that apply to employees.

☐ How to set job priorities and performance standards.

☐ Ways of getting commitment.

☐ Ways of correcting poor performance.

☐ The use of employee evaluation to improve performance.

"What do you intend to accomplish in the next few months?" Diane asked Annette over a cup of coffee in the company cafeteria.

"Well," replied Annette, "the first thing is to develop a new proposal procedure manual by the end of May. Most of our requests for proposals are received in June, and I'd like to be ready. We also need better information from our data-processing section. I'm going to give them a plan in two weeks that will outline specifically the kinds of reports we need. Then there's our telephone problem. Currently, whoever is available answers and then usually has to track someone down who knows what the caller needs. I'm working on a way to funnel all the calls into a single desk that will relay them to the proper person."

"You should write those ideas down; they're good objectives, and I'll bet the boss will be pleased with them," responded Diane.

"I think I will," said Annette, "He just may think they're worth doing."

MAKING THINGS HAPPEN AS A SUPERVISOR

"The supervisor's job is to get results through people," according to Lawrence Appley, past president of the American Management Association. Unfortunately, supervisors may plan, organize, direct, and control with distinction; they may understand employees' latent motivational drives well; they may be the most charismatic individuals around; yet, they may still find that they don't get top results from their workers. One reason that supervisors sometimes fail at getting results, even though they are often well-trained, is that they don't always know how to clearly determine and communicate job objectives to their people. It, however, isn't simply a communications problem. There is more to defining a job well than giving clear instructions.

THE KINDS OF JOB OBJECTIVES TO ESTABLISH FOR YOUR EMPLOYEES

Job performance **objectives** include three basic kinds: **routine objectives** that include duties for the employee; **problem-solving objectives;** and **innovative objectives.** Accomplishing each of these objectives is important to the supervisor in achieving overall job performance. Supervisors must think in terms of the results they want before they formulate objectives for employees.

Setting job objectives with employees is one of the most important and most abused duties of the line supervisor. Not only do supervisors often fail to communicate job objectives, but even when they do communicate them, many supervisors do so ineffectively.

Assigning Routine Duties

Job assignments that create the fewest problems in normal workaday life for supervisors and employees are routine duties. If the supervisor is an office manager in a large office complex, there are certain duties that must be done regularly by that supervisor's people. Work assignments must clearly express job assignments so that they can be accomplished on a regular schedule. Most supervisors seldom have problems communicating these goals to employees. It is usually clear what such jobs require, and employees know that these tasks must be done regularly. Employees recognize the need for performing regular duties, and there is seldom any question concerning what needs to be done, when, and by whom. Only when something unusual happens must the supervisor work closely with the employee.

About the only problem that can develop concerning routine duties is when an employee is not performing to the supervisor's satisfaction (or when the employee overlooks a regular duty). The supervisor can, therefore, direct routine duties relatively easily and take corrective action. He or she can manage such work by exception. That is, the supervisor can look for exceptional items—tasks not accomplished or unusual problems that develop. When exceptions are identified, specific attention can be devoted to these matters.

Problem-Solving Objectives

Working with employees in solving problems is more difficult for supervisors than working with employees on routine job duties. For example, a supervisor might discover that while regular duties are done well by the work crew, there are also recurring problems. Supervisor and employees must work together to solve the problem. But, the way they work together may differ depending on the nature of the problem. It is in solving this kind of problem that many supervisors find the value of quality circles.

Problem solving is not a question of whether or not people do their regular duties well; it is a question of how to overcome or prevent problems—a robot continuously breaking down or someone regularly failing at certain tasks. When supervisors have a problem, they often must solve it with the assistance of subordinates. The supervisor must work with the subordinate by first recognizing the problem and then communicating a solution acceptable to the employee (or by agreeing to use a solution developed by the employee). Ultimately, whether a quality circle is used or not, the supervisor must also seek subordinates assistance in eliminating problems. Solving problems may be the supervisor's biggest challenge.

Innovative Objectives

Setting innovative job objectives with employees is a third supervisory duty. Innovative job objectives are tasks that help employees and the organization to grow. An innovative job objective can be rearranging work schedules to provide better customer service, or it can be a total office reorganization from manual operations to electronic automation. An innovative job performance objective, therefore, is an attempt to improve the results obtained by the organization and its employees. The supervisor leads this activity, but he or she is not the only source of ideas.

DESIGNATING JOB PRIORITIES

Once supervisors realize that their primary job is to get results through people, and that one can do this by setting work objectives, they quickly realize the next step is to pinpoint priorities.

Pinpointing **job priorities** is an easy task. It requires thinking about what needs to be done first, second, and so on. However, establishing job priorities does not ensure that employees will perform according to plans or achieve satisfactory job quantity or quality. In addition to stating what needs to be done, performance standards must be set.

PERFORMANCE STANDARDS—
HOW TO SET THEM

Setting job **performance standards** is relatively easy. Supervisors must establish what needs to be done, where, when, and by whom. However, while setting performance standards is theoretically easy, many supervisors fail. They do not recognize that there are four requirements: (1) to clearly specify job duties as to quantity of work required, (2) to clarify the quality of work expected, (3) to set time schedules and deadlines, and (4) to establish any cost or budgetary constraints that may exist (if employees have any control over these matters).

The Situation. Let's assume that an employee is working as a shop technician in a retail store that specializes in winter sports equipment (snow skis, ice skates, and so forth). The shop technician's job involves mounting bindings on skis. How might this shop technician be supervised in terms of job priorities? For example, the technician must mount bindings on skis, repair scratched and damaged skis, wax skis, and oversee the rental of skis, boots, and bindings to customers who don't want to buy them outright, in addition to renting ice skates and snowshoes.

One way a supervisor can establish performance objectives for the shop technician is to set up a **job performance grid,** as in Figure 8–1. Work performance expectation is specified first in terms of the primary job being done—putting bindings on skis—then in terms of job quantity, quality, timeliness, and cost.

In establishing performance priorities, the supervisor must establish objectives for all four aspects of job measurement (assuming all four are relevant to the employee's job). Establishing performance objectives in one feature of the job—for example, quantity of work to be done—does not ensure that other aspects of the job will be satisfactorily accomplished.

Case History. In a certain retail ski shop in the Midwest, the store supervisor told the shop technician that the expected work standard was

FIGURE 8–1 Job Performance Grid

Area of job responsibility: Mount bindings	Minimum requirements	Average expected performance	Maximum probable	Actual performance
Quantity expected				
Quality expected				
When required				
Cost, budget, or other constraints				

the complete mounting of a minimum of 10 pairs of ski bindings per day. Furthermore, the supervisor told the employee that while 10 pairs was the minimum work standard, the employee was expected to mount an average of 15 pairs each day. In fact, the supervisor told the shop technician that if everything went right, the employee would be expected to mount a maximum of 20 pairs per day.

As it turned out, the shop technician mounted an average of 16 pairs of bindings per day. Was mounting 16 pairs of bindings per day a good performance? One can't really tell unless one knows the *quality* of the job being done, whether or not the jobs were done when the customers wanted them done, and how much time the employee spent mounting bindings (to the possible neglect of other duties). For example, even though the shop technician mounted 16 pairs of ski bindings on an average day, the bindings may have been mounted in a slipshod fashion. What would happen if the employee mounted the bindings but the customer discovered that the ski boots wouldn't stay in the bindings because they were improperly mounted? Even though the bindings were mounted in adequate quantity—16 pairs per day—a poor job was done in terms of quality; the customer would complain, and work would have to be redone.

Supervisors must establish qualitative as well as quantitative standards for work performance. In this example, the supervisor could require 15 pairs of bindings be mounted on an average day in accordance with a qualitative standard. This could be done by telling the employee that the *minimum* performance level expected is that 90 percent of the work done be acceptable to the customer, while the *average* expectation is 95 percent. The *maximum* level probably could be set at 98 percent. The reason that a maximum of 100 percent is not established is to prevent the shop technician from trying to do a perfect job when perfection—in terms of customer complaints—is neither required nor possible. Total acceptability is not an unreasonable standard to expect in a job requiring zero defects—such as piloting an airliner to a safe landing, even though some passengers may complain about the roughness of a certain landing. In the ski shop example, the qualitative standard would hinge on customer satisfaction with the product, an important consideration for any retail service store, as well as on customer safety in using the equipment. In the airline example, the need for 100 percent perfection is less an arbitrary managerial decision and more reliant on common sense.

If supervisors establish performance objectives in terms of qualitative standards, they have managerial control over whether or not the employee is doing the quality job required. In this way, supervisors can determine, by checking on customers' satisfaction with their skis and bindings, for example, whether or not the shop technician is doing a sufficient quantity of work at the set quality standards. The supervisor is in a position to take corrective action, if necessary, in coaching the employee on achieving required performance standards.

SCHEDULING IS ALSO IMPORTANT

The quantity and quality of work that employees do are not the only measures of whether or not they perform adequately. Getting work done on time is also an important requirement. What would happen, for example, if the ski shop employee mounted an adequate number of bindings on skis to the satisfaction of customers, but failed to get the job done on time? Consider what happened in the ski shop when a doctor's wife bought a complete set of skis, boots, and bindings, and asked the store to have the bindings mounted and ready for a ski trip at the end of the week. That was on a Tuesday. The doctor's wife gave specific instructions to the salesclerk that her husband intended to pick up the skis on Friday afternoon because they were flying to Sun Valley for a skiing vacation. Unfortunately, when the doctor came to pick up the skis, the work hadn't been done. Consequently, the doctor was angry, the salesclerk was embarrassed, and a $500 sale was lost because the shop technician didn't get the job done on time as promised.

Note that doing the job "on time, as promised" is a separate problem from the question of whether or not quantity and quality requirements are met. The mechanic could have worked diligently and expertly on every job in the shop between the time the doctor's wife bought the gear and when the doctor came to pick it up. But the mechanic's work would still be considered unsatisfactory by the ski store's owner if the doctor's order *wasn't ready on time*. The mechanic was not doing the work that was supposed to be done, even by working hard and doing acceptable or higher-quality work. In this example, the employee's work-priority system was incorrect, even though the shop technician was conscientious in trying to do a good job. It is not adequate for supervisors merely to tell employees how much work to do and of what quality. They must also tell employees *when* work needs to be done, and in some cases, how much time, material, and money can be involved.

COST AND BUDGETS— ALSO A CONSIDERATION

The final consideration supervisors must make in assigning work and job priorities is the cost or budgetary factor. Payroll time is always costly to the company. This is true whether the employee is mounting bindings on skis, sorting mail in the post office, repairing automobiles at a service station, or working as a croupier at a gambling casino. Consequently, costs, budgets, and expenses, when controllable, must be included in job performance requirements for employees.

The cost of any work almost always increases as the time spent on the job increases. A good piece of work, in terms of minimums, is usually a work order that requires a minimum amount of time at the lowest payroll cost, just as a bad piece of work cost-wise is usually the one that requires the greatest amount of time to accomplish. When reading the job performance grid in Figure 8–2, "minimum acceptable" and "maximum probable" are reversed in respect to desirable and undesirable situations regarding budgetary constraints. The grid shows that it is possible that the minimum time a shop technician might be expected to spend mounting bindings is 65 percent. However, on the average, a mechanic is expected to spend about 75 percent of his or her time in the shop mounting bindings, while the maximum probable standard might be 90 percent of the time (if everything fails). If, in looking at actual job performance, the shop technician spends 80 percent of available time mounting bindings on skis, the employee is spending too much time mounting bindings. This is another reason for establishing minimums and maximums of expected

FIGURE 8-2 Job Performance Grid

Area of job responsibility: Mount bindings	Minimum requirements	Average expected performance	Maximum probable	Actual performance
Quantity expected (bindings mounted)	10 pairs	15 pairs	20 pairs	16 pairs
Quality expected (customer acceptance)	90%	95%	98%	90%
When required (done on time)	95%	98%	100%	95%
Cost, budget, or other constraints (percent of time)	65%	75%	90%	80%

performance. If a person spends too much time mounting bindings and neglects other activities, the job is not being done satisfactorily—even though quantity, quality, and meeting deadlines on time are all satisfactory. Spending too much payroll time on an otherwise satisfactory job reflects negatively on the shop technician's ability to do the job adequately. If the employee did poorly in other respects, it could lead to the employee's dismissal. In any event, a reduction of the time spent doing work would be necessary.

LOOKING AT OVERALL JOB PERFORMANCE

The ski shop technician doesn't receive good job performance marks. Actually, the employee does a sufficient quantity of work but spends more time doing slightly above-average work. So, the shop technician might be considered acceptable on that basis. However, in respect to the total quality of job performance, the best the employee can get is low marks. Too many of the customers are unwilling to accept the employee's work without complaints. In addition, the employee has trouble getting the work done on time. This problem may reflect not only a personal scheduling problem (which the employee has) but also an operational problem (which the supervisor has). If, for example, the supervisor is not telling the shop technician of when the job needs to be done, or if clerks are not telling the shop technician when they promised the merchandise to the customer, there is a managerial problem of *communication* rather than a work performance problem. Or, it could be that clerks are negligent in telling the shop technician when jobs need to be done, or that no system exists for clerks to communicate this information to the shop. Of course, it is always possible that the salesperson told the shop technician and the shop technician forgot. In any event, the case is serious in consequences; it is a problem that must be overcome. Overcoming the problem is the responsibility of the supervisor as well as the individual employee.

GETTING COMMITMENT—THE KEY TO MANAGING FOR RESULTS

The most important ingredient required for supervisory success in attaining desired results is getting employees to be committed to accomplishing objectives. Obtaining employee **commitment** is difficult for some supervisors. The reason, however, is not because of personalities or people's unwillingness to work together; it is how the supervisor communicates work performance objectives. Understanding the concepts of setting performance goals in terms of quantity, quality, timeliness, and cost objectives helps immeasurably in establishing work performance goals. However, there are additional guidelines that can be used to support or reinforce the use of objectives. The guidelines require following basic rules established by experienced supervisors. These rules help ensure that the individual responsible for doing a job will be committed to that job.

Rule One: Performance Goals Must Be Concrete

People resent not knowing precisely what is expected of them at work, particularly if it is not possible for them to measure the results of the work. Sales personnel don't like to be told simply to sell; they like to have a performance quota or standard. This quota might be in terms of dollar volume sold or it might be in terms of prospects contacted. It is a concrete and measurable objective. Performance goals must be concrete if results are to be obtained.

Setting concrete, measurable objectives is imperative in any kind of work, for any kind of supervisor. Production supervisors establish concrete objectives in terms of tons of output or units of material processed; shipping room supervisors are concerned with the number of boxes wrapped or deliveries made. Similarly, a dispatcher should know how many telegrams or messages have been delivered in a given period, the supervisor in charge of robotics should know just what it takes to maintain robots in functioning order, and an office manager should know approximately how many letters can be typed in a given time. There is no substitute for the firm establishment of performance goals.

Objective job performance standards can be established in a variety of ways. Use of raw data figures is usually the best way; that is, dollars of sales, tons of output, or number of units produced. However, raw data cannot always be used—how do you quantify customer satisfaction? Moreover, sometimes raw data are not too meaningful, and standards may need to be developed regarding different situations. It is one thing to tell a pipe fitter to run 200 feet of pipe in a straight line in an open, easily accessible area. It is quite something else to tell the same pipe fitter to run 200 feet of pipe in a boiler room or a cramped crawl space.

Thus, sometimes a ratio or other form of work performance measurement is more meaningful than raw data. In the ski shop, it was easy to require the mechanic to mount 15 pairs of bindings per day. But such a definitive number would not be meaningful in terms of the job's qualitative aspects. For example, it would be unrealistic to allow the mechanic to receive only one customer complaint per week. In the peak of the ski season, even the best mechanics have more than one complaint a week. But in the summer, when ski sales are slow and the shop technician mostly repairs bicycles and strings tennis racquets, the norm should be no complaints about improperly mounted bindings. Consequently, a ratio is often more meaningful—where so many complaints per jobs done is accepted as a measure of performance as opposed to looking only at the number of complaints.

Sometimes even ratios are meaningless. Thus, it may be better to use some kind of scale rather than raw data or ratios. Verbal scales can be used to measure almost anything. For example, verbal scales such as *good, better, best* and *bad, worse, unbelievably rotten* are arbitrary although they show qualitative degrees of job performance. When all else fails, even a written description of the expected work outcome is better than nothing.

Rule Two: Objectives Must Be Realistic

If supervisors expect to have a definite commitment from their employees about objectives, supervisors must establish concrete and measurable objectives as well as realistic objectives. It is one thing to expect workers to do a good job; it is an entirely different matter to expect them to do an impossible task. The best office furniture designer, highly schooled in ergonomics, will still find that no office chair design is ever perfect.

The feeling of impossibility toward various tasks comes from many sources. A supervisor may assign too much work to a conscientious employee, and no matter how much that employee wants to succeed, failure occurs. For example, a totally robotized assembly area is impossible to attain because people must keep the robots repaired.

Also, there is another practical matter to consider. It may be impossible for particular employees to handle a job, not because they can't do it, but because they don't *have control over it*. It would be unrealistic for a hotel manager to expect a bellhop to deliver 10 buckets of ice every hour when no more than 15 buckets of ice might be demanded at that particular hotel in a 24-hour period. Goals must not only be concrete and measurable, they must also be realistic. Inability to attain a particular goal is probably more demoralizing and frustrating to a subordinate than any other working condition. The wise supervisor is well aware of this problem.

Rule Three: Commitment Requires that Performance Goals Be Formally Established

Another requirement for a real commitment to work performance goals is that they be formally established between supervisor and subordinates. This requires that the objectives be written down or recorded so that everyone knows what they are. Reference can be made to the objectives so that they are not overlooked or forgotten.

While it is not imperative that all performance goals be in writing, it helps. The reason is similar to why writing out New Year's resolutions helps. The resolution might otherwise be forgotten. People are far less forgetful and far more committed to obtaining a particular objective if they can see what that objective is and have it clearly in mind. Many supervisors find it expedient to set up performance matrixes (such as what was developed in the ski shop) or to issue formal memos about what an employee is expected to do, when, and how. If this is done, both parties—the supervisor and subordinates—should keep a copy for the record. This is not done as a check on each other, but as a reminder to supervisors that they must support subordinates but not be unduly lax in demanding performance.

Rule Four: Supervisor and Subordinate Must Agree on the Goal

The supervisor should obtain an agreement from subordinates that mutually chosen goals need to be attained. The supervisor must not, however, coerce employees into agreeing to something they really *do not feel can be accomplished.*

Some supervisors are so overbearing that they tell their employees that so many units of work are expected and realistic and then ask employees if they agree. Only a naive employee won't "agree" under those circumstances, even though he or she knows that many units can't be produced. No one gains from such activity. The supervisors lose out by erroneously thinking that they will get a top employee performance, and employees lose because they feel frustrated—ultimately, they may be out of a job.

Good supervision requires encouraging subordinates to participate in developing performance standards. Then, when employees and the supervisor agree through open communication, they are likely to achieve desired results. Most capable supervisors pay plenty of attention to good communication. This is another reason for the popularity of quality circles.

Rule Five: Goals Must Be Attainable

Any goal that is established must be attainable. This point is often overlooked by many supervisors in setting performance standards or expectations with employees. Supervisors need to realize that subordinates don't automatically understand that newly established performance standards are obtainable.

The requirement of obtainability is not lacking in most supervisor's work assignments. Reasonable supervisors will usually ask subordinates to do what can be done. Sometimes, however, the impossible is asked. Often, achieving the impossible is what is expected by supervisors.

Certainly there is a difference between making an impossible demand and stretching the talents or capabilities of employees. Most persons, with proper leadership, have been motivated to do tasks they didn't believe they could do. In retrospect, they realized that the zealous supervisory push was responsible. One can reflect on youthful experiences to remember such achievements: a high school coach who tells the team they can win, and they defeat the acknowledged champions; an aunt or uncle who says, "I believe in you, kid," and causes the youngster to excel; and the friendly neighbor who says, "I've never seen them do a good job against real competition—like you're going to give them," who inspires a seemingly unbelievable performance. How does the supervisor distinguish between work that is attainable and stretches the worker, and the work that is unreasonable? The answer is judgment. It's a feeling. Some people are better judges of that feeling than others. Maybe that's where the idea that supervisors are born—not made—comes from.

For the most part, however, such a feeling can be developed. It requires a great deal of attention to detail. It takes a realistic, practical, and objective look at what an employee can or cannot do. Most importantly, it requires attention to the work assignment. A supervisor can't just make a wish and expect workers to do it. Merely wanting employees to perform well doesn't make them do so. Goals must be realistic and attainable. Goals can be realized by a thoughtful supervisor who carefully evaluates the job performance expectations before demanding performance from workers. Clearly, there is a valuable contribution made by supervisors in their expectations of subordinates in accomplishing success at work.

EXPECTATIONS AND GETTING QUALITY PERFORMANCE

Remember the concept of expectancy theory and its use in establishing clear-cut job performance standards that are *attained*. A worker often is what he or she is expected to be (the Pygmalion effect), and the supervisor can often elicit superior performance with his or her expectations. Just as in *The One–Minute Manager*, it is important for the supervisor to think of all employees as potential winners, and it is just as important to expect those winners to accomplish realistic, attainable goals in the qualitative standards that are defined.

ASSURING QUALITY WORK

The act of a supervisor telling an employee what his or her performance expectations are and getting a commitment from the employee does not ensure that the employee will produce a quality product or provide a quality service. All organizations—manufacturing operations, retail or service industries, or wholesaling institutions—have **quality assurance** and quality-control problems.

Quality control, from a supervisory viewpoint, is making sure that people do the job they are expected to do in a responsible way. While it is up to each organization to determine precisely what efforts will be made in quality control, there are some guidelines that every supervisor should know.

1. Emphasis Must Be Placed on Attaining High-Quality Work. One particular problem that many supervisors fail to understand in trying to get compliance from workers for required performance standards occurs because supervisors do not put sufficient emphasis on attaining quality work from employees. They fail to link how well workers do their jobs to the worker's performance appraisals and performance reviews. To avoid this problem, supervisors must emphasize that any complaints about the quality of an employee's performance will hurt the worker's merit review, and good reports about employee performance will benefit the employee's job performance review.

2. Explain What Quality Is Expected on the Job. Quality work is not something that one automatically knows when one sees it. The preceding portion of this chapter pointed out how a supervisor can establish performance standards in respect to the quantity, time, and cost of a job. In addition, for a worker there is a clear-cut distinction between a good job and a bad job. It is imperative that the supervisor clearly demonstrate those differences in order that workers know how to determine if—and when—they do realize the quality of work being demanded. For example, how can a supervisor in the space shuttle program define what a quality job performance is for an astronaut?

3. Make Sure That Workers Are Told Exactly What Is Wrong When They Do Poor-Quality Work. Most people will not deliberately do poor-quality work. However, many times workers do poor-quality work and don't realize it. Any intelligent supervisor will apprise any employee in specific terms when and why the work is not considered satisfactory and will explain how it can be corrected. Such notification should be made immediately and positively to be effective in obtaining a worker's willingness to correct a poor performance. Again, remember *The One–Minute Manager* concept and the need to accentuate the positive in getting people to do things right. Also, remember the concept of being tough on poor *performance*, not on the poor *performers*.

4. Make a Game or a Challenge out of Quality-Control Efforts. One trick many supervisors use to get subordinates' cooperation in quality-control efforts is to make a game or challenge out of that activity. It is possible that, if regular quality-control checks are being made, a given worker might do better on one day, and another worker does better on another day. Maintaining a weekly performance record, which is updated and posted regularly, has had beneficial effects in many offices and work areas because it gives the individual workers some recognition for having done an extraordinarily good job in quality control. Such activities are considered morale boosters in most work circumstances. However, a word of caution in using this technique: If the same individual wins and wins and wins, it would be best to discontinue the game. Those who begin to feel that they can never be the best sometimes will become so disappointed that they will quit trying.

5. Give Your Workers Cost Feedback Information. Poor quality control in an office means redoing work and wasting employees' productive time and efforts. In a retail store, it means handling customer complaints and returned merchandise. In a wholesaling operation, it means returned or rejected goods. In short, poor-quality work wastes money. Studies of why poor-quality work happens will often show it is because the employee doesn't know about the costs involved. Other times, it is simply easier for an employee to be sloppy and hope that the customer or co-workers will accept poor work rather than exerting the effort of doing quality work. Or, the employee may think it will be cheaper to pass along the shoddy work rather than go to the expense of making it right the first time. All of the foregoing logic is wrong. One must remember the old adage, "When will you have time to do it over if you don't have time to do it right the first time?" Doing work over to make it right is more expensive than doing it correctly the first time.

6. Make Sure that You Are Committed to Doing Quality Work. Most studies of why employees do not care how good their work is indicate that employees often feel that they are taking their cues from their leader—the first-line supervisor. If you see a first-line supervisor who doesn't seem to care about quality—one who is indifferent at best, not only about personal dress but also about the care and effort devoted to the supervisory job—the supervisor's workers will demonstrate the same uncaring attitude. Leadership by example has quite a bit of truth to it. This is especially true with quality control and quality work.

7. Ask Your Workers How They Think Improved Quality Can Be Obtained. This idea comes from the concept of both expectancy theory and the use of quality circles. It is usually true that workers feel they can improve the work environment. But many times workers feel that nobody cares about their ideas, and they allow ideas to wither away rather than offering them to supervisors who act as if they know more than the worker does about how work should be done. Intelligent supervisors encourage their subordinates to offer ideas and suggestions about how a job might be improved—and how the quality of the work being done might be improved, too. This is true even in situations where quality circles are not used or considered inappropriate.

8. Have Quality Briefings. It is always easy to have too many meetings. Having a weekly meeting on quality control is probably not the solution to a problem of poor-quality performance by employees. However, it is good advice for any operating supervisor to understand that irregular pep talks, given at appropriate intervals, can do much toward inspiring employees to obtain extraordinary results in the quality of their work. These meetings show the supervisor's interest in the work employees are doing but, perhaps more importantly, they demonstrate the ongoing interest and *necessity* of obtaining quality job performance.

9. Use Examples of Acceptable and Unacceptable Quality Work. Many supervisors find it beneficial to provide examples of unusually good work and exceptionally bad work. Care must be exercised in picking bad work so that no employees are embarrassed at having their work picked. Thus, sometimes, supervisors are best advised to pick examples from other departments, former employees, or their own sloppy work. However, it is a good idea to use examples of current employees' extraordinarily *good* work as a motivational and morale-building example.

10. Where Possible, Define Quality Work in Tangible Forms, Such As in Writing or Possibly Visual Presentations. People like to see or have some identifiable, quantifiable way of determining what quality work looks like. A boss can say, "Do good work." But doing good work might not be as easy as just talking about it. One motel chain uses pictures of motel rooms after they have been cleaned as examples so that the maids see what is meant by a room that has been cleaned and straightened. The maids can then distinguish between that room and one that has merely been cleaned but left in a state of disarray—such as chairs not set at the table, motel service cards not arranged on the dresser, towels not squared on the towel bar, and so forth.

11. Make Routine Inspections to Highlight High-Quality Work. If the supervisor is blessed with a quality assurance department, that department undoubtedly makes routine work inspections. Any recognition of high-quality work can be made subsequent to these inspections. However, not all operating supervisors have the benefit of such watchdog activity. For supervisors who do not have access to a quality assurance department, it is a good idea to emphasize concern with quality assurance by determining whether or not high-quality work is being produced in an acceptable time frame and then giving the appropriate recognition to employees.

12. Never Permit Sloppy Work to Continue. Studies show that once in a while, under the guise of being a good boss, some supervisors make the mistake of allowing marginal work to continue being produced. Work that is marginal at best and unacceptable at worst cannot be tolerated for any period of time. Thus, when a supervisor finds something wrong with work as it is being done, a halt must be called until the employee is trained to know what quality work looks like and how to produce it. It is a poor supervisor who takes inferior work away from the irresponsible worker and gives it to a good worker to correct. Anyone who does poor work should correct it on their own. That is the ultimate rule in learning how to do acceptable quality work.

WHAT TO DO ABOUT SLOPPY WORK

When employees do not care about doing high-quality work, it is often because of poor communication. Sometimes, no one has even taken the time or effort to explain what is required to employees. Yet, few employees will deliberately do sloppy work. Usually, when they do it is because they do not know how to do the job; they do not know what is expected of them; they do not have sufficient tools, materials, or resources; they do not have sufficient time; no one has explained to them what a good job looks like; nobody seems to care; or a combination of the foregoing.

Personal commitment from the supervisor alleviates most problems concerning sloppy work. If supervisors are concerned, they train the employee adequately and they communicate to the employee what is required. In addition, a good supervisor is aware that the employee has inadequate tools, materials, or resources with which to do the job, or that there isn't time to do the job adequately. The truly effective supervisor is thorough in defining for the worker what the job performance expectations are and in following up to ensure that the employee is doing an adequate job.

It isn't always the employee's fault that quality work is not done. Sometimes, poor quality results because of a defect in the design or technique the employee uses to do the job—and investigation might determine how that design or technique was established. Also, an employee might fail to do a job well because the material or components they must work with are not quality merchandise. Another reason for poor quality work is the layout of the work area or how the material or service must be processed. Some processes are born to lose no matter what happens. Sometimes employees do not have adequate tools or instrumentation with which to work. It is hard to do a high-quality job of machining or cabinet making when the equipment with which one must work cannot provide or hold the proper tolerances. These work design and techniques problems concerning work performance are often the real culprits behind poor job performance.

CORRECTING POOR PERFORMANCE

When a person performs poorly at work, corrective action must be taken. Having established performance standards certainly helps in this matter. But establishing performance objectives for workers and trying to define quality work is only part of the game. The employee must also accomplish the desired job results. In fact, the whole concept of managing by objectives requires not only that supervisors establish performance goals with their subordinates in terms of acceptable quality levels, but that they compare those goals with the results actually attained. This determines the employee's effectiveness.

Thus, if supervisors use a performance matrix, for example, for the work they expect subordinates to produce, they should use the same standards to assess how subordinates are performing. The supervisor should occasionally check to ensure that an employee is performing the job properly—at sufficient quantity, with adequate quality, at reasonable cost, and on time. Whenever a deviation is observed, the supervisor should discuss the matter with the subordinate, find out what's wrong, and work on **correcting poor performance.** This is especially true when work quality is poor. The corrective action may be coaching, counseling, or training, for example. Of course, it is also the subordinate's responsibility to call unusual situations to the supervisor's attention if he or she is not aware of them. The supervisor must recognize, too, that when a poorly performing employee is having a problem, remedial action cannot wait until annual performance appraisal time. As with the concept in *The One–Minute Manager*, an immediate reaction to the problem is essential, be it a one-minute reprimand or a one-minute praising.

Correcting Performance Inadequacies as They Occur

Whenever an employee is not performing satisfactorily, something must be done promptly to correct performance. These conditions should be made *immediately, frequently, in specific and understandable terms, and with a positive orientation*. Let's consider each requirement and see why all five are necessary when performance is unacceptable. Note that these ideas are completely consistent with the concept of *The One–Minute Manager* and the ideas found in the notion of the pursuit of excellence in management.

Immediacy. It does no good to tell someone two, three, or four weeks—or a year later—that his or her performance is not satisfactory. That only permits the problem to continue and encourages the employee to feel that the unsatisfactory performance is acceptable. One must immediately notify a subordinate that the work is somehow unacceptable or unsatisfactory.

Frequency. The employee must be told as often as it occurs that unacceptable work is being done. Such recurring remonstration is not nagging; it is simply part of the supervisor's job. If the employee is not told as often as the poor performance occurs, he or she may get the idea that there are no real standards and that on some days poor performance is acceptable.

Specificity. The where and how of the unacceptable work must be specified. Often, supervisors commit the error of simply telling an employee that work is not acceptable "because." They never explain why. To correct a subordinate's performance, one must specify why the work is unacceptable. Is it too long or too short? Is it oversize or undersize? Is it lacking in consistency—and if so, how can one tell what the right consistency is?

Perhaps supervisors who do not specify what is wrong with work just assume that workers know what is right. But several studies indicate that employees *don't* necessarily know what is right. For example, you probably have had a meal served to you at a banquet. Therefore, you should certainly be capable of serving a meal to someone else at a banquet. If you're to be serving, do you serve guests from their left side or their right side. Is the salad on the left or on the right? Do you serve on a clockwise or counterclockwise basis?

The foregoing questions show that items we take for granted have a correctness to them that is not always absorbed by us. Training is required, and it must be specific. It must be repeated as often as necessary to get the employee to do the job exactly right.

Understandability. The supervisor should describe what good performance is in understandable terms. Practically all jobs have esoteric terms. Most of us know words that other people don't know in certain contexts; certain words have specialized meanings in specialized situations.

If the supervisor talks to a subordinate in incomprehensible terms, the supervisor cannot expect the subordinate to correct his or her performance. John Mee is often credited with the statement, ''Spread the fodder low. There are more jackasses than there are giraffes.'' In other words, a supervisor intent upon giving a subordinate understandable instructions must talk in relatively low-level language—not to talk down to the subordinate, but to avoid lofty terms and expressions that might not be understood.

Because employees don't understand certain phrases does not mean they are ignorant. After all, most of us are fluent in only one language or, at most, two or three. But there are literally hundreds of languages spoken on the face of the globe and, for the most part, none of us understand what millions of other people say. We simply don't understand what their sounds mean. Understandability is imperative if one is to be an effective supervisor and hopes to correct poor performances by subordinates.

Positive Orientation. Most work orders need to be given in a positive way since people do not respond well to criticism or negative statements. We don't like to be told that we're stupid, ignorant, uncaring, unmotivated, and the like. We like to hear that we have desirable attributes, albeit attributes that perhaps need to be capitalized on or reinforced in some way. Therefore, a supervisor who is interested in turning an unacceptable performance into an acceptable performance should consider the benefits of thinking and instructing others in positive rather than negative terms.

SUPERVISING FOR RESULTS—
TYING IT ALL TOGETHER

The effective supervisor recognizes that a good employee expects to do an adequate quantity of work of acceptable quality, on time, and at reasonable cost to the employer. These are realistic expectations. Consequently, whenever supervisors appraise the performance of a subordinate, they must be willing to look at what the employee actually did, as well as what could have been done.

Accomplishing results is the responsibility of the supervisor, who must obtain results from subordinates. It is the obligation of subordinates to perform as required. The supervisor must be neither unduly tolerant of poor performance nor oblivious of especially good performance. There should be a clear-cut set of job performance goals and objectives and clearly established standards of quality job performance, determined in advance, to which the individual employee has agreed and is committed. Then, as time passes, and as employee performance is realized, recognition ultimately can be given to employees who are producing well. Whether expected goals are or are not accomplished can be determined and future improvements can be made. If supervisors do this regularly, they should have little or no difficulty in accomplishing the desired results from all employees.

In addition to the interim checking up and correcting that the supervisor should do, there should also be a time when the supervisor sits down formally with the subordinate and assesses his or her performance. The results attained should be compared with the objectives. Any deviations from the agreed-upon performance should be noted and analyzed. A reasonable explanation should be duly noted and exceptions should be made where required. However, if reasonable explanations do not exist, the supervisor should not tolerate unsatisfactory performance. The supervisor should not allow poor performance over an extended period, especially after offering assistance to a subordinate who performs improperly.

Things to Remember

1. The job of a supervisor is to get results through people.
2. Job performance objectives include:
   a. Routine objectives.
   b. Problem-solving objectives.
   c. Innovative objectives.

3. Once objectives have been set with employees, the next step is to pinpoint priorities.

4. The job performance grid allows supervisors to not only set standards but to measure performance against established standards.

5. Job performance goals must be:
   a. Concrete.
   b. Realistic.
   c. Formally established.
   d. Agreed upon by both employee and supervisor.
   e. Attainable.

6. Assuring quality work requires special management effort that emphasizes immediate correction when errors occur.

Key Words

objectives
routine objectives
problem-solving objectives
innovative objectives
job priorities
performance standards
job performance grid
commitment
quality assurance
correcting performance

Self-Assessment

How much do you understand about the value of objectives and assuring quality in the work place? Evaluate yourself by responding to the questions or items below. If you disagree, have a negative response, or a low answer, mark a 1, 2, or 3. If you agree, have a positive response, or a high answer, mark a 4, 5, or 6.

1. I usually set realistic, measurable objectives for myself both at work and in my day-to-day activities away from work.

1	2	3	4	5	6

2. The higher one sets personal objectives, the more he or she is likely to achieve.

1	2	3	4	5	6

3. In evaluating employee potential, the most useful objectives to look at are problem solving and innovative ones.

| 1 | 2 | 3 | 4 | 5 | 6 |

4. Pinpointing priorities is usually a difficult task.

| 1 | 2 | 3 | 4 | 5 | 6 |

5. The job performance grid is useful in comparing actual performance to expected performance.

| 1 | 2 | 3 | 4 | 5 | 6 |

6. Some supervisors find obtaining a commitment from employees is a difficult task.

| 1 | 2 | 3 | 4 | 5 | 6 |

7. For employee objectives to be successful, they must be set by the supervisor and explained to the employee.

| 1 | 2 | 3 | 4 | 5 | 6 |

8. Supervisory expectations of improved performance have little real impact on actual performance by empolyees.

| 1 | 2 | 3 | 4 | 5 | 6 |

9. Managers must tie performance reviews to quality as much as to productivity if quality is to be achieved.

| 1 | 2 | 3 | 4 | 5 | 6 |

10. Regardless of how hard an employee tries, some jobs will not have the desired quality.

| 1 | 2 | 3 | 4 | 5 | 6 |

CASES

Cop Out

In early 1985, Calcor Operational Programs (COP), a distributor of specialized computer programs, found itself floundering in a highly competitive business. While most of the programs handled by COP were produced by independent programmers and met specific customer demands, several problems occurred all at once. COP had a successful start, business expanded, and more companies and some governmental agencies became regular users of COP products. Profits were good, morale was high, and COP became a model for other computer software operations.

As competition increased and user demands decreased, however, profits began to fall. To cut costs, the work force was reduced, some of COP's regular contract programmers began to produce for other companies, schedules slipped, and the company was unable to meet customer requirements as it formerly had. Trying to regain its former dominance in its field, David Zeour, COP's President and General Manager, decided to institute a management by objectives program. At a meeting with his top staff, David announced the following rules:

1. Company objectives for profits, marketing expansion, product development and research, personnel utilization, customer relations, quality standards, and operating costs will be set and distributed to each department manager.

2. Individual department managers will determine objectives for their departments that support the company objectives. All objectives will be submitted to the General Manager's staff in writing, and department managers' performance will be evaluated based on whether objectives are attained or not. Managers who change objectives once approved by the General Manager, or who fail to achieve objectives, will not receive merit increases in pay and may be replaced if major objectives are not met.

3. Employees will set objectives for approval by department managers. Employees who fail to achieve stated objectives will not receive merit increases in pay and may be replaced if major objectives are not met.

A year later, David Zeour announced that the company was on the verge of bankruptcy, management by objectives was an unworkable system, and that he hoped to merge COP with another major software firm.

1. Why did his plan fail?

2. In what ways can MBO systems be most useful?

3. What types of objectives would employees and department managers set under the system proposed by David?

Bars

There are many ways to evaluate employee performance. One of the most useful ways is to allow employees, in conjunction with their immediate supervisor, to rate themselves based on how well they met pre-established objectives. It is a time-consuming and difficult task unless the supervisor realizes that it is also a valuable way for manager and employee to discuss actual work conditions and how well the employee performs compared to his or her own standards.

A variation of this approach is known as the Behaviorally Anchored Rating Scale or BARS. Employee performance is rated on a scale similar to a thermometer. Each degree, or step on the scale, is related to performance of a specific job duty. If, as an example, department store clerks are required to assist customers, maintain stock properly, make sales entries, inventory stock in their department, assist other employees, and represent the store in both appearance and manner, a BARS chart similar to the one shown below can be constructed.

9	Greets customers, maintains stock, advises customers, knows inventory procedure, makes accurate sales entries, encourages customers to return.
8	
7	
6	
5	
4	Makes sales, gets few complaints, knows most procedures.
3	
2	
1	Does not use correct procedures, waits on customers only when asked.

1. Develop a BARS for yourself using routine objectives from your current job as a guideline. For examples, see any current human resource management text in your college library.

2. What are some of the advantages of rating systems based on objectives?

PART FOUR

Training and Control

Supervisory Time Effectiveness

9

Thought Starter

One of the most popular topics discussed by professional management trainers is how to improve time utilization. Many top managers utilize their time very efficiently and so do some supervisors and employees. Most people, however, are terribly inefficient in their use of available time. Procrastination, vacillation, idle conversation, indecision, poor planning, and allowing too many interruptions all contribute to complaints such as, "There just isn't enough time to get work done." Few resources are as valuable as time. Yet, it is an element of our lives that is often squandered heedlessly. Time is *more* than money. It is our very life.

In Chapter 9 you will learn:

- □ Most people are time wasters.
- □ We can all learn to improve the ways that we use time.
- □ A daily log helps in developing time control.
- □ Formal time analysis can be learned.
- □ Ways you can take charge of your own time.

For the third weekend in a row, Tom Hardin was spending a Saturday morning cleaning up the week's work. "Somehow," he thought, "I've got to find more time." He plunged back into the stack of papers on his desk. After almost four hours, he decided to call it a day, and he reluctantly straightened his desk. "How do some of these other supervisors get away without all the extra time I put in? If I'm doing something wrong, I'd sure like to understand what it is. There's not enough time to finish any of the stuff I have to handle." His thoughts were interrupted by the telephone's insistent ring. Before answering the phone, he knew it would be his wife wanting to know when he would be home.

CONTROLLING TIME

We all waste time. Sometimes the reason for wasting time is obvious. Too often, however, being a time waster is really only a symptom of a deeper problem. Unfortunately, treating a problem's symptom will leave you at the beginning—the problem is still there although the symptom is treated.

Rob Rutherford[1] states that "one way to view time is to imagine having a wheelbarrow filled with 24 hours. That 24 hours gets used one way or another, unfortunately too frequently by things that waste your time." He says that defining a time-waster may seem easy at first glance. A meeting, a telephone call, certain paperwork, the breakdown of the copy machine, social chitchat, and travel time are obvious **time-wasters**. Yet, when a serious effort is made to pinpoint the real cause of wasted time,

---

[1] Robert D. Rutherford, *Just in Time*, (New York: John Wiley & Sons, 1981), p. 4.

it's difficult. To whom is the activity a time-waster—to you or to someone else? When does it become a time-waster—when the meeting runs past the adjournment time and is boring to you, when it doesn't start on time, or when the discussion isn't relevant to your needs? Therefore, what wastes time for an individual or what is perceived as a nonproductive use of time may not necessarily be a waste of time for someone else or in a different situation.

Trying to determine what is a time-waster for you as a supervisor can be accomplished by analyzing the following maxims offered by Rutherford[2]:

1. If you have perceived an activity as a time-waster it probably is one.
2. All time-wasters produce both physical and emotional reactions.
3. All time-wasters have a potential built-in time-waster multiplier.
4. Every time-waster is an inappropriate use of your time.
5. All time-wasters are caused by you, others, or a combination thereof.
6. All time-wasters provide "payoffs" of negative thoughts, feelings, and reactions.
7. All time-wasters can be rationalized.
8. All time-wasters make statements about you.
9. All time-wasters can be replaced by more productive activities.
10. All time-wasters bear a cost/benefit ratio.

Rutherford's point is that anything can be waste of our time. Any project becomes a handicap to us when we let it get out of control. We must recognize what wastes our time and what we can do in terms of **time control**.

TIME EFFECTIVENESS

Time analysis of how a supervisor's schedule is spent is the key to effective utilization of supervisory time. Studies show that few supervisors know how they spend their time and that, even when they do know, they are often unsure what to do about it (if they are using time unwisely). Most supervisors simply lament the fact that there are only 24 hours in a day and seven days in a week.

---

[2] Ibid., pp. 5–8.

If supervisors don't know how they spend their time, they don't know how they misuse their time. Before we can think intelligently about **time effectiveness**, we must be aware of where the time we spend is going. This is especially important for the supervisor who is making the vital shift from doer to supervisor.

According to Peter F. Drucker, one of the best ways to increase personal effectiveness is to improve the way time is utilized.[3] The effective use of time cannot be made in a hit-or-miss fashion—it requires deliberate planning. It also requires critical analysis of how time was previously spent to make future time expenditures more effective.

BECOMING AWARE
OF HOW YOU SPEND TIME

Anyone who has been involved in training supervisors in more effective use of time knows that the question most often raised is: "What can I do to utilize my time more effectively?" There are many ways to determine how we use (and waste) our time. Probably the best and most effective way is to keep a **daily log**.

The Daily Log

Maintaining a daily log is a simple process and can be done in several ways. Figure 9–1 demonstrates a daily log that can be kept by the supervisor who is interested in where time is going. In the log, the supervisor records the time spent in various activities, whom he or she was working with in these activities, and what was accomplished. With the log for reference, a supervisor can analyze what was accomplished and what could have been done to make better use of time.

Another way of determining how time is spent and what can be done about it is the guesstimate. Guessing is less accurate than keeping a log, but it can be useful, for example, if people cannot force themselves to accurately record what they have been doing. Keeping a log requires the accurate recording of starting and ending times for the various activities that supervisors have in their workaday life; a guesstimate does not. Also, the guesstimate works best when the individual spends time in large blocks, on specific activities that are easily remembered, and/or if only a gross measure of how the individual spends time is needed.

The big problem with the guesstimate method is that we frequently

---

[3] Peter F. Drucker, *The Effective Executive*, (New York: Harper & Row, 1967).

FIGURE 9–1

	Monday	Tuesday	Wednesday	Thursday	Friday
8:00 *Morning* 10:00	8:00–8:30 Plan day's work 8:30–9:00 Work with Bob on cash receipts 9:00–10:00 Meeting with Mr. Carnes				
	10:00–12:00 Verify ac- counts payable log				
Noon 1:00 *Afternoon* 3:00	1:00–1:45 Correct problem with Acme, Inc., by phone				
5:00					

forget the little items that take up time—which we tend to lump all together. Also, we sometimes forget the accomplishments we realize—or fail to realize—from our many small activities. Furthermore, many times we may spend large blocks of time on work that is done at a leisurely pace and then we crash on projects that really should take more time than is given. That isn't so bad, but we tend to smooth out our estimates of time spent and lie to ourselves.

Given the guesstimate's inaccuracy and approximation, its use must be limited to the supervisor who cannot spend time maintaining a daily log of activities. The daily log is far more useful and accurate if the supervisor is to develop accurate information concerning how he or she spends time. Without accurate information, the supervisor is unable to determine how to change daily work habits.

Usual Time-Wasters

If individual supervisors are conscious of the many personal and organizational pressures that make so many demands on their time, they will be in a good position to take corrective action. The pressures of time seldom permit individual supervisors to do everything they find interesting or consider worthwhile. In addition, there are always demands made on the supervisor as a result of conditions that were unanticipated. Then, too, many managers have extra work responsibilities because of other unavoidable problems—such as an employee being seriously injured on the job, a prolonged series of machinery breakdowns, or the untimely resignation of a key employee.

Let us look at the likely sources for wasting time. Several studies on the use of supervisory time have found that the following areas are the most common drains upon operating supervisors' time:

1. The telephone.
2. Meetings.
3. Reports.
4. Visitors.
5. Making work assignments.
6. Procrastination on making decisions.
7. Fire fighting.
8. Special requests.
9. Delays.
10. Professional education—reading, briefing sessions, analysis of work records, and so forth.

While few supervisors waste time in all these areas, most supervisors waste time in many of these areas. For example, the telephone is often the top source of time drain for supervisors. Studies show that a common reaction of most supervisors when asked to account for time spent on the phone is amazement. The supervisor may spend as much as 25 percent of his or her time on the telephone—*one third of which is waiting.* Yet, seldom do supervisors guess that they spend so much time on the telephone—especially waiting.

Many supervisors do not believe their time is spent in the way that most studies of supervisory time use indicate. For this reason, informal analysis (such as the daily log) of how the supervisor utilizes time is nearly always beneficial. There is, of course, no real solution to how we waste some of our time. But the pursuit of excellence is always challenging; a 10 percent improvement will amount to about 200 hours per year—which equal about five work weeks per year, a desirable goal.

Formal Time Analysis

With a log of daily activities, supervisors can apply the principles of effective time use. It is always difficult to admit to having wasted time or having used it ineffectively. The acceptance of that fact is essential before any behavior changes can be made concerning the use of time. The principles of effective time use vary in number and often appear mutually exclusive. Yet, they are sound principles and they can help any supervisors trying to improve time management. Effective time use principles include these:

1. Review what has been done to see what could be done in less time.

2. Use whatever shortcuts are available, remembering the principle developed in Chapter 3 that *good enough* is all that is needed for quality performance on the job. Make sure that you are not doing items that your employees could do.

3. Tackle tough jobs first—supervisors who do the difficult work promptly tend to accomplish more than supervisors who take fun jobs first.

4. Assign to subordinates all work that can be expediently assigned.

5. Avoid getting wrapped up in what other people are doing, particularly if your only motivation is inquisitiveness. Curiosity is a time-waster.

6. Give clear and straightforward orders and instructions to subordinates.

7. Rely on the fact that *unfinished* work is more of a motivator than *unstarted* work. In short, get *started* on jobs because then you are more likely to finish them. When was the last time you could paint half a wall, yet how long could you put off starting to paint the wall in the first place?

8. Be decisive and tenacious when implementing supervisory decisions.

9. Establish procedures for what must happen when you are absent. Name who takes charge in your absence.

10. Take some time out of your busy schedule to reflect upon the job and what *needs* to be done, rather than always attempting to be *doing* something. Reflection on work schedules may help you to see shortcuts or ways to save time.

11. Be punctual. This forces you to be self-disciplined and also sets a good example for employees.

12. Try to maintain a reservoir of items to do during idle periods. If you have computer printouts to scrutinize, blueprints to study, or sales manuals to read, save them for periods in the day when you are waiting for someone or while you wait for a ride home in the evening.

13. Guard against digressing in discussions and meetings to unimportant subjects. Learn to use an agenda and stick to it.

14. Never end the workday without a plan for what will be done first the following morning. Getting started in the morning can be a serious time-waster if you don't have some definite action planned.

These principles of effective time use are not always consistent in every instance. Like any other principles of good supervisory practice, most are situational. The basic principles, however, are usually valid and should be remembered by supervisors—with these caveats: (1) time consciousness is more than knowing rules or principles; it is intelligently implementing those rules and principles; and (2) don't try to make yourself into an automaton; it is good to improve your efficiency, but don't go overboard with the process. Taking time management in stride will help reduce stress and keep your subordinates from thinking you are crazy.

A WORD ABOUT THE DIFFERENCE BETWEEN TIME MANAGEMENT AND DELEGATION SKILLS

One important point to remember about time management is its purpose. The study of time management has the purpose of freeing up supervisors' time—presumably to do other, more important business.

But, it also has the purpose of teaching supervisors how to do more in less time.

The problem with this aspect of studying time management is the implication that the supervisor should learn how to work harder and more effectively. Placing heavy emphasis on that objective is, however, self-defeating. There is no point in the supervisor merely learning how to do more work in less time. Success at that skill only results in a hard-working (and effective) supervisor. But that success does *not* ensure that the supervisor will be effective in getting results *through other people*.

Success at getting work done through other people is accomplished by the supervisor's success in using **delegation skills** and making effective work assignments. An aspiring supervisor must realize that success at delegation and making work assignments often preempts success in making yourself more time efficient. Success at both achievements is desirable, of course, but if the new supervisor is lacking in one skill at the expense of the other, he or she should always have a bias toward developing skills at delegating and making work assignments.

GUIDELINES FOR DEVELOPING THE EFFECTIVE USE OF SUPERVISORY TIME

It is always difficult to arrive at the perfect solution regarding time use. Nevertheless, the following postulates, which are based on the study of effective time use by managers and supervisors in several large corporations, can help prevent the inexperienced supervisor from wasting time.

1. Spend some time keeping a written log concerning how you spend the major portion of the work day. To know how to spend time more effectively, you must know how you currently spend your time—especially in redundant or repetitive activities. Everyone can benefit from knowing how time is expended. The supervisor needs to assess how he/she spends time at least occasionally to know what the sources of time drain are on personal activities.

2. Schedule your least interesting tasks when your energy is at its peak. Most people can best do what they don't want to do only when their energy is at its peak. You can best do the tasks you like to do even when you aren't feeling your best. Good supervisors know that unless they schedule their least interesting tasks when they feel best, they procrastinate or put off doing important items that really need to be done.

3. Frequent and regular review of job activities that might be assigned

If these employees didn't take a break for lunch, they could spend more time working. But there will always be the need to allow time for coffee breaks and lunch breaks.

to a subordinate is another key to good supervisory time use. Most supervisors who are effective users of time review their job activities regularly—always asking the question, "Can someone else do that job as well as I can?" If and when they find that someone can do the job just as well, they assign someone to do the job. This frees the supervisor for more important activities.

4. Make sure you have the time to do what you want to do and really should do in performing your job. This is virtually a unanimous comment made by supervisors who are considered effective by their superiors. They organize their activities to do not only the task they must do, but also the items they should do.

5. Regularly analyze your activities to determine how they can be combined or eliminated. A good supervisor regularly makes job analyses to determine how he or she can rearrange or eliminate scheduled activities. This is an obvious statement, but it is quite far-reaching in its effect. Studies show that most bosses who are ineffective in their time use *do not* take the time to scrutinize job activities for repetitive or redundant activities.

6. While most supervisors plan ahead, a high percentage of good bosses indicate that they also occasionally take actions that lead to immediate rewards. The reason for this is that short-run job accomplishment can be rewarding from an ego and morale standpoint. Rather than continually building for the future, many experienced supervisors recognize that some short-run job satisfaction is important—for their own morale, and for the morale of employees. As a result, they will occasionally take or permit actions that are not important over the long run, although they have immediate benefits.

7. Effective supervisors seldom think that they have more work than they can handle. Most supervisors pride themselves in the efficiency with which they dispatch their activities. Efficient supervisors have time to do what is required of them by their managers. They can do this because they can delegate and assign work to subordinates who can handle the jobs required, they schedule work well, and they know how to organize the work for results.

8. Short-time tasks are sometimes postponed in order to get started on long-range projects. One of the most common practices engaged in by successful supervisors is to get started on long-range projects, postponing short-time tasks (such as answering phone calls, reading correspondence, and so forth) until they get major projects started. Most people are motivated to pursue work that is started rather than work that is not started. Studies show that one of the most irritating things to any worker is being unable to finish a job once it is started. Studies also show that most employees fail to be concerned about *not* being able to get started on a job.

9. Effective supervisors have an ability to arrange task priorities based on the importance of task goals rather than on their personal feelings toward accomplishing those goals.

Again, studies show that supervisors who use their time most proficiently do so because they attack jobs based on what is most important rather than based on what they feel most comfortable doing or have the most personal interest in trying to accomplish. In doing so, they are far more likely to accomplish all the goals required of them.

A Quick Look at the Question of Are You Wasting Your Time

Anyone conscientious about changing how they spend their time will worry, "How am I doing?" Answering that question is not easy, but there are a few questions that can be asked which give quick answers and also indicate immediate steps that could be taken to improve time efficiency. These questions include:

1. Can any of my activities be eliminated, delegated, or assigned to anyone else?

2. Can any activities be combined with other activities so that some work can be avoided or reassigned?

3. Can the time required to perform any activities be minimized or reduced by reallocation?

4. Can the sequence of activities be changed to a more logical arrangement?

If supervisors use these questions as guidelines, they should be far more effective and proficient at work and be able to pinpoint where they should focus their time management efforts. They will have increased time available to do the activities they must do, and they will free up some time for, perhaps, refining their skills at delegating and making work assignments.

A WORD ABOUT WORK SIMPLIFICATION AND MOTION ECONOMY

Any supervisor interested in using time wisely knows that time management can be improved by learning some fundamental principles of simplifying work and making efficient movements. This applies to the supervisor's movements and to employee activities and movements. While the supervisor does not need to be a time and motion study expert, some basics are needed. They include the following:

1. Use Rhythmic Motion. One works best when one works with a rhythm. This is true for supervisors as well as subordinates. If the work is repetitive, make sure it is done with a smooth rhythm.

2. Engage in Simple Activities. Work should be done as simply and efficiently as possible. Don't move the body if merely moving the arm is adequate. Always swing the arm in curved paths rather than in straight lines that require starting in one direction, stopping, and returning in the opposite direction. It is far easier to draw a figure eight, for example, than to retrace a straight line from left to right over and over again. It is also more productive.

3. Make Sure that Workers Are Comfortable. People like to be comfortable at work. Don't require someone to stand when they can sit.

Don't require someone to bend over unnecessarily. Standing at awkward angles or assuming awkward positions can be extremely tiring for the worker, it has a negative effect on productivity and morale, and it results in shoddy work. Pay attention to the basic ideas of **ergonomics**.

4. Eliminate Unnecessary Activities. Don't require the setup and cleanup of tools and materials more often than is necessary. Don't require an employee to do something, undo it, and then redo it. Not only is such activity a waste of time, it is also demoralizing and confusing to the worker.

5. Have a Plan for Actions that Are Required. Employees need to know what needs to be done, when, and in what sequence. Furthermore, they need to have proper tools and materials; otherwise, the disorganization will hinder their performance.

Work simplification is an integral part of the supervisor's job, although it is not an area that he/she must master. It minimizes time spent in supervision activities, and it spares the employee wasted time and effort. But, perhaps most importantly, it focuses attention on what motions really need to be done and what is wasted energy and time.

ERGONOMICS AND TIME MANAGEMENT

Ergonomics is the science of fitting the work, the tools, and the machines to the worker—not vice versa. Many inept supervisors, in trying to save time, feel that the worker should adapt to the machine. The aim of ergonomics, however, is to increase the worker's productivity and, *at the same time*, make the worker's life more comfortable.

Ergonomics is becoming a refined science—and there are people who have academic degrees in ergonomics. The supervisor should be familiar with ergonomics out of concern for what the worker does and hopes to do. The supervisor's motive is as much humanitarian as it is an interest in increasing productivity. Everybody wins if some attention is paid to accommodating the employee's physical requirements. Computers have greatly facilitated the ergonomic engineer's job. Now, it is possible to try out different designs via the sophisticated applications of computer technology.

HOW TO MAKE YOUR TIME GO FARTHER—SOME TRICKS OF THE TRADE

There is no substitute for making a log or a guesstimate of how one's time is spent. It is imperative that a supervisor knows how his or her time is spent. However, just knowing where the time goes doesn't necessarily ensure that anything can be done about it. The supervisor must know some basic tricks that experienced supervisors use to free up additional time during their hectic days (see Figure 9–2).

Differentiate between Routine Work, Special Assignments, and Fun Work. There are many tasks that supervisors do on a regular basis. These items seem to get done because the supervisor was either told to do them or they must be done to avoid creating additional problems. Regular work will usually get done. Such work should be done, if possible, at the same time every day so that a minimum amount of time can be allocated for it. Some authorities estimate that 70 percent of most supervisors' time is spent on work that the supervisor must do regularly (which does *not* include running meaningless errands, helping a worker correct a problem that the worker *should* be able to correct alone, and so forth).

Special assignments always occur, however, and when you're asked by your boss to take on a special assignment, it's difficult to say no for fear of being accused of not doing the job adequately enough to accept extra work. Special assignments have another problem—they can be fun; however, they also take up valuable time. As a rule of thumb, supervisors who spend more than 10–15 percent of their time on special assignments are probably being too accommodating of others' demands on their time.

Creative work is always exciting and interesting, but it may not be essential. Unfortunately, most first-line supervisors find that their bosses

FIGURE 9–2 How to Make Your Time Go Further

1. Differentiate which work is most important.
2. Be decisive.
3. Initiate things.
4. Use the exceptions principle.
5. Control your paper work.
6. Learn to be a good reader.

like them to do creative, interesting work. It not only builds the supervisor's morale, but it makes the job more interesting and rewarding. Don't be afraid to undertake creative work; but if you let it take more than 10–15 percent of your time, your regular job duties, special work assignments, and creative work will add up to more time than you can devote to the job.

Think Business and Be Decisive.   Many supervisors find it essential to always think business when decisions need to be made. Specifically, most supervisors avoid indecisiveness and make decisions relatively fast. Good supervisors do not make snap judgments predicated on irrational, unplanned premises. They do, however, avoid repeatedly pondering questions before making a decision. It's the continuous debate about making the decision—rather than deciding—that really erodes time.

Related to being decisive is being definite about dates, times, and promises. Nothing is more frustrating and wasteful than failing to establish definite times for appointments and meetings. Making statements like "the first of next week" or "later this afternoon" frustrate individuals who utilize their time wisely and they cause punctual persons to show up too early. Time, energy, and morale are wasted.

You Be the Initiator; Don't Let Others Make Demands on Your Time.   Telephones, meetings, reports, and visitors are the biggest drains on the supervisor's time. Often, these activities drain time because the supervisor reacts to, rather than initiates, the activity. Intelligent supervisors control their time and do not let the telephone interrupt them. The telephone can be a monster, but no one must answer a phone just because it rings. There is no need to be more than courteously available, even if there is no one else to answer the phone. Ways to minimize telephone interruptions include saying things like, "I'm extremely busy—can I call you back?" or "I'm sorry. . . . unless it's critical, it will have to wait. I have another urgent problem already in front of me."

Telephone interruptions aren't the worst time-wasters. Probably the worst offenders are visitors—the employee who drops in with, "Hey boss, got a minute?" or the superior who says, "Got a minute? There's something I've been meaning to tell you."

It is extremely difficult to tell someone that you don't have time or that they are interrupting you. However, most time management experts agree that simply saying "No, I don't have a minute. Can I get back to you later this afternoon when I do?" is an appropriate response to anything other than "Hey, the lab is on fire! Help us put it out!" Don't permit yourself to be used for the convenience of whoever catches you at any given time. You cannot organize your day on that basis and, furthermore, you're at the mercy of the individual who has picked that particular time. This skill is critical when you have more important matters to consider.

Learn to make notes and memos about persons you must see and telephone calls you must return. It is all right to put off people by asking them if you can get back to them later. Studies show that, when you do get back to them, they often have already decided to make their own decision and they really don't need to see you. In fact, a study by one of the authors showed that in more than 10 percent of the cases where supervisors do get back to the individual who wanted to see them "for a minute," the topic had been forgotten. The critical factor is that people will respect your need for time—particularly when you say, "No, I don't have any time now, but I will see you later at. . . ." But *you must stick to your word and see them at that time*. Supervisors who jealously guard their time (*and the time of others*) have learned that workers will respect them for not being *immediately* available if there is a follow-up at a prescribed time. This also teaches others to be sure they have something important to talk about.

Use the Principle of Management by Exception. Only exceptional circumstances should be brought to the attention of the boss. Routine daily activities and decisions should be made based on preestablished ideas, guidelines, and policies. Supervisors who feel they have to make every decision find that they repeatedly make the same decisions. Having to repeat decisions wastes the supervisor's time, and it destroys morale in the organization. People don't like to feel that they can't learn to make decisions. The supervisor who demands to pass judgment on every question, issue, or problem facing a subordinate will sorely antagonize even the most patient employee.

Control Your Paperwork. When you become a supervisor, you will have much more paperwork than before—except if you had nothing but paperwork to do as a regular employee. How can a supervisor handle paperwork without becoming bogged down by constantly sorting and shuffling papers, looking for records and notes? There are some basic guidelines based on the law of the vital few and the trivial many.

There are a few pieces of paper that are vital to you, while there are many pieces of paper that are of little importance. Experienced supervisors usually recognize three kinds of paper they must cope with: (1) paper that must be acted on immediately, (2) paper that can be delayed, and (3) paper that doesn't need to be acted on and shouldn't be kept around.

How does one succeed in sorting paperwork into those three classifications? One can decide *never* to touch the same piece of paper a second time without taking some definite action on it the first time it appears. Thus, whenever supervisors are deluged with paperwork—be it from the U.S. mails, intracompany mails, memos, communiques, or whatever—they should automatically dispose of paperwork as follows: Read it over and see what needs to be done. If it is for information only, throw it away or file it appropriately. But, get rid of it!

The second kind of paper can be postponed for awhile. That paperwork should not be put back in the pending file without your acting in a way that will *cause* it to come to your attention in the future when it is important. If you have a memo from your boss asking for some information or inquiring about when you can attend a meeting, make a phone call *now* or write the note back to the boss *now* with stipulations regarding your requirements, conveniences, or expectations. Then, that paper is temporarily disposed of and, *when it needs to be brought to your attention again*, you know it is time to again dig out the memo. This way you won't forget about it, and you won't have to read it over three or four times—avoiding the embarrassment of making a last-minute call to your boss apologizing about why something was, for example, not done on time.

The third kind of paper is the type that is immediately important. Usually, no paperwork is so urgent that it must be looked at and immediately acted on. However, there is no point in procrastination. If you are doing paperwork and this kind of paper appears, find the necessary information, make the necessary decisions, and dispose of the paper. You can do this if you set up a definite time every day to do paperwork and if you resolve to finish with each item *as it appears*. If you sort paperwork by these three classifications and take the actions outlined, there will never be a buildup of papers that you must rummage through at the last minute because you had forgotten, overlooked, or not made a decision earlier.

Learn to Be a Good Reader.   Most everyone has heard of speed reading. Speed reading is not really a trick. It is simply knowing how to use your eyes and mind to quickly record and understand written messages. A more coherent understanding develops from the ability to see the big picture rather than reading word after word. Here are some tricks for speed reading:

1.   Read *groups* of words rather than one word at a time. Your mind will enable you to read three, four, and more different words at one time.

2.   Avoid fixing your vision on any particular word. If you want to read for comprehension, keep your eyes moving. The longer you stare at a given word, the more apt you are to forget what preceded that word and not comprehend what follows.

3.   Concentrate. You can't read and also think about last night's bowling score or today's work problems. When you sit down to read, concentrate solely on what you read.

4.   Don't go back over what you have already read. Studies show that poor readers backtrack because they have momentarily forgotten what they have just read. If you continue to read, however, what was read before will make more sense in the context of future material—or else, if it is forgotten, it probably is unimportant information.

5.   Don't talk to yourself. When you read, don't even move your lips. When you say words (even silently) while you read, you slow down. Most people talk at a speed of about 125 words per minute, but they think at a speed of 400–500 words per minute. When you mouth each word you read, you limit reading speed to your talking speed.

6.   Avoid mental blocks. When you read, you find unfamiliar words. Most experienced scholars know a trick about developing a good vocabulary. The trick is that the context in which a word is used often explains the meaning of the word. Don't waste time on trying to analyze what a given word means. Rather, put the word in context and you will probably figure out what it means. If it is totally unclear, however, look the word up in a dictionary. This practice also helps to build vocabulary and enhance your understanding of that word in the future.

7.   Don't avoid reading. Like any other talent, reading is a skill that can improve with practice. If you never read, you will have difficulty doing even minimal reading. If you read prodigiously, your reading skills will be honed so that you can absorb more ideas from printed matter faster.[4]

Taking Charge of Your Time

Work is not accomplished in a vacuum. Successful time managers must take charge of their own time. You must have a partnership with yourself and others concerning how you accomplish tasks.

---

[4] Ibid.

A time-conscious management team is a group of individuals who work together. The team concept is that people can accomplish things by cooperating with each other. This means that you must let others know what you expect of them, what you expect of yourself, and that you have a mutual appreciation of their time and your own. It comes from knowing how to gain and retain respect from others for the use of your own time and the demands that they make on your time and vice versa.

Getting the Respect of Others for Your Time

Rutherford offers two suggestions as to what is necessary for teaching people to respect your time: (1) you must respect your time and make your words and actions reflect that respect, and (2) you must respect the time of others and demonstrate that you also value their time. There are a few items to be aware of in working with others by mutually cooperating in controlling the time demands made on each other. They include:

1. Be aware of how you use and misuse your time—know where your time goes.

2. Be discriminatory in the use of time—make decisions on how you allocate time.

3. Let others know how you feel about their use of your time and what they can expect from you in using their time.

4. Be aware of any unstated agreements you have with other people that invite or enable them to invade your time.

5. Ascertain whether you're making any statements—either verbally or nonverbally—that are inviting or requiring others to make poor use of your time.

6. Respect other people's time.

Any individual who is aware of these rules will probably find that they use their time wisely. They will get respect from others in cooperating with the reasonable utilization of everyone's time.

Things to Remember

1. All people waste time on occasion.

2. Time-wasters can be controlled. Rutherford lists 10 reasons for wasted time.

3. Knowing how time is spent is the key to time control.

4. A daily log is an effective way to learn how time is spent.

5. Formal time analysis based on a daily log is a tool for better time planning. Fourteen time-analysis steps are listed.

6. Supervisors often do the tasks they like first, instead of the tasks that need to be done.

7. Learning to read rapidly and accurately is a significant management time-saver.

8. Ergonomics, work simplification, and time and motion economy can all save time.

9. Six techniques are listed for helping the supervisor and others to have respect for time use.

Key Words

time-wasters
time control
time effectiveness
daily log
time analysis
delegation skills
work simplification
motion economy
ergonomics

Self-Assessment

Evaluate how well you utilize time and what you know about time management. A 1, 2, or 3 response means disagreement or a low response. A 4, 5, or 6 response means agreement or high response.

1. I feel I rarely waste any time at all. I am willing to maintain a daily log to prove it.

| 1 | 2 | 3 | 4 | 5 | 6 |

2. I have good reading skills. Generally, I read faster than 600 words per minute.

| 1 | 2 | 3 | 4 | 5 | 6 |

3. I fully understand the principle of management by exception.

| 1 | 2 | 3 | 4 | 5 | 6 |

4. I understand how to control paperwork.

| 1 | 2 | 3 | 4 | 5 | 6 |

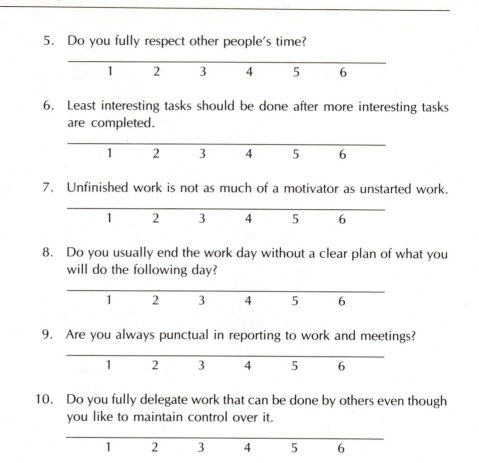

5. Do you fully respect other people's time?

| | 1 | 2 | 3 | 4 | 5 | 6 |

6. Least interesting tasks should be done after more interesting tasks are completed.

| | 1 | 2 | 3 | 4 | 5 | 6 |

7. Unfinished work is not as much of a motivator as unstarted work.

| | 1 | 2 | 3 | 4 | 5 | 6 |

8. Do you usually end the work day without a clear plan of what you will do the following day?

| | 1 | 2 | 3 | 4 | 5 | 6 |

9. Are you always punctual in reporting to work and meetings?

| | 1 | 2 | 3 | 4 | 5 | 6 |

10. Do you fully delegate work that can be done by others even though you like to maintain control over it.

| | 1 | 2 | 3 | 4 | 5 | 6 |

CASES

Time on My Hands   Shelia Kilpatrick was a good listener. It was one of the characteristics that led to her promotion to office manager for Sam's Auto Glass (SAG). People would call her and talk about business and personal matters. Shelia's employees enjoyed discussing daily occurrences with her as well. In addition to employees, customers, and vendors, Shelia was also popular with other supervisors. During an average day, two or three supervisors would visit her office for a cup of coffee and discuss current organizational changes, rumors, and their own plans. From time to time, she would return the visits.

SAG was the largest automotive glass installation and service center in

Columbia. To keep up with the many facets of the business, weekly staff meetings and almost daily special meetings were held by various segments of the organization. As office manager, Shelia felt she must attend all meetings to know what was going on. In some meetings, she had little to contribute because her department was not affected, but she became thoroughly familiar with major problems in each area of the organization. In a conversation with Laurel Pencor, head of purchasing, Shelia complained, "I seem to have less and less time to do my work. I'm always busy, I don't procrastinate, and I work hard. Why don't I have more time?"

"Perhaps you should do what I'm doing," said Laurel. "Every day, I keep a log of my time usage. It's surprising how much more I can get done now that I know how I've been spending most of my work day."

1. Was Shelia a good supervisor? Why?

2. What were some of her most obvious time-wasters?

3. How do you know Shelia was not fully aware of how her time was spent?

A Little Self-Help

Maintain a daily log for four days. Try to be as complete and as honest as possible. You will find that maintaining the log is not as time-consuming or difficult as it may first seem. At the end of the four-day period, analyze your time log and see how many regular time-wasters you can identify. Develop ways to control your major time-wasters. Follow up in two weeks with another log and analysis to determine if any changes have occurred. Some people find that just maintaining a log helps to make them aware of time-wasters and they improve almost immediately in their time usage due to the necessity of making log entries. Many people are reluctant to admit that they waste much of their time.

A second suggestion is to have your reading speed checked. Most colleges and some libraries have standardized reading tests that can accurately determine how fast a person reads nontechnical material. If your local college has a reading laboratory, they will usually administer a test on request.

A third suggestion is to learn to manage by exception in both work life and personal activities. Management by exceptions means distinguishing between what needs to be done and what doesn't. It also means correcting problems and not trying to repair what works. Another aspect of managing by exception is learning to use the experience of others to avoid repeating mistakes that have already been made in performing or learning a segment of a job.

10

The Supervisor and Cost Control

Thought Starter

No one knows the real size of wasted costs in organizations throughout the United States. At one time, it was estimated that 15 percent of the spare and replacement parts made by automobile manufacturers were lost or stolen. While theft by employees and customers is a major concern for some businesses, it not the only reason for cost difficulties. Grocery stores and supermarkets routinely discard thousands of dollars worth of food because of spoilage or out-of-date labels. Manufacturers lose money when parts fail to meet specifications and have to be remade. Restaurant managers know that broken dishes and glasses as well as unused food are a source of loss. Employees who have to wait for assignments, wait for materials, or wait in lines to have material reproduced or to get supplies all add nonproductive costs to an operation. Cost control is an essential management function.

In Chapter 10 you will learn:

□ The difference between cost consciousness and cost reduction.

□ The frustrations of attempting to reduce the wrong costs.

□ Pareto's law of maldistribution and its applications to cost control.

□ Why profitability is usually more important than cost savings.

□ Why many cost-reduction efforts fail.

□ Steps that can be taken to improve controlling costs.

When Carrie Douglas became manager of the Plenty of Things (POT) restaurant, she decided to make a few changes to improve profitability and gain better control of operational costs. She first had two storage rooms built, one in each end of the dining area, for tablewear, cups, plates, napkins, and other supplies. By having two stations, the time required to set up tables was substantially reduced. In each of the supply areas, Carrie limited the number of glasses, plates, cups, and other supplies available to dining room employees. This helped waiters and waitresses to be aware that if breakage occurred, there may not be enough supplies for customers. She also trained her maître d's and hostesses to seat patrons in groups so that no waiter or waitress would be overloaded with work. Carrie arranged and equipped the cooking and dishwashing areas to improve both convenience and safety. Her philosophy was that actions designed to improve service and convenience for both employees and customers could, in the long run, reduce costs. Although her methods and equipment modernization increased costs initially, they also enhanced profits and fully justified the expense.

COSTS AND COST CONTROL

One area of supervisory responsibility that is often minimized, although it is critical to the success of organizations, is **cost control.** There are numerous training programs focused on reducing operations costs, and practically all such programs emphasize the supervisor's responsibility to spearhead cost reduction and control programs. In recent years, however, people who are involved in analyzing operating costs and ways to run an organization more efficiently have changed their emphasis from cost reduction to the more practical concept of **cost consciousness.**

COST CONSCIOUSNESS VERSUS COST REDUCTION

Recent experience has shown that traditional cost-reduction activities of supervisors seldom realize any lasting benefits. Among the many reasons for this are: (1) the emphasis usually is on costs rather than profits (profitability is most important—not how much or how little money is spent); (2) supervisors are misguided in implementing cost-reduction programs; and (3) organizational policy is unenlightened. To understand how the supervisor fails in controlling costs, let's take a look at the supervisor's role in minimizing costs.

The Role of the Supervisor in Minimizing Costs

Controlling costs is usually a matter of *degree* rather than choice. If a supervisor is only *occasionally* aware of the responsibility for maintaining control over costs, the results are disastrous. Only *continual emphasis* allows for effective control of costs.

Once one recognizes that controlling costs is a continual obligation for every supervisor and employee in an organization, it is clear that an effective cost-control program requires emphasis on planning expenditures and use of manpower, materials, supplies, and so forth. But, one word of caution: a common error committed by inexperienced supervisors is an undue emphasis on paper controls rather than positive actions. A balance must be achieved.

Undue Emphasis on Cost-Control Efforts

One of the first problems supervisors confront in attempting to do a good job in keeping costs at an acceptable level is finding sources of financial drain. In addition, many supervisors try to operate (or are forced to operate) without any operating cost plans. Yet another problem is that many supervisors operate with the philosophy that most people are not especially wasteful (or at least not deliberately wasteful), while others operate with the assumption that *all* people, if not *tightly* controlled, will be wasteful of materials, equipment, and time.

A supervisor's biases toward cost control will determine where he or she feels the most wastes occur. Unfortunately, biases may lead to additional difficulties. Sometimes in desperation, a manager will issue a blanket mandate to all supervisors to cut all costs by some figure. This seemingly fair tactic affects some supervisors more than others, because some departments may be operating very efficiently and others may be operating inefficiently.

While intentions to cut costs may be admirable, they may not be productive. For example, to assume that *everyone* can cut operating costs because *everyone* is wasteful is short-sighted and inaccurate. Second, to assume that everyone can cut costs by some flat percentage is an equally invalid assumption. Not all people, no matter how wasteful, will waste the same amount or at the same rate. If some people are doing an especially good job, while others are doing especially poorly, any mandate to reduce costs only handicaps the individual who is doing a good job of controlling costs.

The supervisor had better try, of course, to comply with such a direction. But a smart supervisor will not try to levy such arbitrary performance standards on employees even though top management might practice such ill-advised cost-cutting activities.

Avoiding the Mistaken Emphasis Problem

To avoid the problem of mistaken emphasis in a cost-consciousness program, the supervisor can effectively use **Pareto's law of maldistribution.** Vilfredo Pareto was an Italian philosopher and engineer who postulated what has been called the law of the vital few and the trivial many; the law of maldistribution; the 80-20 principle; and the exception principle. Pareto stated that a vital few (approximately 20 percent of people or things) account for 80 percent of the major problems in an organization, while the remaining "trivial many" (80 percent of the people or things) account for the remaining problems (20 percent).

Pareto's law, while essentially an observation, tends to carry with it the support of time. We can observe this in virtually all human behavior. For example, in practically all societies, a vital few people commit most of the crimes, while the trivial many are honest and law-abiding. Most manufacturers know that only a vital few parts of their products create real trouble in use, while there are a trivial many minor items that could go wrong with the product. Retailers know that most of their customers are repeat customers—not new ones—no matter how much they advertise.

Just as many engineers and behavioral scientists embrace the general idea behind Pareto's law, so must the operating supervisor who looks for potential cost problems. Studies show that in practically all cases where problems occur in a department, they occur primarily in a particular sector within that department. A cost-consciousness program starts with an analysis of the total organizational unit to determine where the bulk of waste is occurring. Then, the supervisor can develop a plan for minimizing or controlling costs for clearly identified functions. This takes the burden off well-run operations and focuses attention on the sources of waste.

The Need to Emphasize Profit Rather than Cost

Supervisors also err in emphasizing dollars of costs or expense rather than profits or the results sought from cost-control efforts. Many supervisors are convinced (perhaps after being erroneously led to believe by their bosses) that minimizing or reducing costs in all areas of activity will necessarily increase profits. The error of this logic is twofold. First, while the supervisor may have subordinates performing a particular function expertly and inexpensively, if that particular function *does not need to be done at all*, then it is a source of profit drain no matter how efficiently it is done.

Second, costs *may not be incurred where they should be*. Consider the sales representatives who are late for an appointment because they were looking for a cheap place to park their car; or the production manager who cheats on equipment maintenance to save immediate dollars, ultimately missing schedules because of later breakdowns. Simply *reducing* costs will not necessarily enhance profitability. It can even hurt profitability.

The intelligent supervisor maintains an awareness of *profitability* rather than merely emphasizing dollars of expenses in developing a cost consciousness in employees. Not only can sole emphasis on costs create operating errors, but many employees and customers may also become irritated by austere cost-reduction activities that merely appear to be cheap. For example, employees become increasingly antagonized if they do not have the appropriate tools, materials, and equipment. Consider the morale of employees required to use manual typewriters when they know word processors are available. Furthermore, customers may resent it if they buy a product—say an expensive electric drill—and find that the cord is ridiculously short; they resent having to beg for butter as patrons in a restaurant. The effective supervisor carefully considers any actions designed primarily to minimize costs by examining the long-run effect such actions will have on profitability—not just the immediate effect on dollars spent.

ERRORS COMMONLY
COMMITTED BY SUPERVISORS

Many of the basic problems encountered by supervisors in minimizing costs in today's businesses result from the use of misguided methods and techniques. Frank O. Hoffman, an expert in cost reduction, has enumerated 12 ways in which supervisors make errors trying to control costs. While all 12 do not merit discussion here, many are relevant. For example, consider the following.

Monday Morning
Pep Talks

One of the more common errors committed by supervisors in trying to implement a cost-consciousness program is emphasizing cost reduction on a scheduled basis—just like the coach giving pep talks at the half of a football game. Unfortunately, in the world of work, the game never really ends. Effective supervisors constantly stress the value of effective cost consciousness and its benefits to the entire organization, but they do *not* do so by making every Monday (or Wednesday or Friday) the day to lecture employees about saving on materials, parts, and supplies. Monday becomes "the day we get lectures about costs," in the eyes of employees. *Continual* and *genuine* interest in controlling costs, not regularly scheduled pep talks, is the supervisory key to good cost control.

Talking Dollars
Rather than
Techniques

Talking dollars rather than techniques is another way in which many supervisors fail in implementing effective cost-consciousness programs. Supervisors who experience success in cost control habitually stress the specific techniques, methods, discipline, or activity necessary to keep costs down rather than dwelling on dollars alone. It does little good for a supervisor to complain that a truck driver is wasting too much gasoline by leaving the engine running while unloading if the driver feels that is the only way to keep the cab warm. It is something else to say, "We could conserve on gas if you would shut the engine off when you *don't need* to keep it running." The employee's attitude toward need may change when the employee can personally decide what is or is not needed—like letting the engine run on really cold days, but being more willing to shut it off on marginal days.

Lack of Personal Commitment and Example by the Supervisor

One significant problem for many supervisors occurs when they are not personally committed to reducing costs. In one case a few years ago, a now defunct manufacturing company's owner had issued a mandate that none of the employees would ever fly first class while on the company expense account because it cost more. Cooperating beautifully, the next time the owner's secretary made a plane reservation for the *owner*, feeling that he was also an employee, she booked him on a thrift fare. When the boss discovered this and confronted the secretary she explained, "You said *no one* was to fly first class." The boss retorted, "That doesn't apply to me." Needless to say, the example made by the boss was extremely important in the development of negative employee attitudes. While the employees did comply with the president's rules in respect to airline travel (he could always fire them if they didn't), his wishes went disastrously unheeded in other areas where it was not so easy to prove deliberate waste—for instance, telephone calls were made when a letter would have sufficed, new supplies were used while old supplies were ignored, and so on.

Demanding Eyewash Rather than Honest Action

Many supervisors fail to reduce costs because they demand reports of efforts rather than tangible evidence. Therefore, employees will often present eyewash—what looks like cost-control efforts—but really isn't. Most persons do not respond effectively to unclear goals. Furthermore, some persons will promise anything, as long as it is not specific what they must do or when. Failure to establish definite dates and times becomes one of the primary causes of supervisor failure in developing cost-consciousness programs because no actual performance is required—just reports and promises.

Failure to Consider Cost-Consciousness Efforts for Promotions or Pay Raises

Few things will actually sabotage a cost-consciousness program quicker than for the supervisor to ignore special efforts made by subordinates at minimizing costs. Most employees don't mind cooperating with cost-control efforts if they see some benefit for themselves. Most workers don't approve of needless waste and don't mind conserving on costs for the company. But, they do want *something* for themselves. If they see no reward for their efforts—the promise of a more professional-looking job title or the opportunity to do a job better or more easily, or if their efforts go ignored or unappreciated by the boss (especially at performance review time), they will lose interest in the organization's cost-control program. It is not that they must be paid for trying to control costs. However, most people have a need to see how doing something can benefit them and/or the organization before they become committed to it. It is the supervisor's job to make those benefits clear and real.

Indicating Disinterest in the Details of the Cost-Consciousness Program

Whenever supervisors indicate by word or action that they are not interested in the details of how a subordinate intends to save money or minimize expenses, they will be unsuccessful at controlling costs. Employees' attitudes, when this happens, sound like this: "Why should I even tell them about my idea to cut costs when they don't care? All they want is to look good. If they don't care how I do it, they probably won't know or appreciate what I have done. Why try?" What could be more damaging for the supervisor's cost-control efforts?

Making the Subordinate Feel like an Informer

One of the most unfortunate things that can occur in a cost-reduction program is for a supervisor to make subordinates feel like they are informing on each other when cost-improvement techniques are discussed. If, in discussing costs with subordinates, the boss assumes an attitude that the subordinates "surely" can think of some way to reduce costs, the subordinates may feel that they are being ridiculed or being forced to tell on themselves and expose areas where they are deliberately or maliciously wasting company funds. In that situation, many persons will deliberately refuse to cooperate for fear of what would happen to them. A good supervisor centers discussions of cost-control efforts on the entire work unit and avoids suggesting that "surely" there is some waste. This is one reason that quality circles have been so successful.

Failing to Provide the Subordinate with Cost Information

Anyone who is responsible for control of costs or minimization of expenses—be it material, supplies, or whatever—has a need to know what items actually cost. If the supervisor fails to give such information to the subordinate, there is no way that the subordinate can make a decision about whether something should be done or not. Consider two office workers whose jobs require that they place long-distance calls for their respective bosses. With no idea that person-to-person calls cost more than direct-dial calls, for example, one worker may unknowingly use the most expensive method even when it is unnecessary. The other employee, knowing how rates are charged and that the party being called is likely to receive the call, may be considered a more valuable employee. By dialing direct, that employee will conserve company funds by making the least expensive calls whenever possible. Yet, the first worker's failure is due to *lack of information*, not stupidity or ineptness. A vital part of a supervisor's job, therefore, is informing employees of the costs they *do* incur and *can* control in their jobs. Don't force employees to make decisions in ignorance.

Criticizing Subordinates for Not Thinking of It Before

Many supervisors get poor results in implementing cost-control procedures because they either inadvertently or deliberately make employees feel stupid for unknowingly doing something wrong or wasteful. Any subordinate who has had this type of abuse bitterly resents the suggestion that he or she is stupid for not having seen the better way. The subordinate will not be cooperative in the future. Consider, in the above example, how the first worker would feel if accused by the boss of being a dummy for not making a station call. Incidentally, person-to-person calls are often *less* expensive if the odds are high the party being called is not in. Do you know which method is best for the company or organization you work for? Systems such as WATS and MCI, developed to lower the costs of telephone calls, *still* cost more than no calls at all and often they run up costs by encouraging unnecessary calls.

The Supervisor's Role in Automation and Mechanization

Cost control and cost consciousness does not derive only from tightening the belt. Methods of doing work often aren't considered by supervisors, especially if the new methods are mechanical, that is, the use of **automation, mechanization,** and **robotization** in equipment that the supervisor knows nothing about.

WHY SUPERVISORS DON'T THINK OF MECHANIZATION

Many supervisors fail to be concerned about mechanical assistance. Other supervisors think too much about it. Machine designers and engineers are the main workers who are "supposed" to think about better ways to do work mechanically. But no one person has all the ideas and, more importantly, people on the job often see applications that the designers and engineers overlook. Many of the best forms of work automation have come from supervisor and worker *suggestions* and, although the person making the suggestion may know nothing of the technical details, the idea (often born from drudgery) needs to be suggested to the design engineer. Supervisors should recognize that much of their responsibility for reducing costs comes from giving their ideas and their subordinates' ideas to the appropriate designers and engineers.

HOW TO AVOID GOING TOO FAR

One word of caution, however, about making design suggestions. While suggesting ideas about a machine or robot that could save production time and effort to the appropriate people is an important supervisory function, supervisors must know that ideas and suggestions are rejected—even *very good* ideas and suggestions. Some suggestions are impractical and are dropped. The originator of the idea may feel rebuked by such action, and it is hard to tactfully reject an idea. So caution your subordinates that any idea submitted may be rejected. Be careful to avoid hurting workers' feelings.

Even excellent ideas are sometimes rejected. This may sound weird, but the explanation for rejecting excellent ideas usually is found in economics. Some terrific ideas are too expensive to be worthwhile. Robotization is generally a good idea, for example—especially for "grunt work" that people don't like to do or dull, repetitive work. But, robots are expensive and it may be cheaper to hire people. Thus, even though an idea for a special machine or robot might be practical and workable, it still may be rejected because of the expense of designing, building, and/or buying the machine.

ORGANIZATIONAL PRACTICES THAT HURT COST–CONTROL EFFORTS

Not all cost-control and cost-consciousness efforts work. Also, it is not necessarily the supervisor's fault. It may be an inherent problem within the supervisor's organization.

The Need for Information

In spite of well-intended efforts to cut costs, lack of adequate guidelines often results in poor decisions, ineffective plans, and costly errors. Scheduling people to stock shelves in a grocery store when the shelves are full is an expensive use of personnel. Equally expensive is the practice of ordering more supplies than is needed, "so we'll be sure not to run out." Adequate operational plans and procedures information are necessary prerequisites to cost control, and the supervisor who feels that he or she lacks these skills should make it known.

PROBLEMS CREATED BY ORGANIZATIONS

Sporadic Policy

Probably the poorest form of organizational policy, with respect to cost control or cost-reduction efforts, results from the attempt to control costs on a sporadic basis rather than continuously. One example is an austerity program implemented on an irregular basis. Governmental agencies, especially, seem prone to this behavior. The traditional attitudes of many employees in such a situation is "Oh, no—here it comes again—time to tighten the belt." At other times, employees and lower-level supervisors react more positively to periodic or cyclical cost-reduction policies.

One problem is that many supervisors feel that unless there is pressure on them from top management, there is no need to worry about anything. They feel that top management will scream when costs get out of line. As a result, some supervisors feel that they are not personally responsible for cost control. In such cases, the supervisor has a difficult time communicating a feeling of serious concern to subordinates for their responsibility in controlling costs of operation.

Another result of not regularly emphasizing cost consciousness is that many supervisors and subordinates will try to conceal certain projects or activities when they see a cost-reduction drive on the horizon. Executives in larger corporations are known to employ the same tactics, and it is easy to understand.

If everyone in the organization knows that each year there are witch hunts for profit drains and unnecessary costs, everyone will try to conceal pet projects. They will deliberately build expensive or time-consuming operations into necessary functions to hide the work that they want done. The consequence is greater complications at work, increased total expenditures, and missed deadlines.

"I'll Get It All Back Later Anyway" Attitude

Some people in a corporate environment with poorly conceived or erratic cost-effectiveness programs, are willing to give up their pet projects—only with the idea that they will get them back when the heat is off. This phenomenon is regularly observed in governmental agencies and other large organizations when, toward the end of the fiscal year, there are serious appropriation cutbacks implemented to stay within the budget. When it appears there will be budget overruns, there usually are across-the-board reductions of expenditures for essential and nonessential programs. It is almost always done, unfortunately, with the knowledge that the project will be rejuvenated in the next fiscal year.

The unwise use of such all-encompassing austerity programs by companies and public agencies can ruin morale and can do much more harm in the long run. Customers and suppliers of a private company using such tactics may become upset because of the lack of delivery, canceling of orders, and so forth.

Experience shows that end-of-year economy moves are seldom economical. When the organization moves into the new fiscal year and has to send material by air freight that otherwise would have been sent by truck or rail, or when it must schedule overtime at time-and-a-half or more to get back on schedule, costs go *higher* than they would have if the program had gone as scheduled. Fiscal, year-end crash economy programs are never good managerial strategy, either from a company standpoint or from an individual supervisor's standpoint.

WHAT NOT TO DO WHEN YOU ARE TOLD TO CUT COSTS

Any first-line supervisor will be asked to cut costs. The enlightened supervisor doesn't want to make any basic mistakes in reducing costs. The really smart first-line supervisor emphasizes cost consciousness rather than cost reduction. But, more importantly, the supervisor wants to avoid making any major mistakes. What might you look out for? There are two different reactions the typical supervisor has when a cost-reduction or cost-consciousness program is to be implemented that should *not* be used.

Don't Be a Cynic

One behavior pattern that the supervisor should avoid is the "old timer," who has "seen it all come and go in the past." These people are usually halfheartedly committed to company cost-consciousness efforts. They simply go through the motions of being committed to a cost-consciousness program, but they really hope it will eventually go away. They are seldom helpful to the cost-consciousness program. Worse, they are hard on the morale of other supervisors trying to do a good job and of workers who are victimized by their halfhearted commitment to controlling costs.

**Don't Be
Overzealous**

As bad as the cynical supervisor who lacks commitment is the supervisor who gets carried away and interprets cost-consciousness efforts as an order to do anything to reduce expenses. These are the supervisors who lay off a person or two, eliminate an extra shift, quit buying supplies and materials, make a big scene about any minor waste, and generally disrupt the entire operation to minimize costs—no matter what it *really* costs. The supervisor who gets carried away has a difficult time implementing a genuine cost-consciousness activity. The "hacking around" done by the supervisor who does anything to eliminate costs gets people mad, hurts morale, and causes employees to worry that they might be laid off.

WHAT TO DO WHEN YOU ARE TOLD TO CUT COSTS

The supervisors who are most effective in cutting costs or implementing a cost-consciousness program really consider what they are going to do and develop a sensible plan to reduce costs over the long run. These supervisors concentrate on the areas where fat can be eliminated and where duplication or waste is materializing, rather than hacking aimlessly at anything that seems to raise operating expenses in their department. These supervisors usually have the best-run operations. About the only time that they are affected negatively by orders to reduce costs is when a poorly informed, upper-level manager simply orders *everybody* to reduce costs by a certain percentage even when a good supervisor's department has been doing well anyway.

HOW TO REDUCE OPERATIONAL COSTS

There is always a time for revitalizing interest in reducing costs that always rise. Thus, it might be wise to think about key areas to be scrutinized on an irregular basis by the supervisor. Some of these tips include the following:

Consider Per-Unit Costs Rather than Total Costs

Every supervisor should know that, particularly in any production or service area, the cost per unit of an item serviced or produced usually falls when the total number of units produced in a given time rises. That is, the costs of running a machine to produce 10 units in a given time may be as high as it would be to run the same machine over the same period while producing 20 units. These economies of scale vary, and it is possible to jam too much through a given machine and break it. But, sometimes it is possible to realize economies of scale that occur because of a rhythm that is produced with higher production levels rather than lower production. Rhythm is important for doing work. People often work better if they have background music (which provides a rhythm). Sometimes it is possible to save the company money by increasing output and, in the process, actually make people's work easier and more pleasant.

Don't Be Stingy

It is an old maxim that to make money one needs to spend money. Another saying is "penny-wise, pound foolish." This is probably true in every organization—be it government, manufacturing, retailing, wholesaling, or service industries. Trying to minimize **operational costs** is seldom accomplished simpy by stopping expenses. There are many cases where people have attempted to save money in the short term but have ended up paying more to accomplish the same goal later.

Time Costs Money

Supervisors who want to economize will often find that costs can be greatly reduced—in those areas where there is idle time, down time, or waiting—such as in an office or a retail store. Under such circumstances, costs sometimes rise slowly over time. Consider an office job where a copy machine is used. Any worker who wants to do a job well will want to use the copy machine. But not everyone can have their own copy machine so somebody must wait. Most supervisors will try to get employees to do all the work that requires the copy machine at the same time. A poorly informed supervisor, however, may permit workers to stand in line at the copy machine or to make countless trips back and forth to the machine rather than do some appropriate scheduling that would eliminate waiting time.

**Look for
Duplication**

Whenever there are duplicated facilities, there is usually some kind of wasted equipment or supplies. Also, unnecessary waste of time results from unnecessary maintenance or start-up and shutdown times. The wise supervisor looks at where people waste their time and efforts, ranging from items such as utilities and energy to supplies, materials, and inventory.

**Recognize that Any
Facility Costs
Money**

Machinery and equipment, space, and undoing and redoing work all cost money. Supervisors who want to minimize operating costs try to utilize space as effectively as possible and take advantage of all available machinery and facilities. If someone can take a fully loaded truck once rather than send the same truck twice with two half loads, it will be cheaper. By the same token, if items can be stored where they can be easily retrieved without having to be unstacked and then restacked, money will be saved.

COST CONSCIOUSNESS:
AN ONGOING PROBLEM

Many operating supervisors ask, "When will things get back to normal so that the pressure for cost cutting will be gone?" Emphasis on cost consciousness will probably never totally go away. Minimizing the cost of operation is part of the ongoing process of any well-run organization, business, or industry. There is no way to escape the concern over operational costs. No matter how effective the supervisor is at implementing and maintaining a cost-consciousness program, a competitive spirit will mean the pursuit of continually lowering operating costs.

Of course, many supervisors overemphasize cost consciousness. A wise supervisor emphasizes cost-saving strategies or cost consciousness continually with an even keel. Successful supervisors find that there are three basic sources for ideas in an ongoing cost-consciousness program: supervisors, employees, and specialists in cost control or efficiency. The supervisor will have confidence in his or her capabilities in finding ideas on how to minimize costs. But that supervisor will also try to get employees' ideas for better cost control. The supervisor will also work with staff specialists in the organization, if they exist, to try to implement ideas that industrial engineers or time-and-motion experts recommend. Unfortunately, first-line supervisors often do not work with their organization's time-and-motion experts or industrial engineers. In fact, many super-

Could anything have been done to
prevent these products from getting
damaged?

"LET'S TAKE A TAXI. THE COMPANY
IS GOING TO PAY FOR IT, ANYWAY."

visors seem to feel that these people are the enemy. Furthermore, unions
and workers often also view time-and-motion people as an enemy trying
to squeeze extra productivity out of the worker. This is an unfortunate,
but real, circumstance in many organizations today.

AN ACTION PLAN FOR CONTROLLING COSTS

Building cost consciousness among people at work is a continuous
process. It cannot be done sporadically, nor can it be done without
thinking by supervisors. A good program devotes attention to the impact
of any action on the overall profitability and functioning of the organization. Six ingredients for a successful cost-effectiveness program are discussed in the following steps.

Step One: Set Objectives

Nothing can substitute for a well-conceived program of maintaining
control over costs at all times. Objectives include dates, times, and
activities to be performed based on a detailed assessment of the various

work areas and resource requirements. Specific cost-control activities must be planned for areas where the most waste is occurring.

Step Two: Make Cost Improvement an Integral Part of Everybody's Job

Most cost-improvement programs exercised by managers fail because employees are not committed to the program. Part of the reason for this failure is that cost-improvement activities are seldom listed as part of an employee's job duty, if they are listed at all. In addition, many bosses fail to consider subordinates' efforts in controlling costs when they appraise employee performance and conduct salary reviews. Any effective cost-consciousness program not only establishes firm objectives but also makes the responsibility for the program an integral part of each person's job.

Step Three: Motivate Employees

Most people understand the need to economize and assume that they cannot simply fritter away the organization's funds. When people knowingly waste funds, it is usually because they harbor certain resentments toward the organization or the supervisor. The effective supervisor works diligently to communicate to employees the need for cost consciousness and how it benefits them rather than simply emphasizing cost reduction.

Step Four: Have Periodic Meetings and Talk Job Techniques

Emphasis should be removed from dollars-and-profits figures and placed on techniques. Most people like mentally challenging games. Many supervisors have found employees, if interested, will develop successful techniques for conserving expenses. A far more fruitful tactic than emphasizing savings is to make a challenge of the task of controlling costs. Consider using a quality circle.

Step Five: Set Up Priorities for Cost Improvement

Not only is it necessary to set specific activities, dates, and objectives for cost-improvement techniques, but priorities must also be set. Seldom can everything conceivable be done to conserve costs, even if all employees are ambitiously behind such efforts. Setting objectives will not, in itself, ensure that objectives will be accomplished. While there may be many ideas for minimizing costs, some ideas will be more fruitful than others. The good supervisor, in discussing techniques with subordinates, will establish what priority will be assigned to each cost-improvement objective.

Step Six: Make Continual Efforts

The message of this chapter can be summarized simply: Make continual cost-improvement efforts. Sporadic cost-reduction methods do not work. They almost always cause the organization to incur more costs— either because of undone work, the need to do work later at a hasty pace, or because employees get angry and take out their resentments on the organization. Continual cost consciousness must be the theme if the supervisor is to be effective in operating efficiently and economically.

Things to Remember

1. Cost consciousness is an often neglected and misunderstood aspect of a supervisor's job.

2. Pareto's law of maldistribution can be applied to cost control.

3. Emphasis on profits rather than costs is vital to a successful economic control program.

4. Profitability emphasis may include cost shifts and cost controls.

5. Cost-control action plans are a necessry part of successful supervision.

6. Cost-consciousness plans should be built on benefits for employees and managers.

7. Most cost-control plans, such as across-the-board cuts, are ineffective.

Key Words

cost control
cost consciousness
Pareto's law of maldistribution
automation
mechanization
operational costs

Self-Assessment

How well do you know methods of cost control? Evaluate yourself by responding to the following statements or questions. A 1, 2, or 3 response means that you disagree or have a negative answer. A 4, 5, or 6 response means agreement or a positive answer.

1. It is the supervisor's, rather than the employee's, responsibility to spearhead cost consciousness.

1	2	3	4	5	6

2. In the final analysis, it is more productive to think in terms of immediate costs rather than long-range profits.

1	2	3	4	5	6

3. Planned expenditures are not as important as steps necessary to reduce costs across the board.

1	2	3	4	5	6

4. In a new organization, would you know where to look to find potential areas of waste and financial drain?

1	2	3	4	5	6

5. Pareto's law implies that it is more important to pay attention to the vital many than the trivial few.

1	2	3	4	5	6

6. Supervisors who ignore employee attempts to control costs will sabotage most cost-consciousness programs.

1	2	3	4	5	6

7. It is important that an analysis of the total organization is made before a plan for cost control is developed.

1	2	3	4	5	6

8. Weekly pep talks have been proven to be an effective means of developing cost consciousness.

1	2	3	4	5	6

9. In establishing cost controls in my work unit, I establish priorities rather than implement all controls at once.

1	2	3	4	5	6

10. Cost-control objectives should be general and apply to all situations rather than specific and aimed at a particular problem.

1	2	3	4	5	6

CASES

A Case of Bills

When Bill and Edwena Thompson opened their Village Off-Set Printing Office (VOPO), they had little idea of how popular it would become in such a short time. As demand increased, they doubled the floor space, added extra people, bought high-volume equipment, and developed a complete stock of various types of paper. Most of the expansion was the result of a $25,000 business expansion loan that was repaid in monthly installments with a 12 percent interest rate. Some of the initial payroll costs were also made from the loan.

Since they stressed high-quality service and quick delivery, the business continued to flourish. Increasingly, more of the business was devoted to large orders from major firms that were unable to handle the printing load with their own equipment. These orders usually were paid within 30 days of completion.

After a few months in the second year of operations, Edwena told Bill that they needed to float a loan to meet the week's payroll. "But we have plenty of business," complained Bill, "and we're taking in lots of money."

"That's true," answered Edwena, "We also have a lot of money going out and lot to be collected. Let's hope the interest on our loans doesn't eat up all of our profit."

1. What kinds of waste may be occurring at VOPO?

2. What simple business fact has Bill failed to recognize?

3. How can Bill and Edwena build cost consciousness into their work force?

Control?

Airjet Corporation Tactical Systems' (ACTS) purchasing department was large and complex. Not only was it responsible for metal fabrication supplies, plastics, supplier-made parts, and equipment, but it also ordered all office supplies and equipment, and plant maintenance supplies, and it was responsible for material control records once products were received. During a routing check of supply records, Elaine Whitney, records and supply supervisor, noticed a number of unaccounted items were missing. No one in her office knew where they were. Some of the items were expendable, such as reams of typing paper, pencils, pens, and gum erasers. "They're the supplies school children could use," she thought. In addition, hand-held calculators, two electric typewriters, and a mixture of other supplies had apparently disappeared into thin air. "It has to be theft," she told her staff of 14 employees. "Someone is taking the material from our supply room without authorization. It could be one or two of our group, but since the room is open to anyone, people from other departments could be taking it as well. In order to reduce costs, I'm going to take the following steps:

1. Janet will control the storeroom. She and I will be the only ones with keys. It will be locked at all times unless we open it.

2. No supplies will be issued without specific authorization from a supervisor.

3. Employees may withdraw only a limited amount of routine supplies to keep in their desks. Limits will be posted on the storeroom door.

1. How well will Elaine's cost-control plan work?

2. How do her employees and other departments feel about the plan?

3. Were there other alternatives that would work as well?

11

The Supervisor's Role in Training Employees

Thought Starter

Training serves more functions than just teaching people how to do a job. It also builds confidence, helps establish a stronger relationship between management and employees, and can encourage the acceptance of responsibility. A major function of training is to reduce the chance for error and shorten the time required for an employee to adapt to a new process or change. Few successful organizations can operate without some form of training. It is apparent that effective training has many positive payoffs. Organizations that pay little or no attention to training new employees and upgrading the skills of current employees will eventually become second-rate.

In Chapter 11 you will learn:

- Development of good work habits is a major training purpose.
- A number of steps are necessary in establishing an effective work environment.
- Supervisors need to recognize and avoid common training errors.
- Principles of effective training can be mastered with practice and dedication.
- Training, like all other management activities, depends on well-executed plans.

A consistent problem at Cross Engineering was the length of time necessary to train new engineering liaison personnel to perform routine statistical computations. "Somehow," Les Unfried told Anne Davis, "we've got to shorten the training period for our new people and, at the same time, upgrade the performance of our employees who've been doing work the old way. The new equipment will make the job easier but it requires new habits." Anne looked thoughtful, "Maybe we can get some ideas from Carl Mahler in personnel. He's just completed a field training program for data processing supervisors. If he's developed some techniques we can use, it's worth a try."

"OK," replied Les, "but the training responsibility is still going to be ours. Let's see what Carl has to offer."

"In five years," stated Bud Hanan, "most of what I know will be obsolete. To just keep current, I will have to be trained and retrained." Bud Hanan is a college instructor who is well aware that training is critical in all work and that instructors in schools and colleges are not exempt. Recently a large community college sent its entire automotive technology staff to an advance automotive systems program sponsored by the General Motors Corporation, just to be updated in newer electronic controls and mechanical technology. Life-long learning has become more than a desired goal. It is a necessity of our times. Much of what is learned, both on the job and in formal training programs quickly becomes obsolete.

At no time in history has effective training become as critically important as it is now. An understanding of training needs determination, design of training programs to meet those needs, and the skills necessary to train effectively are vital components of being a complete manager.

THE SUPERVISOR AS TRAINER

Oliver Goldsmith once stated that "those who think must govern those who toil." No statement is more concise or relevant in its application to the **training** job of the supervisor. The supervisor's job is to get results through people. This means that the supervisor must think about the job to be done; determine who and what are involved; determine when, where and how it is to be done; and then supervise persons doing the job.

If employees have good work habits, do their jobs well, and are supervised correctly, they are always more effective. Thus, when discussing the supervisor's role as trainer, there are several jobs involved. The first one is to ensure that employees develop good work habits. Supervisors, by example and by their relationship with each employee, can develop more effective performances if they *teach* employees good work habits as well as how to do the job correctly.

Training is a universal job of supervisors. Effective supervisors must assume the responsibility for ensuring that subordinates know what the job is, when to do it, how to do it, and why to do it. Especially critical is the need to recognize when an employee's job performance is inadequate and needs improvement. This is especially true in today's highly technical work environments.

There is a multiplicity of ways in which training can be conducted by supervisors. Supervisors should know the options available to ensure that employees are trained as effectively as possible. Before getting into the how-to-do-it of supervisory training, however, we should first look at the supervisor's role as trainer and some of the common errors committed by beginning supervisors in a training role.

KINDS OF TRAINING

There are various **forms of training** a supervisor must provide for employees in order to obtain satisfactory performance. Essentially, they are skill training, knowledge training, and attitude training.

Skill Training

Skill training means teaching a person a specific skill. There are literally thousands, perhaps millions of different skills—the ability to program a computer, to conduct sophisticated lab research, and to operate electronic controls are some of today's challenges, along with old standbys such as the ability to weld, to drive a truck, to spray paint, to hit a baseball, to operate a movie projector, to fly an airplane, to repair an automobile engine, and so on.

When a supervisor teaches a skill, it means that he or she is answering the questions: How do you do this job? How do you program for this process? How do you land on a fog-shrouded runway on an aircraft carrier? How do you use a microprocessor? How do you install carpeting? Skill training exploits available knowledge. It exposes tricks of the trade—little knacks, secrets, and the like that make the difference between hacking away at a job and doing the job professionally.

Knowledge Training

Knowledge training is similar to skill training except that it teaches an individual primarily to think. Knowledge training is like education, although it is job related. For example, what happens when two chemical compounds are mixed? What happens when electrical current sent through a transformer exceeds certain limitations? What happens when one puts too much air pressure in a tire? What happens to an airplane during a takeoff roll when crosswinds exceed 30 knots? An airline pilot, for example, must know if there are sidewinds to the runway that exceed safety limits for the aircraft. The concern is that the plane, in taking off, could receive a sideways lift from crosswinds that could flip the plane. A medical doctor must have knowledge training too. What happens if a person takes X quantities of penicillin? What happens if a person takes Y quantities of penicillin? What happens if a person takes X quantities of penicillin and Y quantities of alcohol?

Certainly an effective supervisor trains employees *how* to do something (skill training). The supervisor also trains employees about what happens *if* something is overheated, left on overnight, gets exposed to another chemical, and so forth.

Attitudinal Training

Attitudinal training concerns the attitude a person has toward his or her job. For example, does a person have a good or bad attitude toward the job? Does an employee want to do the job well, or is he or she willing to defraud the customer, milk the employer, or otherwise take advantage of a situation?

Generally, individuals who have a good attitude toward their job will do a good job, and individuals who have a bad attitude toward their job will do poorly. There are exceptions, of course. A doctor may abhor having to sever a limb from a patient. But that doctor may nevertheless amputate the limb because he or she knows that failure to do so may cause the patient to die.

In training an individual to do a job, the supervisor must give the employee skill training (how to do the job), knowledge training (why the job must be done), and attitudinal training (why something that seems stupid, foolhardy, or irrelevant is imperative).

UNDERSTANDING HOW PEOPLE LEARN

A supervisor must see to it that his or her people are trained to do the job. The first-line supervisor doesn't always do the training. Often, the training can be delegated to someone who is more knowledgeable or experienced at training employees. Larger organizations often have training departments or someone in the personnel department with that responsibility. Unfortunately, in many organizations there is no one qualified, other than the first-line supervisor, to do the training. Therefore, it is important that the first-line supervisor know how to train people.

Knowing how to train employees requires that the supervisor know how employees learn. Learning is not something that people do automatically. While first-line supervisors might think that they learned by observing what others did—and to some degree that is true—not all people are motivated to learn, nor are they conditioned to learn unless something is done to help them in the learning process. The effective first-line supervisor is aware of what it takes for an individual to try to learn various job functions.

Classical Learning

Often, we learn by associating one item with another. This is called **classical learning** or classical conditioning. One way to understand this phenomenon is by explaining Pavlov's dog. Pavlov was a Russian scientist who conducted experiments with a dog. He noticed that a dog would salivate when it was shown a piece of meat. The meat obviously stimulated the dog's salivary glands. Pavlov then began to experiment with ringing a bell as he showed the meat to the dog. Each time the bell was rung and the meat was shown, the dog salivated. Finally, Pavlov got the dog to salivate merely by ringing the bell. The dog had learned to associate the meat with the ringing of the bell. Pavlov's experience is the essence of classical learning. What it means is that we learn to associate one item with another because they occur at the same time or in a logical sequence.

Operant Learning

Operant learning (operant conditioning) means that individuals learn that by doing one item something happens to them that is either good or bad. If by doing a certain item people find that something *good* happens, they will probably want to continue to do it. If, however, by doing another task they find that something *bad* happens, they will presumably stop doing it. Put in experimental terms, if a dog learns accidentally that by stepping on a lever a piece of meat will appear for the dog to eat, it will continue to step on the lever whenever it is hungry. Likewise, if the dog learns that by stepping on a lever it will get shocked, it will soon stop stepping on the lever if it doesn't want to get shocked.

Social Learning

Social learning is another method of learning. Social learning, which is not totally different from classical or operant learning, is learning by observing others. If someone traveling in a foreign country observes that everybody who walks past a particular street corner picks up a rock and throws it across the street, that person, upon passing that corner, will also probably pick up a rock and throw it across the street. This is because the behavior was observed in others, and the individual who observed the behavior assumed that the behavior was normal and expected —perhaps even required.

Can a cat be trained to do things? Do animals learn,
just like people? What does a supervisor need to
know about training and how people learn?

HOW PRINCIPLES OF LEARNING
AFFECT THE SUPERVISOR'S JOB

Classical, operant, and social conditioning (or learning) are the three
ways we learn. The supervisor in training people must use these principles to teach skills, knowledge, and attitudes to employees. Therefore,
the supervisor must understand that people learn in a variety of ways.
They can learn by observing others, by having good or bad things happen
to them, or by associating one item with another.

**Applying the
Principles**

Good supervisors employ all three learning techniques in training
employees. For example, a first-line supervisor attempting to teach someone newly hired to operate a hotel reservation system probably begins by
using basic classical learning practices. The supervisor tells the trainee
the steps that must be taken before the system is turned on. The idea is to
associate one set of items or actions with another set.

The trainer, on the other hand, might use operant conditioning—
pointing out to the trainee what happens if and when certain things
occur. The idea is to show the trainee that when X is done, Y occurs.
Employees learn that when they do something, something else hap-

pens—either desirable or undesirable. For example, if a person goes too fast when driving a car, he or she can hit the brakes and slow down or stop; likewise, if a person pushes the accelerator down too fast, the vehicle might accelerate too rapidly and crash. In explaining to the trainee how to operate equipment, the supervisor uses the principles of operant conditioning. The supervisor also uses operant conditioning in commending the subordinate on his or her ability to learn how to operate the equipment. That is, whenever the employee is told by the supervisor, "You're coming along fine now. That's it—you're doing a good job," the employee is getting positive reinforcement for learning to operate the machine. Positive reinforcement is something desirable happening to the trainee that becomes an integral part of training.

A third kind of learning that might be employed by a supervisor in training the employee is social learning or learning by observing. The supervisor might ask the trainee to observe another operator at work or have the trainee observe the supervisor operate the equipment. The employee learns how others operate and how to handle special situations—such as how to work with an irate customer. Supervisors should strive to employ all of the techniques that can be used to assist the trainee to learn quickly and to assimilate job skills.

THE IMPORTANCE OF WORK HABITS

The *ultimate* responsibility for good work habits comes from the supervisor. It is his or her responsibility to ensure that employees work effectively, proficiently and safely. The manager's position enables him or her to set the tone at work and to control the work group. The supervisor has control over subordinates in their direct relationship and in terms of the group with whom each employee works.

People's working habits develop from a variety of sources. These include early training received while growing up in a family or habits learned at work or at school. Prior work experiences are another source of work habits. In adddition, the group of people with whom one works, and their standards and value systems also affect work habits. Finally, the boss can influence work habits.

TRICKS USEFUL IN INFLUENCING WORK HABITS

Establishing a healthy work environment is the key to successfully instilling good work habits in employees. A good work environment

**FIGURE 11–1   How to Establish a Good
Work Environment**

1. Get your employees started on the right foot.
2. Be aware of employee work patterns.
3. Substitute good work habits for bad ones.
4. Show why poor work is unacceptable and how to improve it.
5. Remember—some jobs look easier to do than they really are.
6. Set a good example.
7. Attempt to get cooperation from employees.

allows the employee to demonstrate and develop good work habits, utilize learning skills, and put talents to their most effective use. This type of situation can be accomplished in a variety of ways (see Figure 11–1), and it comes primarily from what the supervisor does.

Get the Employee Started on the Right Foot.   Many employees do their job well once they are effectively trained. However, some get started on the wrong foot. It is imperative that the supervisor take special steps to ensure that the employee knows how to get started correctly on the job. Few people will deliberately fail to do the job expected of them, but many times they do not know what is expected. If employees are not told that it is considered good form to clean off their desk before leaving at night, they may only do it occasionally—not knowing that it is expected. How can the employee be criticized later for keeping a messy, disorganized desk? The supervisor's role in developing good work habits includes setting examples and informing people of what is expected. In short, the supervisor's role as a coach cannot be minimized.

Be Aware of Employee Work Patterns.   The supervisor should continually question whether or not employees are doing their jobs properly. It is not only necessary that the employee be trained in how to do the job, but the supervisor must also follow up to determine if the employee is actually doing the job as he or she was taught.

Substitute Good Work Habits for Bad Ones.   Many managers have tried to change their subordinate's behavior. Successful managers have found one absolute requirement: don't attempt to change one type of an individual's behavior without substituting a more acceptable alternative. If, for example, the supervisor sees a subordinate who habitually comes to work and heads for the coffee pot after clocking in, some substitution for the need to escape work must be presented before the employee can be expected to change the behavior. Firing the employee will not remedy the situation. Furthermore, a frank talk with the subordinate, while probably helpful, must carry with it the suggestion of more acceptable behavior.

If the Employee Is Doing a Job Poorly, Demonstrate Why the Work Is Unacceptable and How to Improve Performance.   Changing work habits is difficult. The threat of firing or the bonus of incentives such as extra pay is not as effective in improving job performance as pointing out the benefits that can be derived by doing the job correctly. In some cases, a money incentive won't work. In other cases, the incentive may be perceived by the subordinate as too hard to attain. An effective supervisor shows the employee a reason for working better in terms of benefits to the employee. Showing that the work may be less fatiguing, less dissatisfying, or less difficult if done differently is usually better motivation than threats of punishment or promises of financial rewards.

Remember that Some Jobs Look Easier to Do than They Really Are.   The supervisor is not expected to be a master of all jobs. Many supervisors mistakenly think they must be able to show that they can do the employee's job well. Normally the subordinate should be able to do the job *more* effectively than the supervisor, even if the employee is doing it poorly. Many supervisors find that by demonstrating the job as it should be done, even though they cannot do it as efficiently as it needs to be done, motivates many subordinates to do the job better. This happens because the subordinate can then appreciate that the supervisor *recognizes how hard it is to properly conduct the job efficiently.*

Yale Latin, recognized as one of the finest American management trainers, adamantly maintained that supervisors can make progress with subordinates by demonstrating that they know the difficulties of doing the job as well as how it should be done. Bosses on construction crews, supervisors on assembly lines, and heads of data processing departments all must somehow communicate to their subordinates that they empathize with and understand the problems that subordinates experience in trying to do the job. But, they must never tolerate a poor job. The supervisor who knows how difficult a job is can demand acceptable performance from a subordinate, because the subordinate can't say that the supervisor doesn't understand.

Set a Good Example.   Nothing is more infectious in an organization than having good examples set from the top. Even the most naive supervisor knows that a no-smoking rule cannot be enforced if he or she violates the rule. The supervisor cannot expect subordinates to engage in good work habits if the supervisor has poor work habits. It is imperative that supervisors be well organized at their own jobs if subordinates are expected to demonstrate a similar quality.

Attempt to Get Cooperation from Employees. Many supervisors find it effective to get the wholehearted cooperation of the individual worker who has poor habits as well as the group. Thus, the supervisor can rely on other employees to offer the most expert and concrete suggestions if they are selected to help improve the new employee's work habits.

HOW TO GET PEOPLE TO DO A BETTER JOB

Any discussion about what a supervisor must do to train employees would be incomplete unless it addressed the problem of *how* to get an *already* trained employee to do a better job. For this purpose, there is a basic six-step model:

Explain to Employees in Detail the Poor Work Habits You Have Observed. Many employees lapse into poor, lackadaisical work habits because it is easier to fool around than to do the job correctly, or because they do not recognize that their performance has slipped. Therefore, in an inoffensive way, the supervisor should get the employee's attention by explaining what the poor work habits are.

Point Out Why Employees' Poor Habits Concern You, Why They Should Also Concern Employees, and Why They Concern the Organization. Pointing out to someone that he or she is engaging in poor work habits is quite different from pointing out why it concerns you, why it should concern him or her, and why it concerns the organization. The supervisor is concerned about poor work habits due to low morale, low productivity, unsafe working conditions, or violations of legal requirements, or other items harmful to the organization. The first-line supervisor has a *legal* obligation to see that employees are working under safe conditions. If sloppy work habits are creating hazards, it is imperative that the supervisor correct the employees.

Ask for Reasons Concerning Employees' Behavior and Listen Openly to Explanations. There may be a reason why an employee engages in poor work habits. This may often be an excuse rather than a reason. Some of the reasons that employees don't or can't do what needs to be done may be personal problems or that other employees are interfering with work. Other times, it is because employees are unaware of the problem, and they will be happy that you explained the poor work habits and took immediate corrective action.

Indicate to Employees that the Situation Must Be Changed and Ask for Their Advice as to How You and They Together Might Solve the Problem by Developing Decent Working Habits. There is no room for equivocation when you are trying to change an employee's sloppy work habits. Only accept proper work practices from employees. It is essential to ask employees for their ideas on how to overcome their difficulties. The supervisor must be sure that employees have the appropriate tools, equipment, materials, and resources to improve their job performance if the sloppy work is caused by inadequate supplies.

Discuss with the Employee Each Idea that He or She Has and Offer Your Help in Implementing Workable Ideas. When an employee offers a useful idea for changing poor work habits to good ones, it is important that the supervisor discuss the idea thoroughly. Discuss how the idea will be implemented, when it will be implemented, and how success at implementing the new technique will be obtained. The supervisor must also be supportive and offer encouragement to the employee for doing an improved job.

Agree on a Specific Action Plan and a Time and Date When All Problems Should Be Eliminated. After thoroughly discussing how the employee intends to better his or her performance, it is important that a specific action plan be developed and that specific times and dates be established. A follow-up date should be set for a review of how successfully the action plan has been implemented and what else, if anything, needs to be done. There is no reason for a supervisor to tolerate sloppy or inept employee performance. This is particularly true if an employee already knows how to do the job well but isn't motivated to do so.

A particular challenge to a supervisor's training skills is to get employees to do something they already know how to do. In trying to improve work habits, the supervisor meets his or her greatest challenge. It is at this point that the salvation of a poorly performing employee might occur, and it is the point where successful supervisors are separated from the also-rans.

FORMS OF TRAINING

Vestibule Training

No chapter on training employees would be complete without addressing the forms of training a supervisor can use. Two forms are common—vestibule training and on-the-job training. Vestibule training is training conducted on machinery or equipment similar to what the trainees will use when they are on the job, but the training is not done on the production line, at the work site, or where the employee will work.

Vestibule training is done in the vestibule—that is, outside the shop or office. Many school situations are vestibule training. This is especially true for training done on microprocessors and at special schools that teach specific careers such as how to be a travel agent.

Vestibule training is a satisfactory way for the first-line supervisor to train employees. Unfortunately, vestibule training has certain drawbacks. It is relatively expensive to set up, (schools often do it because organizations can't afford to), because it requires separate work facilities away from the work area. This usually requires extra or duplicate facilities, and even though the equipment used by trainees doesn't have to be as new or operational as the actual equipment they will use on the job, it must be reasonably up-to-date, or else they will not learn how to operate the equipment properly. In addition, vestibule training takes the supervisor's time away from the main job of supervising employees already on the job.

Vestibule training also has some decided advantages. The employee is usually not under the gun to produce. Therefore, the trainee isn't as apt to suffer pressures from on-the-job training. This attribute is particularly critical in teaching the employee how to cope with the public, telephone inquiries, or other sensitive contacts with customers or clients. Vestibule training has the advantage of separating the new employee from the firing line, which is conducive to a healthy learning experience: no damage is done to customer relations if the employee makes a mistake or incurs a problem that he or she can't yet handle effectively.

On-the-Job Training

Another frequently used training technique is on-the-job training. On-the-job training is often used as a guise for saying, "We'll throw the employee out on the job and see whether the employee sinks or swims."

On-the-job training, if planned properly and conducted with an attitude of trying to *teach* the employee how to do the job—using classical, operant, and social learning techniques—can be a valuable training experience. The advantage is that the employee does the job and sees what *actually* happens. Another advantage is that the employee can experience the immediate pleasure of doing a worthwhile job by producing something of quality.

The advantages of on-the-job training are the disadvantages of vestibule training. On-the-job training means that no separate training facilities are required. Thus, it is less expensive. Furthermore, employees are producing work while they learn, so they are, to some degree, making money. Trainees also get the excitement of knowing that they are doing the job.

The disadvantages of on-the-job training are that the employee doesn't have the relaxed environment that is so conducive and necessary to learning. Also, an employee who makes a serious mistake during on-the-job training may be embarrassed and may suffer the rebuke of co-workers or clients. A result of embarrassment is usually a feeling of resentment. Furthermore, employees may develop a quitter mentality and not return to work because they feel they can't do a good job.

On-the-job training, like vestibule training, has a place in the supervisor's bag of training tricks. It can be used effectively if the supervisor *truly wants to train* the employee. It is apt to be ineffective if the supervisor simply says "sink or swim."

CREATING A POSITIVE TRAINING ENVIRONMENT

Teaching an employee how to do a job is simple, especially in the right environment. However, because of its simplicity, many employees neglect the environment; they feel it is unimportant. Actually, there are several rules to follow in creating a good **training environment:**

1. Put the employee at ease. It is important to relieve any tension or concern the employee has about being able to master the job.

2. Explain to the employee why he or she is being taught the job. Knowing what is expected when the training is completed in terms of job knowledge, skills, and proficiency helps in learning any skills.

3. Attempt to create interest in the job. This requires that the supervisor encourage the employee to ask questions about the job—what is expected to be learned, what benefits will the employee derive from mastering the job and so forth.

4. Show the employee what the whole job entails and how it relates to other jobs done in the department and organization. The worker may already have much of this information, but it should not be assumed. Don't assume that the employee knows all intricacies of the job. At this point in training, a little repetition is valuable—the failure to tell the employee all about a job usually ensures bad results.

5. Attempt to place the trainee as close as possible to the normal working situation. Both on-the-job training and vestibule training can accomplish this. As soon as possible, the employee should be placed in the new job position to gain familiarity with the work area and co-workers.

AVOIDING COMMITTING COMMON TRAINING ERRORS

Many supervisors fail as trainers for many reasons. Fortunately, most errors can be easily avoided if the supervisor is aware of a few simple rules, as explained below.

Error One: Trying to Teach Too Much

No one learns to be an airline pilot, a brain surgeon, or a computer programmer in one day. Most tasks we engage in as humans require the application of several learned skills. Just as Henry Ford did not personally design and build every part that went into his first automobile—the motor, the transmission, the differential, and so forth—in the same manner, no one can learn a complex job all at once. Rather, people must be taught segments of a job and develop the pertinent skills before they are taught the total operation. For example, learning how to weld is simple for those who know how, but it is complex for the student. The welder has to know the qualities and characteristics of different metals, the equipment being used, which metals can be welded and which cannot, and so on. It is ridiculous for a salvage company involved in reclaiming sunken ships to hire an employee and expect to teach that employee immediately how to use a cutting torch or how to weld under water if the employee doesn't even know how to weld two steel bars together on land.

■ *Rule One:* Don't try to teach a complex job as a complete unit. Rather, break it into understandable parts. Remember to give a one-minute praising when an employee does the job correctly.

Error Two: Attempting to Teach the Individual Too Fast

Supervisors commonly try to teach a job more rapidly than they should. This is because they often are rushed at work and feel that they don't have time, or won't take the time, to train employees. Yet, one of the most grievous supervisory errors is trying to teach individuals too fast. This forces an employee to perform a job for which he or she is not ready. For example, dispatching duties in a trucking firm aren't learned overnight, even if the delivery routes can be memorized in a few hours. It's one thing to be licensed to fly a single-engine plane, but it's something entirely different to be capable of flying a multiengine jet-transport plane two weeks later.

With some job training, there can be too much information to be learned all at once. While it is possible to teach some items more rapidly than others, there are some practical minimums. Too many supervisors feel that training can be done faster than it usually is done. This attitude often surfaces when the supervisor is too familiar with a job.

While some speed can be gained from a properly conceived training schedule, it must be done in a well-planned fashion. On-the-job training, where a person learns while doing the job, does work—*but only when there is a definite plan behind it.* Though some people are sharp enough to learn complex jobs rapidly with no guidance, most people cannot. Furthermore, individuals who can teach themselves usually become discontented with a job that they mastered so quickly; the job may offer no intellectual or achievement challenge to them. In short, any job that can be learned in a short time may not have much real, long-run appeal.

■ *Rule Two:* Don't push employees beyond their learning speed.

Error Three: Lack of Communication Regarding Formal Training Plans

Supervisors commonly don't have a formal plan and sequence established for training employees in the job, and they never tell the employee about it. Many supervisors commit this error because they know the job well themselves, and they feel that people should see all the steps involved and understand the hodgepodge of ideas, demonstrations, and lectures given by the supervisor.

Figure 11–2 illustrates the advantages derived from explaining the training plan being received by employees. In Figure 11–2, Part A, an employee is given a sheet of paper with random numbers on it. The employee is asked to connect the numbers in sequence with a line. That is the only requirement, and, assuming the employee knows how to count from 1 to 48, the employee should be able to do the job.

Experience shows, however, that few people can connect all the numbers correctly in less than two minutes (most take about four min-

FIGURE 11–2   Part A

utes), even though most people can count from 1 to 48. Yet, if the instructor tells people what the plan of the job is (which can be seen by dividing the paper into quadrants as shown in Part B of the figure), and explains that odd numbers are on the left and even numbers are on the right, and that the numbers are grouped at the top and bottom in alternating blocks of four to the sequence, then most people can do the whole project in under two minutes.

The lesson to be learned from Figure 11–2 is that *with a work plan that is explained*, most people can master complicated work. Without a plan, the simple job of counting from 1 to 48 can be difficult and time-consuming.

- **■ Rule Three:** Have a formal plan established for training and let employees know what the plan is.

Error Four: Failing to Recognize Individual Differences in Trainees

Supervisors sometimes fail to remember that everyone is different—especially when it comes to training people. Many supervisors, because they are in a hurry to get the employee functioning effectively on the job, subject the trainee to an already established regimen of training. Supervisors don't understand that some individuals can learn some jobs more

FIGURE 11–2 Part B

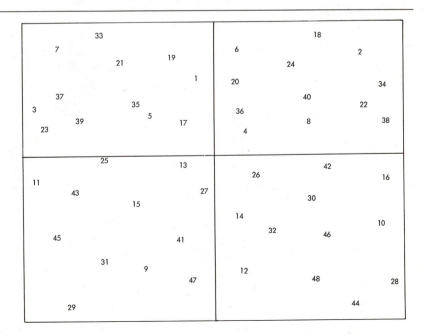

quickly and easily than others. Individual differences can combine dramatically in affecting one's capability for learning how to do a job.

In one company that manufactures electrical transformers, differences in people's learning abilities became apparent in a supervisory training situation. One of the supervisors believed that anyone could wind the wire coils required for manufacturing transformers. Yet, while "anyone" could do it, doing it *right* required a precise manual dexterity depending on the size of the transformer and the wire being used. Men worked more effectively with the heavier gauges of wire, while women functioned more effectively with lighter wire. A select number of women worked especially well with wire so fine that it could not be seen with the naked eye. This process required keen manual dexterity and visual acuity. The women saw their work through magnifying glasses and, for the most part, only women could do the job satisfactorily.

Any supervisor attempting to train employees must realize the individual differences in people concerning the speed with which they learn. The speed of learning is not necessarily a function of intellect, but rather a combination of mental and physical skills. Effective supervisors find that it is helpful to adapt training efforts to individual differences and capabilities of employees.

- **Rule Four:** Carefully analyze trainees' individual strengths and weaknesses concerning learning a task.

Error Five: Failing to Provide Practice Time

Supervisors sometimes fail to provide employees with the time needed to practice and develop skills once they have been learned. All jobs that require any kind of mental and physical skill require practice. Professional golfers practice almost every day, professional bowlers bowl almost every day, and skilled mechanics ply their trades everyday.

It is one thing to know how to do a job; it is quite another thing to develop high skill. Airline pilots know that they don't hop into the cockpit of an airplane that they haven't seen for 20 years and expect to fly it proficiently. For the same reason, it is impractical for the supervisor to expect to teach a person how to do a job and then not give the employee some time to develop some skill.

- **Rule Five:** Give employees time to practice doing the job in order for them to develop proficiency at the task before being required to do it "for keeps."

Rule Six: Failing to Show the Employee the Big Picture

It is an error for the supervisor to show the employee too much of a job too quickly. But, it is also possible not to show enough of the job. Balance is required in determining how much to show the employee and how rapidly. For example, a recent study indicates that employees exhibit more positive work attitudes if they are shown how the job they are learning fits in with other jobs. They learn to do the job more quickly and produce higher quality work as a result.

Few employees really don't care about the work they are doing. Most people like to think the job they are doing is beneficial to people. They like to know how their work fits in with other work, and what the ultimate use of their work will be. The file clerk in a large corporation may perceive his or her job as unimportant. A person who rents cars for a national car chain may feel the same. If no one ever tells them how, where, or when their jobs are important, they may never know why their jobs are important and why they need to be done correctly.

Overkill can occur in training when showing an employee how everything fits together. First of all, time can be wasted if showing the big picture takes too long or is done too frequently. Secondly, some trainees may decide that they would rather do a different job once they see the other kinds of work people do in a different part of the organization.

- ■ *Rule Six:* Trainees should see how the job they are being trained for fits in with the rest of the organization's work and how their efforts in service or productivity are used in a finished form.

Error Seven: Failing to Give Reinforcement

It is always good to reinforce a person in learning anything—the baby learning how to walk, the adult trainee, and so on. It is not enough for an individual to try to do a new job. Without some reinforcement for learning, people find it difficult to sustain a high level of motivation.

The supervisor should recognize that reinforcement need not be tangible. Vocal encouragement and praise in front of others helps to motivate a person in learning to perform a job. If employees can develop a feeling of personal progress and accomplishment on the job, they will usually be highly motivated.

- ■ *Rule Seven:* Extrinsic and intrinsic reinforcements work together far more effectively than either kind does independently.

Error Eight: Intimidation of Employees

While it is uncommon, many supervisors are ineffective as trainers because they intimidate their employees. They can do so in many ways. Some supervisors flaunt their knowledge over the trainee to enhance their egos. Others, by their behavior and attitudes, intimidate unwittingly and unknowingly. Some supervisors feel that it is a good educational device to be demanding. They, too, intimidate employees deliberately, albeit with good intention.

Most people do not like to be intimidated—they find it difficult to learn. They try because they don't want to fail, yet they feel that the trainer looks at them unmercifully closely. As a supervisor, it is difficult to recognize that one may intimidate subordinates while training them. The conscientious supervisor strives to avoid this error.

- *Rule Eight:* the best test to ensure that such intimidation is not occurring is to check with supervisors who see the training situation, who know what is happening, and who might be able to offer advice.

Error Nine: Lack of a Common Vocabulary

Practically all work circumstances have esoteric terms—that is, words, phrases, descriptions, or sayings that don't make sense on the surface but that have specific meanings to people who are knowledgeable about the subject. The supervisor who is training an employee must use such terms only when necessary and explain them when they are used. Talking a language the employee doesn't understand not only intimidates the employee, but it almost ensures that the employee will be confused and not get as much as possible from training exercises.

It is one thing for a supervisor to be unaware that an employee doesn't understand the phraseology used in training, but it is unforgivable for a supervisor to use such words knowingly to impress the trainee. Of course, the trainee will need to learn specific language. Consider, for example, that a medical student must learn Latin to communicate effectively with other medical students and physicians, and the machine operator must learn specific terms or nomenclatures for materials, equipment, operating machinery, and so forth. Also, just as the medical student must know the specific names of various anatomy parts, the computer programmer must know certain precise meanings in computer language, and the insurance salesperson must know specific insurance terminology.

- *Rule Nine:* Use language designed to help the trainee understand what is being taught. Avoid language that will confuse and explain esoteric terms.

Error Ten: The Pygmalion Effect

The **Pygmalion effect** is the tendency to be what you are expected to be. The Pygmalion effect comes from a story about the sculptor who wanted a statue to come to life so badly that, ultimately, it did. When applied to training employees, the situation might be one where the supervisor is so sure that an employee will not learn something that the employee (in the supervisor's eyes) becomes "impossible to teach" long before the employee has had a chance to learn.

Usually, the Pygmalion effect is a bias against the employee. When it is, it is called the *horns effect* because it is done on purpose, since the supervisor doesn't like that employee for some reason—racial, ethnic, sex, age, or other biases. Other times, it is done unknowingly by the supervisor. But, in either case, the impact is devastating on the employee's ability to learn a job or a skill.

Naturally, the Pygmalion effect can also work the other way—although not necessarily to the trainee's advantage. That is, the supervisor might think the employee will do a great job because the supervisor *wants* the employee to do well. Unfortunately, this might be likened to a halo effect, where the supervisor thinks the employee can do no wrong and becomes blind or oblivious to the employee's shortcomings in handling the job. Because of this, disaster can occur. For example, the supervisor might permit the employee to operate machinery or equipment long before the employee is really qualified to do so. But, from a morale standpoint, assuming that the employee will never be able to do the job is probably more devastating to the employee's training and development than is the problem of the halo effect in thinking the employee is better than he or she is. However, errors of both kinds—the halo or the horns—must be avoided by the supervisor.

- *Rule Ten:* Make sure your expectations of the trainee are realistic and appropriate.

Things to Remember

1. Effective trainers recognize several types of learning:
   a. Classical learning
   b. Operant learning
   c. Social learning
2. Trainers also understand different types of training:
   a. Skill training
   b. Knowledge training
   c. Attitudinal training
3. Ten common training errors are listed. Skilled trainers are familiar with all of them.

4. Successful training programs center on establishing good work habits. Several methods of obtaining good work habits are reviewed.

5. Vestibule training and on-the-job training are the two most common forms of training. Classroom training is a form of vestibule training. Systematically supervised training at a real workstation is on-the-job training.

6. Building good work habits is an ongoing process and a legitimate management function.

Key Words

training
skill training
knowledge training
attitudinal training
classical learning
operant learning
social learning
forms of training
training environments
Pygmalion effect

Self-Assessment

Rate your knowledge of training by completing the following questions or statements with a 1, 2, or 3 if you disagree or have a negative response, and a 4, 5, or 6 if you agree or have a positive response.

1. Once a skill has been developed and perfected, no additional training will be needed.

1	2	3	4	5	6

2. Examples set by supervisors are one form of training.

1	2	3	4	5	6

3. Swift, but not necessarily harsh, punishment is the most effective way to improve work habits.

1	2	3	4	5	6

4. Supervisors must be able to perform all of the tasks they supervise better than their employees.

1	2	3	4	5	6

5. To be a good trainer, you must be able to do a job better than your employees.

| 1 | 2 | 3 | 4 | 5 | 6 |

6. It is usually better to break a task into separate parts to be learned rather than try to teach the whole job at once.

| 1 | 2 | 3 | 4 | 5 | 6 |

7. Psychologists have shown that most people learn at approximately the same rate.

| 1 | 2 | 3 | 4 | 5 | 6 |

8. Some employees are naturally skilled and require little or no practice to improve skills.

| 1 | 2 | 3 | 4 | 5 | 6 |

9. A common training error is failure to show how the job being learned relates to other jobs in the organization.

| 1 | 2 | 3 | 4 | 5 | 6 |

10. Both positive and negative reinforcement work in training situations.

| 1 | 2 | 3 | 4 | 5 | 6 |

CASES

Do It Again, Stupid   Burt Hall was manager of Southwestern Investment Company's (SIC) central statistical analysis department. His department was responsible for analysis of market trends, sales data, economic forecast data, and regional demographic changes. As first-line manager over 12 highly skilled people, his job was in some ways more enjoyable than that of the other supervisors. One of Burt's primary difficulties, was however, new employee training. Most new employees came from other departments in the company and they knew basic computational techniques but not the precise type of reporting completed by Burt's group. When new employees joined his team, Burt felt obligated to do most of the training person-ally. He wanted to establish good work habits and get to know the employee better. It was unfortunate that he knew little about training.

"It's perfectly simple!" exploded Burt to the almost tearful Myra Hall, who had just been transferred to his department from personnel. "Why can't you do it right?"

"I'm trying my best, but this is my first time with a program like this."

"Here, let me show you again, I'll do the whole thing over. You watch every step." As Burt began, he found the computer would not produce the results he expected. In frustration, he called Jerry Stypes, Chief of Programming.

"Oh, didn't someone tell you," said Jerry, "that program has an error. It gives the right results only part of the time."

1. What must Burt do to improve his training techniques?

2. What should Burt have done before his session with Myra?

3. In the future, should Burt do the training or get someone else? Why?

The Business of the United States

Often we hear the quote that the "business of America is business." In a speech presented to the Sacramento, California, Comstock Club, Austin Kiplinger, publisher of the *Kiplinger Letter* and the magazine *Changing Times,* stated that most people entering the job market today can expect to change their jobs, if not their careers, five times during their work life. Kiplinger meant that technology changes, modifying the ways that orga-nizations work, changing the expectations of employees, and making a diverse education more important than ever.

Recognizing the dynamic nature of many jobs, universities are now offering classes via television aimed directly at professionals who may have graduated in engineering, chemistry, or electronics but are not current in their knowledge.

Community colleges have recognized the trend even longer, and across the nation, they have a primary role in retraining people by upgrading current skills and teaching new skills. Some people have said that technology and change have gone as far as they can go. However, change never stops. Newer skills continue to emerge as necesssary components of our society and the prospect of closer internationalization of economics and large organizations become closer to reality. It appears that Austin Kiplinger was correct when he stated that the business of the

United States is not just business: "The business of the United States is education."

1. Comment on Mr. Kiplinger's focus on the importance of education. Why does he think it is so important?

2. How have skill requirements changed where you work or have worked?

3. What will be the major roles of educational institutions in the future?

PART FIVE

Communicating and Working with People

Communications:
A Supervisory Tool

12

Thought Starter

Human beings interact through communication. When we see another person, something is communicated. Their size, approximate age, sex, physical condition, and how they feel are all transmitted to us instantly. Communication is a vital part of our lives. Even though communication is part of our fundamental living patterns, managers in organizations frequently identify communication as their most difficult and pervasive problem. Why is communication difficult?

Our lives are filled with failures to understand and to be understood. We make incorrect assumptions, do not listen, and prefer to provide our own point of view rather than understand others'. Yet, success in science, business, government, education, or any other field depends on effective communication.

□ Communication involves both understanding and being understood.

□ Two major problems prevent effective communication:
   The sender fails to transmit a clear message.
   The receiver fails to understand the message.

□ Management communication involves influencing others.

□ Common barriers to communication.

□ Bridges to effective communication.

□ How to improve listening skills.

□ The importance of body language.

□ The importance of choosing words.

"Our purpose," Lila Anderson emphasized, "is to create a master planning system that will obviate previously delineated, procedurally based contingency methods. Furthermore, a plot of the asymptotic relationship between the time variable and those related to potential growth indicates increasing additional requirements." She pointed to a colorful chart. "Are there any questions?" Not a murmur was heard at the conference table. "All right, have your suggestions in my office as soon as you can," Lila concluded.

Carl looked at Buster McKinney. "What did she say, Mac?"

"Not a damn thing as far as I can tell," Mac snorted.

"I don't even know what to ask, much less what to suggest," said Carl.

THE SUPERVISOR AND THE NEED FOR GOOD COMMUNICATION

Most of the workaday life of the typical supervisor is spent in some mode of **communication.** To be effective, first-line supervisors must be skillful in communicating with subordinates and superiors, and others they associate with at work.

Good communication requires more than the ability to speak to others and to pay attention to what they say. It requires the *ability to make oneself understood and to understand others*. It is a well-known fact that people communicate well without talking or listening. Consider the message communicated by comedians doing pantomimes, or the ability of deaf persons to understand what others do and say by lip reading and being alert to other visual and sensual signs. There is a significant nonverbal component in person-to-person communication—body language, gestures, and the tone of voice. Effective communication requires: (1) the ability to be alert to what is happening, (2) the ability to transmit ideas effectively to others in the organization, and (3) the ability to absorb ideas communicated by others.

One of the primary responsibilities of the supervisor is to communicate *effectively* with employees. He or she must convey messages to employees and receive messages from them. Dr. Ralph Nichols, an international authority on communication, states that managers devote nearly 70 percent of their working hours to communicating with superiors, subordinates, and peers. This means that a supervisor who earns $20,000 a year is being paid $14,000 to communicate effectively with people.

HOW TO (MIS)UNDERSTAND EACH OTHER

For many reasons, supervisors misunderstand and are misunderstood when they communicate with others. Sometimes they don't pay attention. Other times, they don't *try* to communicate. Sometimes, communication breaks down because of interference.

Supervisors don't have to be experts in all forms of communication. They do not have to know what a communications channel is or how senders and receivers can verify understanding the messages they exchange. However, a supervisor must understand the basic reasons for good communication and the processes involved. The communications-influence model in Figure 12–1 can help.

Usually, when two or more persons misunderstand each other or fail to communicate effectively it is because of one of two problems:

1. What the sender of the message wished to communicate was not clear.

2. The receiver of the message failed to understand the message sent by the sender.

Effective communication doesn't necessarily mean only understanding words or messages accurately. For example, just because someone understands the message does not guarantee the right kind of action. That is, a first-line manager may say to a subordinate, "Clean up this mess." The subordinate may understand and accept the message. The subordinate may then close off a work area and clean up the mess, forcing a shutdown of activity in surrounding work areas.

Something more must transpire between a sender and a receiver than

**FIGURE 12–1 Communications-
Influence Model**

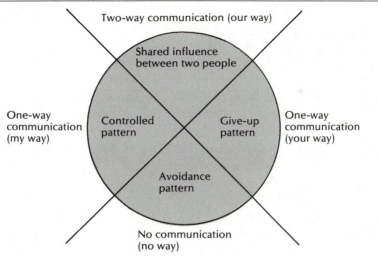

giving, receiving, and accurately understanding a set of instructions. There must be some clarification of the meanings and intents, goals and alternatives, and possible results for a given course of action initiated as a result of the communication process.

HOW THE SUPERVISOR CAN INFLUENCE OTHERS

The supervisor, in communicating with subordinates, wants to influence them. That is, the supervisor wants to transmit an idea to the subordinate—or whoever else they communicate with.

This process of influencing people takes a variety of formats. It is never a one-way process. For example, in using the communication process to analyze how a first-line supervisor can influence the behavior of associates, some basic questions must be asked: Does the supervisor wish to build commitment from subordinates by providing opportunities for them to participate in decision making? Does the supervisor only want people to conform to a stated company policy? Depending on what is desired, it may be important for the supervisor to draw out the ideas, feelings, and experiences of others. For example, if the supervisor wants to reconcile conflicting views between subordinates and the supervisor, the open communication of ideas is important. Yet, it may be desirable to totally avoid someone else's ideas because it would only force the discussion of an undesirable issue.

THE COMMUNICATIONS-
INFLUENCE MODEL

The idea behind the communications-influence model in Figure 12–1 is that communication processes are mainly influence processes. That is, words, idea, facts, and feelings are *communicated* to others in order to *influence* others' behavior. **Communication patterns** produce understanding, acceptance, and desired actions from the individual a person communicates with.

Shared Communications Pattern

There are four forms of communications-influence that the supervisor should be aware of. One form occurs when two people are influencing each other, what is called the shared communication pattern. Shared communication processes *work best* when it is desirable to inform or to stimulate others. This is the basic concept of two-way communication that is probably the most desirable communication process.

In the shared-influence pattern, influence flows back and forth between any two people (see Figure 12–1). This requires two-way communication. It does not require either person to win a position from the other; rather, both sides must be willing to listen, explore, assess, and evaluate each other's ideas.

The shared two-way communication process is instrumental in helping people explore ideas. That is, by sharing information and ideas with others, people can learn the opinions of others and try to understand opposite points of view and/or reactions. Perhaps the epitome of this idea occurs among people romantically involved. Both partners want to influence the other favorably by giving and receiving information and ideas about how the other feels.

The Controlling Pattern

At the left-hand side of Figure 12–1 is the controlling pattern of the communications-influence model. The controlling pattern helps the communicator to influence the situation and stay in control of the person being communicated with. Supervisors do this to win an argument or to get other people to do what the supervisor wants them to do

There are two basic modes for controlling the process of influence through communication. One is to persuade others; the other is to dominate others.

Persuasion. When people use the controlling pattern, they try to assert their ideas (demonstrated in the model as "my way") over other people. Persuasion may be defined as showing the advantages of "my" course of action over alternative course of action ("your way"). Supervisors who are prone to tell other people what to do inevitably engage in the controlling pattern as they communicate with others. When this happens, there is a heavy emphasis on the supervisor telling other people how work has to be done, what's right, what's wrong, and what should happen next.

The Enforce-Dominate Mode. The other mode used in the controlling pattern occurs when supervisors with an extreme need for power want to assert authority over others and dominate them. Thus, they use the my-way technique. Such comments as, "The boss wants us to get this out by noon," and "I've listened to you people talk before, and it's never worked out, so here's the way we're going to do it" are expressions of the enforce-dominate style.

The Give-Up Pattern

The give-up pattern is the opposite of the controlling pattern. In this method, the individual surrenders most or all influence. This is done for a variety of reasons, such as to get the approval of others or as the result of despair over a situation.

The give-up pattern is an impoverished method of communication because it requires the acceptance of other ideas and precludes others from benefiting from the ideas of an individual who gives up and doesn't offer any feedback. Thus, the individual who is in the give-up mode simply acquiesces to the feelings, thoughts, desires, and ambitions of others. When individuals go along with what someone else wants, they give up something. But the strategy of "Okay, I don't agree with you, but I'll go along with your plan" is less costly to one's morale and influence with others than the submissive style of "Right or wrong, you're still the boss." In both situations, the loss of the individual's input to the organization is unfortunate, because nothing worthwhile materializes from the person who gives up.

When Supervisors Should Use the Give-Up Pattern. Most first-line supervisors are *not* inclined to use the give-up pattern. Most supervisors are strong-willed enough to engage in shared communication, or they will avoid confronting an issue (the avoidance pattern), or, usually with subordinates, they will exercise my-way control and tell the subordinate what to do utilizing the controlling pattern. However, there are occasions for using the give-up approach:

1. When the other person has most of the facts and experience required to handle the problem, and the supervisor has little or none.

2. When the problem is highly personal and is not work related, and it would be imprudent for the supervisor to say how he or she feels about the issue.

3. When the other person is highly motivated and/or emotionally committed to the problem and may not be rational.

4. When there is a high degree of risk that the supervisor cannot make a correct judgment or offer appropriate advice to an individual he or she works with.

The Avoidance Pattern

In the avoidance pattern of the communications-influence model, the communicator avoids any real contact with the person he or she communicates with. Like the other three patterns, the avoidance pattern can go in two directions. One path is flight. In the flight response, the individual flees the situation and abandons any communication efforts. Comments from the avoidance pattern include: "Well, I've done all I can," or "That's not my job."

The other avoidance pattern technique is the fight response. In the fight response, people think there is some communication because the individual exercises emotions and feelings. But, the avoidance reason, while a bit harder to understand in the fight mode, is nevertheless *avoidance* and, therefore, noncommunication. When individuals fight, they lash out (figuratively, for the most part) at another (safe) object against which they can displace their emotion—like the golfer who throws the golf clubs into the lake or the tennis player who throws the racket into the net at the frustration of having lost. Even though they lash out, they are not communicating anything other than their basic frustration. Typical comments that indicate the fight reaction in the avoidance pattern are "I'm fed up with what they're doing. Why the hell can't they straighten things out?" or "That sure was a stupid mistake." The fighter tends to build hostility toward the individual(s) to whom the comments were directed and rarely contributes to the problem-solving process.

The avoidance communications pattern is not helpful or desirable in most general communication processes. However, there are some cases where the technique is desirable. They include instances involving a legal, moral, or ethical issue that the supervisor lacks the knowledge or the ability to handle, or when an individual feels frustrated, fearful, or lacks understanding of the situation.

THE MAJOR NEED FOR SHARED, TWO-WAY COMMUNICATION

The supervisor cannot answer every question that occurs in the work relationship, but being employee-centered is useful in the two-way communication process. Nevertheless, there is always the problem that employees don't believe that they are being told the truth or else they feel they are not being told the *complete* truth.

With the problems inherent in communication, it is importnat that the supervisor understand what is *appropriate* for discussion. When talking with an employee, it is a good policy to communicate openly and honestly. This is also true in matters concerning things that may cause controversy, misunderstandings, problems for subordinates, or employee attitude and morale problems.

BODY LANGUAGE AND WHAT IT CAN TELL YOU (OR ABOUT YOU)

No discussion of effective communication for supervisors would be complete without some mention of body language. Body language includes thoughts communicated by an individual through the use of the body, voice, choice of words, expressions, and so forth (as opposed to what is actually said). Body language is the *way* we communicate, including the gestures, mannerisms, and inflections we use, as well as *what* we are saying and to whom. Body language is not limited to people who can understand it. In fact, body language is an important factor in the communication between man and beast. Consider a dog's behavior in a situation with a man who hates dogs. The man may say, in loving tones, "Come here, sweet animal, but the animal will not come. The animal knows that the man actually hates him, although he may not know why. He knows because of the way the man talks, the way he stands, and even the way he smells. In contrast, consider the situation where a hunter may get rough with a favorite bird dog after the dog has done an especially fine job of locating a downed bird in high grass. Everything the hunter is doing would be considered negative—swearing, slapping the dog, and so on, but the dog loves it and the hunter loves it, and they both know it. That is body language.

The Supervisor and Use of Body Language

All of us use body language. Controlling body language is primarily a matter of intent. However, there are some basic rules that a supervisor can use to become a more effective communicator. Communication ability is not just a function of what is said or written; rather it is unseen, felt, and sensed in the process. In body language, there are three kinds of difficulties that operate against effective communication of a message:

Improper Posture, Motion, or Balance of the Body. Supervisors who have awkward posture; who commit unusual, strange, or irregular motions; who are imbalanced in their bodies because they sit or stand too close to the employee; who commit unnecessary and irritating nervous movements such a making various distracting gestures and facial expressions, will find their ability to communicate with employees severely hampered. Not only are the close proximity, awkward motions, or posture of the supervisor's body annoying to the employee, but many imbalanced movements of the individual's body can cause the employee to focus more attention on the manager's body language than on what is being said. Supervisors must avoid any especially nervous or irritating habits in communicating. They must also not tip off others about their thoughts if they are negotiating with an employee or a union representative.

Improper Use of the Vocal Mechanism. The voice can also cause serious barriers in communicating. Poor breath control, causing loss of words and sounds, may only be part of the problem. Speaking too rapidly or too slowly can interfer with the chain of thoughts and cause misunderstanding. Speaking too softly or too loudly irritates and distracts the listener and gives him or her great difficulty in understanding what is being said. Finally, poor articulation, the slurring of words, and the use of incomplete sentences may cause a communication problem. Communication may falter because the words are not said or are not understood correctly, and communication will break down when body language is distracting.

Improper Choice of Words. The third kind of body language that may cause misunderstanding is improper use of words and phrases. A foreign accent, for example, can be distracting. A limited vocabulary may make the listener bored with a subject or distracted from what is said. In addition, profanity may distract the listener. Finally, poor grammar can create communication barriers that are difficult to overcome.

PARALANGUAGE

While the study of body language and the communications-influence model is important, it isn't always what is said or how it is said that counts. Sometimes, the total context is most importnat. Actions can speak louder than words, as in body language, but that isn't all. A supervisor must not say or *do* anything that could offend or put an employee at a disadvantage. The supervisor must learn what the employee thinks, feels, and recognize different forms of body language.

Avoiding Turnoffs

To assure that supervisors focus on what the employee says, they must not assume anything. When employees express what they believe, the supervisor should be thankful that they are honest enough to not avoid the issue. When an employee starts to say something, the supervisor may not always want to hear it. Because of that, the supervisor may indicate nonverbally that he or she doesn't want to listen by assuming a physical posture that discourages the employee from talking. Turning away from the employee and crossing one's arms, for example, usually communicates a don't-try-to-tell-me attitude.

When a supervisor assumes a posture that communicates a don't-try-to-tell-me attitude, for instance, it is called **paralanguage,** or partial communication. Words aren't said in paralanguage, but meanings are sent. It is like sign language. The other party knows what is happening, but nothing specific is said and body language doesn't explain it all. Paralanguage can, on the other hand, encourage an employee to open up, to express feelings, and the resulting two-way communication can improve an employee's morale.

False and Misleading Statements

Another example of paralanguage is an attempt to understand "where the employee is coming from." People may voice a feeling they do not really have, like an envious child apologizing for breaking a peer's toy that the first child wanted. The child, in apologizing, says the words "I'm sorry," but is inwardly happy. An inexperienced supervisor tries to understand the *real reason* someone is saying something because he or she may not mean what is being said.

Avoiding Overreacting

Jumping to hasty conclusions is also a problem. Effective supervisors never react too quickly to what is said. They don't get panic-stricken when someone says something they disagree with. When a supervisor panics, he or she reverts to the one-way, my-way control situation or the no-way avoidance pattern of the communication-influence model. A supervisor can also be too concerned about what an employee communicates with either words or paralanguage. However, it is wiser to be too concerned in two-way shared communication than to not be concerned enough.

KINDS OF SUPERVISORY COMMUNICATIONS PATTERNS

There are many supervisory communication patterns. Probably the best pattern is face-to-face communication, because it promotes shared, two-way communication and best utilizes paralanguage.

Written communications tend to be one-way and they usually result in my-way control. Written communications include memos, letters, reports, notices, posters, displays, and visual aids. Written communications are usually more formal than oral communication. It is advisable for first-line managers to avoid written communication when possible in favor of using the spoken word. The one exception to using oral communication is when future reference is necessary for what is being communicated.

Another more formal type of communication is the planned conference or group meeting with the supervisor's employees. A supervisor who is good at conducting meetings where information is encouraged from the participants may realize benefits of shared, two-way communication. This is especially true in quality-circle meetings. Unfortunately, even with the best intention, many problems occur in the communication process.

BARRIERS TO EFFECTIVE COMMUNICATIONS

There are numerous reasons that supervisors fail to communicate effectively or fail to receive messages correctly. These reasons can be broken into three classes: **psychological barriers, sociological barriers, and sensory barriers** within the individual. A careful review of these impediments to effective communication should help the manager in

DON'T TRY
TO CONFUSE
ME WITH FACTS.
MY MIND IS
MADE UP

Does this sign tell you something about
why some people do not communicate
very well?

understanding what some of the roadblocks are in effectively communicating with subordinates.

Psychological Barriers to Effective Communication

Failure to Understand Personal Motives. There are numerous psychological barriers that cause supervisors to be less than effective in communicating with employees. One major problem is when the supervisor does not understand his or her motives. If supervisors are not fully aware of what or why they want something done, they may be oblivious to subordinates' objections. Supervisors may fail to be thorough in communicating to employees exactly what they want done.

Tendency to Prejudge. Supervisors may have a tendency to prejudge or evaluate others; they show premature approval or disapproval. If the supervisor assumes that the subordinate is incompetent in handling a particular job, he or she may not be able to communicate effectively the need to do the work, even though the subordinate can handle the job. The supervisor's attitude is perceived as negative by the employee, while the employee's attitude is perceived as negative by the supervisor.

It's-Impossible Attitude. Some supervisors adopt an attitude that something is impossible or highly unlikely. In talking to subordinates, they communicate an air of "I don't see why you think that can be done. I don't think it can be done at all." When this happens, the subordinate naturally feels that what he or she is trying to tell the supervisor will not be accepted and, consequently, there is no point in raising questions or voicing objections. This is also true when the subordinate assumes a similar attitude toward the supervisor. If the subordinate thinks it can't be done, and the supervisor doesn't recognize this attitude, the supervisor may issue an order that will go totally unheeded because the subordinate has a psychological block against doing the job.

Assuming an Air of Incredulity.   Some supervisors fail at receiving messages correctly from subordinates because they don't believe what the subordinate is saying. Whenever they assume an attitude of "How did you ever get that notion?" Supervisors discourage subordinates from communicating effectively. This air of credulity can work the other way: A subordinate can also act as if he or she can't believe what the supervisor is saying. In either event, communication will break down and conflict will occur.

Being Flip about Matters.   Some supervisors are flip about serious situations and this stymies communication. If, for example, a boss laughs about or plays down the orders he or she gives to subordinates, they may not feel that the order was really meant seriously. The supervisor has scuttled his or her communication effectiveness. Again, the effective supervisor should be aware of similar behavior in subordinates or superiors. Serious statements can be misunderstood because of the seeming lack of importance placed on orders in how they are expressed.

Refusal to Listen.   Some supervisors grossly discourage communication from either supervisors or from subordinates, because they refuse to listen. If a person makes it clear that he or she wishes to hear no more about a subject, it is impossible to carry out effective communication with that individual. A point of impasse is reached quickly; words are not understood, messages are not read, and body language is not interpreted.

Feelings of Self-Righteousness.   Nothing has a more negative effect on communication between a boss and a subordinate than the individual who feels and acts self-righteously. Self-righteousness nearly always leads to heightened emotions and misinterpretations. False images are developed, people feel persecuted, and a general tone of uncooperativeness develops. It is not always possible to avoid emotional barriers in communicating, but effective supervisors always guard against the trap of self-righteousness.

Rejection of a Source as Being Valid.   Some supervisors fail to communicate effectively because they worry too much about the source of information being communicated to them. Many times, in listening to employees, they feel that a particular person couldn't know something or is too naive to communicate a particular idea to them. As a result, supervisors can categorically reject what is being told to them; later, they realize their mistake.

The Know-It-All Problem. Some supervisors consider themselves more knowledgeable about their work than anyone else in the organization. They assume an air of superiority toward employees and fail to elicit useful responses. Often, they fail to listen to employees because they feel that employees don't know what they are talking about. This is a form of prejudgement, but it is different from simply assuming that someone is ignorant.

The I'm-No-Good Syndrome. Another cause of ineffective communication for many supervisors is their failure to recognize employees who feel inferior or intimidated. Just as the supervisor can feel superior and lord over those who report to him or her, many employees sometimes feel inferior toward their bosses and feel that they cannot understand, cannot adjust to, or cannot learn what the boss is trying to tell them. Many employees feel they cannot do the job and consequently they fail. The results are practically always catastrophic, and the source of the problem resides in the supervisor's inability to communicate and the subordinate's inability to understand or listen effectively.

Sociological Barriers to Effective Communication

The Generation Gap. Some supervisors fail at communicating effectively because of the generation gap. Many times, older persons have difficulty communicating with younger people. This is not because the two age groups don't understand each other. They both understand the words. The problem is one of *acceptance* rather than definition. In many cases, the generation gap manifests itself as if people came from different cultures. The problem is sociological in that neither party tries to understand the other because they feel so alienated from each other.

False Role Expectations. Most people feel that others in our society should play a definite role. For example, subordinates typically expect bosses to behave in a particular way. Bosses, in turn, expect subordinates to act in a particular way. When neither behaves accordingly, it can cause suspicion, distrust, and an ultimate communication breakdown. The supervisor who acts out of his or her role (for example, by playing big brother) can seriously disturb the relationship with a subordinate. Similarly the subordinate who acts out of his or her role (say, by assuming to be next in command) may have difficulty in effectively communicating with the boss.

Protection of One's Prestige.   Many people have a definite idea of what their position is or ought to be in society and in the work community. This usually means that they have a personal commitment to protecting their perceived role and its importance. Whenever they view something as a threat to this role, it may cause a communication breakdown. Be it from a superior or a subordinate, if a person feels he or she is being discriminated against, that person develops mental blocks against listening to what is being said or else builds up tremendous resentment toward the communicator and is unwilling to understand the communication.

Two Minds, Two Interpretations.   Not all people interpret messages in the same way. What is seen, heard, smelled, touched, and understood can vary greatly. One person may feel that a pat on the back is given in good faith with friendly gusto; another individual may feel offended by the same pat on the back, as if it were condescending. We perceive things as a function of what we hear, see, smell, touch and in relation to our perceptions of the surroundings.

If an environment is perceived as friendly, we feel more comfortable and intepret things in a good light. If our surroundings appear hostile, our perceptions may be defensive. Good communications can be distorted by the physical setting and how the individual perceives the environment. One physical setting may connote various ideas in different people's minds. One person may get worried by being called in by the boss; another person may be elated at a similar call.

Sensory Barriers to Effective Communications

We must not overlook one of the most serious causes of miscommunication—some form of sensory inadequacy. For example, if a person is hard of hearing or has poor vision, he or she will not be able to hear or read as effectively as others. Furthermore, that individual may not be as alert to surroundings (in respect to sensory inadequacies), yet he or she may be more alert in terms of other senses due to overcompensation. Thus, good communication between a boss and a subordinate involves more than simply hearing and seeing. Any sensory defect can hinder how a person perceives messages. A person who is hard of hearing may feel that the supervisor deliberately talks in low tones so that the hard-of-hearing employee cannot hear. This can build tremendous resentment with a consequent disruption in work. An employee with poor hearing may feel overly gratified toward a boss who goes out of his or her way to talk loudly, or he or she may feel the boss who talks in loud tones is oversolicitous. There is no set answer to the **sensory barrier** problem, but the good supervisor must be sensitive to it and make necessary personal adjustments.

BRIDGES TO GOOD COMMUNICATION

The list of barriers to effective communication at work is not meant to be exhaustive. However, it helps the supervisor recognize that good communication is not easy. If the supervisor is to be effective in communicating, he or she must know the causes of communication problems.

No matter what is done in trying to communicate, in all likelihood, many of the aforementioned communication problems will still exist. There is no sure method of effective communication. If the supervisor follows some basic rules, he or she may be able to get the message across effectively. Given that the typical supervisor may spend 70 percent of his or her time communicating, it is well worth a try. Here are some **communication bridges:**

The Need for Empathy

One of the first skills in effective communication is to be conscious of the need to empathize. To empathize means truly understanding the feelings of others. Empathy means that supervisors must be able to understand as best they can the opinions and attitudes of employees. Supervisors who can sense the feelings of employees and clients will try to express themselves in ways that are meaningful and understandable.

Genuine Concern for the Problems and Difficulties Faced by Others

A second bridge to effective communication is having a genuine concern for the person you communicate with. Whether a supervisor tells employees that it is time for them to go on a coffee break or critizes employees for having ruined a sale, he or she should be concerned about the effect of the message on employees. Being blind to the overall effect can cause serious blocks to effective communication. However, if there is a genuine concern for the employee expressed in an understandable fashion, the supervisor should have little difficulty in communicating effectively.

Avoidance of Defensiveness

Some supervisors fail in communicating with subordinates because they are defensive. They worry that the employee will not get the job done, they worry that the employee will think they are unreasonable, and so forth. Whatever they are defensive about, if that feeling surfaces in how they communicate with subordinates, a breakdown in rapport may occur. When such defensiveness is obvious to the subordinate, he or she is likely to misinterpret what the superior is trying to say.

Being Knowledgeable

Another bridge to effective communication between a manager and employees comes from being knowledgeable. When the supervisor knows what he or she is talking about, there can be more effective communication about the how, when and why of what needs to be done. However, a word of caution is needed—the supervisor must avoid a know-it-all attitude.

Avoidance of Bias and Prejudice

Address the employee in an unbiased and unprejudiced manner. A supervisor may tell an individual to do something, but if he or she suggests via body language, tonal quality, or other physical symbols that the subordinate is the wrong race, sex, or religion to handle the job, the supervisor will not get compliance. Instead, major communications problems will surface. The real key to effective communication is the avoidance of bias and prejudice.

Practice Listening

Any supervisor wanting to communicate with subordinates effectively must listen to them when they voice any feelings, observations, or objections concerning the job. **Good listening** is a tough job. However, poor listening limits the effectiveness of communication. Alert listening and perception of the subordinate's feedback will enhance the supervisor's communication.

Being Particular about the Location Used When Communicating

It is one thing to communicate in a quiet office. It is something else to try to communicate to an employee on a foundry floor, at a construction site, or in front of any onlookers in a store, restaurant, hotel, or other service establishment. There is a right place and a wrong place to conduct effective communication. *Sometimes* the exigencies of a particular situation preclude calling an employee off to a quiet little nook to discuss problems. Effective supervisors can often do something about where and how they talk to their employees. The supervisor must know what makes a good place for more effective communication. Another item to consider is the time of day—it may be just as important as the place picked for communicating to an employee.

HOW TO VERIFY COMMUNICATIONS EFFECTIVENESS

Many supervisors assume that once something is said that's all that needs to be done. Few people have a perfect memory, however, and something is always overlooked or forgotten. The supervisor who becomes impatient or reluctant to repeat messages that have been given to subordinates will find the effectiveness of his or her communication limited. Few people resent repetition if it is not overdone. This is especially true if something was missed or forgotten the first time. The supervisor should repeat messages willingly if there have been misinterpretations or portions forgotten.

If the judge is hearing your case, do you want the judge to be a good listener? Shouldn't you, as a supervisor, be a good listener, too?

Using the Trick of Having Messages Repeated

If you ask someone to repeat to you what they heard, you can often validate whether or not your message was received correctly. Of course, if the message is repeated in the exact words, there is the chance that the message has only been memorized but not understood. Therefore, a sure-fire scheme to ensure and verify communication is to ask the receiver to repeat to the sender what the message was. If the receiver of the message can repeat the message accurately to the sender, especially in different terms, the sender can be reasonably assured that the message was properly interpreted.

The foregoing idea does not ensure *compliance* with the message, but it *does* mean that the message was properly understood. Many supervisors who are effective communicators will not only ask subordinates to repeat certain messages, but they will also ask them to state those messages in different terms. Thus, subordinates demonstrate an understanding of a message's intent.

Observing Others

Most of us know that we learn through actual experience and observation of other people. The child learns certain manners and gestures from parents; the entertainer learns certain moves from watching other entertainers. Why not note how things are perceived by the persons you communicate with? What happens if an individual says yes but frowns? What happens if an individual smiles sardonically while agreeing to an order that you know he or she doesn't like? We have all seen a time when someone has agreed to do something verbally that we knew they were not committed to or would not do well.

The only way such obvious breakdowns in communication can be interpreted is by careful observation. Supervisors should learn to make mental notes of weaknesses and strengths of individuals, especially their idiosyncracies and other behavioral patterns that tip off whether or not they are listening and how they interpret what they are told. Any supervisor who is capable of avoiding such breakdowns in communication with subordinates or superiors will go a long way toward avoiding misunderstanding.

Using Memos

Years ago it was stated that "oral messages don't go." Many people have advocated that if supervisors are really serious about communicating they should write it down. Written messages can be useful or they can be a waste of time. It depends on the situation and the reason. One manager wrote memos to himself (which isn't necessarily so bad), but went to the extent of having his secretary type them up!

Written messages are more permanent and less apt to be forgotten or overlooked. However, they are also more rigid. They lose the feeling of warmth and humanness. Written messages can also leave unsaid what should have been said; they provide little opportunity to be clarified. They can also be inaccurate and misinterpreted. Because of the shortcomings of written memos, the supervisor must not always write out messages. Important messages can be committed to written form to eliminate some problems of spoken words. But, the supervisor should know the shortcomings of written messages.

Although supervisors might not write out everything, they can improve their note-taking capability. When a person receives instructions and takes notes, he or she is less apt to forget what was said. Furthermore, the note taker can embellish or add to those notes. The only problem with taking notes in an effort to improve communication is that some people, in writing notes, fail to listen or perceive other items that are happening or being told to them. Many students have failed examinations because while they were writing detailed notes about one idea they failed to hear the new idea.

DEVELOPING LISTENING SKILLS— THE KEY TO SUPERVISORY AWARENESS

No matter how aware we are of the barriers to effective communication and the bridges that help overcome those barriers, there is one skill that many supervisors still lack—effective listening. According to Erle Savage, senior partner of the Pidgeon-Savage-Lewis Corporation of Minneapolis, there is a tremendous loss of information between a manager and subordinates. In fact, supervisors' supervisors tend to receive only about 30 percent of the information transmitted to them by upper management in the organization. Furthermore, they were, in turn, ineffective at passing on information; their subordinates received only about two-thirds of the information they *did* get. First-line supervisors weren't any better, either.

Such a tremendous breakdown in communication, with the concomitant loss of information about what happens in the organization, is a result of ineffective listening. Most people feel that all it takes to be a good listener is to wash one's ears and pay attention to what one is being told. Unfortunately, such a prescription does not work. There are many reasons why we fail to heed what is communicated to us, and we are just as susceptible to these problems as anyone else in the organization.

How to Improve Your Listening Skills—10 Rules for Good Listening

Improving listening skills is easy. The techniques are essentially the same; all one needs to do is practice.

Be Interested in the Subject.   One item that can really impair listening skills is not being interested in the subject one is listening to. If someone thinks, ''I am not interested in the details of that job,'' or, ''That doesn't apply to me, so I am not going to pay any attention; I am just going to think about my fishing trip next week,'' he or she will not be an effective listener no matter what is said.

Overlook Any Distractions Concerning How the Message Is Delivered.   No one likes to listen to things that are irritating. For example, some of us don't like to listen to persons with speech impediments and we may ''tune them out.'' But consider the consequences of tuning out a message from a stutterer who screams at you, ''Run! Run! The . . . the dam br-br-broke.'' Failure to heed the message could result in your death. It is one problem to be irritated by a poorly delivered message, but it is not sensible to let such irritants keep you from paying attention to what is being said.

Stay Relaxed.   Many supervisors get overstimulated about various items. They don't like it if someone picks on their pet peeves or attacks any of their sacred convictions. As a result, some supervisors fail to listen when they hear certain words, statements, opinions, or suggestions. For example, if one subordinate says, ''That crummy idiot didn't do his job,'' and you happen to be a compassionate person, you may fail to listen to the bigoted message. While it may be commendable to be unbiased and charitable toward others, it is still important to listen to what happens. When there are important messages to be communicated, people should not let personal biases or preferences keep them from paying attention to what the message is.

Try to Get the Message, Not the Facts.   Many people want only the facts. However, simply going after the facts does not ensure that you will get the message. Studies show that people who listen for the total message tend to get far more of the information correctly—and retain that information far longer—than people who concentrate on detail. Consider how confusing it would be for someone to explain the rules of college football if you had never seen a college football game. Getting the facts, without seeing the game played, doesn't contribute much to an understanding of the game. Remember, details can always be filled in later if one gets the basic message.

Try to Understand the System Used to Communicate the Message. Many people feel that messages can be communicated in only one form. In speaking, for example, one must start with a subject, then a verb, and then the object of the sentence. While rules of good grammer help with effective communication, they are only an aid. Many languages—German, for example—start with the verb, then the subject, and then the object of the sentence.

In short, attempting to mold everything into a rigid (as opposed to logical) format that fits rules *you* learned may preclude you, as a listener, from getting the message. Invariably, people will talk and write in certain ways. While talking and writing may not always follow rules of good grammar, they can still get to the point. If you were working in a restaurant and a foreigner came in and said, "Hungry I am. That I want," and pointed to something on the menu, you could understand what the foreigner was trying to communicate. Understanding is the name of the game in effective communication.

If You Are Listening, Listen. Failure to pay attention is one of the most grievous errors made in communicating. It is especially serious when it is done deliberately. How many times has the scene been played where the wife hears the husband grunting, "Unha, unha," while she tries to discuss a matter with him knowing he isn't listening? It is usually obvious to a speaker if someone is not paying attention. This is especially true when listeners are faking attention. Not only does faking attention cause other breakdowns in interpersonal relationships between the speaker and the listener, it means that the faker will not get the message. In short, if you should be listening, pay attention! Don't mentally tune out the speaker or feel that you can con them into thinking that you are listening when you are not.

Avoid Unnecessary Distractions. As a listener, you may not always be able to pick the place where you must do your listening. With such handicaps to effective listening, you must try harder to overcome other difficulties by being more attentive. Failure to do so means that you could get the wrong message.

Clarify in Your Mind What Is Being Told to You.   Many persons mentally try to avoid technical items. They sometimes don't understand what they are told, and they are afraid that they cannot possibly understand. While some persons cannot understand what is told to them, this rarely happens in a work situation. If employees are fit for their job, they usually can understand what they are told. Persons who fall into the habit of saying "I can't understand anyway" are simply giving up. They may never be effective communicators.

Overcome Slurs.   Many times, we can be completely distracted in listening to other people because of slurs or slights we perceive from them. Sometimes these slurs are direct—such as racial or ethnic slurs. However, many other forms of slighting can also occur that are not as obvious. Some people get emotionally distraught if they are in a meeting or conference where the leader doesn't recognize them or minimizes their suggestions or input. When this happens, many people become resentful and rebellious. This rebellion results in their total rejection of the speaker, the meeting, and the message being communicated. While it is never fun to be involved in such situations, they do occur. Effective communicators and managers will not let such slurs overwhelm them and their ability to understand the messages that are being communicated.

Using Thought Power.   The average English-speaking person talks approximately 125 words per minute, while he or she can think at a speed of 400–600 words per minute. The ratio of average talking speed to average thinking speed is about 4:1. This ability gives us a tremendous amount of thought power that we can use in listening to someone. If listeners use this thinking power, they can listen to what a speaker says, reflect upon what the speaker has said, and have time left to predict what the speaker is *going* to say. In this manner the listener can get the whole message in mind and be actively involved in the communication process.

The rules for active listening are not easy to follow. If the typical supervisor fails to receive 70 percent of the information sent down by top levels of management and spends nearly 70 percent of the time communicating, it is imperative that listening skills be fully utilized. This, in turn, enables the first-line manager to be a more effective communicator, which will ultimately make him or her more valuable to the organization.

Things to Remember

1. Effective communication is an essential ingredient of good management. It requires the ability both to understand and to be understood.

2. Communication processes are primarily influence processes.

3. There are four primary influence patterns:
   a. Shared communication patterns
   b. Controlling patterns
   c. Avoidance patterns
   d. Give-up patterns

4. Body language is as important as spoken language.

5. Paralanguage includes the total context of the communication.

6. Barriers to communication include psychological, sociological, and sensory.

7. Bridges to communication barriers include empathy, concern for others, avoidance of defensiveness, being knowledgeable, avoidance of bias and prejudice, listening practice, and appropriate location.

8. Learning good listening habits is an essential ingredient of effective communication.

9. The total message is more important than just the facts.

Key Words

communication
psychological barriers
sociological barriers
sensory barriers
essential bridges
good listening
paralanguage
turnoffs
overreacting
communication patterns
communication bridges

Self-Assessment

This test is somewhat different than those tests found in other chapters. It measures how you feel about your communication skills compared to others. Communication involves understanding and being understood. In your ability to understand and be understood, compare yourself to the following people. As you make comparisons, think of your present place of work or a place you have previously worked. Comparisons are made by giving yourself a score of 1–6 for each of the categories of comparison. If you feel you are less skilled in understanding and being understood than the name in the category, mark a 1, 2, or 3 depending on the strength of your comparisons. If, on the other hand, you are more skilled in understanding and being understood than the name in the category, mark a 4, 5, or 6 depending on the strength of your comparison.

Category	Rating (1–6)
Your immediate boss.	_____
Others at your level.	_____
Those with lower rank or less seniority.	_____
All people in the organization.	_____
Total Score	_____

Your instructor will explain how to evaluate your score.

CASES

Listen Closely

Two candidates were competing for final selection as Chief of Police: Bill Tunstall, a veteran of many years, and Ron Bates, who was younger, better educated, and better liked. Both men were captains and both had distinguished records. When Ron was selected by the Columbia City Council, Bill Tunstall did not try to hide his bitterness. "A college education doesn't make a good cop. Experience does, and I have experience." Although he had always worked well with Ron, some of his bitterness was directed toward Ron's relative youth and formal education.

In a recent meeting with his top staff, including Bill Tunstall, Ron announced, "We are going to reorganize how beats are assigned. Each area of town will have its own team and team leader. Our underlying motive is for police officers to work in the same area and become well acquainted with local citizens, be able to identify outsiders, and establish credibility in the community. Instead of our usual morning meetings for assignments, each team will meet and map out its own plan to meet the needs of the area to which it is assigned." After the meeting, all of the top officers except Tunstall congratulated Ron on the new plan.

In a meeting later that day, with his own group of lower-level officers, Bill repeated Ron's message. "Here we go again," he stated in a sarcastic voice. "We're going to have a reorganization," he said as he paused and turned his fist in a thumbs down sign, "of how beats are assigned. "His face and voice registered disgust. "Each area of town" (at this point, Bill drew a laugh by making a tiny square on the chalkboard behind him) "will have its own team and team leader." Here, Bill drew another laugh for the mock surprise on his face. The meeting continued in the same vein as Bill used the exact words Ron had delivered in a very different fashion.

The next day, headlines on the Columbia *Courier* read, "COUNCIL AND TOP POLICE OFFICERS ENDORSE REORGANIZATION—COPS HATE IT."

1. How did Bill change Ron's message?

2. In what ways do body language and paralanguage modify meanings?

3. If asked what he said to his group of police officers, how would Bill Tunstall reply?

People Don't Listen

Most people have had amusing and unamusing experiences with mistaken messages. Several years ago, I tried to sell a used radial-arm saw in order to replace it with a newer model. I called a local company that published a weekly classified booklet and asked that my 10-inch, radial-arm saw be advertised in the next issue. To my surprise, the ad appeared in the following issue. It stated, "Radio alarm saw 10 inches. Call after 5."

A friend of mine and I just missed an excursion train through part of a mountain park we both wanted to see. We decided to exchange our tickets for the late afternoon tour. As we neared the ticket counter, one of the guides approached and said, "Missed your train?" My friend, whose hearing is not the best, stuck out his hand and replied, "Glad to meet you Mister Paine, my name is Harold James."

One of the more publicized communication errors occurred approximately 40 years ago at the end of World War II. After the bombing of Tokyo by American forces and the issuing of a surrender-or-else ultimatum, the Japanese announced a policy of *mokusatsu* in their newspapers. *Mokusatsu* has two meanings in Japanese. It can be interpreted as "no comment," meaning that more time is needed to make a decision, or it can mean "ignore," a refusal to recognize your message. The Japanese diet (ruling body) needed additional time to make decisions on the terms of surrender and meant the "no comment" interpretation to be used. American translators however, interpreted the message as "ignore."

1. Give examples of communication misunderstandings you have experienced.

2. What barriers caused the misinterpretations to occur?

3. Can you give examples of deliberate misinterpretations of messages?

13

Resolving Conflict and Building Strong Working Relationships

Thought Starter

Many first-line managers spend only about 35 percent of their time with the people who report directly to them. Some of the remaining 65 percent of their time is spent on administrative duties, but most of it is spent in meetings with other managers, specialists such as budget and cost accountants, safety inspectors and engineers, customers, representatives from various vendors, union officers, and a wide spectrum of others. This is particularly true of large, complex organizations with high demands on all management personnel.

To get work done, it means that supervisors must build effective working relations with members of their work group and with all outside contacts. Rivalries often exist between similar departments and friction occurs. In other instances, strong, cooperative, and supportive relationships develop that have benefits for all segments of the organization.

In Chapter 13 you will learn:

☐ No one works alone. Jobs are interdependent; each supports the other in some fashion.

☐ Decisions and actions in any part of an organization affect the other parts.

☐ Establishing effective working relationships with other segments of the organization is essential.

☐ At least four strategies are possible in resolving conflict.

"Betty, is there any way you can help me with this one?" asked Pete Langley over the telephone. "If I don't get this data by tomorrow morning the shucks will hit the fan. Arlene needs it for her presentation to the top brass and she's already asked for it twice."

"Pete," replied Betty, "you know we have a priority system and there are four jobs ahead of yours. You don't even have an approved work order. What could I charge it to?"

"Tell you what," answered Pete. "Next time you are short on data entry help, I'll send Mike over for a couple of hours. He's one of the best, even though he works for me now. Not only that, but you trained him."

"Well, OK, you'll get your report, Pete, but I want that approved work authorization before Monday morning," said Betty.

A familiar phrase in politics is the Latin quid pro quo. It literally means something for something. In more common organizational politics is means "You scratch my back, I'll scratch yours." It's the basis for much of what occurs in most organizations.

CONFLICT AND STRESS AT WORK

Many managers feel that they are alone in their work and that they have no one to go to when they need help with their activities. They know they can talk with managers and that they can occasionally find answers in working with other departments. But, for the most part, many supervisors feel that they alone are totally responsible for the organization and for getting results.

307

One of the more challenging yet often overlooked jobs that supervisors must engage in is working effectively with others at their own level or at a higher level. No supervisor is an island. He or she must relate with other supervisors, department heads, and specialists within the organization, as well as with subordinates and superiors.

All kinds of **stress** and **conflict** occur at work. These situations must be handled well by supervisors. Yet, many people don't know how to handle conflict when it arises; therefore, they suffer from tremendous stress. Especially when difficult situations arise, it is common for supervisors to feel that they are working alone. Enmeshed in their workaday responsibilities, they feel solely responsible for getting results. They feel the wrath of higher levels of management when problems occur. Concern for their own responsibilities, however, often blinds them to other parts of the organization's operations.

This blindness is not a matter of shortsightedness or not caring. Rather, it occurs because supervisors are so busy that they don't have time to look around and conceptually integrate the various aspects of the operation, that is, to see the big picture. This attention to their own work often creates a my-department-is-the-only-one attitude with some supervisors.

WHY BOSSES IGNORE OTHERS' PROBLEMS

Why would a supervisor feel that his or her department is the only one that really matters? Is it because of smugness, conceit, arrogance or ignorance of the contribution of others? Or, is it because the supervisor is too busy and wants, above all, to do a good job? The answer is probably none of these. The supervisor's tunnel vision often results from being comfortable with what he or she understands and, therefore, places the most importance on.

For example, if you are in a part of the nation that has adequate water, you may be oblivious to the problem of water rights in more arid states. Conversely, residents of arid states tend to think that the issue of water rights is a significant problem.

In other words, while we often are aware of other person's problems, somehow their problems don't seem important. Perhaps the problem is best summarized in an old joke: A recession is when your neighbor is unemployed, and a depression is when you're unemployed. What is necessary to remedy the situation? Essentially, the supervisor must develop an awareness of the importance of other functions, operations, and activities within the organization.

INTERDEPARTMENTAL RIVALRY

Home Office versus Field Force

Interdepartmental rivalry might be the best term to describe a classic problem in organizations. For example, the home office and employees in the field are often at odds. Home office personnel feel that their activities are the most important: "After all, if we don't control those guys in the field, we'll be in trouble with our customers. We'll lose all our sales and the company will go down the drain." Field personnel, however, state: "If we listen to those guys in the home office, we'll be lucky to make any sales. They don't know what is happening out here."

Purchasing versus Auditing

The rivalry between the home office and the field force is classic, and there are other standing rivalries—for example, the purchasing department versus the auditing department. The purchasing department has to get material, parts, machinery, and equipment to the production people so that they can produce a product, but the auditing department inhibits the purchasing department. The auditing department always wants to see approved purchase orders. The auditing department doesn't want to see anything bought that doesn't have three firm bids solicited. The auditing department has rules and regulations that, if not followed, mean that favorite customers are not paid, ill will is created with suppliers, and so forth. The auditing department has the responsibility to the organization's shareholders: "If we don't control the purse strings adequately, this company will be in chaos."

Production versus Sales

Another standing feud often exists between production and sales. The sales department promises to deliver everything yesterday; the production department knows it will be six months before they finish the job they're on and that it's ridiculous to speak of a delivery schedule of anything less than between now and next year.

Everybody against Everybody

And so it goes. There are other classic rivalries that create conflict. One is quality control people versus production people; another are the feuds between the people in data processing and the people in the finance department. Many of these traditional rivalries are wholesome if they do not get out of hand, which is the first-line supervisor's job. This means that the supervisor must know the functions and activities of other departments that his or her department interacts with. It's not necessary that a shop supervisor completely understand all of the quality assurance engineer's problems—just understand them a little. But the quid pro quo is that the quality assurance engineer must also understand the problems of production and, while not passing inferior or unacceptable production, work with that production supervisor to accommodate both sets of needs and, above all else, to satisfy the customer.

This is also true concerning the purchasing and auditing departments. The auditors are the shepherds of the corporate funds. But, the purchasing department has to spend money so that the organization can engage in its activities. The acquisition of materials needs to be controlled, but problems always surface. Customers get into most-favored positions. Sometimes customers are sole suppliers and have to be treated very nicely. Supervisors who openly discuss their interdepartmental problems can make giant strides toward alleviating conflicts.

The same remedy applies to the rivalry between production and sales. While people in sales want to promise anything that the customer wants, they must understand that production is not a magic act. There are certain limitations of material, machinery, equipment, back orders, and the like. Production can't just drop one job to satisfy a customer because doing so is usually at the risk of dissatisfying another customer.

WHY SUPERVISORS ARE NOT ALONE ON THE JOB

All large organizations employ a number of managers, supervisors, foremen, and other personnel. How these supervisors relate with each other is not merely a matter of camaraderie, good fellowship, or the sharing of common experiences at work. It is improper for the supervisor to feel that he or she is alone on the job. Most supervisors are far more dependent on *others at their own or higher level* in the organization than they realize.

Consider that in most larger companies and organizations, many of the operating departments must interact with each other if the job is to be done correctly. What happens if a supervisor in department A decides to reschedule a work sequence that will have a direct effect on the work schedules of another department. Let us assume something simple—say the supervisor of department A decides to schedule vacations for 20 percent of his or her employees during the first two weeks of August and 20 percent during the last two weeks of August, whereas only 10 percent had been permitted to be gone at any time in the past.

Such a shift in schedules will cause an *additional* 10 percent cutback in the production of department A in August. Production will be cut back by 10 percent because of usual vacations plus 10 percent more because of the added 10 percent of the work force on vacation from department A during August. If another unit, department Z, is *dependent* on the production of department A to do its work, that extra 10 percent cutback in hours will adversely affect department Z's production schedule.

If the supervisor of department A neglects to inform the supervisor of department Z of the change, the supervisor in department Z will have more employees at work than required (assuming there is no backlog of work). This will raise department Z's per unit labor costs or force department Z to lay off people. Furthermore, the supervisor in department Z will have to decide what to do about production schedules for department Z's people when department A returns to work in full force. Should the supervisor in department Z then schedule overtime work?

The impact and importance of this example on the second supervisor (department Z) is obvious. The problem could be avoided, however, if both supervisors planned ahead recognizing that vacation schedules must be coordinated. That is precisely the point! There *must be* **interaction** among supervisors that provides **interdepartmental cooperation.**

HOW TO DETERMINE WHAT INTERACTION IS NECESSARY

Given that many departments may be dependent on each other— seldom is A dependent on B and only B, and so forth—supervisory cooperation can be complex. A single supervisory decision can overwhelm the total organization. The reasons can be oversimplified to a lack of careful communication between supervisors. Yet, the solution is not as simple as improving communications. In a complex organization, if one supervisor feels separate and removed from other parts of the organization, myriad problems can be generated.

For the supervisor to recognize whom he or she is dependent on and interdependent with in the organization, supervisors must know the different work relationships on the job. The best way to do this is to analyze the job by asking questions such as:

1. What work from other departments, organizations, and persons precedes the work in my department?

2. What work from other individuals, departments, and organizations follows the work in my department?

3. Who are the other supervisors whose units do work similar to work in my department?

4. What actions and activities of my department have an effect on or exemplary value for all supervisors and departments within the organization?

5. How does my personal and departmental performance affect my superiors' performance of their jobs?

6. What effect might my department's actions have on my employees or the employees in other parts of the organization?

The Need to Get Along with Other Supervisors

Experienced supervisors know that it is extremely difficult for supervisors to cooperate with each other at all times. Often, it is more difficult for supervisors to cooperate with each other than it is for their subordinates to cooperate with each other. The reasons for this difficulty are their achievement needs, what they want to do, and what they feel is necessary. Effective supervisors want their units to perform well. As a result, most supervisors feel that what their department does is extremely important, often, they feel that their work should take precedence over other matters. This often causes problems with other supervisors who feel the same way. Let's look at what happened at a large midwestern mail order establishment a few years ago.

CASE HISTORY

A supervisor came to work on a Monday morning and discovered that the fire sprinkler system had been triggered over the weekend and had doused much of the paperwork left on employees' desks. Most of the paperwork involved mail orders for products that the company was selling. Needless to say, everyone in the department was upset, and the amount of cleaning and deciphering was overwhelming. Adding to their irritation was having to straighten up a mess that should not have occurred.

Close investigation disclosed another problem. The sprinkling system had been activated because the heating system had gone awry and had caused the building to get so hot that it triggered the automatic sprinkling mechanisms. The maintenance department was also upset about the situation, but for a different reason—problems in the boiler room and with the heating system. Unfortunately, because of the building's design, the repair of the boiler room problem required that the service people go through the mail-order room to work in the boiler room. This fact antagonized the already unhappy supervisor of the mail-room operations because it slowed their cleaning process. As a result, he became uncooperative toward the maintenance superintendent, who was trying to restore the heating system to satisfactory operation. Every effort made by the maintenance supervisor seemed to complicate the problems of the mail order supervisor, and the two were not speaking to each other by noon of the first day.

The situation should not have occurred, but it did. When emotions are not high, people can look at a situation and see how pointless and absurd some arguments are. But when personal involvement in the problem occurs, it is difficult to be wholly objective. How can the conscientious supervisor avoid conflicts at work or at least avoid an ineffective situation? A few guidelines may be beneficial for the new supervisor.

COPING WITH CONFLICT SITUATIONS

Wondering how to win in a conflict situation at work is always of interest to supervisors. Most supervisors know that conflicts arise between most supervisors because of their tremendous achievement drives. They all have a sincere desire to win. To win in conflict situations, one must try not to force others to lose.

Many scholars in recent years have studied organizational behavior and have decided that there are four types of **conflict resolution** in various situations between people: (1) **win/win solutions,** where both persons win; (2) **win/lose solutions,** where one person wins and the other person loses; (3) **lose/win solutions,** where one person loses and the other person wins; and (4) **lose/lose solutions,** where both persons lose. Only the first choice—the win/win attitude—is acceptable in today's working community if a supervisor is to be successful.

To understand the solutions, consider the attitudes that people bring to work. Supervisors instinctively have a tremendous desire to win. That desire makes them good supervisors. Unfortunately, that desire is sometimes converted into a desire to beat other people. This forces the supervisor to have a win/lose attitude. Win/win attitudes mean that the other person doesn't have to lose. Supervisors with a win/win attitude feel that they will win and that other persons will also win. When two supervisors are in a conflict situation and *both* have a win/lose (or lose/win) attitude, the outcome is fairly predictable: one person will win and the other person will lose—or they both will lose. It is impossible for both supervisors to win in this situation, especially if one supervisor is intent on beating the other. In fact, many supervisors who have an extreme win/ lose attitude also feel that if they must lose anything, they intend that the other person loses something as well. Many supervisory relationships are nothing more than a "I will win and you will lose, or we will both lose together" situation, *which means that a lot is lost in the organization.*

The Intelligent Way out of Conflict

The only effective way out of any serious conflict between two supervisors, department heads, or other individuals is for them to assume an attitude that everyone can win. The supervisor who assumes a win/win attitude wants to win. But he or she also recognizes that other supervisors (or workers) need to win, too, if they are to be satisfied with the situation and not set out to get the first supervisor.

The win/win attitude is the basic rule that most labor arbitrators follow to get harmony between companies and unions. For example, an employee who files a grievance under a union contract may have been wrong because he or she did not do a job that the supervisor assigned. The supervisor, in making the job assignment, may have been unduly harsh and undiplomatic in making that assignment and may have violated the *unwritten* law that all employees take turns doing an especially undesirable job. The supervisor could have accidentally assigned the same job to the same person three days in succession. Who is at fault— the employee for refusing to do the job or the supervisor? Both persons are at fault. The question in the arbitrator's mind, however, is how can each person win?

Many arbitrators remember win/win solutions when it is obvious that both sides have reasonable arguments for what they did. While some labor situations are of the win/lose variety (an employee hit a supervisor and must be discharged, or the company erred in promoting a person with less seniority over a person with more seniority), seldom are the cases so clear-cut. Consequently, in any kind of conflict, the supervisor is better off recognizing that the conflict exists and thinking about how he or she can best resolve the conflict so that both parties win. If both parties in the conflict assume a win/win attitude, the results will be more acceptable to each side.

Some General Guidelines for Conflict Situations

It is one thing to talk about resolving conflict from theory; it is something else to keep cool in a conflict situation. We must have a few guidelines concerning how to maintain dignity and aplomb when tempers are high and arguments occur.

1. Always Avoid Out-and-Out Fighting. Some people enjoy a good fight. This is especially true when they are around archenemies and have developed animosities and deep personal hatreds over the years. But, if two supervisors continually fight with each other, going out of their way to thwart each other's efforts, the situation usually worsens. If managers really want to analyze their performance and effectiveness in an organization, they must carefully question themselves about how they work with other people. Do they draw lines and dare people to step over them, or do they work to cooperate with other individuals?

2. Avoid Petulance and Impatience. Whenever a supervisor gets involved in today's competitive business world, it is easy to become impatient with others. This is especially true when plans go awry, and when it looks as if other people are deliberately sabotaging each other's operations, schedules, or plans. However, for a line supervisor to sulk over being put in second position or feeling that he or she has been taken advantage of only adds salt to the injury. Maturity in business means the ability to maintain self-control even in disappointing circumstances.

3. Control Your Temper. Fighting, arguing, and bickering are undignified and bad for the total organization. One need not feign affability if angry. However, effective supervisors never lose their tempers, shout, or plan to sabotage another supervisor's operations. Observant people can easily detect anger because it causes a certain amount of physiological and psychological change in a person. Even untrained observers can see the effects of adrenaline racing through the body of an individual from the look on his or her face, the flush around the neck, the increased rapidity of breathing, and so forth. These physiological and psychological changes cannot only be seen, but when they happen, they hinder that person. For example, if people are extremely angry, they may not think rationally and they may be impetuous—like insisting that either the other supervisor resign or that they will resign.

Not only can lack of control over one's temper cause a supervisor to act in a way that may harm his or her career, such behavior may also encourage the antagonist. Consider what happens if the antagonist *delights* in seeing the other person emotionally distraught. If the antagonist senses that minor goading can cause terrific emotional reactions in the supervisor, the antagonist may do so to get the supervisor more upset.

4. Remember to Try to Do What Is Best for All Concerned. Many supervisors, when they get into conflict situations, somehow get their value systems distorted. Some people feel that they come first, the company comes second, and everybody else is last. This is an unfortunate attitude because it means that if the supervisor loses, everyone loses. Success at work comes from a team effort rather than individual performance. This means that if the supervisor keeps his or her value system in line, everyone can win.

5. Don't Ignore Emotional Attitudes of Other People. Many supervisors underestimate their opponents in conflict situations because they ignore their opponents' emotional attitudes. People's fears and antagonisms can be deeply rooted. It is hard to have a win/win situation if a person is not cognizant of others' emotional attitudes and outlooks. The other person's point of view must be considered if one hopes to resolve existing conflicts effectively.

6. Don't Minimize Any Problem that Seems Important to Someone Else. Many supervisors fail to resolve conflict situations satisfactorily because they don't recognize how serious the conflict really is to other persons. For example, a conflict over interdepartmental schedules may look to you as resolvable by having the other supervisor just schedule overtime. But, in the other supervisor's eyes, the solution may not be so simple. The other supervisor may have promised an employee that he or she could take some vacation time to visit a sick relative and, as a result, the supervisor is reluctant to renege on that promise *regardless of the effect on production schedules*. Being aware of other people's problems and the importance they put on those problems is an asset for a supervisor in conflict situations.

7. Don't Use Surprise Tactics. People get easily upset by any kind of shock situation. Most of us like to know what to expect. When we know what to expect, we can be partially prepared to handle the situation. But when something hits out of the blue, it is difficult to react to the situation effectively. Many supervisors attempt to avoid conflict situations by making a determined effort to communicate to other employees and supervisors what they plan to do, when they plan to do it, and how they expect to do it.

8. Don't Expect Too Much. It is also important to recognize that it is possible to win too much—especially if winning means that another person loses. Sometimes winning the major portion of a war entails losing certain battles during the campaign. This is especially true in working with people. Experienced supervisors find that if they have certain pre-conceived ideas that they *must* win, they usually have to give up some of those expectations if a mutual accord is to be realized and both sides are to win.

9. Don't Make Judgments. A major problem in resolving conflicts occurs because the parties involved in the disagreement pass judgment about the propriety of another individual's activities rather than describe only the circumstance as it is. Nothing can be accomplished by saying to one's adversary, "You're wrong when you do thus and so," or "That is bad whenever. . ." If a person wants to resolve a conflict with others, he or she is best advised to describe the situation rather than give opinions about it.

10. Do Not Generalize. Generalizations are not well-suited for success in resolving a dispute with another individual. Little can be gained by saying, "You are always wanting additional time off," or "I've never heard any of you volunteer for overtime," and so forth. It is seldom true that people always do things or *never* do things. If a person wants to resolve a difference of opinion with other persons, he or she must deal with specific facts rather than generalities. Generalities tend to polarize the opponents' position and solidify them in their desire to win and conquer rather than to resolve the conflict.

11. Work Only with Workable Items. Some situations can be changed, such as who gets to use which machine and when someone takes a break. But some things cannot be changed, like how tall a person is or skin color. When a person is involved in a circumstance involving conflict with others, the conflict should be resolved by working with what can be changed and avoiding what cannot be changed. The supervisor who intends to resolve conflicts must steer discussion toward what can be altered or rearranged and not get lured into fighting over what cannot be changed.

12. Avoid We/They Distinctions. Another trick in resolving conflicting interests between two supervisors is to avoid making statements that underscore their differences. Comments such as "You guys always. . ." or "What they always do is . . ." merely underscore a divisive situation. It is unlikely that one person is *always* the good guy and someone else is *always* the bad guy. In a dispute, persons tend to polarize their positions to paint the picture as black or as white as possible. This is especially true when another person is called in to arbitrate—say, a superior level manager over two first-line supervisors who are having a difference of opinion. Anyone who wishes to be adult about resolving differences should not make statements that *further* divide the disputants.

13. Depersonalize the Issue. Nothing is gained from getting personal or hitting below the belt. Comments such as ''If your mother had taught you to think . . .'' or ''What can you expect from a . . .'' tend to cause adversaries to fight that much harder and be that much more adamant in their efforts to win at the other's expense.

14. Focus on What You Want to Do. Ask for the purpose of any statement or allegation made in a conflict situation. For example, if one supervisor says to another supervisor, ''I think we ought to get rid of all those hand-pushed dollies,'' the other supervisor might ask, ''How would that accomplish our goal of improving safety and still providing service to my people?'' or ''What do you intend to gain by doing that?'' Often, when individuals know what they want to accomplish and can articulate the expected benefits, a workable alternative can be obtained in the dispute.

DEVELOPING INTERDEPARTMENTAL COOPERATION

Changing a conflict situation to cooperation is difficult. It is naive to believe that it can always be done. However, if we are willing to bring conflict to a level of cooperation, the odds are good. On the other hand, if an effort is not made to give both sides a winning way out, if possible, the conflict will probably worsen. Given that nobody can always win in a clear-cut win/lose situation, it is advisable for any clear-thinking supervisor to use the win/win conflict-resolution technique rather than look for a clear-cut decision. This is especially true for emotional situations where it is unlikely that any individual is all right or all wrong.

Personal Styles of Conflict Resolution

Attempts have been made to describe the individual styles that first-line managers should use in coping with people in conflict—be they superiors, subordinates, or peers. Blake and Mouton (as well as Jay Hall, L. L. Cummings, D. L. Harnett, and O. J. Stevens)[1] have identified five styles regarding how supervisors resolve personal conflicts:

The Tough Battler. The individual who is the **tough battler** has one purpose in life—winning. This person has little concern for the needs of others and views winning as the only acceptable outcome of any conflict situation. Losing is seen as reducing a person's status. The tough battler is usually willing to sacrifice others' feelings for the sake of winning.

The Friendly Helper. The opposite of the tough battler is the **friendly helper.** This person is extremely concerned about how others feel about him or her. Since this person's primary motivation is to be accepted by others, he or she is most apt to give in and let others win, avoiding at all costs hurting someone in the process. This person gives in to the tough battler because he or she desires to avoid all conflicts in pursuit of harmony within the organization.

The Lose/Leave Style. The person who operates in the lose/leave mode sees any confrontation as a hopeless, useless, and punishing experience. He or she prefers to avoid conflict and wants to be physically and emotionally removed from it. This lose/leave person is different from the friendly helper in that the former does not compromise principles for the sake of harmony but simply escapes.

The Compromise Style. The individual who is inclined to compromise in resolving conflicts believes that getting something—half or even a little less than half—is better than getting nothing at all. Anyone who uses this style is intent on letting everybody win something. This person may enjoy the maneuvering required in finding an acceptable middle ground among the conflicting interests. This person usually vacillates between expressing anger and trying to smooth things over; he or she wants to find a workable solution.

The Problem Solver. The problem solver actively attempts to satisfy personal goals and the goals of others in the conflict situation. This

---

[1] R. R. Blake and J. S. Mouton, "The Fifth Achievement," *Journal of Applied Behavioral Science*, 1970, pp. 413–26; L. L. Cumming, D. L. Harnett, and O. J. Stevens, "Risk, Fate, Conciliation, and Trust: An International Study of Attitudinal Differences among Executives," *Academy of Management Journal*, 1971, pp. 285–304; J. Hall, *Conflict Management Survey* (Conroe, Texas: Teleometrics International, 1969).

person sees conflict as beneficial to the organization if others cope with it maturely. According to Alan C. Filley, the problem solver (1) sees conflict as natural and helpful, (2) demonstrates trust in others and candidness with others, (3) feels that everyone's attitudes and positions need to be aired, (4) sees everyone as having an equal role in resolving the conflict, and (5) does not sacrifice anyone for the good of the group.[2]

Effectiveness of Various Conflict Resolution Styles

Filley and Cummings state that only three of the five conflict resolution styles are commonly utilized by supervisors.[3] They are the tough battler, the friendly helper, and the problem solver. Tough battlers usually end up in a stalemate when resolving conflicts with others. However, when the tough battler is confronted with a friendly helper, the battler will win. The battler also wins a majority of the time when interacting with the problem solver. Thus, statistically, the win/lose battler wins most of the time except when he or she is forced into a stalemate when confronted face to face with an equally staunch battler.

YOU MAY NOT WIN WHEN YOU WIN

Statistically, if a person is a win/lose battler, he or she should win more than he or she loses. But this does not mean that the win/lose battling style is necessarily the most desirable style for a supervisor to employ in conflicts with others. When one person beats another person, there may be a toll taken that causes *everyone* to have lost something because of the demoralizing and discouraging impact the loss has on the loser. Also, if a person loses too much in a conflict situation, reprisals may affect the winner in behind-the-scenes sniping and opportunism directed from the loser toward the winner.

HOW TO PLAY IT

In practice, one can say when a win/lose style (tough battler) might be more appropriate than the problem-solving style (theoretically the best) and the friendly-helper style (probably the least acceptable of the three

---

[2] A. C. Filley, *Interpersonal Conflict Resolution* (Glenview, Ill.: Scott, Foresman, 1975), p. 52.
[3] Ibid., p. 55.

most common styles). The win/lose strategy usually works best in situations where the stakes of winning are high and especially if the disputants won't ever have to work together or cooperate with each other in the future. On the other hand, when the stakes are low and people must continue working together, most people will feel more comfortable in the problem-solving or friendly-helper mode.

Most people will adopt a style of conflict resolution that they have found to be successful in past conflict situations. The problem-solving or integrative style usually gets the best results. But the difficulty is that problem-solving techniques may be too time-consuming and, thus, too expensive a method to employ. Furthermore, the friendly helper alternative may not be acceptable to an individual because he or she can't deal with losing from an emotional stance.

STRESS, CONFLICT, AND DOING YOUR JOB

Virtually no one is immune from stress and conflict. Unfortunately, stress and conflict can create tremendous difficulties for supervisors and everyone else at work.

The Stress of Job Pressures

The more successful anyone becomes in their job, the higher they rise in the organization. That rise usually means greater job pressures. There is evidence of this pressure in all walks of life. The severe problems generated for any supervisor as a consequence of stress occurs in a variety of ways. One consequence of too much stress is overeating. Obesity is a national problem in the United States. Other reactions to job-related stress are high blood pressure and tension-related health problems. A third outlet that many people seek for releasing stress induced by job pressures is substance abuse—the chronic misuse of alcohol, drugs, and other illicit substances.

The Insidious Nature of Stress

Stress and its effects build up silently. People who begin to suffer from stress often do not realize it is happening. Furthermore, they are often surprised to discover that they are exhibiting stress-related symptoms. Usually some signs of stress are visible to co-workers. When stress is bad enough that the individual notices the problem, extreme effort is required to overcome the problems.

The Supervisor and Stress

Supervisors must be aware of stress. They may see it in subordinates, and they need to be aware of their own stress. Although everyone experiences stress, it does not need to "drag anyone down."

Before discussing how to handle stress, here is a partial list of job pressures that particularly affect supervisors. They are:

1. Growing responsibility—whenever anyone takes on a more responsible job, he or she also takes on more stress in almost any organizational structure. This is especially true if someone takes a supervisory position that he or she really doesn't want. In that case, the stresses can be unbearable.

2. There is increasing competitiveness at work. In today's high-tech environment, everyone is gravitating toward similar job skills. Competition for the best jobs is getting tougher, and stress comes with competition.

3. Social legislation that affects how supervisors can (or cannot) treat employees creates innumerable stress-related problems for the supervisor trying to be fair, honest, and conscientious at work.

4. Age differences often account for stress between individuals at work. This is especially true if the supervisor has significantly older or younger individuals whom he or she must supervise.

5. The knowledge explosion—without question there is an explosion of knowledge and technology in our society. The rate of change in technology within every profession is increasing astronomically. This technology puts tremendous stress on the supervisor to "keep up."

Stress Overload

Stress is often associated with supervisors, especially those supervisors who strive to get ahead in the corporate structure. While this is not necessarily statistically accurate, many people think stress-related problems are mostly generated at supervisory and managerial levels within the organization. A major problem occurs when someone gets overloaded with stress. Overload is the point where a person can no longer process or handle additional stress. Most people are assumed to arrive at some stress threshold and once they pass that point, "something snaps."

The main help for an individual's coping with stress is being aware of when stress is becoming chronic. Stressful conditions can occur in many forms for someone about to reach an overload situation. Some stress symptoms may appear as anxiety and tension, while others may occur as pain and various physiological and psychological changes in the body.

An individual suffering from stress overload may experience a decline in self-esteem, may become confused and disoriented, and may suffer from hallucinations and other extreme symptoms. When an individual suffers heavily from stress, his or her whole ability to function effectively at work is impaired. Ulcers, migraine headaches, and other stress-related conditions are real hazards for anyone suffering from stress. Supervisors must be alert to the symptoms of stress.

Helping People with Stress

A supervisor who recognizes a stress overload in himself or herself or in subordinates will try to help alleviate the situation. Unfortunately, most help has to come from the individual being affected, although professional counseling is certainly advised for anyone suffering from stress-related symptoms.

What to Do about Stress

Much has been written and discussed in recent years about stress-related problems on the job. Many systems have been devised on how to avoid stress or how to cope with stress when it hits a supervisor or a subordinate. Some of the systems that are touted by persons knowledgeable in **stress resolution** include the following:

1. Conduct a thorough self-appraisal about how life affects you. What sends you up the wall? Are you impatient, perfectionistic, overly demanding (or not demanding enough), indecisive, or what? Are you bothered when you have no control over a situation?

2. If you can identify what creates stress, you can suggest solutions to deal with the problems. For example, if you are impatient or perfectionistic, be aware of this and work to control these characteristics to your advantage. If you are indecisive, learn to develop decisiveness and subscribe to the rules of effective decision making for supervisors. Learn to establish schedules, set priorities, and develop ground rules for decision making.

3. Learn to relax. There are a variety of ways for learning how to relax. One method is to practice some form of meditation. Sit in a comfortable position and consciously block out what produces tension from your mind. This can be done alone, but professional help is immensely valuable in accomplishing this goal.

Learn to engage in activities that totally distract you from your problems. This might include watching television or going for a walk. Another way of learning to relax is vigorous exercise. Most experts recommend that some form of vigorous exercise helps to relieve tension and stress. Experts caution that it is necessary to see a doctor *before* engaging in a vigorous exercise program.

4. Obtain professional help if you feel that you or another employee is in serious trouble due to stress. Psychologists, psychiatrists, and counselors help people to overcome mental stress-related problems. Medical doctors are helpful in referring you to other professionals. Also, it is not unusual for clergy to help people in coping with stress, particularly if it is related to personal problems.

In summary, it is difficult to confront stress. However, help is available. No supervisor should have to suffer from stress-related problems, nor should he or she have to suffer from the stress-related problems of subordinates. In sum, when a stress-related problem occurs, the following rules are helpful:

1. Don't ignore the problem; face it for what it is.

2. Don't attempt to run away from the problem—you probably can't escape it.

3. Don't try to minimize the stress-related problem or lie to yourself about what the problem is.

4. Don't wait and see what happens—do something about stress-related problems.

Things to Remember

1. All kinds of stress and conflict occur at work.

2. It is easy for the "my-department-is-the-only-one" attitude to develop.

3. Interdepartmental rivalry is a classic organization problem.

4. Supervisors are not alone on the job.

5. Interaction with other departments cannot be avoided.

6. To win in conflict situations, don't force others to lose.

7. Win/win attitudes help everyone.

8. Problem-solving attitudes are the most productive attitudes in organizational settings.

9. Stress often builds without the affected person realizing fully that it exists.

10. Most stress overload can be alleviated with assistance from others.

Key Words

stress
conflict
interdepartmental rivalry
interaction
interdepartmental cooperation
conflict resolution
win/lose strategy
lose/lose strategy
lose/win strategy
win/win strategy
tough battler
friendly helper
compromise
problem solver
stress resolution

Self-Assessment

Here are some statements and questions related to conflict, stress, and conflict resolution. If you disagree with the statement or question or have a negative response, mark a 1, 2, or 3. If you agree or have a positive response, mark 4, 5, or 6.

1. People who suffer from stress often do not realize that it is happening.

       1   2   3   4   5   6

2. Increased personal stress usually means an increase in job-related stress.

       1   2   3   4   5   6

3. If there is a winner, there must also be a loser.

       1   2   3   4   5   6

4. Win/lose, tough battlers are likely to win an argument or conflict situation.

       1   2   3   4   5   6

5. Problem solvers see conflict as natural and desirable.

        1   2   3   4   5   6

6. Changing a conflict situation to one of cooperation is usually not difficult.

        1   2   3   4   5   6

7. It's a good idea to generalize rather than be too specific in attempting to resolve a conflict.

        1   2   3   4   5   6

8. It is easier for supervisors to get along with each other than for their subordinates to cooperate with each other.

        1   2   3   4   5   6

9. Supervisors are sometimes blind to other organizational needs because of their own concerns.

        1   2   3   4   5   6

10. Some acute stress symptoms are excessive perspiration without exercise, loss of appetite or compulsive eating, digestive problems, tension headaches, irritability, insomnia, alcohol abuse, sudden loss of energy and apathy, and general feelings of anxiety. Do you have any of these symptoms?

        1   2   3   4   5   6

CASES

A Matter of Principle

Upward movement in an organization is sometimes called a vital shift. For employees who move from a nonmanagement assignment to first-line management, the shift can be especially difficult during the early period of learning and adjustment. Vic Flynn never wanted to be a manager. It just happened. After three years with Metals Electrolysis Continuous

Coating Associates, he became supervisor of the coatings area. MECCA, as the company was called, applied special coatings to a variety of metals used in the chemical, electronics, aircraft, and space exploration industries. Processes were exacting and required complex control. Prior to his promotion, Vic had been a union secretary for a work force that was a large mixture of minorities with only a few Caucasians. He was frequently called the "token white" by other union officers. When a supervisory vacancy occurred, Bob Downey, the plant superintendent, asked Vic to fill in. Vic thought it was a temporary position until Bob handed him a copy of his official change of status.

Vic immediately found that his relationship with his union friends changed. Those employees who reported directly to him acted uncomfortable when Vic made regular work assignments. He did not like telling people what to do, and he disliked correcting people he had worked with for three years. Vic found that he analyzed reports well, and he was never late in submitting required paperwork. From time to time, Vic would go to Bob and ask if his old spot was still open. Bob always assured Vic that his current assignment was where management wanted him to be. When the first union grievance was filed against Vic for doing work that he should have assigned to a union employee, Vic realized he was management. Since he worked swing shift and slept late in the morning, he spent less time with his family. He got less and less sleep and lost weight. Almost daily, he felt like quitting and looking for work somewhere else. His only benefit, he often thought, was a slightly larger paycheck. At the end of his third month on the job, Vic was confronted by Henry Tyson, the union president. "Vic, I want to tell you that you're management now and the people in your crew want you to act like a manager. We all know you have it in you. Learn to stand up for the company and for your people. If you have to fight the union, fight hard. We think that there won't be many conflicts." When Vic later told Bob Downey of his conversation with Henry, Vic said, "Henry's a good man." In the following days, Vic did not feel as alone as during his first few weeks. At least two people had faith in his ability even if he was uncertain at first. Last year, when Bob retired, Vic became MECCA's youngest plant superintendent.

1. Why was Vic so uncertain about his role at first?

2. What could Bob have done to help Vic through this period?

3. What were some stress symptoms shown by Vic?

Conflict Revisited   William James was called the father of American psychology in much the same way that Frederick Taylor was known as the father of Scientific Management. In his first text, James wrote that people become tired, not necessarily because of hard work, but because of conflicts within themselves. Anxiety and stress are caused (James did not use the term *stress*) by unmade decisions. If there is an opportunity for a promotion but a person is unsure whether it is what he or she really wants, anxiety and tension (stress) will build until the decision to accept or not accept the opportunity is made. Similarly, if a person is offered two equally attractive opportunities, the same type of tension can occur. A third type of conflict occurs when a person dislikes a situation he or she is involved with and sees no way out. Anytime a difficult decision must be made, we experience stress.

When internal conflicts and on-the-job demands are equally stressful, stress overload will likely occur. We experience the pressures of unmade decisions and we must deal with conflicts outside ourselves. For many persons, the result can be withdrawal, abrupt personality changes, and a variety of physical symptoms. James suggested two approaches to deal with stress. One suggestion is to make decisions about our lives and learn to accept the consequences. We must also do the same with the conflicts of other people. Conflict resolution is often a decision about what course of action to take—within ourselves and externally.

1. Can you think of difficult decisions you have had to make? How did you feel before making the decisions?

2. Can you recognize stress overload in yourself and others? How?

3. What are some practical approaches to conflict resolution with others?

Power and Politics

14

Thought Starter

One of the realities of organizations is that many persons, especially persons in management, like to acquire and use power. One way to get power is to use politics. Power and politics can be positive and benefit an organization. They can also benefit individuals. Individual power used as ego fuel is largely negative. It creates fear, resentment, and opposition.

All managers have certain types of legitimate power. If a person can hire, fire, evaluate performance, make or recommend pay increases, make work assignments, issue schedules, recommend promotions or reassignment, influence policy, implement procedures, or discipline workers when necessary, that person has power. Power is the degree of influence a person has over others; it is derived from many sources.

In Chapter 14 you will learn:

- The concept of the company man or woman.
- What it takes to get to the top.
- The meaning of political awareness.
- Sources of power.
- Types of power.

Anna Bradley was supervisor of employee services for Atlas
Engineering for many years. Her work unit handled insurance
claims, special travel funds, helped employees in emergencies,
and sometimes supervised company social gatherings like the
annual picnic. Somehow, Anna seemed to know more than
others about what occurred in the organization. She was able to
sort rumors from facts, she usually knew about reorganization
and personnel changes before they were announced, she was
aware of new management changes before others, and she was
highly supportive of most management actions.

Anna had her own network of information gatherers and
transmitters. If a person was not part of the network, they did
not share the information. Many lower-level and some mid-
level managers made it a point to regularly have coffee or lunch
with Anna. She was never out of invitations.

Obsequious is a word seldom used by most people in normal conversation. It means fawning or ingratiating behavior; people who are obsequious are overly solicitous of someone else's good favor. Few people
want to appear obsequious in their relations with other people. Yet, it is
almost axiomatic to suggest that if an individual is to succeed in an
organization, she or he must be aware of the power and politics within
that organization and that being obsequious contributes to success in
power and politics.

BEING MAZE-BRIGHT

No supervisor wants to be perceived as overly solicitous of anyone in
the organization. However, it is extremely important that individuals

331

know how to get along with each other and how to cooperate; this is the concept of being **maze-bright.**

Concept of the Company Man and Woman

Unfortunately, many individuals get branded as **company people.** In 1956, William H. Whyte, Jr., described what he called "the organization man."[1] This was the individual who seemed to sell out to the organization and behave as if the company or organization is always right while other employees within the organization may be wrong. He wrote about the individual who is tremendously interested in getting ahead in the organization. This individual will do virtually anything to get ahead.

In bygone years, individuals who had a bad case of this ambition were called "the company man (or woman)." Once someone was branded a company man, he (or she) was thought to always be blindly in favor of everything that the organization did, essentially going against fellow workers and subordinates. They were people seen as doing anything and everything necessary to get the results the organization required with a blind devotion to the organization's goals, which they perceived as necessary, appropriate, and just.

Today, the world has changed somewhat. When William H. Whyte, Jr., wrote his book, most supervisors were male. But more than that has changed. The laws governing work relationships have also changed. Employees have more rights to be independent in actions and thoughts regarding what and how they do their jobs.

However, there is still a great need to have employees who are adamantly supportive of organizational goals (within limits concerning legal, moral, and ethical questions). There is still a need to have persons who are willing to ensure that the organization accomplishes necessary goals and objectives for the organization to stay in business and provide products and services to customers. Today's supervisor must be bright and have a **political awareness** of what makes things happen in the organization; the supervisor must also be aware of the needs of employees within the organization.

The Need for Company People

Company people are essential to the functioning of large organizations. Probably the most compelling of their traits is that they equate personal interests with the organization's long-term development and

---

[1] W. H. Whyte, Jr., *The Organization Man* (New York: Simon & Schuster, 1956).

success. Company people believe that they will benefit most if their organization prospers; their belief in the organization's success may transcend their own interests. These people care about the organization they work for and its development. They are as motivated by the hope for success as they are by fear about the organization's projects, organizational interpersonal relationships, and their own careers. When these people are separated from the organization, they feel insignificant and lost; while part of the organization, they place themselves on the cutting edge of the organization's success.

On the positive side, people who are considered company people derive a special importance from belonging to the organization. The organization may provide them with a sense of belonging, responsibility, and a feeling of loyalty. However, there also are negative feelings: Feelings of little self-worth and the fear of losing their place in the organization. They tend to worry about the organization and ask questions like: "How am I doing?"; "Are we falling behind?"; and "Do others understand what is going on—where we are going and how we are going to get there?"

Company people tend to feel that they are in a hostile environment when they are outside their organization. This makes them feel dependent on the organization; however, it also heightens their sensitivity to the emotions of people, workings within the organization, especially organizational politics. They feel that politics are extremely important. Power centers within the organization are territorial in nature, and company people are acutely aware of who belongs where and why organizational matters happen as they do.

Because of their understanding of internal organizational politics, they participate and contribute heavily in forging alliances, making the necessary compromises necessary to develop complex projects, and bring them to fruition. They resent both people who are too perfectionistic, which is perceived as uneconomical when it is not required, and the overzealous game players who use people solely for personal gains in the organization.

RISING TO THE TOP

Company people function especially well when they get to middle management and higher in the organization. They clearly see the object of every project, the reason for every organizational division, and the overall goals and objectives that they are trying to accomplish. As they move up the ladder of success, they enjoy additional responsibility, and they are often seen as extremely trustworthy and conscientious about their attainments within the organization.

Problems in Being Overly Politically Aware

Company people tend to be overly politically aware. They are all for the success of the organization. But, because of attitudinal outlooks, sometimes they have difficulties at work. They often overvalue the company in relationship to their family life and because of this they are often accused of being workaholics; and often their nonwork involvements suffer substantially.

Another problem with the company person's outlook is that while their work tends to reinforce a responsible attitude in the organization, it may also strengthen a negative syndrome of dependency. That is, they may submit to the organization's authority and betray themselves to gain security, comfort, and ease within organizational positions.

Another problem for company people is that they often defer to superiors and, because of this, they seem to lack principles. They tend to get ahead because the people in power are usually flattered by the courtly treatment they receive from company people. But, they are not necessarily held in high esteem by those superiors.

Probably the biggest failing of company people is when they arrive at the top of a situation. They are often seen as too weak to deal with the challenges at the top of any organization. Often, they are thrown aside by the really powerful people in the organization who, although appreciative of the company person's past contributions to the organization and praising of their concern for humanistic values, nevertheless feel that company persons cannot make the really tough decisions of top-level management. The supervisor who aspires to higher levels in an organization must be aware of the need for power and politics within the organization. It is not sufficient for success in an organization to merely be obsequious with one's superiors. Having the necessary toughness and capability for making decisions is also imperative if one is to rise in an organization. Of course, many people do not wish to rise in the organization.

THE BASES OF POWER WITHIN AN ORGANIZATION

Some definitions of leadership suggest that a good leader is the individual who can use **power** and resources to effectively **influence** various combinations of employees, tasks, and work loads.

Power and Influence

Power is an essential ingredient in effective leadership and getting ahead in an organization. However, power is only one factor of leadership. The two concepts are not synonymous. Power comes in a variety of forms. The bases of power in an organization are: (1) **legitimate power,** (2) **reward power,** (3) **coercive power,** (4) **expert power,** and (5) **referent power.** Let us look at each of these sources of power to understand how they affect one's job and how they can be used advantageously by the aspiring supervisor.

Legitimate Power

Legitimate power is power that usually parallels one's position in an organization. That is, someone is in a position of authority based on their position in the organizational chart or their level within the organization. Legitimate power is the power of the office rather than the power of the individual. Because of that, it can be delegated from one individual to another.

Kings and queens have legitimate power. Similarly, in an organization, people who have the position often have a degree of power. However, just because someone has a position does not mean that they have insurmountable power. In many organizations it is common to hear of people being "kicked upstairs." This usually involves stripping the individual of any real power (in terms of reward and coercive power) while granting them a title that carries some legitimate power.

In the lower organizational levels, supervisors often have legitimate power because of their job title. But, they often feel they lack that something extra to get other people to work up to their potential. Sometimes that is because they are faced with strong informal leaders who possess other forms of power such as referent or coercive power. Other times, it is because they are reluctant either to use the power that they have or to cultivate other sources of power for themselves.

Legitimate power, while it comes from the organization, is not necessarily what it takes to get tasks done in an organization. Legitimate power is probably more useful at top organization levels (where other forms of power tend to abound, too) rather than in lower organization levels. An ineffectual supervisor strives to get work done in an organization as a consequence of using legitimate power. Perhaps that is because legitimate power in an organization's lower levels doesn't go very far—a supervisor's legitimate power just isn't like the president's legitimate power.

Reward Power

Reward power is the ability to give people rewards in return for their performance and behavior within the organization. The person who has reward power has control over material rewards—money, promotions, and so forth. These people seem to get tasks done by making a request of someone. But that request is usually overtly or covertly coupled with a promise of reward for complying with that request. It is, therefore, often a supervisor's reward power that can stimulate people to perform within the organization as they should.

In supervisory terms, reward power gives an individual supervisor the opportunity to dispense merit pay, to offer promotions, or to make a recommendation for some individual reward such as time off or a specialized job assignment.

Reward power in organizations is an extension of classical ideas about motivation. That is, if someone does what they are supposed to do, they will presumably receive a reward. If the employee produces appropriately, there will be suitable compensation.

The supervisor interested in using reward power, however, must understand that reward power can only be derived by a leader who has some unilateral discretion over the dispensation of rewards to subordinates. If an individual is not perceived as having such power, reward power does not exist and is ineffectual.

Coercive Power

Coercive power is where someone has the ability to administer various sanctions or punishments to individuals within the organization. Coercive power does not necessarily derive from one's position within the organization. It comes from the individual who controls some kind of substantive and material penalties. The individual using coercive power gives an order that is coupled with some threat of punishment for non-compliance.

Coercive power can often be seen in a police situation. A police officer has virtually no power over a citizen other than coercive power. The police officer can issue a ticket or arrest individuals for not doing what they are supposed to do. But that police officer could probably offer little, if any, reward to individuals who do what they are supposed to do. In the managerial arena, some individuals have more coercive power than legitimate power or reward power.

Reward power and coercive power are not complementary. For example, a first-line supervisor might have the power to recommend someone for a raise or a promotion, but he or she has no power to fire individuals, reduce their salary, or inflict any real, material penalties on a poorly producing or misbehaving employee. This often occurs in a labor union situation. The boss can reward the individual in some ways, but he or she does not have the coercive power to reprimand or discipline the individual because that is left to higher management levels and the relationships that management has with union leaders.

One of the most perplexing problems facing organizational supervisors is when they feel void of any coercive power. If an individual cannot be coerced in any way—particularly by being fired, given a disciplinary layoff, or given a pay decrease, then how can the supervisor get an individual to perform? Nothing will happen if the supervisor has no coercive power. This is one reason that many supervisors feel impotent in union situations.

Expert Power

Expert power is primarily concerned with knowledge, skill, or expertise. Many people are experts at many things. It is the expert power that subordinates bring to work with them that overcomes or overrules legitimate power, and perhaps even the reward power and coercive power of the boss. Usually, expert power is present because the individual has had special training, experience, or knowledge that no one else has. The individual with expert power is a resource for doing certain tasks or accomplishing certain goals.

People using expert power always investigate the situation, ascertain what is happening, and give or withhold information to others in the organization. A supervisor who has great expertise has expert power. However, some supervisors don't know what they're talking about; this can be painfully obvious in their relationship with subordinates.

One interesting point about expert power is that it often is bestowed on the supervisor by the subordinates of the individual with expert power. For example, having an educational diploma does not make an individual an expert. It also does not mean that an individual is automatically perceived as an expert. While there may be indications that the individual is well-schooled, it does not mean that they necessarily *have* that expertise—or that people perceive them as having that expertise. Because students and other members of the academic community will make a decision about a Ph.D.'s expertise in a particular area, they give that individual expert power.

Subordinates cannot make decisions about one's reward, coercive, or legitimate power (although they may affect whether or not an individual is perceived as holding legitimate power), but they do decide about giving or not giving expert power. Any supervisor who feels that he or she

has expert power had better be sure that their subordinates perceive him or her as having expert power. Expert power is mostly a function of one's followers. Expert power is a real source of power and facilitates supervisors in being successful at getting results through the people that work for them.

Referent Power

Referent power is difficult to define. Referent power usually occurs because an individual has been particularly strong, successful, or has some kind of charisma that attracts other persons. The fundamental resource of the individual with referent power is the approval of the people who bestow power on them. People who exercise referent power state what they think concerning their ideas about work and other persons accept what they say.

Referent power is an intangible part of any supervisor's personality that permits him or her to emerge in a leadership situation. It may be personal magnetism, charisma, or any of the indefinable qualities of an individual.

Television advertising says more about referent power than anything else. Celebrities who speak for or about products may have no expert knowledge, but they nevertheless have credibility in giving advice about why the viewer should purchase a certain product. Television endorsements use referent power. References make a difference. If a person says so and so is good, and the individual making the statement is perceived as credible, then that advice will stick.

Within the workings of any organization, referent power can be significant. An individual within the organization who is perceived by the supervisor as having strong referent power will be very influential to that supervisor in making decisions. For this reason, the internal politics within the organization—particularly backbiting, informing, and other nefarious behaviors—can be critical and can lead to character assassination within an organization. The individual with referent power "gets to the supervisor" and puts in a bad word; the individual informed on may well get into trouble. Supervisors should understand referent power and how people with referent power in the organization may try to influence or dominate the supervisor's behavior and decisions.

SOME BASIC THOUGHTS ABOUT POWER

In any organization, power is extremely important in how successful a person will be and what happens to them and the organization. There are some basic ideas concerning an individual's power in an organization that are relevant to supervisors wondering about the power and politics of an organization. They include the following:

1. If a low-level person in an organization has important expert knowledge not available to higher-level individuals, that person will have power over his or her superiors.

2. Anyone who has a strong enough position in an organization that he or she is difficult to replace has great power over persons who can easily be replaced.

3. Experts are more difficult to replace than nonexperts.

4. There is a strong correlation between the amount of effort a person is willing to exert in any area of influence and the power that he or she can command over that area of influence, if for no other reason than because of the development of expert or coercive power.

5. Any supervisor who is unwilling to become knowledgeable on a subject runs the risk that subordinates will obtain power relevant to that supervisor.

6. The more attractive an individual is, the more likely he or she will obtain access to individuals in an organization and develop some power to control those persons.

7. The more central a person is in an organization, the greater access he or she has to persons who have information and the higher the degree of probability that he or she will develop power for influencing what happens in the organization.

Being Aware of the Organization

It is important for anyone wanting to be a successful supervisor to understand the power and politics of any organization. Power stems from many sources. Power can be cultivated. Power can be used.

Not all people who have power use or abuse it. There are many legitimate uses of power. An effective organization will not develop unless some individuals are willing to wield power. They must develop their power from whatever sources they can: legitimate, reward, coercive, expert, or referent power.

The main idea for any aspiring supervisor to remember is that power must be used. Also, a person must be politic in the organization. However, rising to the top of any organization—success at being a company person—requires that the individual understand the politics of the situation and the necessity of how to wield power wisely.

Things to Remember

1. Supervisors must be politically bright.
2. Company people are essential to the functioning of large organizations.
3. Company people function best as middle or higher-level managers.
4. Power is an essential ingredient of effective leadership.
5. There are five basic types of power:
    a. Legitimate power.
    b. Reward power.
    c. Coercive power.
    d. Expert power.
    e. Referent power.
6. Awareness of the organization is a management necessity.

Key Words

obsequious
maze-bright
company people
political awareness
power
influence

legitimate power
reward power
coercive power
expert power
referent power

Self-Assessment

If you disagree or have a negative response to the questions and statements listed below concerning power and politics, answer with a 1, 2, or 3. If you agree or have a positive response, answer 4, 5, or 6.

1. Reward power and coercive power are closely related.

| 1 | 2 | 3 | 4 | 5 | 6 |

2. Legitimate power is the power of the office rather than the person.

| 1 | 2 | 3 | 4 | 5 | 6 |

3. Legitimate power is probably more useful at lower levels of management than at higher levels of management.

| 1 | 2 | 3 | 4 | 5 | 6 |

4. Expert power is not useful to managers, but it is useful to non-managers.

| 1 | 2 | 3 | 4 | 5 | 6 |

5. Referent power is more intangible than other forms of power.

| 1 | 2 | 3 | 4 | 5 | 6 |

6. Nonmanagement employees with special expertise may have power over their supervisors in some conditions.

| 1 | 2 | 3 | 4 | 5 | 6 |

7. Expert power may be granted to a person whether he or she has real expertise or not.

| 1 | 2 | 3 | 4 | 5 | 6 |

8. Not all people who have power use or abuse their power.

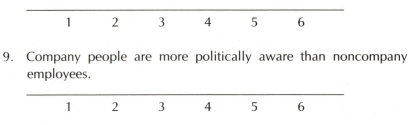

    1   2   3   4   5   6

9. Company people are more politically aware than noncompany employees.

    1   2   3   4   5   6

10. Being maze-bright means knowing the importance of relating well to others in the organization.

    1   2   3   4   5   6

CASES

The Size of Things

Psychologists have been fascinated for years with the symbols of power used in different societies. In parts of Africa, power was once measured by the weight of the chief's wives: the fatter the better. Young women were kept isolated in huts and fed until they were walking mounds of fat. The king would often sit on one to impress visitors. In our society, power is often associated with size and quality. Big cars, big offices, big houses, and big buildings are all associated with power. Although there are many exceptions, a number of studies have shown that taller people have greater opportunities for success than people of below-average height. Other power symbols are related to education and social values. People with higher levels of education are often given credit for knowledge that they do not have. In our country, we seem to still believe in the principle of distributive justice. Distributive justice means that we want the most powerful members of our society to have the symbols that go with that power. We want our boss to have a nicer office than others at her or his level. We want the top manager to have a bigger salary and greater rights.

In some ways, the concept of distributive justice is universal. Greater respect is given to persons we perceive as powerful than persons who are believed to be weak. Persons who rise in organizations are often motivated by the need for the symbols of power as much as power itself.

1. What power symbols are evident in your work place?

2. How do job titles relate to power?

3. How are politics and the concept of distributive justice related?

The Old Shell Game

Sooner or later, many people learn simple political games that enhance their status. Military people in basic training quickly learn that if a person can carry a clipboard with important looking papers on it, few people will challenge where they go or give them unwanted assignments. One political game is to appear important whether you are or not. Astute organizational politicians learn to build alliances both within the organization and outside. Strong relationships with key customers, suppliers, or governmental agency representatives are a security blanket. They are generally willing to support you if needed.

A slightly different form of alliance is to build friendships and strong associations with people who are part of the top management information network. A network is a loose association of people at different levels in an organization who know and trust each other, at least enough to keep each other informed and to issue warnings if trouble is brewing.

Although some organizational politics can be dirty, most of the politics is harmless and useful. Regardless of our feelings about the word *politics*, it is a reality of organizational life that must be recognized and learned like any other management skill.

1. Give some examples of politics that you've witnessed in work situations.

2. Gamesmanship rarely pays off in the long run. Why?

3. What is the usual basis for trust in an organizational setting.

PART SIX

Supervision, Discipline, and the Law

15

Unions, the Supervisor, and the Law

Thought Starter

Union-management relations have changed over the years. Recently, there has been a move toward increased cooperation as both sides have realized that they share similar goals. It is still difficult, however, to supervise employees who are union members. Flexibility in making work assignments, enforcing discipline, and applying work rules are frequently limited by labor contract agreements.

As American business and industry has changed, and as the blue-collar work force has been reduced, unions have lost members and political clout. They are still an important and powerful segment of our work force that cannot be ignored or slighted by management. While the long-range future of labor-management relations is not clear, we are witnessing an important period of change.

In Chapter 15 you will learn:

☐ Supervisory responsibilities in labor relations.

☐ Major labor laws and their importance.

☐ The role of the union steward.

☐ Labor relations terminology.

☐ Why job security is a continuing major issue.

When Rand Furniture expanded it became unionized. Few management people had first-hand experience dealing with collective bargaining agreements and few supervisors knew the meaning of many labor-management concepts. Kathy Cummings was employed as the company's labor relations specialist and her first task was creating training sessions for managers. Her topics included management rights, union security, seniority provisions, grievance ajudication, economic packages, and other issues.

At first, Kathy's topics seemed a mystery, as did the collective bargaining agreement itself. After the first session, most managers realized that the agreement was essentially a set of personnel rules agreed to by both management and employee representatives. It was a legal document that could be changed only by mutual agreement. Both management and employees were required to adhere to its rules.

THE SUPERVISOR AND THE UNION

Most companies do not have a **union.** In addition, unions are on the decline in the United States. However, the first-line manager must work with and understand **labor relations** and unionism. The first-level supervisor is not only the first manager the worker must look to for direction and instructions about doing a job, but he or she is also the manager whom the worker looks to for protection of employee rights. If the supervisor does not protect these rights, employees sometimes join unions.

One reason that the supervisor must know his or her role in labor relations is that the employer is held responsible for any action that the first-line manager takes in dealing with employees or the employee's representative, the union. Any action that the first-line manager takes in relating to employees (or the union) has the same legal impact as if top management or the company's owners had taken the action.

Because first-line supervisors are saddled with interpreting labor relations law as it applies to employees, they must be intimately familiar with labor laws, a **labor contract** that exists in their organization, and all rules and regulations that cover the work situation. There are many problems and pitfalls in which a person can become snared if he or she is unfamiliar with the law and labor contract provisions at work.

LABOR RELATIONS LAW

Labor relations law is the body of law that governs the relationship between the employer, the employee, and the employee's representative, the union. Labor relations laws are primarily viewed as federal laws in most supervisors' minds. However, every state in the United States has laws that govern working relationships in certain situations. Therefore, the supervisor must be aware of federal and state regulations.

Some Basic Terminology

At the outset, it is necessary to develop a vocabulary applicable to the relationship of the union, the worker, and the first-line manager.

The Labor Contract. The labor contract is a written agreement negotiated between management and the union that governs the conditions of employment. The labor contract is a formal document specifying such items as how hard people are expected to work, how much they will be paid for work, what happens if disagreements occur in interpretation of the labor contract, and other job-related matters.

Collective Bargaining. Collective bargaining is the process by which the labor contract is negotiated and enforced between the employee's representative, the union, and the company. Under federal law, employers must bargain in good faith with the union and the union must bargain in good faith with the employer. The bargaining results in the labor contract.

The Union. The union is the organization designated by the employees to represent them in collective bargaining with the employer. Most unions are national or international in scope. When their membership is solely within the United States, they are usually called national unions;

when the membership is from inside and outside the United States, they are usually called international unions.

Local Unions.   Local unions are the local representatives of the national or international union. As the local post office represents the U.S. Postal Service, the local union represents the national union organization.

Unfair Labor Practices.   Unfair labor practices are what both employers and unions can be found guilty of if they violate the rights of each other or the workers. Unfair labor practices have been defined by federal labor laws and are enforced by the courts by such enforcement units as the National Labor Relations Board.

The Grievance Procedure.   The grievance procedure is the process in the labor contract that specifies what happens and what can be done when an employee feels that he or she has not been treated fairly under the labor contract provisions. The grievance procedure is clearly defined in Chapter 16. It usually consists of several steps that must be followed as the worker, the union, and the employer resolve differences of opinion concerning the labor contract provisions.

Arbitration.   It is sometimes impossible for the union and the company to agree on what is meant by the labor contract they negotiated. When these disagreements occur someone must decide what was really meant when the labor contract was written. The individual designated to make this resolution is the labor arbitrator. The labor arbitrator is an unbiased third party whose job is to decide what is meant by the labor contract. For example, a labor contract might say that "an employee can be suspended for violating a significant safety rule in the plant." But, what is meant by "may be suspended" and "a significant safety rule"? That language might have seemed meaningful to the parties who negotiated the labor contract, but it may have two or more widely different meanings in applying the rules on the job; arbitration helps to clarify those meanings.

WHERE UNIONS CAME FROM

The Guilds

Unions have not always existed in society. In fact, unions are a relatively recent phenomenon. Unions actually owe their beginnings to the days of the highly skilled craftspersons of the past—the artisans

A Teamster's union hall.

working in guilds. Originally, unions were organizations of skilled crafts-people—coopers, smithies, printers, and so forth—who worked as employers rather than employees. In medieval times, people either were unskilled laborers doing menial tasks or they were highly skilled artisans doing specialty work.

In the late 1800s and early 1900s, there were laws enacted that significantly affected unionism—the Sherman Antitrust Act of 1890 and the Clayton Antitrust Act of 1914. These laws limited worker participation in union activity. Both laws concerned the definition of whether or not participating in union activity was an illegal conspiracy. The serious student of labor relations history should investigate this issue in detail. However, for our purposes, these laws were instrumental in defining what unions could and could not do. For the most part, these laws, as interpreted by the courts, seemed to be antiunion.

It wasn't until the early 1930s and the Great Depression, with the resulting national turmoil, that labor unions and participation in labor activities actually became accepted and legal. This change occurred with the 1935 passage of the National Labor Relations Act, commonly known as the Wagner Act.

WHY THE LAW SUPPORTS UNIONS TODAY

Why did the United States, in 1935, pass a law highly supportive of labor union activities? It was largely because of the changing times and popular acceptance of the notion that unionism was the protector of workers' rights. How did this happen?

In the days of the guilds, unions were employer organizations. They were considered illegal conspiracies and were somewhat limited in their activities by laws that decided if their activities were either criminal or civil. Until the early 1900s, because of the Industrial Revolution and the mechanization of most jobs, the work environment required fewer un- skilled laborers and needed mostly semiskilled or highly skilled workers.

In the days of the guilds, it was easy to determine whether someone was highly skilled or not—you were either an accomplished silversmith, or you were a simple metalbender. However, by the early 1900s, there were large factories with many mechanized operations because of the Industrial Revolution. It took some skill to run the machines in these factories. But, no longer could the working person be classified as un- skilled. Workers either had a high skill such as printing, silversmithing, or bricklaying or a moderate skill such as machine operation. Because the Industrial Revolution reduced the need for the highly skilled person and increased the demand for the semiskilled person, a larger percentage of the working population had to be included in the semiskilled class. This semiskilled class became the backbone of today's working class.

As more people joined the semiskilled working class, they began to feel the need for union protection. That is, when a person was working on a semiskilled job, he or she could be replaced relatively easily. Thus, workers had *some* job security in that it would be inconvenient to fire the worker and then hire and train another. But workers did not have *much* security. Thus, while semiskilled workers could rely to some degree on skills to ensure employment, they were not irreplaceable. Because of this, they became highly motivated to find protection from capricious employers who might fire them at will.

HOW THE LAW CONSTRAINS
TODAY'S SUPERVISORS

There are several types of **constraints** placed on first-line supervisors today by labor laws, the labor contract, and the unions. The constraints concern any action that a supervisor might take that would have an injurious effect on an employee's job, how the employee does the job, how the employee is paid for doing the job, or an action that would lead to an argument over something an employee can or cannot do based on the employee's involvement or association with a union.

There are also serious constraints imposed by unions and labor laws controlling the supervisor's actions such as firing an employee, giving an employee a suspension or a temporary layoff, assigning disagreeable work to the employee, giving an employee difficult, or dangerous work to accomplish, unreasonably or assigning work that is out of the employee's area of expertise. In addition, the supervisor is severely limited in changing work procedures, processes, tools, and materials that the employee might be required to work with; deciding how the employee might be disciplined for acting unwisely at work; and deciding whether or not the employee can be moved from one job to another, even if the new job is a promotion or carries a pay increase.

There is far more than meets the eye in the existence of unions and the provisions of labor laws for constraining what a supervisor can or cannot do at work. If a supervisor neglects a worker's grievance about a working condition, the supervisor might be in trouble. If the first-line manager assigns jobs in an arbitrary, unfair, or discriminatory way, that supervisor may also be in trouble. Whenever a supervisor gives an order to a worker that violates safety codes or common sense, difficulty may ensue. Any supervisor who is inclined to be overly bossy or throw weight around can create problems and difficulties for himself or herself and for the organization. Labor laws, regulations, and union contracts protect and defend the rights of the worker against capricious behavior by first-line managers or anyone else representing company management.

The Need to Know the Contract

Because of the many constraints placed on a supervisor by unions, labor relations law, and the labor contract, the supervisor must understand specifically what can and cannot be done under the labor contract. For example, most labor contracts specify what is called the wage and the effort bargain.

The *wage bargain* determines how much someone will be paid. It also stipulates amounts paid for specific jobs, when overtime is to be earned by employees, how much overtime will be paid, how much vacation and/or sick leave pay an individual is to receive, when wage increases will be granted, whether or not an individual will be paid a guaranteed minimum number of hours if called in to work, and many other matters concerning how and how much the employee is paid.

The second portion of the labor contract usually concerns the *effort bargain*, an agreement on how much work an individual needs to do to satisfactorily perform his or her job. The effort bargain includes the hours of work, classifications of employees' work, what is considered satisfactory employee performance, and so forth. The effort bargain attempts to delineate how much effort an individual must put into his or her job to be considered an adequately performing employee.

If a supervisor is not aware of what the labor contract requires concerning the employee's effort, the supervisor can again run afoul of employee rights. This can happen when the supervisor demands too much of the employee. Either the company fails to get adequate performance or the supervisor gets into trouble because the worker initiates a grievance against the supervisor's extreme work demands.

Whether or not the operating supervisor is clearly aware of what a labor contract requires depends on the supervisor. While a blissfully unaware supervisor can learn many contract provisions by being hammered for contract violations, the only way to effectively function as a supervisor of unionized employees is to know what the labor contract requires. The best way to do that is to read the labor contract and discuss it with other supervisors or managerial personnel. Supervisors have been fired for breaching or violating the labor contract—perhaps through ignorance—causing a serious infringement upon the rights of the union or unionist, costing the organization a significant sum of money.

UNION ORGANIZATION AND STRUCTURE

No chapter on labor law and the labor contract as they affect first-line supervisors would be complete without a word about the union counterpart of the first-line supervisor. **Union organization and structure** is based on a hierarchy. Naturally, the international union has a president, vice president, and operating department heads. The international leaders, however, usually serve in political roles, and most of their impact is felt at the national level by influencing the enactment of labor laws, legislation, or rules and regulations that will favorably affect the union. The first-line supervisor need not be concerned about the upper levels of union leadership. The union leader who is important to the first-line manager is the local union representative because this is the labor contract watchdog.

THE STEWARD AND BUSINESS AGENT—UNION COUNTERPART TO THE FIRST-LINE SUPERVISOR

At the local level, most unions have a local union president. This person is usually a zealot and popular among the members of the local

union. However, this individual is in charge of the entire local and, unless the entire local is employed by one employer, the union president has many different plants, stores, offices, or other operations to look after. Local unions usually have many different representatives who assist their president. These assistants or **union stewards** go by various titles. On the production floor or in assembly-line work, they are usually called shop stewards. This individual is the counterpart of the first-line supervisor in industrial work.

In nonindustrial work (usually craft work—construction jobs, for example, where extensive skill is required), the person who represents the union's interest is also a steward but not as powerful as the industrial steward.

What happens when employees are unhappy about how they are treated at work? Whenever members of the bargaining unit feel that they have anything to complain about, those employees—union members or not—will take those grievances to the shop steward. It is the shop steward's duty to take the issue up with the first-line supervisor. This is where the first-line supervisor is confronted with the entire matter of union-management relations. It is here that the issue needs to be resolved peacefully. If not, major issues, fights, and disputes about labor relations will occur.

WHY EMPLOYEES JOIN UNIONS

Employees join unions for many reasons. Many employees join the union to make more money. However, many labor leaders argue that more money is not the primary reason to join unions. Job security is a significant reason; employees tend to feel that the union gives them protection and helps to prevent the employer from taking unfair advantage of them.

There are other reasons that workers join unions. Not only can a union help give them security and protection against capricious company action (especially supervisors), but the union also tends to help people keep their jobs. The union has the obligation to protect people whose work is satisfactory but who could be discharged because of arbitrary feelings of supervisors—personality clashes and other subjective reasons.

The union also gives the employee a voice in matters that concern wages, hours, and conditions of employment. The union also provides a fraternal situation. Union meetings play a big role for some employees in how their free time is spent. This is especially true for the staunch unionist who regularly attends meetings, and organizes and participates in other union functions. Unions provide social functions for their membership, ranging from beer busts to sponsoring cultural activities such as art fairs, concerts, and plays.

It is easy to understand why some employees join unions. All of the above reasons are voluntary in nature, but sometimes it is mandatory for employees to join unions. In states that permit union shop agreements (about 30 states do so), an employee may be *required* to join a union as a *condition of continued employment*. But for whatever reason an employee joins a union, the union is a third party in the legal relationship between the line supervisor and the employee. The union's goals and activities must be considered by the supervisor if he or she is to be effective with employees. Ignoring the union is not realistic. Attempting to crush the union is also an unwise policy for any individual supervisor.

WORKING WITH THE UNION

Unionism in the 1980s is on the decline. But while it is declining, it is not gone. The union has primary purpose of protecting the employee from unwarranted acts by the employer. Particular effort must be devoted to understanding what the union wants, for such understanding helps supervisors to work with the union and its services to everyone's advantage.

Protection of the employee against unwarranted activities by the employer and unknowledgeable or malicious supervisors is the primary union goal. However, as an institution, the union has other goals. One of these goals is financial strength for itself (as an institution) and for its membership.

In addition, unions promote as much security for themselves as possible. This means that unions want everybody to belong; there is security in large numbers. Because of their institutional status, unions want recognition. This means that they try to get credit and visibility whenever possible.

From the supervisor's standpoint, it can be assumed that the union is biased in favor of the employee. However, this bias should not be confused with the idea that the union is necessarily antimanagement or unjustly prejudiced in favor of the employee. While some radical union leaders occasionally act totally prejudiced against management, the serious union leader, including the lowest level shop steward, seldom is guilty of such behavior. The union steward is the person the line supervisor will most commonly work with especially in work involving disciplinary matters. The union steward is the lowest ranking union individual who has any real authority in handling disciplinary matters, grievances, or complaints that employees have against the company or the supervisor. Stewards are really just workers, but the employees elect them to protect their interests and the union's interests at work on a daily basis.

What If You Run into a Real Union Zealot?

On occasion supervisors run into unionists who "ride their badges." Riding a badge means that the employee is hiding behind the union for protection and taking advantage of that protection. People who do this often also engage in malicious and wanton activities designed to antagonize the supervisor or otherwise foul up the organization.

Of course, union members are not the only persons who ride the badge. On occasion, a union leader may take advantage of the situation. Some union stewards, when they are in a strong union situation, carefully calculate the mischief they can cause and still be protected by the union or the labor contract.

The union's existence does not necessarily give the employee or the union leader the freedom to act with impunity. Other artificial constraints control and dictate employee behavior as well. Governmental constraints such as the Civil Rights Act and the Occupational Safety and Health Act are applicable. Company regulations also have an impact. Some of these other constraints have the same protective affect on the employee who wishes to engage in calculated malicious behavior as the union does. All these regulators can provide the employee with an artificial barrier to hide behind.

SUMMARY

When reviewing the existence of a union in an organization, the union's primary interest should be protection of the worker in legitimate matters concerning the employee's pay, hours, and working conditions.

It is impossible to enumerate all the areas that the line supervisor needs to concern himself or herself with in considering how to cope with a union situation. However, there are a few basic rules that an operating supervisor should know if a union contract exists at his or her organization. These rules include the supervisor's obligation to recognize the union if a contract exists (and the obligation *not* to jeopardize the company's position with the union if a contract does *not* exist); the obligation to protect management's rights to manage the organization; the requirement to be explicitly fair and impartial regarding wages and salaries as they have been negotiated; the requirement to observe established hours of work, shifts, vacation schedules, breaks, and so forth; and knowledge of the various fringe benefits that any unionist may receive and the conditions where those fringe benefits are payable.

The supervisor must also understand the grievance procedure, especially the necessary steps and mechanisms prior to when the personnel or industrial relations department might process a grievance. He or she must also understand the various job security devices that are in the labor contract—seniority, bumping rights, job rotation requirements, and so on—as well as an understanding of the basic labor contract's terms, duration, and what is required of the supervisor, the employee, and the union.

APPENDIX—THE LAWS OF LABOR RELATIONS THAT AFFECT FIRST-LINE MANAGERS

There are many laws that affect first-line managers and their ability to supervise. The laws that exist are too numerous to mention. But there are some laws that daily affect the supervisor's job. These laws include the **National Labor Relations Act (Wagner Act) of 1935,** the **Labor Management Relations Act (Taft-Hartley Act of 1947,** the **Labor Management Reporting and Disclosure Act (Landrum-Griffin Act) of 1959,** the **Equal Employment Opportunity Law (Civil Rights Act) of 1964,** the **Walsh-Healey Public Contracts Act of 1936,** the **Wages and Hours Law (Fair Labor Standards Act) of 1938,** and the **Occupational Safety and Health Act (OSHA) of 1970.** Let us look at the major provisions of each of these laws as they affect first-line supervisors and their relations with workers, the union, and supervision.

The National Labor Relations Act (Wagner Act) of 1935

In 1935, Congress enacted the Wagner Act, which stated that it was United States government policy to promote collective bargaining. This meant that any business covered under provisions of the law (today this covers almost all work done by companies engaging in interstate commerce) had to, at the election of workers, bargain collectively with the worker's representative—a duly appointed or elected union. In a large percentage of working organizations—particularly in the highly industrialized areas of the Northeast and the far West—most workers are governed under labor contracts negotiated by labor unions. These labor contracts specifically define the wage and effort bargain made between the worker and the employer, which is enforced by the first-line supervisor and the union. Thus, the Wagner Act specified the conditions where the worker can negotiate the terms and conditions of employment—often constraining the operational practices of the first-line supervisor. The first-line manager must understand that these constraints defined in the labor contract have the full force of the law behind them in enforcement of the contractual provisions. They are no different from any other legal contract.

Special Provisions of the Wagner Act. The Wagner Act specifies that collective bargaining be used for workers who want unions to represent them, and it also specifies certain rights of the worker and unfair practices of employers. These rights permit employees to join unions, to be free from an employer's harassment because they have joined a union, to participate in union activities and to be free to express themselves through union membership. The Wagner Act provides workers with relative freedom from interference for participation in union activities and also protects them from discrimination because of union involvement. An employer, or an employer's representative who violates these rights has committed an unfair labor practice.

As a watchdog to ensure that employers and their representatives (first-line supervisors) did not interfere with or discriminate against the worker in participating in union activities, the National Labor Relations Act (Wagner Act) established the National Labor Relations *Board* (NLRB) to enforce employee rights as provided under the law. Thus, supervisors often hear complaints and comments about unfair labor practices that they allegedly engage in, such as interference or discrimination because an employee participates in union activities. When a first-line manager (actually the company) is accused of unfair labor practices, the complaint is lodged with the National Labor Relations Board, which must investigate, determine whether or not such discrimination occurred, and take appropriate remedial legal action.

The Labor Management Relations Act (Taft-Hartley Act) of 1947

The Taft-Hartley Act, which amended the Wagner Act in 1947, provides the first-line manager with some operational running room. The amendment was enacted because of the experience of United States employers in trying to comply with provisions of the 1935 law. Union abuse of rights under the 1935 law left a bad impression on employers and the general population—so bad that the 1947 amendment to the Wagner Act was passed over the veto of the President of the United States—which definitely reflected the strong feelings of the population.

The Taft-Hartley Act of 1947 provides protection to the employer against the arbitrary and capricious activity that unions became noted for between 1935 and 1947. The 1935 law made it an unfair labor practice for a company to refuse to bargain collectively with the duly elected representatives of workers. However, the 1935 law did *not* make it illegal or unfair for the duly elected representatives of workers (the union) to refuse to bargain collectively with the company. The originators of the Wagner Act never thought that unions would refuse to bargain, but they did. In fact, between 1935 and 1947, it was common for unions to *refuse* to bargain collectively with the company; instead, they told the membership to go on strike and severely cripple the company's performance.

This problem became particularly acute following the end of World War II. At that time, the United States was short of many consumer goods—automobiles, refrigerators, and so forth—because all industrial productivity had been geared toward supporting the war effort. Consequently, unions capitalized on the opportunity to blackmail employers into giving extremely high wage increases by threatening (or refusing) to bargain over wages and hours when existing contracts expired. Because employers could sell anything they produced, they would do anything to keep their employees at work and, therefore, they could be coerced by unions in to agreeing to inflationary wage increases. This union practice created one of the most inflationary periods in United States history. Thus, in 1947, because of the galloping inflation caused by union refusal to bargain with employers, Congress passed the Taft-Hartley amendment to the Wagner Act, requiring unions to bargain in good faith with employers just as employers must bargain in good faith with unions.

There were other provisions of the 1947 law that applied to labor relations. The 1947 law defined other union obligations to employers and specified unfair union labor practices. The law made it illegal for a union to attempt to force an employer to discriminate against *nonunion* employees, or for the union to coerce employees to join a union if they didn't want to, or to charge excessive fees of employees who did wish to become union members. In addition, the law said it was an unfair labor practice for the union to force an employer to pay for services that were not performed—the practice known as featherbedding, where an employer was forced to pay a union member for doing work that the union member did not perform.

The Labor Management Reporting and Disclosure Act (Landrum-Griffin Act) of 1959

The Landrum-Griffin Act was passed because of reporting corruption in unions during the 1950s. It was designed to help protect the individual worker *from the union!* During the 1950s, unions sometimes took advantage of members by requiring excessively high dues and initiation fees, and they engaged in other forms of extortion. To eliminate these practices, the 1959 law required reporting and disclosure of the internal financial operations of labor unions and labor leaders, and it also required that labor union leaders disclose any membership in subversive organizations such as the Communist party.

The Landrum-Griffin Act is designed to keep labor leaders honest with union members. It is designed to prevent unethical practices by the union and its leaders, and to prohibit activities between the union and the company that interfere with or frustrate the due process of collective bargaining. It is also designed to prevent the misuse or misallocation of union funds by union leaders and to eliminate racketeering practices.

The Equal Employment Opportunity Law

The Equal Employment Opportunity Law of 1964 prohibited employers or employers' representatives (first-line supervisors) from discriminating against employees or job applicants because of race, color, sex, religion, national origin, or age. There are legitimate situations where an exception to this law may exist. For example, a person might discriminate in employment because of religion, if a person is an employee of an educational institution run by a religious denomination; a person might also discriminate on the basis of sex where persons are employed as fashion models. It would be absurd for a male to model women's clothes or a woman to model men's clothes. Other than in circumstances where it is necessary to have bona fide discrimination because of race, color, sex, religion, national origin, or age, the practice is illegal. First-line supervisors must be blind to race, color, sex, religion, age, or national origin in making job assignments or in designating promotions. The Equal Employment Opportunity Law was designed to protect designated minority groups from employment discrimination. This law is not a union management law. Rather, it is directed at employers, and employers must comply with it whether or not a union exists in their organizations.

The Walsh-Healy Public Contracts Act

The Walsh-Healy Public Contracts Act concerns work done under government contracts that exceed $10,000 in value. The Walsh-Healy Act prohibits hiring boys under 16 and girls under 18 of age for certain jobs, and it limits basic work hours to 8 hours per day and 40 hours per week. When more hours of work must be engaged in on government contract work that falls under this law, the employer must pay time and a half for all overtime work. Furthermore, the law sets strict standards for safety, health, and working conditions that must be maintained in the work environment. This law means, for the first-line supervisor (who is involved in government work under provisions of the law), that rigid requirements are established in the number of hours that can be worked and the age limits of individuals who can work on the job.

The Wages and Hours Law (Fair Labor Standards Act)

The Fair Labor Standards Act restricts the employment of children 14–16 years of age to nonmanufacturing and nonmining jobs. It does not permit the employment of children 16–18 years of age in hazardous jobs including driving or helping a driver of a motor vehicle. The law also sets minimum wages and prescribes that time and a half must be paid for all hours worked over 40 hours per week. The law also defines what is work and what is not. Working, as defined under provisions of the Fair Labor Standards Act, is actual engagement in the work. It specifies that standing in line to receive one's paycheck and cleaning up at the end of the work day (such as changing clothes, washing, bathing, or checking out from work) are not considered work, *unless* the union agreement specifies that it is work.

The Wages and Hours Law also sets guidelines for determining which supervisors must be paid overtime work and which ones need not be paid overtime. The law establishes classifications of exempt and nonexempt employees; that is, some supervisors are exempt from overtime provisions under the Fair Labor Standards Act and some are not. An employee who is considered exempt from overtime provisions is classified as an executive. Such an individual must be a supervisor of a recognized department or division who regularly directs the work of two or more employees and exercises discretionary powers including hiring and firing and making recommendations about the hiring, firing, or promotion of subordinates. The exempt person must also not perform nonexempt (nonsupervisory) work more than 20 percent of the time, and he or she must receive a salary of at least $155 per week. These laws are constantly changing, and if there is any doubt regarding your situation, contact a local representative of the Department of Labor's Wage and Hour Division.

A first-line supervisor who is an exempt employee ought to know that condition. Likewise, supervisors who might be classified nonexempt might find that the law is on their side and provides for the payment of overtime when they work more than 40 hours per week.

THE OCCUPATIONAL SAFETY AND HEALTH ACT OF 1970

Not only should the supervisor shoulder responsibility for teaching safe work methods, but it is also the law. The Occupational Safety and Health Act (OSHA) of 1970 requires that all work areas, conditions, sites, tools, and equipment comply with certain minimal standards. The law also requires that the supervisor and employer cooperate to ensure that those conditions are met and maintained. The law provides heavy fines and penalties for the employer, the supervisor, and the worker if OSHA regulations and requirements are not met.

The following items are some of the rules a supervisor ought to remember about his or her responsibility for safety. Some are not legal matters, but they all will help to preclude problems.

1. Safety records and what kinds of accidents have occurred in the supervisor's organization should be noted and publicly acknowledged.

2. Safety equipment and clothing should be provided to employees, and an emphasis should be placed on how to use the equipment and clothing correctly. It is the supervisor's responsibility to train and encourage employees to use the equipment and clothing they have and to enforce rules requiring the use of safe methods and techniques in doing the job.

3. Recognition should be given to workers who have a good safety record. Positive reinforcement and operant conditioning can be used to encourage employees to work more safely. This will encourage other employees, through the process of social learning, to observe what safe workers are doing and how they can obtain the same safety records.

4. If the first-line supervisor is not concerned about safety, employees will not be concerned either. Safety consciousness is contagious. If a supervisor talks it up, so will the employees, and that process will help break some of the traditional resistance to safety programs.

5. Investigate whether there are accident-prone employees in your department. Psychologists argue that some people are accident-prone. This is because they view certain ominous life situations as nonthreatening. They, therefore, do not take adequate precautions. When an employee develops a record of having several accidents (certainly if they occur over a short period), a thorough investigation must be made of how this employee views work situations that the employee may think are safe but others do not. The employee should be singled out for help in identifying accidents that they may be subjected to in their workaday life.

6. Have some employees who are particularly concerned about safety serve as safety leaders and perhaps even conduct meetings in which they suggest ideas and offer recommendations about how the work circumstance could be made more safe. This emphasis on safety will underscore your commitment to a more safe operation and will also promote assistance from several of your employees.

7. Manage the situation. Managing the situation means setting up work so that people want to work safely. Materials and equipment must be available and designed to facilitate in cleaning up spills, putting away

tools and sharp objects, and generally making it easy for people to maintain a safe working area so that the situation dictates that they eliminate existing safety hazards.

8. Use periodic retraining programs—particularly when new methods or techniques are used that may involve certain safety hazards or create conditions where employees might not know how to cope and would be at risk.

9. Find out what other organizations do in safety programs. Promote novel ideas because they are practically always motivational The aspect of competition can be created—the supervisor convinces employees that they can be as safe as another company's employees who do similar work.

10. Welcome all ideas and suggestions made by employees concerning what changes might be made and particularly concerning identification of areas where unsafe conditions may materialize. Employees like to have their suggestions heeded. Always take note of—and the required action to eliminate—unsafe working conditions if they are brought to your attention by an employee.

Things to Remember

1. Most companies do not have unions.

2. Unions reduce management flexibility.

3. The union contract is a legal document that regulates conditions of employment.

4. Collective bargaining is the process by which the labor contract is negotiated and enforced.

5. The union represents employees in bargaining collectively with the employer.

6. Unfair labor practices are defined by the federal government. They are illegal actions for both employers and unions in their dealings with each other.

7. Supervisors need to know the union contract and union representatives.

8. Union stewards represent employees in day-to-day disputes with management. Business agents operate the local union organization.

9. Some of the primary laws affecting union management relations are:
   a. Labor Management Relations Act.
   b. Reporting and Disclosure Act.
   c. Walsh-Healy Public Contracts Law.

    d. Wage and Hour Law (Fair Labor Standards Act).

    e. Equal Employment Opportunity Amendment.

    f. Occupational Safety and Health Act.

Key Words

union
labor relations
labor contract
collective bargaining
local
unfair labor practices
grievance procedure
arbitration
constraints
union organization and structure
union steward
National Labor Relations Act
Labor Management Relations Act
Labor Management Reporting and Disclosure Act
Equal Employment Opportunity Law
Walsh-Healy Public Contracts Act
Wages and Hours Law
OSHA

Self-Assessment

    Listed below are some questions and statements about union-management relations. If you disagree or have a negative response to an item, mark it 1, 2, or 3. Should you agree or have a positive response, mark 4, 5, or 6.

1. First-line managers, by law, speak for all management when dealing with unions.

      1   2   3   4   5   6

2. There were no unions before passage of the National Labor Relations Act of 1935.

      1   2   3   4   5   6

3. Job security is a primary union goal.

      1   2   3   4   5   6

4. The Civil Rights Act and its Title VII amendment are not labor-management relations laws in the strictest sense.

	1	2	3	4	5	6

5. A primary purpose of the Fair Labor Standards Act was to establish national overtime pay provisions and minimum wages.

	1	2	3	4	5	6

6. First-line managers need not be concerned about upper levels of union leadership.

	1	2	3	4	5	6

7. First-line managers deal primarily with the union steward in day-to-day union-management matters.

	1	2	3	4	5	6

8. Unions have not always existed in our society.

	1	2	3	4	5	6

9. Union agreements do not limit the types of work assignments that a supervisor may give an employee, but they restrict the amount of work the employee is required to perform.

	1	2	3	4	5	6

10. The Occupational Safety and Health Act applies only to organizations with union-management contractual agreements.

	1	2	3	4	5	6

CASES

Carry on Mike   Mike Bradford was one of the most competent production control specialists in the Tomlison Manufacturing Company's operations. In addition to scheduling, Mike did special follow-up on parts that were behind schedule in the manufacturing process, and he rescheduled operations when possible to ensure completion by the established due date. On special projects, Mike was usually assigned to a group that ensured special attention to critical components of the item being manufactured. Tomlison Manufacturing Company made pumps, valves, and other components for use on submarines, naval vessels, and aerospace fuel systems. Their work was precise and exacting.

In its contract with the International Association of Machinists, management agreed that no union employee's work would be assigned to nonunion workers. Machinists operated machines, custodians cleaned, dispatchers moved parts from one workstation to another, and so forth. Union employees and management were bound by the union-management contract to adhere to established job descriptions. When one of the engineers on a special project wanted to see a valve part that had just been machined, Mike volunteered to get one. The part was approximately the size of a standard pencil. Mike walked to a table where a number of parts were waiting before movement to a final inspection station. He picked the part up, carried it to the engineer for examination, and then returned it to the table. The next day, Karen Hurst, shop dispatcher, filed a grievance against the area supervisor for letting Mike move the part. Parts movement was, by job description, dispatcher's work.

1. Was Mike wrong in moving the part? Explain.

2. Why would Karen file a grievance over a small item?

3. Were the rules governing parts movement reasonable in this case?

Now I See You, Now I Don't

Unfair labor practices include concepts such as promises of better conditions by management to avoid union problems, interrogation of union members by management, threats by either union or management representatives, and spying on either union or management activities.

When the United Chemical Workers union began organizing employees of Poly-Ethylene-Products (PEP), it was a long and difficult process. Some employees felt that the union would be beneficial; others doubted its value. Some workers thought that management would become hardened against employees if there was a union and most enjoyed good relations with their immediate supervisors. To explain the benefits of a union, organizers from within the work force and from the United Chemical Workers state headquarters periodically held meetings after work to explain the union's position.

On March 14, Diane Watson, a plant supervisor, was in a drugstore across the street from the Elks Club where a union organizing meeting was being held. When the meeting ended, Calvin Potts walked across the street to pick up a magazine and saw Diane. "Hi, Cal," Diane said. "Been to a meeting?"

"Yeah," answered Cal. "I'm still not sure about this union stuff."

"Were there many people there?" Diane continued.

"Sure were, and most of them you know. I think most of them are convinced the union is a good thing," stated Cal. "See you later." Neither Cal nor Diane knew that their conversation was being heard by Robin Lester, one of the state headquarter organizers for the United Chemical Workers. Two weeks later, an unfair labor practice charge was registered against the company by the United Chemical Workers Union for spying and interrogation.

1. Was Diane spying in the legal sense?

2. Were Diane's questions to Cal a form of interrogation?

3. Did either Cal or Diane understand the law concerning unfair labor practices?

16

Maintaining Discipline and Handling Grievances

Thought Starter

Grievance procedures exist in organizations without unions as well as in organizations with union-management contracts. In most cases, procedures are more highly structured where contracts are in force than when management has some latitude in interpreting its own policies. Grievances occur when an employee feels strongly enough that he or she has not been treated fairly by management that a formal complaint is filed.

When there is a strong antagonistic relationship between an organization and a union, grievances become a way of life for supervisors. Endless hours are spent in meetings trying to resolve disputes ranging from type of work assignment to overtime distribution. While many union stewards and most employees do not like extensive involvement in grievance hearings any more than management, some people find that it is a way of exerting a special kind of power and they are constantly looking for management errors that can be the basis for a grievance.

In Chapter 16 you will learn:

- Grievances should be settled at the lowest step in the procedure.
- There are two kinds of grievances: clinical and legalistic.
- Discipline is positive and necessary in the work place.

- **All supervisors should know ways of maintaining discipline and handling grievances.**
- **A supervisor's fairness is the best defense against grievances and the best method for maintaining discipline.**

At Reliance and Printing Company (RAP), the labor contract states that employees called in for unscheduled work must be paid for a minimum of four hours work at one and a half times the base rate. If an employee called in on a Saturday completes a job in an hour, the employee will receive four hours pay at time and a half, the equivalent of six hours of straight-time pay.

On Monday afternoon, shortly after he arrived at home, Leon Ames, a pressman for RAP, was called and asked where the day's run report was. "It's on my desk, as usual," he replied. "You can start the next run with the color layout. The press is all set up." The next day, Leon and the shop steward appeared in the pressroom supervisor's office. "We want Leon to receive call-in pay as required by the contract or we will file a grievance."

The supervisor sighed, "It's going to be another one of those days."

DISCIPLINE IN THE ORGANIZATION

Discipline is not a dirty word. It is positive and is necessary at work. Discipline, in an organization, ensures productivity at work and helps to maintain an orderly workplace. Thus, the supervisor is responsible for

371

maintaining discipline in the organization. This is true whether the workplace is an industrial plant with fumes, heat, and so forth, or a hospital that is cool, comfortable, and hygienic.

People at work get into trouble that requires **disciplinary action.** How the supervisor maintains discipline at work has a lot to do with how pleasant the workplace is, how safe it is, and whether or not work gets done on time. If supervisors are unreasonable in maintaining discipline, there will usually be employee rebellion. When that happens, the union may step in (even when no union existed before) and attempt to protect employees from heavy-handed behavior.

The Objectives of Discipline

Any supervisor, in establishing and maintaining discipline in an organization, should:

1. Foster or promote mutual respect between self and subordinates.
2. Keep employees basically satisfied with their jobs and work conditions. Attempt to maintain the work environment according to established rules of conduct and good citizenship.
3. Teach people to perform their duties efficiently, effectively, and safely.
4. Ensure a predictable work output.
5. Maintain a safe and orderly workplace for everyone.

Rules of Discipline

In maintaining organizational discipline, supervisors should follow these guidelines:

1. Give clear, precise, and simple instructions.
2. Know personnel policies and procedures (including the labor contract, if one exists) and the basic rules, regulations, and policies governing the conduct of work.
3. When problems occur, move promptly to prevent a volatile situation.
4. Attempt to determine what has caused problems—bad blood between employees, a misunderstanding of a supervisory order, sheer ignorance by the persons involved and so forth.
5. Determine what action to take based on the facts: what the participants claimed happened, how serious the violation is, what disci-

plinary action has been taken in similar situations, and whether or not there are mitigating circumstances.

6. Make records of any statements, opinions, and all factual information that comes to light in the investigation.

7. Once the matter is disposed of and appropriate records are made, forget about the incident. Nothing is more likely to lead to the end of a supervisory career than harboring grudges and taking it out on other people.

To maintain discipline in the organization, the supervisor must remember that he or she is not in a popularity contest. The supervisor has a right to protect management and the company from unjust claims, but he or she also must protect employees.

Steps in Disciplinary Action

The following list is a procedure that many supervisors follow in taking disciplinary measures. The steps help to protect the rights of the employee, the company, other employees, and the supervisor.

1. Investigate the disciplinary matter thoroughly.

2. Check with the personnel department to find out what has been done in any previous disciplinary matters that are similar.

3. Investigate the background of employees involved.

4. Determine what has caused the disciplinary problem.

5. Determine, in consultation with the personnel department, what to do *before* the action is taken.

6. Document all relevant statements and allegations.

7. Make a record of what was done; make sure that the personnel department gets a copy of that record.

AVOIDING PROBLEMS WHILE MAINTAINING DISCIPLINE

Disciplinary problems arise no matter how alert a supervisor is. To be on top and maintain discipline within an organization when employees misbehave requires that the first-line supervisor sometimes "lean" on employees. Sometimes the supervisor has to issue unpopular orders or directives. As a consequence, **complaints** can materialize, and sometimes they will escalate into substantial grievances. A good supervisor is aware of the problems and issues that can cause **grievances** and attempts to preclude them as follows:

1. The Supervisor Should Pay Attention to Employee Complaints. Some people just complain, but others have genuine grievances. A supervisor should never overlook or minimize—or, worst of all, ridicule—any expressed grievances.

2. Don't Try to Settle Every Grievance that an Employee Has. While supervisors should try to talk out every employee complaint and be reasonable in the process, it is too much to expect that all complaints can be satisfied simply by talking. It is more important that, when grievances *do* occur, a fair hearing be given as soon as possible; if the employee has justification for the complaint, appropriate steps must be taken to alleviate the situation.

3. Determine the Facts of the Situation. Most supervisors who end up with egg on their faces do so because employee grievances have occurred and the supervisors have only part of the story. A supervisor cannot be a total fact finder. But with a degree of diligence, a thoughtful supervisor can eliminate much of the confusion concerning a grievance and can shed light on what steps to take.

4. Whenever You Are Forced into Making a Decision about a Grievance, Be Definite in the Answer You Give. It is unwise to hasten a decision concerning an employee's complaint, but you must be relatively decisive. The first-line supervisor is paid to make decisions when decisions are warranted. Workers respect supervisors for decisiveness, particularly if they know the decision is based on a careful analysis of the facts and that the supervisor has not played games or unnecessarily prolonged making the decision.

5. Try Not to Make an Employee Eat Crow or Be Embarrassed by Your Unfavorable Decision Concerning a Grievance. Many grievances that blossom into full-blown employee relations disputes do so because the employee has been psychologically hurt or humiliated by a supervisor who wouldn't listen or who belittled the employee. Sometimes, the supervisor "wins the battle and loses the war," because the employee waits to get the supervisor later.

6.   It Is Better to Prevent Grievances before They Occur.   Be adept at handling grievances when they materialize. Supervisors often do not sense the breeding ground for gripes and grievances that can mushroom if left unheeded. A great deal of insight or empathy is not necessary to know what makes employees unhappy. While it is impossible to eliminate every potential problem, some things can help. For example, the supervisor can analyze past grievances to see if anything *still* exists that might cause the old problem to reemerge in a new form. History does repeat itself, and reflection is helpful as a tip for pending problems.

7.   Anticipate What Current Activities Could Erupt into Hard Feelings.   The supervisor should try to sense how people feel about the current situation—that is, are they happy or is there bickering, complaining, snide comments, or other indicators of dissatisfaction between workers, between workers and the supervisor, or between workers and the organization? Indicators of latent hostilities are signs of future grievances that may haunt the first-line supervisor.

SOME CONSIDERATIONS IN DISCIPLINING AN EMPLOYEE

It is good to talk about how to avoid having to handle problems, gripes, and grievances when they occur because such grievances may mushroom into full-blown disputes. Yet, disciplinary matters do sometimes occur, and a supervisor should never fail to discipline or reprimand employees when they have misbehaved at work. It is important to consider some of the relevant problems that may materialize—and that might be prevented—when the first-line manager must discipline an employee. Some of the considerations include the following:

1.   Engage in Constructive Discipline.   Often, supervisors forget the purpose of discipline. Whenever employees have misbehaved, the intention of any disciplinary measures leveled against them is to *correct* their behavior; it is not to punish them. Punishment seldom, if ever, is effective at changing behavior, and it often breeds resentment that later materializes as "getting the boss." Also, a supervisor should discipline *all* employees who violate work rules. Past practice shows that the supervisor, by leveling punishment on one employee and not on another person, is being discriminatory. An equal yet considerate administration of discipline is required.

2. There Is Usually Some Underlying Emotional Stress or Unhappiness that Causes an Individual to Perform Poorly. The supervisor must be alert and sensitive to both employee and personal needs. Sometimes employees bring nonwork problems to the job—financial difficulties, health, or love-life problems. Again, counseling and understanding may go a long way in helping someone, whereas rigid discipline will not.

3. Most Employees Respect Supervisors Who Are Firm and Fair. Employees expect supervisors to discipline them when they deserve it. In fact, they may find fault with the supervisor *if the supervisor fails to discipline employees* when they deserve it. On the other hand, they expect just and equal treatment. An individual who is disciplined expects to be disciplined to the same degree as another person guilty of the same infraction.

4. Never Make a Disciplinary Decision When You Are Angry or Upset. People do not think well when they are emotionally distraught. This is true of both workers and first-line supervisors. Because people do not act sensibly when they have lost their tempers, it is good to postpone taking any disciplinary action until you have gotten over any emotional feelings. There are several ways to do this, even though a situation may argue for immediate action. One way is to take a walk—or to tell the worker to take a walk—or postpone seeing the worker for an hour or two after the incident has occurred. You and the employee both need a chance to simmer down. One trick some supervisors use is to send the offending employee home for the day. This gives the supervisor time to regain his or her thoughts and possibly consult the industrial relations department about the propriety of any decision he or she will make concerning the employee—*before* the decision must be rendered. It's always possible to pay the employee for the remainder of the day if the supervisor was off base in sending him or her home.

5. Avoid Listening to Other Workers' Advice about Handling a Situation. While the supervisor should consult the personnel department about what to do in maintaining discipline, it is *always* inadvisable for the supervisor to consult other workers on disciplinary matters. Similarly, it is *usually* inadvisable to consult the union steward. The exception arises in situations where the company or organization has a policy requiring that union representatives be consulted. The reason for this is that there is much to be lost by other workers or the union steward in doing anything other than siding with the offending employee. Consequently, they may offer bad advice or information.

6. When You See a Problem Brewing, Adequately Warn the Employee that His or Her Persistence in the Behavior Will Lead to Trouble. Whenever you give a warning to an employee about pending behavior problems, ensure such warnings are more than idle threats. Remember, if you always give warnings but never carry them out, people will disbelieve you. It is like crying "wolf" too many times. Warnings must be enforced if they are not heeded. Any rule that is not enforced is merely advice. Remember, however, that when warnings are given, it is the ideal time to engage in constructive discipline, because that is the opportunity to correct the employee without having to invoke any punishment.

SOME DIFFERENT SLANTS ON DISCIPLINE

Any chapter on discipline would be incomplete without mentioning two activities that some organizations use to establish discipline. One item is to give an employee time off with pay in a misbehavior situation. The other item is the use of **employee disciplinary groups.**

Time Off with Pay   Some companies report success in disciplining employees by giving them time off with pay. Time off with pay does not appear to be much of a disciplinary tactic. In fact, it could be construed as rewarding an employee for misbehaving. However, when an employee is given time off from work with pay, everyone knows that the employee is being disciplined. Furthermore, there is the implication that the company is vitally concerned about the employee's behavior and that the employee's wage is immaterial. By continuing to pay the person, the company may convince the errant employee that his or her wages are not nearly as important to the company as is his or her behavior.

Employees who have been disciplined with time off and pay usually report they had a "funny feeling" about having the day off. They knew they were being disciplined, yet their pay was not reduced. Most workers say that it causes them to think differently about why they were ordered off work. Some employees report that it causes them to reject feelings of being treated unfairly or vindictively by the supervisor—a paramount reason for trying to impose constructive discipline.

**Employee
Disciplinary
Groups**

Another experiment—employee disciplinary groups—is obtaining moderate to very successful results. This sort of discipline has been around for centuries. It is based on the idea that one's co-workers should determine the discipline.

Psychological experiments show that co-workers, who really know what is happening with the problem employee, can usually accurately determine what discipline will be appropriate and effective better than a supervisor. Someone who is not privy to the employee's feelings will have to go by the book and use progressive discipline practices. Co-workers, on the other hand, may know that an employee is deliberately misbehaving at work and they are, therefore, in a better position to discipline the employee.

Companies with successful employee disciplinary groups are usually not unionized. Also, they may have been lucky not to have employees complain about unfair practices or discriminatory treatment. Any organization that tries to implement an employee disciplinary group must be aware of labor laws and regulations that, in many cases, require all employees be treated the same; therefore, when one employee is disciplined more severely than another for the same infraction, legal problems could materialize.

Usually, employees who want to participate in employee disciplinary groups also want a safe and productive work environment, and they are not inclined to unionize or go to the courts with claims of unfair treatment. The organizations with employee disciplinary groups that are popular among the majority of workers have not experienced extreme difficulty with violations of a labor contract or employees' legal rights. Many professional organizations have a self-imposed disciplinary process as an integral part of their group. Supervisors should be wary of violating a worker's rights under a labor contract or various labor laws. He or she should get approval from higher management before attempting to implement an employee disciplinary group.

COMPLAINTS AND GRIEVANCES—
STEPS TO FOLLOW WHEN
THEY OCCUR

Handling complaints and grievances is best done between supervisor and employee or between the supervisor, the employee, and the union steward (if the organization is unionized). It is desirable for complaints and grievances to be disposed of amicably among the individuals in-

FIGURE 16-1

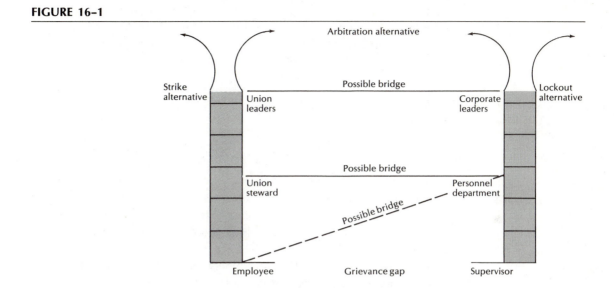

volved. Figure 16-1 shows the usual **grievance procedure** that is followed in most organizations if grievances cannot be disposed of at their point of origin by the supervisor.

As seen in Figure 16-1, the supervisor can always go to the personnel department or the industrial relations department for assistance in handling any grievance (assuming the company or organization is big enough to have a personnel department). Likewise, the individual employee can go to the personnel department, or in a union situation, the employee can go to the union for advice. Going to the union usually means calling the steward or going to the grievance committee for additional assistance.

The supervisor should avoid higher steps in the grievance process unless the matter is extraordinarily serious and cannot be resolved amicably at the ground level. If an extremely volatile grievance occurs at work, the personnel or industrial relations department or the union grievance committee might take the complaint to a third level—between corporate and union leaders. If the issue cannot be resolved at that level, it may be taken up with an arbitrator.

As shown in Figure 16-1, any grievance can go to the top. There is always the possibility of a minor situation—a complaint or grievance concerning a trivial matter—mushrooming out of proportion and causing serious problems at work such as a strike or walkout. This can hopefully be avoided by the supervisor as long as all parties' rights are protected. This is why settling issues before they are formally sent up the grievance ladder is important. The supervisor needs to know how, when, and where to impose discipline fairly.

WHY GRIEVANCES OCCUR AT WORK—CLINICAL VERSUS LEGALISTIC COMPLAINTS

Benjamin Selekman years ago established that there are two reasons for complaints occurring at work. One reason is **clinical grievances;** the other is **legalistic grievances.** Selekman was concerned that a stated grievance often is not the *real* cause of the grievance, but it is the only way that the employee can get his or her complaint to be heeded by management.

For example, assume that Mary Smith is a supervisor in the labeling department of a large retail store. Kristine Finn works for Mary; she runs one of the labeling machines. One morning, to stop what Mary feels is too much talking at work, she chews out Kristine. She really "leans" on Kristine for wasting too much time talking to Jan Page, who also runs a labeling machine. Can Jan and Kristine cause a problem for Mary over this discipline? Probably not. Why? Because Kristine and Jan have no *legal* beef. The supervisor's comment concerned their work behavior.

However, let's say that later in the afternoon, Mary forgets to let Kristine go on her scheduled 2:30 break. In addition, Mary forgets to send Kristine on her break all afternoon. Because Kristine did not get a break she is legally entitled to, she has grounds to file a complaint or grievance. She has every right to file the complaint, and she can make trouble because she was deprived of her legal job benefits. Kristine does not *have* to file a grievance. But because she is mad at Mary, she *will* likely file a grievance to make trouble. It is hard to say whether the grievance is a result of Kristine not getting her coffee break or because Mary chewed her out.

Selekman, in discussing the difference between legalistic and clinical approaches to effective supervision, argues that the effective supervisor tries not to force legalistic behavior in such a situation. The source of the grievance has nothing to do with the coffee break; rather, it happened because of the way Mary related to Kristine.

The real grievance cannot be legally debated, and the issues brought up in a grievance procedure must be items that can be legally debated.

For the employee to "get" the supervisor, she had to look for an excuse—having no coffee break—to make her case. Although it is not the real issue, it is what she can fight back about.

Many complaints and grievances in a working situation are the results of intangible, interpersonal factors rather than legalistic matters. Selekman demonstrated that the effective supervisor should be clinical in his or her approach to handling problems with employees. He or she must look for the real cause of the grievance rather than the stated cause. The stated cause may be that she didn't get a coffee break, but the real cause was the personal affront Kristine Finn felt she received from Mary.

How Legalistic Should the Supervisor Be?

It is always difficult for a supervisor to determine how legalistic he or she must be in handling a grievance and in maintaining discipline at work. On the one hand, the supervisor cannot be too soft, because he or she risks giving up many of management's rights to manage. On the other hand, common sense says that humanistic understanding goes further than rigid, autocratic behavior. It is a trade-off between trying to settle the problem satisfactorily and protecting the legitimate rights of the employee, the company, the union, and other workers by asserting rigid rules.

BEING FIRM BUT FAIR

Being able to say that any disciplinary action taken is *warranted* is crucial to ensuring that a supervisor's actions are justifiable. An easy way to ensure **fairness** is to ask certain questions regarding the need for imposed discipline or punishment (see Figure 16–2). Some of these questions might include:

1. Is the Cause for Disciplinary Action a Known Violation of Policy? When determining that a disciplinary problem has occurred, the supervisor should first determine if the problem occurred as the result of a violation of company policy. The way to ensure this is to ask: If the problem were a violation of a known policy, is that policy posted on a company bulletin board or otherwise generally known to all employees? Also, did the employee ever receive a personal copy of the policy, and is that policy stated in an easy-to-understand wording? Is the rule reasonable in that it contributes to the orderly, efficient, and safe operation of the business, or are there extenuating circumstances as to why the

FIGURE 16–2   Disciplinary Checklist*

1. What is the cause of the disciplinary problem?
2. Who is involved in the disciplinary action?
3. What has been done in the past when this disciplinary problem occurred?
4. What is the employee's record in respect to previously violating this particular rule?
5. Has the employee been involved in any disciplinary procedures in the past year?
6. Has the employee ever received any formal warning concerning this or any other related disciplinary matter?
7. What was the probable cause that initiated this disciplinary problem?
8. Is there any evidence that the employee deliberately created the disciplinary situation?
9. What disciplinary choices are available to the supervisor? Especially, what choices are available and/or mandated under the labor contract and what has been done in the past?

* Supervisors in some companies use this checklist to ensure that they are appropriately investigating every aspect of a disciplinary problem. It helps guard against action that might result in an employee grievance against the company or the supervisor.

employee might have felt the rule did not apply to the situation that occurred? If the answer to any of these questions is no, the supervisor should rethink the seriousness of the rule violation in determining how to exercise disciplinary action.

2.   What Has Happened to Other Employees Who Have Violated the Policy or Order?   This question concerns the nature and severity of the rule violation. Given that it has been established that the rule was knowingly violated, the next issue is determining how serious a problem has occurred. At this stage, the supervisor must learn whether or not other employees have violated the rule and, if so, what kinds of disciplinary action they received. Also, it must be determined whether records of similar rule violations are available and how the company coped with them. It must be determined whether or not the employee who has violated the rule has the worst (or among the worst) records of all employees in respect to violation of that rule or order. Obviously, the worse the record of the employees, the more severe the disciplinary action that will be taken. This is true because the employee who is a habitual offender may exhibit a chronic attitudinal problem in that he or she doesn't care whether or not the rules are followed. The first offender doesn't necessarily act from a don't-care attitude. In fact, the first offender

Have you ever had a boss chew you out?
Was the boss being fair with you? Have
you ever filed a grievance because you
were treated unfairly?

may not know that something should or should not be done. As a result, the wise supervisor does not treat the first-time offender as severely as a chronic offender. Only by determining the actual intensity of an employee's offense can the supervisor ensure that he or she will handle the disciplinary situation properly.

3. What Is the Employee's Record Concerning This Policy or Order? Determine how the employee has acted regarding the specific rule or order that was violated and whether or not he or she has been warned about the violation in the past. If an employee has been warned on previous occasions, especially if the warnings were written, the discipline placed on the employee is more severe than if the employee had never been warned. Again, the employee *should* know what the rules are, especially if they have been posted on a bulletin board, written out, or verbally communicated to him or her. Unfortunately, this is not always the case.

4. Has the Employee Ever Received a Final Warning Concerning the Policy Violation? If an employee has ever received a final written warning for violating a rule, he or she must be treated severely. It is not always certain that the employee understood the seriousness of the final warning—so that the delivery of the final warning and what was actually said must be clearly ascertained before definitive steps are taken. But, in most cases, if an employee violates a rule that he or she had already received a final warning about, the employee needs to be terminated.

5. What Triggered the Violation of the Policy? Some rules are violated unknowingly or, at least, not deliberately. For example, a car driver may make an illegal left turn because the "no left-hand turn" sign was removed by a prankster. Similarly, an employee may violate a rule out of sheer ignorance rather than maliciousness. Most rule violations are fairly trivial when they are violated unknowingly. Common sense usually precludes people from doing really dangerous or unreasonable acts that would jeopardize the safety of other employees. Thus, the supervisor should determine the nature of the incident that caused the employee to violate a rule or order.

6. What Evidence Is There that the Employee Wantonly Violated a Rule or Regulation? Before a supervisor metes out punishment to an employee, he or she must determine the names of all people involved in the situation, including witnesses, dates, times, places, and any other pertinent information that may help determine the extent, severity, and deliberateness of the violation. The supervisor, in doing this, is looking for any extenuating or mitigating circumstances that may help the employee prove that an especially severe penalty—or *any* penalty—is unwarranted. Such a determination may also mean the opposite; a more severe penalty may be necessary.

7. Are the Intended Disciplinary Measures Appropriate for the Offense? Is the discipline related to the seriousness of the offense, and is it consistent with the employee's past record? Guidelines for answering these questions can be developed by looking at how others have been treated for similar violations and if their penalties considered the employee's service in the organization. In taking disciplinary actions, the supervisor must be as honest and straightforward as possible. If the employee has a bad prior record, has been with the company for a long time, and has involved other people in serious offenses, the punishment should be far more severe. However, new employees having limited time with the company, who are acting individually and not affecting others,

Why is this experienced supervisor probably right?

should not be treated as harshly. If the supervisor hands out penalties haphazardly, he or she will cause a serious breach of supervisory trust.

FAIRNESS AND DISCIPLINE

Any supervisor is subject to having to handle employee grievances and/or misbehaving employees. Handling such matters correctly at the time the issue develops is critical to the supervisor's success or failure. The good supervisor must be fair in disciplinary matters. Fairness has many dimensions, however. The supervisor must be fair to the employee, to the organization, to himself or herself, and to the other employees who may be affected by the disciplinary situation. For example, consider how difficult it is to be fair when two employees play tricks on each other, get angry, and start a fight. Who started the fight, and how can corrective disciplinary methods be applied?

Maintaining effective discipline at work takes on many facets. In addition to the supervisor's concern for fairness, he or she must also remember that any aggrieved employee, at any time, may take matters into his or her own hands, either physically or in trying to get other persons involved. These persons may be employees, supervisors, customers, or union leadership. The supervisor must know that other persons can have an influential effect on the disposition of any employee grievance or complaint. Being fair is of paramount importance; if the supervisor is not fair, someone or something (often a union) will require that fairness be assured.

THE GRIEVANCE PROCEDURE— WHAT YOU NEED TO KNOW UNDER A UNION CONTRACT

Operating supervisors in a union situation often get into trouble because they don't understand how to handle the **grievance procedure** specified in the union contract. While it is difficult to be precise about how the line supervisor needs to act under a specific labor contract, some generalities can help. No two labor agreements are exactly alike, but many of the clauses have a common basis. Here are some of the guidelines:

1. Any beginning supervisor operating in a union situation should *read the contract*. He or she will usually find it is easily understood.

2. Union leaders and stewards like to cooperate with supervisors *if possible*. Again, while it is possible to find union leaders who "ride their badges," they usually try to work out any *genuine* misinterpretations under the contract. A solid working relationship with the union steward serves the supervisor well.

3. Certain impasses are likely to be reached between a supervisor, an employee, and a union steward. When this happens, the supervisor must know the grievance procedure and how to handle himself or herself when real trouble is brewing.

4. The grievance process in all labor contracts ensures that all parties who have complaints will have their complaints dealt with in a fair and uniform manner within the organization and under union contractual provisions. For example, if an employee questions working conditions or

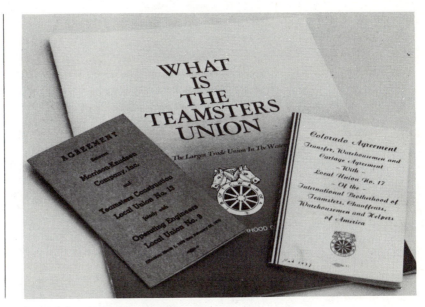

Some labor union contracts.

the way he or she is treated by a supervisor, the employee has the right to have his or her grievance considered by management. The grievance process assures the employee that this hearing will occur even if the employee's supervisor doesn't want it to occur. The grievance process is a device that forces the company to have an open-door policy. The employee is invited to discuss any grievances, gripes, or disputes that he or she feels are not being dealt with effectively in normal work relationships.

5. It is imperative that the supervisor knows what to do when an employee files a grievance. To be prepared:

a. The supervisor must understand what the contractual words mean *in practice*. See Figure 16–3 for a list of common terms in labor contracts. Most labor arbitrators, in resolving disputes, look at prior experience, past practices, and other relationships between the union, the company, and the employees. Trying to handle a grievance without knowledge of past company practices is dangerous for the supervisor.

b. The supervisor should be aware that no supervisor can act as an all-powerful being whose every wish must be complied with. The grievance procedure was developed to prevent that behavior.

**FIGURE 16–3   Common Due Process
Terms Used in Labor
Contracts**

Past practice.   This phrase, in labor relations usage, is the same as *precedent.* Both terms refer to the company's past practice in cases similar to the one at hand. Supervisors must be cautious to take action consistent with past practice because arbitrators look for consistency between past and current practices.

Due process.   It refers to the rights an employee has under the labor contract. It means that any discipline applied to a worker must be consistent with the detailed, methodical, and procedural steps specified in the labor contract. Failure of a supervisor (or a company) to give an employee due process usually results in the employee being given one more chance, regardless of what the employee's violation was. Arbitrators will determine that, if the employee was not given due process, he or she was not appropriately treated and must be given another chance.

Just cause.   It refers to the idea that the supervisor, in attempting to impose discipline, must have just cause for initiating the disciplinary action. Just cause precludes a supervisor from irrationally and capriciously imposing discipline on an employee.

Progressive discipline.   Term that means disciplinary actions taken against a subordinate become progressively stronger or more punitive. An employee may be given only an oral warning for a minor infraction of a work rule the first time. A second rule violation by the same employee brings a stiffer warning, although it may still be oral. If the infraction occurs again, a written reprimand may be issued. Should the infraction occur again, a second written reprimand (containing the warning that the next infraction will warrant a disciplinary layoff of one day without pay) will be made. The progressively tougher discipline may ultimately end in termination of the employee for a minor infraction if the employee persists in doing the same thing willingly and wantonly.

c.   The supervisor must recognize that whatever he or she says or does is legally viewed as a *representative of company management.* If the supervisor tells an employee that he or she is fired, upper management can rescind that order; but for purposes of the grievance, the employee *was* fired by the company. This means that the union can call a strike even though top management is willing to put the fired employee back to work. In short, when the supervisor acts, the company acts, and consequently the supervisor cannot get away with impetuous behavior.

d.   The supervisor should remember that almost anything he or she says or does can be the subject of a labor arbitration or labor grievance. The supervisor must not be flip in relating to the union, the union steward, the employee, or workers as a group. It is imperative that he or she have a thorough and provable case before doing anything drastic. Experienced supervisors know that they must build a record of what has transpired in any kind of disciplinary matter with an employee. It is never sufficient for a supervisor to make a decision on a grievance and then insist that the decision be followed. He or she may have to prove later that the matter was handled properly. At a minimum, this means the supervisor must have the foresight to see what will logically follow from his or her behavior. Good supervisors quickly learn to look for help, to develop records, to take down names of any necessary witnesses, and to make notations of any other data that might be used as evidence in a later situation—be it a grievance or an arbitration hearing.

e. Supervisors know that the company will try to back them when they make a decision. However, the company has no obligation to back the supervisor when he or she has made an unwarranted decision. The supervisor will not gain the respect of other supervisors or subordinates by being sloppy. Thoroughness of action and fairness are the best guidelines for supervisors. Their ability to prove themselves in a situation is unimportant.

In short, the existence of the union probably doesn't require the supervisor to do anything more or less than he or she would do without a union. But, the union is a watchdog and it can be unleashed by an employee who is ill-treated. So, with or without a union, learn to treat employees correctly in discipline and you won't have a problem.

Things to Remember

1. Discipline is not a dirty word. It is positive and necessary.

2. Good discipline is based on mutual respect, rules of conduct, training, predictable work output, and safety.

3. It is necessary to understand effective disciplinary action steps.

4. Good supervisors avoid problems while maintaining discipline by following a set of reasonable rules for themselves.

5. Constructive discipline involves emphasis on correction rather than punishment.

6. There are several types of disciplinary actions ranging from reprimands to time off with or without pay.

7. In some cases, employee disciplinary groups are an effective means of ensuring discipline.

8. Clinical grievances are based on feelings and emotions.

9. Legalistic grievances are based on rules or contract provisions.

10. Being firm but fair in a grievance situation is a desirable supervisory attitude.

11. Where unions exist, supervisors must understand the grievance procedure.

Key Words

discipline
disciplinary action
complaints
grievances
employee disciplinary groups
clinical grievances
legalistic grievances
fairness
grievance procedure

Self-Assessment

Here are some statements and questions concerning discipline and grievances. Respond with a 1, 2, or 3 if you disagree or have a negative answer or a 4, 5, or 6 if you agree or have a positive response.

1. Discipline implies punishment.

1	2	3	4	5	6

2. Supervisors must protect both employees and their organization.

1	2	3	4	5	6

3. Supervisors should not try to settle every grievance that an employee brings up.

1	2	3	4	5	6

4. In grievance hearings, it's good discipline to show others, as well as the employee, how the employee was wrong.

1	2	3	4	5	6

5. Good supervisors never admit they made a mistake to employees.

1	2	3	4	5	6

6. Failure to discipline employees when needed can result in a loss of respect for the supervisor.

1	2	3	4	5	6

7. When a problem arises, it is a good idea to let it cool off for a few days before taking any action.

1	2	3	4	5	6

8. Any grievance can go to the top.

1	2	3	4	5	6

9. Often, the stated cause of a grievance and the real cause are not the same.

1	2	3	4	5	6

10. Due process means that you should act first and ask questions later.

1	2	3	4	5	6

CASES

Dirty Linen

Wanda Broadley liked working at the receiving counter for the Hotel and Linen Supply commercial laundry. Her job was to sort and identify linens, uniforms, table wear, and other items that came in for cleaning. While the job was somewhat dirty, in that she handled soiled materials, she enjoyed talking with the delivery people, being away from the noise and heat of the cleaning operations and, to a large extent, being her own boss. When Sue Williams, the shift supervisor, told her to cut down on the time spent talking to delivery people, Wanda was upset and angry.

Two days later, she asked Sue for a transfer to another assignment. "You're one of our best employees," stated Sue. "If I transferred you, there is no one else who knows receiving and sorting as well. It would mean training another person and a loss of efficiency. It's bad enough when you go on vacation." Wanda again approached Sue, this time with a written request for transfer. When Sue failed to approve the request, Wanda filed a grievance. It stated that Sue was discriminating against her by keeping her in an undesirable assignment where she was exposed to soiled and perhaps dangerous materials for long periods. If a transfer was impossible, she demanded hazard pay for exposure.

In a subsequent grievance hearing, Sue's position, that management could assign people anywhere within their job description, was upheld. Even though the matter was settled for the time being, Sue was puzzled by Wanda's action.

1. What was the real cause of the grievance?

2. Did Wanda have a legitimate case?

3. What position would you take as a union steward representing Wanda?

Signs of Trouble

There are few tangible ways of determining if discipline is breaking down in an organization. Here are a few; in all cases, current practices must be compared to past actions to determine the extent of discipline problems.

1. Increased tardiness.

2. Excessive unexcused absences.

3. An increase in errors.

4. Increased failure to meet required deadlines.

5. Excuses blaming equipment, materials, other departments, or faulty instructions when these have not previously been common problems.

6. Avoidance of supervisor.

7. Extended lunch and coffee breaks.

8. Early shutdown of work before the regular work period ends.

9. Increases in minor accidents.

10. Development of a hostile climate.

1. Select three items from the list and develop a plan for changing them.

2. List some reasons why discipline may break down.

3. Are most people self-disciplined? Explain your answer.

PART SEVEN

The Supervisor and Social Responsibility

17

Beyond Profits and Productivity: Legal, Social, and Ethical Responsibility

Thought Starter

One of the fastest-growing and most significant fields of law during the past 20 years is called *pro bono publico* law. Loosely translated from the Latin frequently used by lawyers, it means "for the benefit of the public." Pro bono law is designed to enforce law that protects the public interest. Many of these laws are directly related to issues such as environmental pollution by work organizations, assurance of equal opportunity and equal treatment in the workplace for employees or applicants, and protection of employee privacy. More recently, pro bono law has dealt with conditions of termination, especially for managers who feel that they have lost jobs through no fault of their own. Frequently, in the workplace, social responsibility describes management actions taken in the public interest. Such actions go beyond the creation of profits or increased productivity.

In addition to protecting people and the environment as required by law, organizations are also responsible for acting honestly, without malice, and within the spirit of both legal and societal standards of behavior. Ethical behavior is another management concern that is closely related to social responsibility. First-line managers are involved directly in both social and ethical responsibilities as required by law and expected by society in general.

In Chapter 17 you will learn:

☐ Government regulations determine many personnel actions that involve first-line managers.

☐ Attitudes, beliefs, and values are much more difficult to change than the enforcement of legal requirements.

☐ What is ethical is sometimes difficult to determine.

☐ First-line managers need to know what laws may affect their work.

☐ As societal values change, so do laws and their interpretations.

"It's more difficult for a young attractive woman to get promoted than one who is older and not too attractive," argued Vicki Bartish. "I don't agree at all," shot back Ron Backman. "Looks are an asset. There's no doubt in my mind that young, good-looking women in key jobs improve the organization's image."

"Well, it shouldn't," stated Vicki flatly, "There is no way you can convince me that looks have anything to do with performance. Performance is what should really count."

"I agree," said Ron in a thoughtful voice, "but I'm not sure that's the case all of the time."

Although Vicki and Ron did not settle the complicated issue, it is one worth examining. Is it right to promote a person because of their sex, appearance, ethnic origin, age, religion, or any reason other than being the best applicant for the position? Managers faced with the necessity of meeting affirmative action goals may treat factors such as ethnicity and sex as job qualifications in the same sense that experience is treated as a qualification. Equally difficult are intangibles such as

395

personality, verbal skills, and level of education. How much weight should these factors carry? If a manager genuinely wants to be fair and ensure that the best candidate is chosen, what should really count in selecting a person for promotion? It can be a difficult question to answer.

SOCIAL RESPONSIBILITY AND THE LAW

From the point of view of the first-line manager, **social responsibility** is any activity that helps to assure fairness and honesty in personnel practices, protection of employee health and safety, protection of the environment, and protection of the consumer and the community which that organization serves. It includes all activities designed to protect the interests of employees and the public in general. Management, at all levels, is also concerned with the image of the organization as a good citizen in the communities it serves. Companies like Exxon, Mobil, Xerox, IBM, United Technology, and many others spend millions of dollars in advertising and public grants (such as those made to the Public Broadcasting System, PBS), to create an image of good citizenship.

Beginning with the Civil Rights Act of 1964 and continuing through most of the 1970s, many laws were enacted to assure that work organizations would promote social goals such as nondiscrimination, environmental protection, effective energy and resource utilization, and the welfare of employees. Supervisors are most concerned, on a daily basis, with laws related to personnel actions. Figure 17–1 outlines some major personnel laws and their purposes.

In addition to these major legal provisions, there are other laws that are related to the supervisor's personnel activities. All states, as an example, administer federal unemployment compensation laws. An employee who is either laid off from work due to economic conditions or who is terminated without just cause is eligible for unemployment compensation in an amount fixed by both the state and federal governments. Part of the compensation comes from company funds. Most organizations prefer to avoid unemployment compensation payments unless such payments are unavoidable. Employees injured while working are eligible for workers compensation, payments designed to offset both medical costs and loss of pay. Since insurance rates are based on the number of payments made to employees, most companies strive to keep injuries at a minimum. While there are many other laws, few have the impact of **Title VII** of the **Civil Rights Act** of 1964 and its 1972 amendments.

FIGURE 17–1 Major Social Legislation for Personnel

Title VII of the Civil Rights Act of 1964, as amended in 1972 (frequently called the Equal Employment Opportunity Act).	Prohibits discrimination in any personnel act based on race, color, religion, national origin, or sex.
Age Discrimination in Employment Act of 1967; amended in 1978.	Prohibits discrimination in any personnel act related to applicants or employees between the ages of 40 and 70.
Vocational Rehabilitation Act of 1973.	Prohibits discrimination in any personnel act by the federal government or any company with government contracts because of physical condition if the person can adequately perform an assigned task.
Vietnam-Era Veteran's Readjustment Assistance Act of 1974.	Designed to promote access to government contractor employment by Vietnam-era veterans.
Pregnancy Discrimination Act (1978 amendment to the Civil Rights Act of 1964).	Prohibits discrimination in any personnel action based on pregnancy.

Supervisors and Title VII

When the Civil Rights Act of 1964 was enacted by Congress, it was divided into sections dealing with specific areas of discriminatory practice such as education, access to public facilities, access to public businesses, and employment. Each section of the act was called a title. In 1972, Title VII of the act—dealing with employment—was rewritten and amended to prevent discrimination based on race, color, religion, national origin, or sex. A special government body, the Equal Employment Opportunity Commission (EEOC), was designated as administrator of Title VII provisions. Title VII covers all employers and labor unions with 15 or more employees or members. Indian tribes, employees of members of Congress, and members of bona fide private clubs are exempt from the law's coverage. All personnel actions such as hiring, training, promotion, transfer, demotion, layoffs, disciplinary actions, work assignments, tests, interviews, and changes in pay or job duties are affected by provisions of Title VII.

As a result of Title VII, several concepts have been developed that directly affect supervisory actions:

Protected Class. Any person or group who, because of race, color, religion, national origin, or sex (also included are people age 40–70 and the physically handicapped) might be discriminated against is a member of the protected class. In some cases, where discrimination has occurred, an applicant or employee who is a member of a protected class may be given special consideration for employment, promotion, training, or other personnel action. Membership in a protected class may be considered part of the qualifications necessary to fill a specific job if there is evidence of past discrimination. During the early enforcement of equal opportunity law, emphasis centered on ending discriminatory practices against blacks, Hispanics, and other racial or national groups. More recently, emphasis has been placed on integrating women into work previously performed almost exclusively by males.

Disparate Treatment. Action by a company or supervisor that clearly treats a member of a protected class differently from other workers is known as disparate treatment. Restricting some jobs to men or women only, or not promoting black or Hispanic employees on a basis proportional to white employees are examples of disparate treatment. Supervisors who behave differently toward members of a protected class than toward other employees may be accused of disparate treatment.

Disparate Effect. Some personnel practices not intended to discriminate against members of a protected class may unintentionally create an illegal practice. Recruitment by word of mouth is an example. Employees, in such cases, usually recommend people like themselves. Another example is the requirement of a high school diploma when a job does not require specialized education or training. Disparate effect has the same legal penalties as disparate treatment. Both practices are illegal.

Reasonable Accommodation. No person can be forced to perform work that violates his or her religion. Some employees, for instance, may have religious prohibitions against working on Saturdays or Sundays. If work is required on those days, the supervisor must try to develop a schedule that will accommodate religious prohibitions. If it is impossible to "reasonably accommodate" such employees, however, the employees may be forced to accept another assignment or, in some cases, resign. In all cases, the employer must demonstrate an attempt to accommodate religious prohibitions of employees.

There have been two significant administrative guidelines to the Civil

Rights Act that also directly affect supervisors. In 1978, the Equal Employment Opportunity Commission and the Office of Federal Contract Compliance Programs (OFCCP), which enforces equal opportunity in government contract employment, published the *Uniform Employment Guidelines*. The guidelines set forth rules for selection of employees and the criteria used for determining whether or not an organization is complying with the law. Supervisors who are part of the selection process need to be familiar with major guideline provisions. In interviews, for instance, the guidelines imply that applicants must be asked the same questions. Panel interviews, rather than only a single-person interview, are also recommended. Perhaps most difficult to achieve is the 80-percent rule. Under current law, a company must monitor the applicants available for work from both majority (usually white males) and minority applicant groups. When majority applicants are selected, 80 percent of the number selected must also be from minority groups. Say 100 white males apply, and 50 are selected; then, if 100 minority applicants apply, 80 percent of 50, or 40 minority applicants must also be included in the work force. As the number of applicants varies, the selection process becomes more complex. Large organizations usually have trained personnel specialists that monitor hiring ratios and try to help supervisors maintain a balanced work force in terms of protected classes.

Sexual Harassment—a Special Problem

A second important ruling made in 1980 establishes guidelines for **sexual harassment**. When men and women work in close proximity, and usually when women report to men, sexual remarks or conduct is almost inevitable. If sexual conduct interferes with work or causes employee stress it may be classified as harassment. Harassment on the basis of sex is a violation of section 703 of Title VII. While it is still uncertain what legally constitutes sexual harassment, some interesting questions are raised. Is telling a dirty joke to a woman a form of harassment? If a person is promoted because of consenting to provide sexual favors to the employer, can other employees claim harassment? Do flirting, terms of endearment, suggestive remarks, and touching constitute harassment? According to recent rulings, sexual harassment includes behavior such as sexual advances, requests for sexual favors, and other verbal or physical conduct of a sexual nature directed toward an employee or applicant. Three general rules apply:

1. If toleration of or submission to sexual advances is made a condition

of work, harassment exists. Under the law, no one can be forced to give in to keep his or her job.

2. No one may be given a poor performance evaluation for refusing to accept sexual advances or to provide sexual favors.

3. Hostile, intimidating, or offensive conduct of a sexual nature that interferes with work performance is also classified as harassment.

While the rules have been made, employees may, in some cases, make accusations of harassment when none is intended. Friendly, outgoing behavior may easily be misinterpreted. What appears to be sexual conduct may not be. An attractive young person may be promoted because of knowledge, skill, and competence rather than because he or she has become sexually intimate with someone in a higher-level position in the organization. Supervisors should be aware of a reverse harassment that occurs when an employee makes sexual advances toward the boss to gain specific favors or to place themselves in a power position through subtle blackmail. Rejected employees of this type may accuse the supervisor of making the very advances that the supervisor declined.

Ethics—Right and Wrong

To cover up mistakes, missed schedules, or poor decisions, some supervisors may deliberately accuse others of causing the problem, make false excuses, or cover up errors by hiding them in paperwork. While wrong, such conduct is almost an accepted reality of modern work. Supervisory **ethics**, doing what is right, is often difficult. If the organization has a no-gambling rule and the supervisor tolerates or even participates in seasonal baseball or football pools circulated by employees, is the supervisor wrong? Crushing what most employees see as an innocent game may have worse consequences than enforcing a rule.

Of a more serious nature is the routine pilfering of supplies for personal use by either the supervisor's or the employee's family and friends. Granting extra uncharged time off to employee friends and making favorable job assignments are also unethical practices.

Ethical practices are always judged by their consequences to the people involved and whether they violate the rules of either the organization or society. One of the most difficult ethical positions a supervisor can be placed in is that of becoming a whistleblower. If a supervisor—or an employee—sees or has knowledge of deliberate unethical practices by a boss or by the organization, should it be reported? If, for instance, sales figures are inflated to raise stock prices, should the records supervisor report the truth? If a product does not meet advertised quality standards, should a quality control supervisor report the truth? If a supervisor's boss orders that the real cost of a job be covered up by reporting incorrect charges, should the supervisor obey the boss?

There are endless decisions faced by supervisors daily that involve ethical positions. While there is no rule of thumb as to what is clearly right, most experienced managers know that judgment and a set of personal ethical guidelines are necessary. Some people are guided by the "what they don't know won't hurt them" principle; others are guided by a firm set of personal convictions. In general, successful managers approach ethics with a strong sense of right and wrong but realize that there may be extenuating conditions and exceptions to almost any rule. While not making undue allowances, they temper their judgments with the reality of work conditions.

Conditions of Work and Rules of the Game

In addition to problems related to equal employment and ethics, supervisors are also concerned with **conditions of work** such as safety, schedules, shift assignments, overtime distribution, and equity. Equity refers to equal treatment of employees. It does not mean treating all employees alike in on-the-job personal relations. It is concerned with fairness, assuring that work is not piled on an employee because he or she is a good performer or, unfortunately, sometimes out of personal dislike for the employee by the supervisor. Most managers strive for fairness, try not to play favorites, or depend on one or two employees more than others. It is important that they be seen as equitable in their treatment of everyone. Whether they are hard-nosed, strict, and rule enforcing, or more flexible, people-oriented, and less authoritarian, consistency in behavior is important. Employees are frequently unnecessarily disturbed by seemingly inconsistent supervisory behavior, often expressed as "blowing hot one minute and cold the next."

One of the most important supervisory functions is related to assuring employee safety. Under the Occupational Safety and Health Act of 1970 (**OSHA**), individual supervisors and companies may be held liable for exposing employees to health-impairing substances and job conditions. While worker compensation laws supply a degree of economic security to people who can no longer work because of job-related injuries or illness, the supervisor is ultimately responsible for assuring safe, healthful working conditions. Large organizations usually have safety engineers, safety inspectors, or other personnel trained to help supervisors in providing safe conditions at work. Insurance companies that provide work-men's compensation insurance also provide advice and direction in assuring occupational safety. From a profit-oriented picture, on-the-job safety pays off. Good safety programs result in fewer absences from work, improved morale, and better equipment and facility usage. Richard Grinnold, of the Industrial Relations Research Association, has pointed out that OSHA has yet to prove it has been worth the millions of dollars it has spent in regulation. Conventional safety programs provided by organizations and insurance companies may be more effective. Of all the government's regulatory agencies, OSHA has been the most controversial and frequently the most costly.

Employee Welfare and Organization Health

Work organizations have evolved into providers of benefits that support employee welfare and provide income for other needs and desires. Supervisors must recognize that employees receive three separate types of income in most job situations. Of the three, pay for attendance is the most important. The term *attendance,* rather than *time worked,* more accurately describes the fact that, in a given job situation, some employees contribute less than others to the organization's goals and yet, they are paid equally with employees having the same job classification. They are paid for attendance rather than productivity, quality, or creativity. When supervisors deal with employees on a day-to-day basis, it is important that employees who do more work receive more approval, recognition, responsibility, and if permitted by rules the organization, money. Nonperformance or minimum performance, if rewarded, will only breed additional minimum performance.

A related pay issue is pay for time not worked. In the United States, vacations, holidays, breaks, and related legitimate pay for time not worked exceeds 300 hours per year, excluding sick leave. Supervisors have control, frequently not exercised, over the most significant loss of time that is not legitimate. Extended breaks, extended lunch periods, startup time (usually a coffee break) at the shift's beginning and also after lunch, and shutdown time before lunch and at the shift's end can often consume large periods of time. It has been estimated that factory workers waste less time than any other group, and they are about 55 percent efficient. Office workers waste more time and are less than 50 percent efficient. When lost time plus legitimate paid time off is added together, it is our belief that many, if not most, employees who are paid for 2,080 hours of work per year (40 hours per week for 52 weeks) actually work approximately 1,000 hours. Supervisors have the primary responsibility for developing methods to reduce the large loss of time that can occur in many places of employment.

A third type of pay is the benefits that employees receive in hospitalization, medical, dental, and other insured health coverage, as well as retirement. While supervisors have no way of controlling employee benefit use, they must constantly know their costs. Abuse of sick leave is a common method used by some employees to supplement paid time off. In the absence of company policies or labor agreements requiring medical certification of illness, supervisors must keep careful records of sick leave patterns that point to abuse in order to take appropriate corrective action.

Chemical Dependency Rehabilitation (CDR)

Chemical dependency rehabilitation (CDR) is a term sometimes used to describe programs developed by work organizations to assist employees with drug or alcohol dependency. Many supervisors may make the costly mistake of ignoring drug and alcohol problems, universarily recognized as illnesses rather than disciplinary problems, and only act when it is too late to help employees with chemical dependencies. Some organizations have special programs and policies designed to assist employees and supervisors faced with drug- and alcohol-related problems. Effective supervisors learn to recognize the symptoms of chemical dependency and take appropriate action—referral to competent counseling or medical agencies. It is necessary, with the prevalence of chemical dependency in our society, for first-line managers to fully understand related company policies as well as identification of sources of assistance.

BEYOND SUPERVISION

Productivity, quality, stability of the work force, costs, schedules, equipment, supplies, and achievement of organizational goals are some of the first-line manager's primary tasks. Beyond those, however, the supervisor is also a servant of society and an administrator of employee well-being. Most of all, effective supervisors are developers of people. Like good coaches, they want employees to develop skills, knowledge, attitudes, and a desire for achievement that will help the organization and the employee. Successful individuals make successful group members. Successful groups make successful supervisors. Successful supervisors make successful organizations.

Things to Remember

1. Social responsibility and the law:
   a. Social responsibility includes activities that protect the interests of employees, the community, and the public in general.
   b. Supervisors are primarily concerned with social responsibility law related to personnel.
   c. Equal employment is a major area of the supervisor's social responsibility.

2. Title VII:
   a. Title VII of the Civil Rights Act prohibits discrimination based on race, color, religion, national origin, and sex.
   b. Supervisors are responsible for enforcing many provisions of Title VII.
   c. Special terminology of equal employment needs to be understood by all supervisors.

3. Sexual harassment:
   a. Title VII, section 703, prohibits sexual harassment.
   b. Any action requiring sexual consent or toleration of sexual conduct as a condition of work is illegal.
   c. Many questions relating to sexual harassment have not been resolved in court.

4. Ethics:
   a. Ethics is concerned with right and wrong.
   b. Supervisors must develop an ethical code based on both judgment and personal principle.
   c. In some cases, there is no clear right or wrong.

5. Conditions of work—rules of the game:
   a. Equity, fairness in the treatment of employees, is an important management function.
   b. Employee safety is an important supervisory function.
   c. The Occupational Safety and Health Act has proven to be expensive and frequently controversial.

Key Words

social responsibility
Title VII
Civil Rights Act
sexual harassment
ethics

conditions of work
OSHA
employee health and welfare
CDR (chemical dependency rehabilitation)

Self-Assessment   Respond with a 1, 2, or 3 to the questions or statements listed below if you disagree or have a negative response. If your response is positive or you agree, answer with a 4, 5, or 6.

1. The Age Discrimination Act does not apply to people less than 40 years of age.

1	2	3	4	5	6

2. Women have been, and still are, subject to disparate treatment.

1	2	3	4	5	6

3. Sexual harassment is not a serious violation of the Civil Rights Act, but it remains an ethical problem.

1	2	3	4	5	6

4. There is an increase in top-down management.

1	2	3	4	5	6

5. Safety is the responsibility of the Occupational Safety and Health Administration.

1	2	3	4	5	6

6. Ethics is a matter of law more than social standards.

1	2	3	4	5	6

7. Work organizations have little or no real responsibility for the welfare of employees.

1	2	3	4	5	6

8. Supervisors should try to handle chemical dependency problems themselves before referring the affected employee to a counseling or medical agency.

1	2	3	4	5	6

9. Ethics are always judged by the consequences to the people involved.

1	2	3	4	5	6

10. Equity means treating all employees alike.

1	2	3	4	5	6

CASES

Maria Is Miffed

Maria Rodriguez worked her way through the ranks of Kerrick Department Stores to her current assignment as general office manager. Nearly all of the company's office clerical staff reported to her. She was proud of the quality and promptness of work generated by her department. Duane Foxworthy, manager of administrative services, was not only an admirer of Maria's effectiveness, but her immediate manager as well. "We're going to get the green light for the installation of the new high-density, totally networked automated office system," he said with a smile. "Some of our current word-processing equipment can be phased out. With the new, high-speed equipment and advance programming, we should be able to phase out about 10 clerical positions."

Maria did not smile back. "That's downright unethical," she replied angrily. "Many of our employees have been with us for years. It's a damned shame and just plain unethical to replace them with electronic machines. We reduced enough when we installed our old word processors. Now you'll be hurting some of our best senior people."

"Hold it," retorted Duane. "We'll try to find new jobs for them and we'll keep as many as we can. In any case, some of your people are ready for retirement. Maybe we can work out something with personnel to give them special early retirement benefits. We're not uncaring, and you know it."

"It's still unethical," murmured Maria as she walked back to break the news to her department members.

1. Is Duane's position unethical, as Maria stated?

2. Why is Maria so defensive?

3. How do you feel about machines replacing people?

Hal's Harem

When the news broke, it broke big. Not only was Hal Harvey being terminated, but there was a good chance that charges would be filed against him by 12 of his employees. Hal was originally hired as a drafting technician for Sizeman Engineering and Technical Company (SET). During his five years with SET, he rose to the head of drafting services. When the company began converting to computer-assisted design, Hal set up a model training program for the new department. He hired technically trained people who were capable of taking engineering specifications and making the appropriate computer entries that resulted in first-rate engineering drawings for use in the construction industry.

In filling vacancies in the new department, Hal hired primarily young, single women with dependents. His explanation to the personnel department was that most of them had good keyboard skills, technical training, and all desperately needed well-paying assignments. Although there were jokes about Hal's Harem, no one took it seriously until Peggy Snyder blew the whistle. "Let me tell you," she began, in an interview with Karen Krista, chief of personnel, "The only way to keep a job is to do what he asks after work. None of us like it, but it's the price of keeping our jobs. When I refused to spend the night with him, he said he'd make life less than happy for me, and he has. I'm quitting, and the others are afraid to talk." A follow-up with other women in the department proved Peggy was truthful.

1. How can unpleasant incidents like Hal's Harem be avoided?

2. What responsibility do supervisors have to follow up on suspicions?

3. Why are sexual harassment cases more difficult than others to prove?

Words and Terms

Abdicator A manager at any level who refuses to make decisions, assign tasks, or define goals. Abdicators depend on employees to do their own managing.

Accountability The obligation and process by which an employee reports job progress to his or her supervisor. In some cases, holding a subordinate liable for responsibility in fulfilling job assignments.

Achievement The degree of success in properly completing a task or set of tasks. It sometimes is used to designate the completion of a difficult, non-routine goal.

Administration Management duties that are concerned primarily with policy and procedure development, report analysis, and planning rather than direct operational activities.

Agreement In this sense, a labor contract. A written document relating to wages, hours, and working conditions by which both management and employees must be guided.

Alternative In the decision-making process, any of several possible solutions to a problem. A good decision usually depends on development and examination of several workable methods of achieving a goal.

Ambivalent A type of worker who, while usually intelligent and capable, is not a high achiever. Ambivalent workers shun necessary work that does not appeal to them. Often, they are frustrated by their own behavior.

Appraisal Any evaluation of an employee's performance.

Arbitration The use of a third, noninvolved person to settle a dispute between two parties. Usually used in unresolved disputes between union members and management.

Ascendant A worker who is highly motivated by recognition, responsibility, and achievement. Unlike the ambivalent worker, the ascendant employee welcomes and accomplishes all work assignments.

Aspiration level The degree to which a person is motivated to achieve personal goals and the difficulty of those goals. A high aspiration level would be indicated by a person wanting to be the best in any endeavor.

Attitude A characteristic way of acting toward a person, idea, or assignment. Attitudes range on a continuum from highly positive to extremely negative.

Attitudinal training Any training designed to develop specific attitudes, frames of reference, or feelings toward work and an organization.

Authoritarian A management style where all decisions are made by the manager. Workers do only what they are told.

Authority The right, granted by either ownership or higher management, to decide, direct, control, and approve or disapprove the activities of others. It includes all decision making rights granted by position and delegation in an organization. In some cases, the term *authority* indicates expertise or knowledge of a particular field.

Autocratic The belief that only those with power and authority can make valid decisions. One who is authoritarian.

Automaton Acting as a robot. A worker who performs repetitive tasks and is never allowed to make decisions.

Back-up technique An alternative course of action for use when a planned course of action proves inadequate or impossible.

Bargaining unit Another way of referring to the union in a particular organization.

Basic needs See Physiological needs.

Behavior Any overt or covert action displayed by an individual. The term includes expressed attitudes, beliefs, ideas, opinions, and physical activities.

Behavioral science The study of human behavior using scientific methods of observation. It utilizes knowledge and techniques developed largely from psychology, sociology, and anthropology.

Benefits Often mistakenly called *fringe benefits,* it refers to two types, direct and indirect compensation. The first benefit is pay for time not worked, such as vacation pay, holiday pay, and paid break periods. Another class of benefits is *contingent benefits;* they include medical insurance, hospitalization, sick leave, and other benefits available to employees but not necessarily used equally by all members of an organization.

Body language Any body movement that sends messages to others deliberately or unintentionally. Posture, hand movements, facial expressions, sitting position, and quickness or slowness of movement all communicate something to others.

Budget Planned expenditures for a specific time period.

Bureaucracy A form of organization based on highly standardized jobs, procedures, and methods with little room for individual decisions or judgment. A form typically adopted by large organizations, especially governmental organizations.

CDR (Chemical dependency rehabilitation) Any action or service designed to correct dependency on alcoholism and drug addiction by employees.

Call-in pay   Minimum amount of pay for work an employee was called in to do, whether the work is performed or not. It is common practice to pay employees at least four hours of pay for reporting to work, even if less time or no time is spent working. In some cases, employees may be paid more or less than four hours depending on company policy or union agreements.

Civil Rights Act   Passed in 1964, amended in 1972 and in subsequent years, the Civil Rights Act prohibits discrimination based on race, color, religion, national origin, or sex.

Classical learning   Usually called classical conditioning, classical learning states that people learn to respond in set ways to stimuli that are associated with reward or punishment. A response to red stoplights is an example. Because of the conditioned response to stop, most people will automatically stop without thinking.

Classical school of management   All management theorists who contributed to management philosophy prior to 1926. Those theorists who advocated methods, procedures, and organizational techniques as prescriptions for management ills.

Company people   Employees usually in management, professional, or administrative work, who strongly support the organization and work for the organization's success as much as their own gain. They see personal success tied to organizational success.

Compensation   Any reward for effort. It usually refers to money given in return for tasks performed.

Complaint   A gripe or *unwritten* grievance. Complaints are usually symptoms of underlying discontent.

Contingency theory of leadership   The belief that the most appropriate leadership style is dependent on the conditions and forces affecting the work situation. Demonstrated by the Ohio State studies, no one style is best for all situations and circumstances.

Contract   Any formal or, in some cases, implied agreement. In union-management relations, an agreement on personnel and work rules including wages, hours, and conditions or work between the union and management. Contracts are binding on both employees and managers.

Control   The acts of setting standards, measuring performance, and taking corrective action. Control is a basic management requirement.

Coordination   As a primary management function, according to some writers, coordination involves utilizing whatever techniques are available to ensure a smoothly functioning, effective organization. In another sense, assuring that goals, priorities, and needs are adequately communicated and controlled.

Cost control   Utilization of management effort to optimize performance and minimize costs per unit of output.

Counseling Techniques used to inform, correct, instruct, and change attitudes. In work organizations, it involves the supervisor assisting an employee in solving work-related problems.

Country club leadership A management style based on making employees happy or satisfied more than directing their activities toward specific task accomplishment.

Cow psychology Daniel Bell's term for human relations. Bell believed too much effort was being made to make people contented rather than productive at work.

Decision A choice of action. Choosing a course of action from several alternatives.

Decision grid A technique for making decisions; it considers such variables as cost, schedules, quantity, and quality.

Delegating Authorizing or directing another person to take some action or perform some task.

Democratic management A management technique that stresses maximum employee participation in the decision-making process. Employees, by common consensus, decide the course of work activity.

Differential piece rate Developed by Taylor and modified by others, a method of payment for units produced rather than time worked. When more than the standard number of units is produced, the rate per unit is increased for all units produced.

Directing The act of giving instructions, orders, or direction to another person. A primary management function.

Disciplinary action Any corrective action directed toward changing behavior, attitudes, or methods of work. Actions taken to ensure that work rules are enforced.

Discipline The act of preventing or correcting errors or improper attitudes. Training that makes punishment unnecessary.

Disparate effect Any unintentional act that has the effect of treating one person differently from another or denying equal opportunity because of race, color, religion, national origin, sex, age, and physical condition.

Disparate treatment Deliberately treating one person differently from another or denying opportunity because of race, color, religion, national origin, sex, age, and physical condition.

Dissatisfiers According to Herzberg, those job requirements such as pay, benefits, policies, and working conditions whose absence dissatisfies workers but whose presence does not satisfy employees.

Due process The guarantee of a fair hearing, of the right to present one's side in a dispute, and the guarantee of fair and equitable treatment.

Efficiency expert A person whose primary efforts are directed toward work simplification, cost reduction, and methods improvement. The original industrial engineer.

Effort bargain In a union-management contract, the amount and type of work required of an employee in a specific job classification.

Ego needs The psychological needs of feeling worthwhile, self-esteem, and desire for recognition. The need for others to see you as an adequate, worthwhile person.

Empathy The ability to understand how another person reacts, feels, and thinks without becoming emotionally involved. Putting yourself in another person's place or feelings.

Equal Employment Opportunity Act In 1972, Title 7 of the Civil Rights Act of 1964 was amended to establish the Equal Employment Opportunity Commission in an attempt to end discrimination in employment and other personnel actions. It has proved to be one of the most significant pieces of social legislation in this century.

Ergonomics A special area of industrial and human engineering that seeks to design equipment, workplaces, lighting, and other environmental conditions to enhance human productivity and reduce job fatigue.

Ethics Principles and beliefs based on what is right or wrong in specific situations. Based on societal values of good and bad.

Expectancy theory The theory that the strength of a behavior (the amount of effort) directed toward achieving a goal is determined in part by the value of the goal and whether there is a realistic expectancy of achieving the goal.

Experimental problems Problems that have been experienced rather than imagined or hypothesized.

Expert power Influence based on knowledge, skill, or special abilities.

Feedback Information received as a result of some action or communication.

First-line management Any manager who supervises nonmanagement personnel as a primary assignment. Commonly called supervisors or foremen. The first level of management.

Forecasts Projections of future events based on analysis of current and past occurrences. Present planning for the future.

Friendly helper A management style based on positive, helpful actions that avoids conflict in favor of compromise or agreement.

Fringe benefit Any benefit in addition to pay for time worked.

Function Any major activity. An organizational unit such as manufacturing, sales, accounting, maintenance, quality control, and so forth.

Goal priority Objectives or tasks arranged in order of importance. The most important tasks receive first priority, and so on.

Go-no-go decisions   Decisions to either take an action or not take one. Such decisions are often crucial but poorly planned.

Grievance   A written formal complaint made by an employee regarding alleged work rule violations, injustices, improper assignments, or other allegedly incorrect actions on the part of the company, a member of management, or a co-worker.

Guesstimate   A guess based on past experience with little or no formal analysis.

Guild   A group of artisans or skilled craftspersons who met, in preunion periods, to reach agreements on work standards, training, and minimum pay for certain jobs.

Hawthorne Studies   Studies made in worker behavior at the Hawthorne, Illinois, plant of the Western Electric Company in 1926. The Hawthorne Studies led to the development of the Human Relations movement in management.

Hierarchy   An organizational form with levels from low to high. Any system that uses levels of importance, responsibility, or authority.

Hierarchy of Needs   A. H. Maslow's belief that human needs range from low-order needs, such as physiological and safety needs, to high-order needs such as social, psychological, and self-actualization needs. High-order needs are important only after low-order needs have been at least partially satisfied.

Human Relations Movement   The group of management theorists who believed that worker effectiveness was dependent on well-founded interpersonal relations.

Impoverished leaders   Managers who see their role primarily as message carriers and do not take a strong interest in either people or the tasks that need accomplishing.

Incentive   An external motivation, such as money used in exchange for getting added effort from employees.

Incredulity   Disbelief in what another person says or seems to do.

Indifferent   A person who works for bread and only bread. The job has little importance other than its monetary benefits.

Innovative objectives   Job objectives other than routine or problem-solving objectives. Such objectives are concerned with new or improved methods, systems, or organization forms.

Integrate   To blend together in a workable combination; to coordinate.

Job description   A formal listing of tasks and responsibilities composing a single job.

Job design   Usually associated with job enrichment, job design includes all activities directed toward making jobs more interesting and increasing employee involvement in job decisions.

Job enlargement   The addition of tasks to a job in an attempt to make it less routine and more interesting.

Job enrichment   A technique of adding increased and nearly total responsibility for the outcome of a job to make it more satisfying.

Job performance grid   A method of evaluating job performance, considering quality, quantity, costs, and schedule adherence.

Just cause   Action taken based on evidence and due process. In union-management relations, a disciplinary action taken by management because of evidence of misconduct or rule infractions.

Knowledge training   Training that involves information, principles, procedures, policies, and methods rather than skills or attitudes. It is sometimes called *cognitive training*.

Labor contract   See Contract.

Labor Management Relations Act   Often called the Taft-Hartley Act, the LMRA is the most important labor law in the United States. With the exception of government organizations, railroads, airlines (covered by the Railway Labor Act), and agriculture, it is the primary labor law for all organizations in the United States that deal with unions and the collective bargaining process.

Leadership   The act or actions required to motivate groups of people toward goals that are important to both the leader and followers. Motivating people to action because they feel the leader's judgment and actions will help them achieve their own goals.

Legalistic grievances   Grievances based on a section or article of a union-management contract (often called an agreement).

Legitimate power   Often called position power, it is the power associated with a specific job level. Upper managers have greater legitimate power than lower-level managers, who have greater legitimate power than nonmanagement employees. Power to assign work, recommend hiring and discharge, recommend or make promotions, discipline, or any similar management activity are examples of legitimate power.

Line function   An organizational unit that contributes directly to the end product or service of the organization.

Line management   The management of a line function or a line-like organization.

Line organization   That part of the organization not considered staff or internal services. The part of the organization that includes line functions.

Loading the dice   Deliberate emphasis of some facts over others to create either a favorable or unfavorable impression or belief.

Local   Locals are the basic organizational unit of unions. They are the union organization in a specific geographical area or company.

Lockout   Management's counteraction to a union strike or threat of strike. The closure of a plant to union employees in the event of a contract dispute.

Lose/lose strategy   The attitude that if "I can't win, neither will you." Any actions taken to ensure that no one else will achieve goals if one's own goals are not being achieved.

Management   The use of resources such as manpower, money, machines, materials, and methods to achieve an organization's goals. In some cases, it is "getting work done through others," as authorized by higher management or by ownership.

Management levels   The classification of managers by organizational level. Usually top or executive management, middle management, and first-line or supervisory management.

Managerial Grid   A training and evaluation technique developed by Robert Blake and Jane Mouton that assumes the primary concerns of management are people and production.

Martyr complex   An attitude of suffering and sacrifice. The belief that circumstances continually place a person in a position where work objectives cannot be achieved. Sacrificing one's self for the organization.

Maximization   Obtaining the absolute upper limits of an organization's or individual's capabilities.

Maze-bright   Being able to understand the intricacies of an organization. Knowledge of where the real points of power and influence are as well as who is listened to and who isn't.

MBO (Management by objectives)   A management technique concentrating on results through the achievement of stated objectives.

Mid-level management   Managers who supervise other managers and who also report to higher levels of management.

Motion economy   See Motion study.

Motion study   The study of the movements people make during the performance of assigned tasks to reduce waste motion and increase productivity.

Motivation   Any set of needs that is a stimulus to action in order to satisfy or alleviate tensions caused by the needs.

Motivation-hygiene model   Herzberg's postulation that two distinct types of need exist in any work situation. Needs that maintain the individual, such as money, company policies, benefits, and working conditions are called hygienic or maintenance needs. Needs for recognition, achievement, responsibility, and self-fulfillment are motivators.

Motivator   A stimulus that creates a need and prompts action to satisfy or alleviate the needs.

Need psychology   Any motivational theory based on the concept that behavior is caused by both felt and unrecognized needs.

Objectives   Desired results or goals.

Ohio State studies   A continuing series of studies at Ohio State University investigating various aspects of leadership. The findings have greatly increased understanding of the leadership process.

Operant learning   Conditioning of habits based on reinforcement of desired behaviors with rewards (or punishment in avoidance behavior) and feedback to let the person or animal know they have succeeded.

Operational objectives   The goals necessary to sustain the activities of an organization. (Shoe stores *must* sell shoes. Furniture manufacturers *must* make furniture.) Not to be confused with profit or financial objectives that are related to policy rather than operation.

Optimum   The best for existing conditions. An automobile may be capable of running 102 miles per hour or standing dead still (maximum and minimum) but it may perform best at 55 miles per hour. Optimum sizes, rates, schedules, quality, and cost are all vitally important in well-managed organizations.

Organization   The arrangement of work into logical, coordinated, interrelated units.

Organization levels   In management, first-line supervisors are the first level of organization, mid-managers are usually the second and third level (in large organizations), and executive management is the top level.

OSHA (Occupational Safety and Health Administration or **Occupational Safety and Health Act)**   Some states, as well as the federal government, have enacted OSHA functions.

Paralanguage   Meaning given to speech by voice inflection, tone, emphasis, loudness, timbre, or other quality rather than the literal meanings of words used.

Pareto's law of maldistribution   Pareto's famous statement that 80 percent of all errors and problems are caused by 20 percent of any population.

Participative management   A form of management leadership that encourages employees to participate in the organizational decision-making process as it affects their jobs.

Past practice   In the absence of specific contract langue, what has been policy or practice remains in effect.

Performance   The quantity, quality, and rate that an employee does an assigned task.

Physiological needs   Biological or maintenance needs. Sometimes called primary needs. They include air, food, water, warmth, elimination, sleep, and so forth.

Piece rates   Pay for pieces produced rather than time worked.

Planning   The act of predetermining courses of action by deciding who, what, when, where, and how a task or set of tasks will be accomplished.

Policy   A broad general statement declaring the intent of an organization in handling various internal and external activities.

Power   Influence of another person or group of persons. Also power is influence in making and implementing decisions.

Problem-solving objectives   Generally nonrecurring, nonroutine situations that require the recognition and solution of problems before a work objective can be completed.

Procedure   A written statement of how to do a task.

Production   Any output: pieces, units, sales made, sheets of paper typed, forms completed, and so forth.

Profitability   The comparison of an act or expenditure to determine its cost-effectiveness. Will it yield or only add to costs?

Program   An organized effort to accomplish a set of tasks in addition to the central effort of the work unit.

Progressive discipline   Discipline based on successively harsher actions for each successive infraction, such as a reprimand for the first violation, a layoff without pay for the second and termination for the third.

Protected class   Any group protected from discrimination because of race, color, religion, national origin, sex, age, or physical handicap.

Psychological needs   According to Maslow's hierarchy, those needs associated with self-esteem, worthwhileness, status, recognition, and achievement. Ego needs.

Pygmalion effect   The idea that what someone expects you to be is what you will probably appear to be, at least in their eyes.

Quality   Degree of correctness or perfection in the performance of a task.

Quality circles   A technique for developing employee involvement in decisions through regular meetings designed to define and solve productivity and quality problems.

Quality control   A formal system to determine product or service quality.

Quid pro quo   Literally Something for something. Favors for favors. "You scratch my back, I'll scratch yours."

Rate   Number of units produced or services performed in a period of time.

Reasonable accommodation   The legal necessity to attempt to accommodate a person's religious beliefs in making work assignments.

Reinforcement   Repetition of a motivating stimulus to get an action or behavior repeated.

Relay test assembly experiment   Elton Mayo's famous experiment that proved management attitudes are more important to productivity than working conditions.

Responsibility   Obligation to perform tasks or duties.

Revisionists   Management theorists who, through the utilization of behavioral science techniques as well as observation and analysis, have revised and modified earlier management theories. Rensis Likert, Chris Argyris, Peter Drucker, Warren Bennis, William Reddin, Leonard Sayles, and many other current management analysts belong to the revisionist group.

Robotics   The use of computerized, automated sensing equipment in the work place to perform tasks ordinarily done by people.

Routine objective   Day-to-day requirements of a job.

Salary review   Review of factors such as performance, seniority, and tasks assigned to determine if an employee should be granted pay increase, and if so, how much.

Schedule   Time allocated to perform a task or deliver a product or service.

Scientific Management   Management according to principles developed by Frederick W. Taylor and his adherents. It stresses methods improvement, work simplification, and industrial engineering techniques to increase productivity and lower costs.

Self-actualization   Maslow's term that describes the good feeling resulting from finding and doing what an individual feels is most satisfying. Satisfaction in the effort rather than its rewards.

Self-fulfillment needs   Self-actualization.

Sexual harassment   Any sexual proposal or act that is a condition of work, a threat to an employee, or an interference with job performance.

Situational leadership   Leadership that arises from the position, conditions, and forces affecting the person leading and those being led.

Skill training   Training involving eye-hand or other body movement coordination to perform a set of tasks. Mechanical assembly, typing, driving a vehicle, and painting are examples.

Social learning   Learning by observing and copying others. Adapting to a situation by observing and modeling others.

Social needs   Maslow's term of needs for affection, belonging, love, and acceptance.

Social responsibility   Acting in the best interests of the public, the employees, and the organization.

Social system   Any stable interrelationship among people. The term usually refers to people engaged in a common effort or held together by a common purpose.

Span of control   The number of persons one manager can effectively supervise.

Staff function   Organizational units or assignments that provide specialized internal services to the line or producing segments of the organization.

Staffing   Acquisition and assignment of personnel.

Standard   Expected level of performance. In some cases, what is determined to be average performance for an average worker in average conditions.

Standard time   Length of time for an average worker under average conditions to perform a task as determined by time studies of a number of workers for a predetermined time.

Supervision   Directing, assigning, correcting, organizing, controlling, and motivating the efforts of others. Getting work accomplished through others. First-level management.

Tenet   A rule, law, or well-founded principle.

Theory G   Geneen's theory that managers should avoid adopting a specific theory or management style. They should, instead, be guided by their own judgment of what is best for a given set of conditions.

Theory X   Douglas McGregor's designation for traditional management based on the assumption that people are basically lazy, self-serving, irresponsible, and in need of strong, close direction.

Theory Y   McGregor's assumption that under proper conditions people seek work, accept responsibility, want to help the organization, and can, to a large extent, effectively manage themselves.

Theory Z   The belief that mutually supportive efforts by managers and employees working in partnership is desirable in achieving organizational success.

Title VII   Passed in 1972, the Equal Employment Opportunity provisions of the Civil Rights Act of 1964.

Unfair labor practices   Any action by management or a union that is prohibited by the Labor Management Relations Act (Section 8). Examples are coercion, interrogation, promises to gain special consideration, and spying on the other side's activities.

Uniform Employment Guidelines   A set of federal rules for assuring equality of employment opportunity. Published in 1978 by the Equal Employment Opportunity Commission.

Unit   A work group, division of labor, function, or members of a union, such as a bargaining unit.

Unity of command   The principle that every person should report to only one other person.

Variable   Any set of conditions that is not fixed. The aspects of work that are not routine.

Wage and Hour Law   Same as the Fair Labor Standards Act. Established minimum wages, national overtime standards, and minimum ages for certain kinds of work. Exempts managers, professional employees, administrative employees, certain classes of technical employees, outside salespeople, and independent contractors from coverage by the law.

Walsh-Healy Act   A similar but more stringent set of Fair Labor Standards (wage and hour) for government contractors.

Win/lose strategy   Actions taken to ensure that if an individual is correct or has favorable results in a disputed situation, that the other parties to the dispute will be incorrect or have unfavorable results.

Win/win strategy   Actions taken to ensure that both parties in a dispute or conflict situation will achieve favorable results or not be considered totally incorrect or inadequate.

Wobble   Union-management term for jurisdictional dispute.

Work simplification   An outgrowth of Scientific Management, work simplification seeks to break any given task into small elements that can easily be learned by a new or untrained employee with minimum expenditure of time or effort. It also seeks to make existing jobs easier. A special field of job design.

Index

*This book has been set Linotron 202 in 10 and 9 point
Optima, leaded 3 points. Part numbers and titles are
30 point Serif Gothic Extra Bold. The size of the type
page is 35 by 46 picas.*